August 2009

NINETEENTH-CENTURY IRELAND

To all students of nineteenth-century Ireland

*

# Nineteenth-Century Ireland

## *A Guide to Recent Research*

*edited by*

LAURENCE M. GEARY

*and*

MARGARET KELLEHER

UNIVERSITY COLLEGE DUBLIN PRESS

PREAS CHOLÁISTE OLLSCOILE
BHAILE ÁTHA CLIATH

First published 2005
by University College Dublin Press
Newman House
86 St Stephen's Green
Dublin 2, Ireland
*www.ucdpress.ie*

© the editors and contributors, 2005

ISBN 1-904558-28-3

All rights reserved. No part of this publication
may be reproduced, stored in a retrieval system,
or transmitted in any form or by any means, electronic,
photocopying, recording or otherwise without
the prior permission of the publisher.

Cataloguing in Publication data available from the British Library

Typeset in Ireland in Plantin and Fournier by
Elaine Shiels, Bantry, Co. Cork

Text design by Lyn Davies

Index by Jane Rogers

Printed on acid-free paper in England
by Antony Rowe Ltd

# Contents

# Preface

✳

In *Irish Historiography 1970–1979*, which was published in 1981, the editor J. J. Lee wrote that the volume's nine contributions were 'not intended as bibliographies "but as individual essays in the assessment and interpretation of achievement in the field of Irish history"'. Lee's volume, like its predecessor, T. W. Moody's *Irish Historiography 1936–1970* (1971), quickly established itself as an invaluable source for students, researchers and teachers, and continues to be an influential work. Twenty years later, Irish historiography has expanded greatly, not least in the case of the nineteenth century where unprecedented interest is evident and new perspectives are emerging. This collection takes as its model the 1981 Lee volume and builds on its achievement, adding new subject areas to traditional historical categories. The essays assess and interpret developments from 1990 onwards in the field of nineteenth-century Irish studies, and from a range of disciplinary perspectives, including art history, women's history, music, cultural studies, and the history of emigration.

As many of the contributors note, interest in nineteenth-century studies has never been greater, and contrasts sharply with previous neglect of many aspects of that century's history and culture. However, many of the changes that have taken place in studies of nineteenth-century Ireland have yet to be fully recognised or sufficiently examined. As Gary Owens remarks, in chapter 2, 'while the quantity of work being produced on nineteenth-century Irish social history has never been greater and its quality has never been higher, the gaps in our knowledge have never appeared wider'. The aim of this review is to provide an in-depth analysis of current work in nineteenth-century Ireland, together with 'the factors and fashions' which have determined these approaches, to use Gearóid Ó Tuathaigh's words, and the changes, 'if any', that have been effected in our understanding of that century and its significance. According to Ó Tuathaigh, the 1990s was a decade which 'saw new and interesting questions posed for the writing of nineteenth-century Irish history'; influentially for the future, it also saw 'the emergence of new ways of posing such historical questions'.

Each contributor was invited to review recent studies of nineteenth-century Ireland in her or his discipline, published since 1990 approximately. The eleven essays included here offer both a wide-ranging analysis of current research and suggestions for future studies. Consequently, the scope of each essay extends far beyond the usual parameters of review articles: each contributor not only reviews key publications in the field but also evaluates current trends in research and, crucially, identifies areas of research as yet unexplored. The select bibliography that concludes the volume is a central part of the overall review, offering readers a useful and accessible guide to recent research in nineteenth-century Irish studies.

A particular strength of this review is the diversity of disciplines represented: not only political, social and religious history (as in the 1971 and 1981 volumes), but also women's history, anthropology and sociology, art history, music, diaspora studies, historical geography, language shift and literary studies. Through the connections and contrasts between essays, the volume is a significant guide to current intersections between disciplines, enabling readers to trace the evolution of various subject areas and the ways in which they have influenced each other. As Joan Vincent and Marilyn Cohen note in their review of anthropological and sociological studies, many traditional disciplinary boundaries have become blurred in recent years. Matthew Stout's essay draws from the rich fields of archaeology, landscape history and historical geography, in its review of 'place-based' histories. On the other hand, many contributors identify missed opportunities to develop other interdisciplinary possibilities – such as the historical use of visual culture (discussed by Fintan Cullen) or the incorporation of women's history (Maria Luddy). While some comparative methodologies have developed, others are conspicuously absent, most strikingly, perhaps, the lack of discussion of language shift and language change among many of the new practitioners of Irish studies, as Niall Ó Ciosáin highlights in his contribution.

Once the choice of disciplines was made, it was left to individual contributors to determine the parameters of each discipline and this constitutes an explicit and intriguing subject within many chapters. Some essays construct new models of analysis with the potential to prove definitive in their fields; see, to name just some examples, David Miller's tripartite model of religious history, Sean Ryder's elucidation of current literary methodologies and Harry White's discussion of Irish musicology. The decision not to include a separate chapter on the commemoration of the Famine was made for a number of reasons. Other individual subjects – Daniel O'Connell, for example – could be considered; and a number of useful survey articles already exist. Most importantly, it is now time to reintegrate the historiography of the Famine within the larger historiography of nineteenth-century Ireland and to study the changes it has made; the attention paid to this question by many contributors within this volume – Matthew Stout, Gary Owens, Gearóid Ó Tuathaigh, Maria Luddy, David Miller and J. J. Lee, among others – points the way in this regard.

These essays are designed for general readers, non-specialists and specialists alike, and provide an accessible introduction to each of the eleven disciplines represented here. We hope they will be of benefit to students in a variety of subject areas, not least those who wish to move beyond traditional disciplinary boundaries in advancing the study of nineteenth-century Ireland. 'The most important task for the future', as J. J. Lee points out in the final chapter in this collection, 'remains exactly the same as for the past – the testing of the concepts with which we work, and the testing of the evidence on which interpretation is based'.

The idea for this collection arose from the work of the Society for the Study of Nineteenth-Century Ireland and we are grateful for the support and collegiality offered by fellow committee members: Claire Connolly, Tadhg Foley, Colin Graham, Carla King, Leon Litvack, James H. Murphy, Christina Hunt Mahony and Clíona Ó Gallchoir. We wish to express our thanks also to James S. Donnelly, Jr, Sara Wilbourne, Andy Storey and Sheelagh McCormack. Barbara Mennell, of UCD Press, has provided expert guidance throughout the publication process. Financial assistance towards this publication was received from the Publications Fund of the National University of Ireland and we gratefully acknowledge this assistance.

LAURENCE M. GEARY
MARGARET KELLEHER
*Cork and Maynooth, July 2004*

# Contributors to this volume

❋

MARILYN COHEN is Assistant Professor of Anthropology at Montclair State University in New Jersey. She has published widely on the Irish linen industry, including *Linen Family and Community in Tullylish, County Down, 1690–1914* (Four Courts, 1997) and as editor of the interdisciplinary volume *The Warp of Ulster's Past: Interdisciplinary Perspectives on the Irish Linen Industry, 1700–1920* (St Martin's, 1997).

FINTAN CULLEN is Professor of Art History at the University of Nottingham. He is the author of *The Irish Face: Redefining the Irish Portrait* (National Portrait Gallery, 2004); *Sources in Irish Art: A Reader* (Cork University Press, 2000) and *Visual Politics: The Representation of Ireland 1750–1930* (Cork University Press, 1997).

J. J. LEE holds the Glucksman Chair of Irish Studies, New York University and is Professor of History, University College Cork. His publications include *Ireland 1912–1985: Politics and Society* (Cambridge University Press, 1989) and *The Modernisation of Irish Society, 1848–1928* (Gill & Macmillan, 1973).

MARIA LUDDY is Reader in History at the University of Warwick. She has written extensively on the history of women in Ireland and was joint editor of *The Field Day Anthology of Irish Writing*, volumes 4 and 5 on *Irish Women's Writing and Traditions* (Cork and New York University Presses, 2002).

DAVID W. MILLER, Professor of History at Carnegie Mellon University, is the author of *Church, State and Nation in Ireland, 1898–1921* (Gill & Macmillan, 1973) and *Queen's Rebels: Ulster Loyalism in Historical Perspective* (Gill & Macmillan, 1978). His current project is a book under the working title *Ulster Presbyterians and Irish Catholics in the Famine Era, 1829–1869*.

NIALL Ó CIOSÁIN teaches history in the National University of Ireland, Galway. He is the author of *Print and Popular Culture in Ireland 1750–1850* (Macmillan, 1997), and of articles on book history, popular culture and the Great Famine.

GEAROID Ó TUATHAIGH is Professor of History at the National University of Ireland, Galway. He is the author of *Ireland Before the Famine 1798–1848* (Gill & Macmillan, 1972; rev. ed. 1990)and has published widely on the subject of nineteenth-century Irish history, and on Irish language and culture.

GARY OWENS, formerly Professor of History at Huron University College in the University of Western Ontario, now lives in County Laois. He has written extensively on the theme of mass mobilisation in nineteenth-century Ireland and the interplay between popular culture and nationalist politics. His most recent work deals with a violent incident during the Tithe War and its memory.

SEAN RYDER lectures in the Department of English at the National University of Ireland, Galway. He is editor of *James Clarence Mangan: Selected Writings* (University College Dublin Press, 2004), co-editor of *Gender and Colonialism* (Galway University Press, 1995), and co-editor of *Ideology and Ireland in the Nineteenth Century* (Four Courts, 1998).

MATTHEW STOUT lectures in early medieval history, landscape history and medieval archaeology in the Department of History, St Patrick's College, Drumcondra. He is author of *The Irish Ringfort* (Four Courts Press, 1997), co-editor of the *Atlas of the Irish Rural Landscape* (Cork University Press, 1997) and a general editor of the Irish Rural Landscapes series published by Cork University Press (2002, 2004).

JOAN VINCENT is Professor Emeritus of Anthropology, Barnard College, Columbia University. She has published widely in the fields of historical ethnography, with extensive field research in the Irish Northwest. Her most recent publication is *Seeds of Revolution: The Cultural Politics of the Great Irish Famine* (Palgrave, 2004).

HARRY WHITE is Professor of Music at University College Dublin and President of the Society for Musicology in Ireland. He has published extensively on the cultural history of music in Ireland and on the music of the Austro-Italian Baroque.

# CHAPTER I

# Political History

✳

*Gearóid Ó Tuathaigh*

The most remarkable fact which confronts any commentator intent on reviewing recent writings on the politics of nineteenth-century Ireland is the sheer volume of publications which have appeared since the beginning of the 1990s. The bibliographical surveys of the major historical journals have continued to grow in bulk and length, reflecting increasing numbers (both full-time academics and a host of independent scholars of different backgrounds) involved in historical research and publications (including local journals and independent publishing projects), sustaining an extraordinary public interest and involvement, throughout the island, in 'doing' local history.[1] A second daunting fact facing such a review as this is the manner in which general scholarly understanding of 'the political' has become enlarged during the past generation. This, as we will indicate later in this essay, is largely owing to the central role which ideology has come to occupy in writings on nineteenth-century Ireland by cultural critics and theorists, and indeed by scholars in a variety of disciplines. 'Writing' nineteenth-century Ireland's political history is no longer a vocation for historians only.

Faced with such a mass of publications, the reviewer might easily succumb to the temptation to list only the major publications, with their tributaries clustered respectfully in the footnotes. Or, alternatively, one might seek to offer as complete a listing as is possible, conscious of the fact that the inevitable name-congestion that would result would tax the patience of any readers other than those whose primary concern is with seeing their own work cited. The approach adopted in this essay seeks to avoid, or at least to reduce to a tolerable level, the shortcomings inherent in both of these approaches. In the first instance we will seek to identify a number of key approaches which have been especially influential in the writings of the 1990s, and also some of the factors and fashions which have made these particular approaches so challenging and fruitful (fruitful, that is, in terms of the originality of the writings which they have generated). Following this brief consideration of key approaches,

the essay will seek to identify what exactly has changed in our general understanding of the politics of Ireland under the Union as a result of these writings.
This, necessarily selective, evaluation will follow a broadly chronological
approach to political developments in nineteenth-century Ireland.

The analytical perspectives and intellectual approaches which have been
particularly influential in recent writings on the politics of Ireland under the
Union may be classified as follows:

1  the growing awareness of and engagement with ideology, and the examination of the role of ideology in determining the agenda of politics at every level;

2  the exponential growth in local history research and publications, which
has resulted not only in the contours of the political map of nineteenth-
century Ireland becoming much richer in detail, but also in the full complexity
of Irish politics – leadership, mobilisation, issues, conflict – being sharply
revealed under the intimate scrutiny of local realities and the particularity of
local circumstances;

3  the increasing tendency for historians and other scholars to consider and
to write about Ireland's historical predicament in a comparative context, the
precise comparisons invoked reflecting the issues or episodes under consideration, the evidence available, the imagination and the ideological position of
the different commentators;

4  the emergence of a rich and ideologically sympathetic historiography of
Irish Unionism.

Before turning to a brief consideration of these areas and approaches of
particular interest, it may be useful to make a few general observations on the
context in which these particularly rich seams of writing on the politics of
nineteenth-century Ireland have occurred. Firstly, anniversaries provided a
powerful stimulus to historical writing during the 1990s; some anniversaries
more so than others. Secondly, as with the historiography of the 1970s and
1980s, the unfolding political prospects in Northern Ireland have played an
important role in shaping the terms in which the political history of the
nineteenth century has been considered and written about. Specifically, there
has been a new emphasis on finding or devising 'frameworks' of accommodation, based on parity of esteem and the principle of consent, and an insistence
that, within an integrated British–Irish polity, east–west, north–south and
intra-Northern Ireland relationships be embodied in new constitutional and
political arrangements and structures. This focus on new 'frameworks of
accommodation' has inevitably influenced the academic consideration of the
alternative routes to accommodation and coexistence (between Britain and
Ireland and between nationalists and unionists within Ireland) which were

canvassed and which might have been taken in Ireland at various times from the 1790s to 1920.

Current political preoccupations and possibilities have created an intellectual climate conducive to a re-examination of anything that smacks of an overly determinist historiography of Irish nationalism and Irish unionism polarising implacably towards the inevitable settlements of 1920–2. Roy Foster has perceptively noted (indeed over two decades he has contributed decisively to creating) this intellectual disposition: the willingness to address 'plurality, variousness and ambiguity' and to 'escape imprisoning historical perspectives'.[2] Foster also identifies the connection between current political preoccupations regarding Northern Ireland and changing emphases in historical writings:

> As the sterility of the extremist option becomes clearer, and intellectual opinion in the Republic and the North is more and more prepared to see ambiguities, difficulties and obstacles that bedevil the traditional versions of our histories, it is interesting to notice unfashionable subjects coming back into the historical spotlight – among them John Redmond, and the political era between the fall of Parnell in 1891 and the Easter Rising in 1916. This is beginning to be seen, not necessarily as a demoralised and sterile landscape, redeemed by the Easter sacrifice, but as a period when new options were tried, new alliances cautiously tested out, and traditional identities debated and examined.[3]

While Foster correctly identifies one particularly rich site of new writing (i.e. the 1890–1916 period), his own assumptions regarding 'the traditional versions of our histories' need careful attention. For example, it is open to question whether the interrogation by leading historians of traditional Irish (particularly Ulster) Unionist history was not a good deal more sympathetic during the 1990s than had been the case over the three previous decades with the more robustly impatient interrogation to which the 'traditional version' of Irish nationalist history had been exposed.[4]

★   ★   ★

Turning from these demonstrably contemporary factors and their influence on the emphases – in theme, tone and period – which they encouraged in the writings of the 1990s; the increasing engagement with ideology has been one of the most striking features of recent writings on the politics of Ireland under the Union. The more narrow and conventional view of politics which prevailed in most traditional histories of modern Ireland has been replaced by an intellectual reflex in which all contested issues are 'political'. All actions and interventions, by individuals or groups, based upon ideas, assumptions or prejudices, need to be examined and understood in ideological terms.

The construction of the myths, the mindsets, the material conditions and the political mechanisms, which are the prerequisites for effective political mobilisation at any aggregate level, has been the focus of intense ideological interrogation among scholars. The examination of the role of ideology in constituting the agenda of 'politics' (i.e. of purposeful action to achieve or to resist change in the structures of power) has been greatly fructified in recent years by the contributions of scholars from a variety of academic disciplines, and by the resolutely interdisciplinary approach of the leading contributors. Thus, cultural critics (strongly informed by theoretical models) have engaged historical 'sources' (not all of them documentary in character) in ways which, it must be admitted, have been unsettling for many conservative historians unwilling to contemplate the implications of any body of theory for the assumptions they hold or for the practices which they follow in 'writing history'.

But despite resistance from many reputable historians, the new, theoretically informed, approaches have encouraged a challenging dialogue involving anthropologists, economists, political scientists, cultural critics and, indeed, historians, on virtually every aspect of historical change and development in nineteenth-century Ireland. The several volumes published in the 1990s by the Society for the Study of Nineteenth-Century Ireland give a good indication of the richness of this recent dialogue and of the variety of perspectives and discourses to which it is hospitable.[5] As the editors of one of these volumes have rightly pointed out: 'the Irish were enthusiastic participants in the ideological strife which characterised the economic, social, political and cultural domains of the nineteenth century'.[6] The editors go on to offer a particular explanation for this ideological ferment in nineteenth-century Ireland:

> The reasons for this are various, but have much to do with the inescapable effects of the 'unfinished business' of colonialism and imperialism in nineteenth-century Irish culture. The unresolved contests between Gaelic and English cultural values, between modernity and tradition, between peasantry and gentry, between Protestant and Catholic – all were such highly visible conflicts in nineteenth-century Ireland that ideology found itself continually in a state of exposure and confrontation, unable to 'naturalise' itself and achieve hegemonic invisibility.[7]

Both the language of this extract, and the proposition itself, serve to alert us to another crucial aspect of the intense attention in recent years to ideology in the study of nineteenth-century Ireland: that is, the fact that a number of key discourses have had a powerful presence in this discussion of ideology and political development during the Union era. These are, principally, post-colonial discourse, which has been widely influential among scholars from various disciplines (but whose applicability to Ireland's historical condition,

4

from the sixteenth century, has been strongly contested), and gender discourse.[8] Each of these has encouraged, in varying degrees, a systematic comparative approach to the consideration of nineteenth-century Ireland, though a comparative approach has also been increasingly evident in the work of scholars who would not locate themselves primarily, or at all, within the two discourses just mentioned.

Postcolonialism has been a particularly hospitable discourse for cultural critics and theorists working from a broadly neo-Marxist position. Its most distinguished (and prolific) exponents have an impressive command of theoretical literature, are original and ambitious in interrogating a wide range of historical sources for the writing of Irish history (written texts, other forms of representation and symbolic systems), and have brought a bracing comparative dimension from, in particular, Africa, India and the Caribbean to their consideration of the condition of Ireland.[9] Seamus Deane's demand that 'everything must be re-read' encapsulates an approach which has resulted in many startlingly original and close readings of texts, episodes, individual historical actors (writers, politicians), all bearing upon the political condition of Ireland in the nineteenth century, but not in that century only.[10] There has been criticism of the application of the postcolonialist model to Ireland on several grounds – not least that it is an excessively schematic and totalising framework unsuited to the multiple ambiguities and contradictions of Ireland's relationship with Britain and with the British empire in the modern period.[11]

What is surprising, perhaps, is the failure of Irish historians in particular, and of Irish scholars in general, to explore seriously or systematically, in an Irish context, the insights into socio-cultural divisions and their political implications which have come from the original work of the subaltern studies group of Indian scholars.[12] One might have expected, for example, that the language shift in Ireland and the creation and development of a language appropriate to mass political mobilisation during the nineteenth century would have suggested itself to scholars as particularly suited to investigation from a subaltern studies perspective. But no such focused project emerged. Yet there can be no doubting the contribution made by critics writing from a postcolonial perspective to the history of mentalité, cultural production, representation and conflict, and to the study of political consciousness in nineteenth-century Ireland. The colonial model, of course, is not to be applied crudely or mechanically to the range of relationships between Britain and Ireland or indeed to the analysis of social formations, political divisions and competing cultural projects within Ireland itself. The ambiguities and contradictions of Ireland's participation in the British imperial experience is but the most obvious area which poses questions for the 'colonial' version of Ireland's historical condition. It is also the case that historians and economists reviewing Ireland's economic 'performance' in recent centuries are more inclined to place

Ireland, for comparative purposes, in the league with other small European states (whatever their political relationship with more powerful neighbours) than with colonies or former colonies of the European empires of the nineteenth century.[13]

The impact of the gender discourse has been registered at a number of levels of reflection and writing on nineteenth-century Irish political history. Firstly there is the writing of women's history: the continuing project of reclamation, of re-voicing (from all the available sources) women's witness and agency in the main public sphere of political contest in nineteenth-century Ireland. Here, substantial progress has been made, building upon the pioneering baseline work of historical scholarship on women's history in Ireland which began in the 1970s. There have been a number of biographical studies of leading women activists, as well as studies of collective political participation (as political activists or as propagandists) by groups of women, whatever their political objectives, in the cause of nationalism or of unionism, socialism or the specific agenda and interests of women themselves.[14]

The systematic building up of the research resources for women's history, including women's presence in the public domain of politics, was greatly advanced in the 1990s by the Women's History Project.[15] This has been a considerable achievement. While women's role in the public politics of nineteenth-century Ireland was the subject of many notable publications in the 1990s, it is probably fair to say that the more ground-breaking work in women's history has been in the area of the economy and the world of work (within and outside the home, paid and unpaid), though of course these spheres are themselves instinct with political questions.[16] The integration of this substantial body of work on women's history into general political histories of nineteenth-century Ireland remains to be accomplished. Or, at least, it remains to be accomplished in a more satisfactory manner than that which Maryann Valiulis has wickedly characterised as the 'add women, and stir' recipe for intellectually low-cost, conscience-saving insertions of women into settled narratives of political history.[17]

Perhaps an even more radical advance is to be found in writings which have sought to situate gender at the centre of the historical process: that is to say, the different witnesses of women and men to historical events and processes, the ways in which and through which these gender differences have been conditioned, how they are constituted and how they are represented in different historical narratives. This work has its focus on the particularity of Ireland's historical experience but is firmly grounded in theoretical literature on gender.[18] Several collections of essays and a number of single-author studies and reviews explored the complexities of gender discourse (and of its relationship with, for example, the discourse of class or of nationalism) in the Irish historical experience.[19]

6

Laura E. Lyons has argued persuasively for the value of this kind of gender discourse, not only as a perspective for finding new and subversive ways of looking at 'familiar' political episodes in Irish history (e.g. the land war, local politics), but also, and more importantly, as a key for generating new questions about power and the historical process, and indeed about the encoding of our versions of the past in a particular language in the writing of history.[20] Lyons has rightly identified Margaret Kelleher's book on the Famine as a particularly challenging example of this new radical 'gendering' of historical questions and answers during the past decade.[21]

Taken together, both women's history and the application of gender discourse to historical analysis and writing made an original contribution in the past decade to writing on nineteenth-century Irish political culture. How influential that impact has been on the general body of historians of the nineteenth century is open to question. Few serious historians of modern Ireland are nowadays utterly ignorant of or insensitive to the fact of gender difference and to some, at least, of the implications of that fact for the kind of historical questions which they ask. At a minimum, for some this reflex probably does not progress much further than asking such questions as: Were women involved in this episode/movement? Was there a women's perspective on it? What answers can the available sources give us to these or similar questions? These are not unworthy questions for any historian, but a modestly growing minority of Irish historians are now more alert than was the case even a decade ago to the fact that such words as 'involved' or 'sources' are not the innocent words they once seemed to be.

The gendering 'reflex' in posing questions about historical change in Ireland is still a practice for a minority. Most professional Irish historians (as indeed is the case with most traditionally trained professional historians in many countries) still shy away from the more difficult (in terms of accessibility of language as much as in conceptual complexity) areas of social theory, even from theories regarding the writing of history itself. A few wear this indifference to theory as a badge of honour. Nevertheless, the interdisciplinary exchanges in Irish historical enquiry are more numerous, more open and more regular than they were a decade ago, and the writing of nineteenth-century Irish history reflects, even if slowly and unevenly, this changing intellectual climate.[22]

⋆　　⋆　　⋆

Turning from these observations on certain key approaches in recent writings on nineteenth-century Ireland, let us now see if we can identify what significant changes, if any, in our understanding of nineteenth-century Irish political history have been effected. As indicated earlier, we will proceed chronologically, adverting, selectively, to major thematic issues as they arise.

The extent of politicisation and socialisation in Ireland during the closing decades of the eighteenth century, and the legacy of these processes for the early nineteenth century, has been one of the themes to benefit enormously from research and publications coinciding with if not necessarily prompted by the anniversaries which arrived in the 1990s. Of course, the debate had already begun on the politicisation and the growth of sectarianism in the 1790s.[23] But during the 1990s the work of a number of scholars, but particularly of Tom Bartlett and Kevin Whelan, transformed our understanding of the politicisation of the 1790s and of the complex strands and the rhythms of political engagement which marked the emergence of the Catholic Question at the centre of Anglo-Irish relations and of Irish politics in the aftermath of the Union.[24] Whelan's identification of the 'underground gentry' of strong, assertive Catholic big farmers, constructing (by shrewd manipulation of popular memory) a 'legitimist' status for themselves as the authentic 'stock' of leadership of their Catholic communities, clarifies one vital element of the potential political resources available to O'Connell. The claims of the strong farmers to legitimacy as 'traditional' leaders of the rural Catholic community had, of course, to contend with the multiple sources of class tension and conflict within the rural society at a time of population pressure and economic strain. But Whelan's version of the long-term victory of the Catholic big farmers is worth quoting, even in summary form:

> this new big-farm group had consolidated its interests in Irish economic and political life by the early nineteenth century . . . They constructed themselves, not as a peasant class but as proprietors-in-waiting, who would reclaim a patrimony of which their noble ancestors had been unjustly stripped. . . . That big-farm class also constituted the backbone of the emergent Catholic nationalist project which was largely constructed and given organised political form by O'Connell. . . . O'Connell's Catholic nationalism appealed to history for authenticity and legitimacy, using an idealised past to destroy the decadent present, thereby liberating the desirable future. In other words, it would utilise (or invent) tradition as the binding force shaping and perpetuating the Irish nation. That paradigm would flourish in the nineteenth century, as the Enlightenment politics of the United Irishmen lost impetus and definition under the challenge of romanticism, nationalism and sectarianism, and as Irish society petrified into sectarian rigidities.[25]

Bartlett's careful presentation of the various ways (including mass militarisation, increasing socialisation at fairs, markets, religious events, and the extensive politicisation of the 1790s) through which Catholic socialisation was strengthened, presents us with a new context for considering O'Connell's achievement. Moreover, the crucial importance of the 'veto' controversy in the changing shape and temper of the Catholic political leadership by the second decade of the Union has been clearly established in his and other recent writings.[26] The fact that some of the older, politically more cautious (and, from a government perspective, more accommodating) bishops, such as Archbishop Troy, had now to take account of the views and political demands of a more assertive and increasingly confident Catholic bourgeois lay leadership marks a significant transition from the late eighteenth century.[27] The role of the priests as allies of the emerging Catholic middle-class lay leadership ensured that political contacts between Catholic prelates and government ministers, or their respective agents, were now only one part (albeit a crucial part) of a wider and politically more complex matrix of interests and negotiation routes within the overall context of church–state relations. A number of recent studies of leading Catholic bishops confirm this development, complementing Bartlett's presentation of the 'emerging' new Catholic leadership by the early nineteenth century.[28]

In the light of the writings of the 1990s, notably by Bartlett and Whelan, one can plausibly see O'Connell as not so much having to create out of nothing, as it were, a mobilised and disciplined mass political movement in the 1820s, as having to lead, to manage and to motivate for particular political objectives (and to do so brilliantly) a Catholic community already substantially politicised, socialised and habituated to collective action.[29] On the other hand, the 'veto' issue also brings into focus a further political development inherent in the rise of the new, confident Catholic leadership: namely, the gradual squeezing of liberal Protestant support for reform on the Catholic rights question. The more accommodating position of liberal Protestants – well-disposed towards movement on Catholic relief, in relation to the 'veto' question and to the general reasonableness of giving the government some guarantees (and gratitude) in respect of any further Catholic relief measure – was ultimately rejected by the emerging Catholic leadership. This left many liberal Protestants feeling bruised and unappreciated, uncomprehending or fearful of the seemingly unbridled scope of Catholic demands. Discreet, accommodating and politically quietist Catholic bishops and gentry were no longer, it seemed, setting or controlling the agenda of Catholic political demands.[30]

The strengthening of confessional communal politics was driven by other political imperatives. For the Catholic leadership – bishops, priests or bourgeois laity, rural and urban – the handling of the challenge 'from below', at a time of intensifying demographic pressure and social tension based on access to land and to the fruits of the land, was a pressing issue. In these conditions, confessional politics were preferable to class politics and conflict (and, it may be said, more feasible, more easily organised, given the State's apparatus of control and its capacity and disposition to deal firmly with violent challenges to the institutions of property). While references to O'Connellite popular political movements as 'Catholic nationalism' ignore or elide many of the more interesting developments in Irish nationalist thought from the late eighteenth and through the nineteenth century, the significance of strong confessional coherence on the demand for Catholic emancipation in the 1820s clearly shaped the 'challenging collectivity' which directed the anti-tithe campaign of the 1830s and which provided the backbone of the Repeal movement in the early 1840s.[31]

This new evaluation of the elements of the Catholic question – and, in Bartlett's phrase, of 'the rise of the Catholic nation' between the late eighteenth and the first quarter of the nineteenth century – does not necessarily diminish O'Connell's towering presence, or the appreciation of his genius as a leader of mass political movements. In fact, studies of O'Connell during the 1990s, while understandably still heavily under the massive shade of Oliver MacDonagh's major biography of 1989, have added further weight to his claims to being considered a major and influential European figure, and have generally confirmed his political significance in the general British (as distinct from the specifically Irish) context of early nineteenth-century radicalism.[32] The published proceedings of the regularly held O'Connell Workshop have included a number of valuable contributions on his historical role and achievements.[33]

If politicisation, socialisation, Catholic mobilisation, and church–state relations have benefited from several seminal publications, the sheer volume of local studies, of parliamentary and popular politics, which has appeared in recent years, demands a ruthless selectivity from the reviewer. Firstly, the ambitious county history series of Geography Publications had published volumes on 14 counties by the end of the 1990s,[34] each volume containing essays on aspects of political history, either by established scholars already published in their field or by young scholars presenting the first fruits of research. The contributions generally relate to such mainstream themes as O'Connellite politics, the Famine, Land League and Home Rule politics, elections, electioneering and local representation. Moreover, a number of other county histories (again with multiple authors) have appeared, independently of the Geography Publication series,[35] while a much larger (and, in terms of academic professionalism, more variable) corpus of shorter local studies have appeared, which often have either included political chapters or, in some instances, have been primarily concerned with local political developments.[36] While these publications on the whole may not have radically altered our large-scale, overall map of the political landscape of nineteenth-century Ireland, the best of this work in local history (and a lot of it is very good indeed) has greatly enhanced our understanding of the contours of politics at local level.[37] If we include the short studies of the excellent Maynooth series of publications on local history,[38] we begin to get some sense of the range, excellence and increasingly professional standard of publications in Irish local history since 1990.

One particularly rich site, as far as key aspects of nineteenth-century politics are concerned, has been Cork, city and county, which merits brief and, of necessity, invidiously selective comment. For the pre-Famine period, Peter Jupp and Stephen Royle have published a challenging study of local electoral politics, based on a careful and imaginative use of poll-books (a source for electoral behaviour not in over-supply for nineteenth-century Ireland). The study confirms the strengthening of confessional polarisation and tension in Cork in the second quarter of the century, while noting that this polarisation was not total. The study is revisionist and original in the best academic sense.[39] We will have occasion to cite Cork again later, in noting the importance of case studies in the contributions to later nineteenth-century politics; but for the pre-Famine period it is worth emphasising that the Jupp and Royle contribution is only one of scores of excellent contributions which, if space permitted, one could and would wish to cite.

If the emergence of an assertive Catholic politics (in terms of a widely shared sense of historical victimhood, rhetorically embellished and politically 'managed' in collective political mobilisation for the specific political objectives of emancipation, 'justice for Ireland', administrative reforms, educational rights and repeal) is one of the key areas in which the 1990s produced a rich historiography, the publication in 1997 of Jacqueline Hill's meticulous study of Dublin's Protestant politics, concluding with the decades of O'Connell's ascendancy, marked a major contribution to the study of popular Protestant Unionism.[40] (Dublin rather than Belfast was the first Irish city to experience organised Protestant popular support for the Union.) This work both builds upon and calibrates much more closely the earlier work of W. J. Mc Cormack and of Hill herself on the origins and popular meaning of 'Protestant ascendancy'. It demonstrates the particular anxieties and prejudices which galvanised opposition to Catholic advances (however incremental) in the political and civic life of Ireland, and in particular in Dublin, from the emancipation crisis of the 1820s through the Whig decade of reforms. The shift from a late eighteenth-century pride in 'our' institutions (the Protestant parliament in College Green, the unreformed Dublin corporation) to a determination to fight to prevent the erosion of Protestant privilege by Catholic advances – along with the clear hardening during the nineteenth century of Protestant Unionist resolve to resist any suggestion of a devolved government for Ireland (Repeal or later Home Rule), in which Catholic numbers and political interests would be dominant – was a protracted and complex political process, the decisive phase of which is carefully evaluated by Hill's work.[41] But this political process – the strong gravitational pull of virtually all Irish Protestants towards Unionism and, ultimately, towards Conservative politics – was a process which also in time affected liberal Unionists in Ulster, as the work of Brian Walker, among others, has already demonstrated.[42]

If Jacqueline Hill's study demonstrates the abandonment of a 'patriotic' eighteenth-century position by popular Dublin Protestantism, and its move to resolute Protestant Unionism (under the polarising pressures of Catholic revival, popular political mobilisation in O'Connell's mass movements, the reform spirit of the 1830s, and the stimulus of Protestant evangelical zeal), the story of Irish Tory attempts in the Repeal years to remain both patriotic and Unionist produced a series of publications in the 1990s which have significantly altered our view of the alternatives to Repeal. Such alternatives were contemplated and actively canvassed during the 1830s and particularly the 1840s, and an alternative critique of the Union, *as it operated*, was provided by a group of patriotic Irish Conservatives who were fundamentally supportive of the Union as a concept and as a potentially benign constitutional framework for Ireland.[43] Thus Spence, Boyce, and Jackson, among others, have re-examined Isaac Butt and his fellow-Trinity Tories of the *Dublin University Magazine* in order to explore the terms in which this particular strain of 'patriotic' constructive Unionism was articulated in the O'Connell era.[44] Samuel Ferguson has also been favoured with critical essays and a major biography.[45]

Nor does this cluster of Tory patriots exhaust the range of alternative political options (alternative, that is, to Repeal and to its direct opposite, the *status quo*) canvassed during the 1830s and 1840s and which attracted scholarly interest in the 1990s. The federalists and Whig reformers have been revisited by Robert Sloan,[46] while, at the other end of the political spectrum, the Young Irelanders, and their constitutional no less than their cultural politics (the politics of representation and rhetoric) have benefited richly from the investigation of their cultural politics by cultural critics concerned with ideology, with the project of the *Nation* newspaper and the publishing agenda of the Young Irelanders, with their use of language and symbols, their concept (and constructs) of Irish identity and their systems of representation of Irishness.[47] That literary and antiquarian 'patriotism' (if not quite full-blown cultural nationalism) could provide common (though in terms of lineage increasingly contested) ground for certain political Unionists and for the cultural nationalists of Young Ireland (some of whom would soon be on their way to becoming political separatists, at least for a time) emerges strongly, in all its complexity and contradictions, from the writings of the 1990s.[48] In addition to the works already cited, we might note the welcome appearance of a number of biographical studies of such leading Young Irelanders as John Blake Dillon, Thomas Davis, William Smith O'Brien, Charles Gavan Duffy and Fintan Lalor.[49]

The political ideas, objectives and agendas of any political movement may be more easily located in the writings of the leaders and the chief propagandists of a movement, but mass political mobilisation in the O'Connell era was also rich in symbols and rituals, laden with historical and mythical significance or devised to achieve particular outcomes of popular sentiment and mobilisation. Gary Owens has been especially engaged in examining these public rituals and the use of political symbols in the O'Connellite mass political campaigns, his approach again illustrating the pervasive concern with ideology in recent writings on Irish political history, a concern with the construction and control of 'meaning', through which specific political outcomes and directions become imaginable and political action possible.[50] The work of Brian Walker has provided similar commentary on some of the rituals and symbols managed and manipulated in the creation of Ulster Unionist popular myths and memory throughout the nineteenth century.[51] Indeed, studies of visual representation of Irish material (in painting, public sculpture – not all explicitly historical in nature) have also evidenced this concern with ideology and 'political' purpose.[52]

In sum, the political dimensions of pre-Famine Ireland have been enormously enriched by the writings of the 1990s. This has been the case in respect of the more traditional or conventional historical accounts of the rise of Catholic political consciousness and confidence, the strong forces making for the polarisation of political loyalties along largely confessional lines, and the generators and tempo of political mobilisation. But the new emphasis on ideology, the fructifying influence of cultural critics on the debate, and the increasingly detailed evidence of 'local realities' emerging from a burgeoning local studies sector, have combined to give us a richer historiography of the pre-Famine period. Above all else, the complexity of political positions (of Catholic prelates, reformers, patriotic Unionists, and a variety of political and cultural nationalists) warns us against the danger of oversimplification, of collapsing all politics into a simple story of polarisation. The 'search for stability'[53] in the immediate post-Union decades involved many circuitous routes, and strange companions sometimes shared part of these journeys and reconnoitres. Complexity did not begin or end in Ireland: for those drawn to parliamentary politics, Westminster provided a challenging and new setting for political engagement.[54]

If anniversaries were critical in prompting the flood tide of studies on the 1790s, culminating in the bicentenary of the 1798 rebellion, the sesquicentenary of the Great Famine also prompted (or at least hastened to completion) an enormous output of academic publications of a generally very high standard. So far as writings on the political dimension of the Famine are concerned, ideology has also loomed large in many of these publications, together with studies of the politics of poor relief, the politics of resistance and the politics of recrimination. Local studies of the Famine's impact have proliferated, and a large number are exemplary, in their use of sources and their awareness of the historiographical debate on the wider ramifications of the calamity.[55] The response of nationalist political leaders to the catastrophe has been examined in several of the main anniversary collections of essays on the Famine, and such politically sensitive issues as the level of evictions and the extent and methods of popular 'resistance' have also been re-examined.[56] But two major works of the 1990s, relating specifically to the political dimension of the Famine – in fact relating to the formulation and implementation of government policy – demand special mention. These are Donal A. Kerr's *'A Nation of Beggars'? Priests, People and Politics in Famine Ireland 1846–52*, published in 1994, and Peter Gray's *Famine, Land and Politics: British Government and Irish Society 1843–50*, published in 1999.[57]

The late Donal Kerr's work is a worthy sequel to his acclaimed earlier work on the Catholic Church and Peel's policy on Ireland in the first half of the 1840s. It is a model of the close, archive-based analysis of a key junction in public policy, the relationship between the Whig government of Lord John Russell and one of the major social and political forces (both institutionally and in terms of its popular influence) in Ireland – the Catholic Church. Government policy is scrupulously deciphered by Kerr, as are the dealings, direct and indirect, between the government and the Catholic bishops; and, in turn, there is a rich documentation of the pressures to which the Catholic bishops were subjected by the horror of events as they unfolded and by the appeals and advice they received from priests, charitable groups and a large number of individual correspondents. While a number of contextual biographies of churchmen published in recent years have been impressive,[58] the sheer range of Kerr's researches and his assured and judicious handling of the play of political forces – issues of motive and manoeuvre, of conscience and calculation, moral obligations and political realities, the sheer force of character and personality – give to his account of the Catholic Church and the Russell government's engagement with the crisis of the famine years in Ireland a unique authority.

Equally impressive, though quite distinctive in its focus, is Peter Gray's major book. Acknowledging the work of earlier scholars in the field of famine relief policy,[59] Gray situates his analysis of the origins and evolution of government policy on Ireland during the Famine within recent literature on ideology and political economy, on Protestant evangelicalism, and on the debate among the thinking (and policy-making) classes on both sides of the Irish Sea on what was described as the 'Irish land question'.[60] Gray eschews polemical or recriminatory flourishes; he is careful and balanced in his handling of evidence and in his judgements; and this, accordingly, gives all the greater weight to his conclusion that providentialism was indeed a critical aspect of a general outlook which determined the mindset of key figures charged with formulating and implementing government policy (especially relief policy) in Ireland during the Famine. As he concludes:

If any general conclusion can be drawn, it is that the Whig–Liberal government as a whole, and even its moralist ideologues, were less responsible for the social sufferings of the later 1840s than an attitude of mind that suffused the British political public, and set the parameters of State activity. The belief that the blight was a providential visitation, sent to bring Ireland into a higher state of social and moral organisation through a necessary measure of pain, shaped contemporary attitudes and subsequent apologetics. The dominant British 'memory' of the Famine thus centred on the notion that the physical and moral condition of Ireland had indeed been raised as a consequence of the providential advent of the potato blight, primarily through a 'free trade in land' and (somewhat euphemistically) mass voluntary emigration.[61]

The role and policy of the government during the Famine is a core concern of Kerr and Gray. But the questions posed by their work relate to a more general issue, namely, the role of the state in Ireland in the early and mid-Victorian years. To assess the particular role of the Victorian state in Ireland requires, of course, a familiarity with the role of that state throughout the different parts of the United Kingdom under the Union, and demands an assured grasp of the political (and ideological) world of Westminster and of those whose intellectual influence shaped the official mind of the day. Here, also, both Kerr and Gray succeed in identifying the particularity of the Irish case (in government thinking and policy), while at the same time confidently negotiating the high politics and the world of ideas, assumptions and prejudices operating at the metropolitan centre.[62]

The administrative 'experiments' undertaken, or forced upon, British governments by the special circumstances of Ireland after the passing of the Union, has been the particular territory of Oliver MacDonagh for several decades. Since 1990 there have been a number of new contributions in this area from Virginia Crossman.[63] In particular, her *Politics, Law and Order in Nineteenth-Century Ireland* focuses on the political framework in which the law was administered. As Crossman remarks,

> Levels of crime, and of agrarian crime in particular, came to be seen as a key indicator not only of the state of the country but also of political competency. The perceived extent of crime and disorder thus acquired a crucial significance. It was assumed to reflect the capacity of government, firstly to protect life and property, secondly to solve the land question, and thirdly to persuade people that the law existed for their protection and that it was in their interests to support it. Disorder was by its very existence a political issue.[64]

It might be added that equally political were the issues relating to recruitment, administration and deployment of the army and of the police forces in nineteenth-century Ireland, and in these areas also important new work has been published.[65]

The impact of the Famine on the political agenda was immediately felt in the sharp emphasis on land questions. Scholars have described the shift in the intellectual climate in Britain in which Ireland's problems (and the solutions to them) began to be recognised as requiring analysis in Irish terms rather than in 'normative' English terms (particularly in relation to land ownership and landlord-tenant relations). In this context, the major work by W. E. Vaughan on the land question in the mid-Victorian years combines subtle commentary on the politics of land with analysis of the economic and social aspects of its ownership, occupancy and use.[66] Indeed, in addition to the emergence of land as a key priority (a predictable political consequence of famine trauma), the immediate post-Famine political agenda of religious rights and privileges, of Irish education and the role of the churches therein, has been the focus of a modest level of scholarly attention, together with a welcome review of parliamentary politics in the 1850s and some further embellishment by Theo Hoppen of his major work on the electoral system and its operation.[67] A notably more ambitious study, over an extended period, was Oliver Rafferty's interpretative study of Catholicism in Ulster, which is constantly challenging in identifying and explaining some of the factors which gave its particular character to the Catholic community, and its concerns, in Ulster.[68] Irish Protestantism, and in particular Ulster Protestantism and its evangelical impulses, also benefited from major new work during the 1990s.[69]

The particular manifestation of Irish nationalist disaffection which finally prompted Gladstone to address this post-Famine Irish agenda of reforms (land, education, church rights and status) in the later 1860s was, of course, Fenianism. The 1990s saw some new work on certain aspects of Fenianism in Ireland. R. V. Comerford nuanced his own highly influential account of the origins and character of Fenianism; also there were a few biographies of minor figures and a small crop of corrective articles on relations between churchmen (bishops and defiant priests) and the Fenians, with one substantial reappraisal by Oliver Rafferty of the Catholic Church's response to the Fenian movement.[70] But there is need for a fresh examination of the politicisation of the rank and file Fenians (in the towns and cities in particular), and of the relationship of Fenians at local level to social and labour questions.[71]

By the final quarter of the nineteenth century, with further franchise extension and the irreversible (if, in the event, extremely slow) march towards adult suffrage already under way in the United Kingdom, the political 'wishes' of the people were still deemed to require careful 'reading' and scrutiny by the great and good (in other words, the people had to be educated to take a responsible view of the general good of society rather than concentrating on their own 'narrow' class interests) before issues became ripe for settlement at

Westminster. This ripening was to be painfully protracted in the case of women's suffrage.[72] But the case was different with regard to the Irish nationalist demand for Home Rule, which assumed centre stage importance in the politics of the 1880s. If the 1990s had seen little major new work on the Fenian movement of the 1860s, then the opposite was the case for Irish political movements and events of the last two decades of the nineteenth century, where the volume of publications was exceptionally heavy: in relation to the politics of the land struggle, of Home Rule, of Parnellite, anti-Parnellite and post-Parnellite politics. Again, we may remark that anniversaries (of Parnell's fall and death in the crowded year 1890–1) have played their part in filling the shelves. But other factors have been at play also. In fact, perhaps the most striking and, in terms of Irish historiography, most influential new direction in the 1990s writings on Irish political culture of the later nineteenth century was the growth of a strong and sympathetic historiography of Irish Unionism from the mid-nineteenth century through to the climacteric of the partition settlement of 1920–2.[73]

On Parnell and Parnellism, it seems fair to say that the essence of Paul Bew's characterisation of Parnell's politics still largely holds the field. Predictably, in view of the paucity of direct evidence on his motivation and intentions, Parnell's continuing inscrutability means that most of the assessments of him are strongly context-bound and inferential, both in respect of his 'rise' (to 1886), the difficulties of the later 1880s and the final tragic year of 1890–1.[74] But even the possibility (plausibly suggested by Patrick Maume) that he may have taken a Fenian oath in the early 1880s[75] has not seriously threatened the current orthodoxy that he was a political survivor (as Roy Foster has again insisted, in reaffirming the importance of his Wicklow gentry and family background).[76] Other orthodoxies include the following: that there was a strong element of social conservatism in his 'vision', especially in his aim of securing a continuing role in political leadership for the largely Protestant landlord class; that his grasp of the depth of Ulster Unionist opposition to Home Rule was defective (even if, at the least, he gave some indication near the end of his life of the need to conciliate: yet he saw Ulster as being an integral part of a Home Rule Ireland); and that his final year was not a year of deranged or wildly despairing political recklessness and flirtation with separatism and separatists, but rather a calculated and rational (if emotionally charged) attempt to reconstruct a political position for himself and for the Irish Home Rule party as independent of the main political parties in Britain as Parnell's party had been prior to 1886.[77] As the several collections of essays on Parnell and his movement emphasise yet again, a verdict on Parnell's ultimate political purposes (if indeed he had such definite ends clearly worked out) remains, and will continue to be, a matter for debate.

If the Parnell enigma continued to attract scholarly interest, perhaps the real bonus of the 1990s, in terms of the historiography of Irish nationalism, came in the form of studies of other Home Rule leaders, new major studies of the land question and of its relationship with the 'national' question (i.e. the question of devolved or 'national' self-government for Ireland), and significant publications on the meaning or political content and on the basis of support for Home Rule itself.[78] The post-Parnellite decade has seen a bumper crop of publications, with William O'Brien, in particular, under examination by several authors.[79]

Two substantial contributions on the political ramifications of the land question, based on theses completed some years ago but each taking due account of recent scholarship, are Philip Bull's *Land, Politics and Nationalism: A Study of the Irish Land Question*, and Donald Jordan's case study of land and politics in Mayo.[80] While Bull's book revisits the land question as the 'engine' of the popular movement for national self-government (in essentially Lalorite terms, but with close attention to the decisive changes in the class balance – and, by extension, the political interests – which had taken place in rural Ireland between the Famine and the land war), Jordan's case-study takes a long-term view of the dynamics of conflict over land in County Mayo. Jordan's local detail (including very valuable statistical material) is handled with assurance and the particular dynamics of the local tensions in Mayo (where Jordan's findings generally confirm and amplify the earlier commentaries on Mayo by Lee, Bew and, more recently, Gerard Moran) are effectively integrated into the general historiography of the land question in late nineteenth-century Ireland.[81]

While ranging widely over the land question in the nineteenth century as a whole, the main focus of Philip Bull's interest is William O'Brien and his United Irish League; and Bull's verdict is consistent with Paul Bew's contention that by the early twentieth century conciliation versus confrontation was the stark choice facing those nationalist politicians who had ridden the land question as the engine of popular mobilisation for home rule during the previous twenty years. Thus, for Bew, in the period 1890–1910 'two competing interpretations – one conciliatory and the other militant – fought out a battle for supremacy in Irish politics. . . . At its high point, the conciliatory principle was embodied in William O'Brien's All for Ireland League', in a determination to reconcile all classes and creeds (including landlords and other elements of the Protestant ascendancy) in moving towards consensus politics in the development of a new Ireland.[82] Bull also registers, and regrets, the failure after 1903 of conciliation and of O'Brien's enlightened strategy to reconcile Irish Protestant landlords to some version of a 'shared' national future (under devolved government) with the nationalist and Catholic majority in Ireland. For Bull, this failure of conciliation was due, ultimately, to the 'inability of the political culture to free itself of the habits of mind and action created by the land issue'.[83] These habits were confrontational, class-riven, and resonating in sectarian recrimination and accusation. But, following the land legislation's creation of the basis for a peasant proprietorship, these habits, if further encouraged (as, for example, was the case in the campaign against the ranchers) could only prove divisive and sterile even within the Home Rule nationalist community, where many wealthy ranchers were now stalwarts of the national demand for a devolved Home Rule parliament. The dynamics of class tension, even as the land question was 'settled' by legislation between 1881 and 1906, emerged strongly in the writings of the 1990s, not only in the works already cited but also in David Seth Jones's examination of the anti-grazier agitation and in a series of articles by Padraig Lane on the perspective and predicament of the agricultural labourers during the decisive phase of the land struggle.[84]

The benign view of O'Brien and of the conciliationist opportunity in early twentieth-century Ireland is strongly endorsed in most of the significant contributions on the Parnellite and post-Parnellite period written in the 1990s and since. Not surprisingly, John Dillon suffers in this historiography, being seen as an excessively insecure and unimaginative political player. Tim Healy, for his part, has been awarded a full biography, which has not quite succeeded in making him any more attractive as a person (or as a political colleague) than earlier critical portraits had suggested, but which does provide a much richer account of the complexity of his calculations, his ability to sniff changes in the political wind (which ultimately guaranteed him a place in the new political order of the Irish Free State after 1922), and of his sheer tenacity in the close-quarters political combat in which he spent his entire career.[85] Justin McCarthy has been favoured with a short biographical portrait by Eugene Doyle: it is a fair assessment of McCarthy, but not one that suggests that he was a major political influence (by force of personality or ideas) in his own time, any more than was the erratic F. H. O'Donnell, who also found a biographer in the 1990s.[86] John Redmond still awaits a full-length modern biography, though Paul Bew's sympathetic short study is characteristically perceptive and humane.[87] Nevertheless, the impression abides that Redmond was somehow lacking in a certain kind of political authority, even after he became titular leader of the virtually united Irish Party after 1900. It is not merely that some of the veteran leaders of the original Parnellite party – Healy, Dillon, even O'Brien – did not defer to him, but that he simply did not project himself with sufficient authority (or ruthlessness) to earn or to demand such notice from his colleagues. Indeed, the biographical studies of the other prominent Home Rule figures of the Parnellite era serve principally to underline the very exceptional character and leadership qualities of Parnell himself.

Detailed local studies of the Home Rule party remain relatively few, notwithstanding a number of good essays in the county history series and a generous supply of articles in various journals on specific aspects of local politics and elections in the Home Rule era, not least in the opposition to Home Rule among Protestants in predominantly Nationalist areas.[88] The Maynooth series on local history has given us one very welcome portrait of a local MP, newspaper proprietor and pillar of the party in Sligo.[89] The significance of newspapers in the creation of a bonded nationalist community, as well as the structure of the nationalist press in late nineteenth-century Ireland are superbly discussed in Marie-Louise Legg's *Newspapers and Nationalism: The Irish Provincial Press 1850–1892*.[90]

The underlying realities of power-in-the-making which can be identified in all of the flux of political contest and calculation in the Home Rule era are the concerns of two very different books by Emmet Larkin and Senia Pašeta.[91] Larkin's impressive volume provides heavily documented support for his already well-known contention that the configuration of power (and of power brokers) which emerged in Ireland in the final quarter of the nineteenth century was, in effect, the embryo of the later dominant social and political formation of the early Irish Free State.[92] Pašeta's short study raises valid questions on the formation (and objectives) of the Catholic elite (again the leaders-in-waiting of the new Irish state) at the turn of the century. Two further interpretative works on the politics of Home Rule demand special mention. Margaret O'Callaghan's highly original reappraisal of Conservative Party strategy under Balfour makes a good case for considering Balfour to have succeeded (not least through the device and the evidence of the Special Commission on Parnellism and Crime) in effectively associating Home Rule and the Parnellite machine with crime and intimidation, a key verdict in achieving and maintaining a broad alliance for Unionism. Her case is argued with great gusto and style.[93] Alan O'Day, who must share the palm with George Boyce and Alvin Jackson as the most prolific writers of the past decade on the politics of modern Ireland, produced what his publisher justifiably announced as 'the first account of Irish Home Rule to explain all of the self-government plans, placing them in context and examining the motives behind the schemes'.[94] O'Day offers useful (if not always immediately accessible) theoretical and comparative positions, within which to situate the Irish Home Rule debate. More fundamentally, however, he makes a 'clear distinction between moral and material Home Rulers. The former appealed especially to outsiders, some Protestants and the intelligentsia, who saw in self-government a means to reconcile Ireland's antagonistic traditions. In contrast, material Home Rulers viewed a Dublin government as a forum for Catholic interests'.[95] While this central distinction will strike many as over-schematic or reductionist, the work as a whole offers a welcome reappraisal of the Home Rule demand throughout its political life.

Within the historiography on Irish nationalism, the recent work which perhaps best illustrates the complexity of post-Parnellite politics, and the much more dense interpenetration of cultural and electoral politics – both among mainstream Home Rule party loyalists and among the 'mosquito' groups which began to emerge in numbers around the turn of the twentieth century – is Patrick Maume's *The Long Gestation: Irish Nationalist Life 1891–1918.*[96] It is, by any standards, an engrossing account of the sheer energy, variety and complexity of the different forms of nationalist political action: in electoral or protest politics, or indeed in the numerous cultural and industrial revivalist projects, some of whose participants may not have intended or acknowledged as having an explicitly political objective, but which, in the nature of things, were objectively part of the project of building up a 'self-reliant' Ireland. Maume's level of detail, and the matrix of connections, between people and organisations, which he establishes, may at times tax the stamina and concentration of even the most attentive reader. But his work is a significant achievement and repays the closest attention. The work also reinforces the established version of the extraordinary personality clashes and mutual suspicions and antagonisms which marked the political leadership (in parliament and in the country) of the Irish Party after the fall of Parnell and, indeed, long after the nominal 're-uniting' of the party under Redmond; the erratic political manoeuvres of William O'Brien described here may also act as a corrective to other more favourable recent portraits of O'Brien.

The distinctive perspective of women political activists on both the land struggle and on Home Rule has been noted for some time. The 1990s brought a good crop of biographical studies, and also a number of reflective contributions on the distinctive political agenda of these women – in industrial and labour issues as well as on the franchise question; and on the critique which some women provided of both the priorities and the political methods which characterised the male-dominated national political movements.[97] The international dimension of women's political engagement emerges as a significant characteristic in turn-of-the-century Ireland.

Constitutional and land issues did not monopolise the political agenda of late nineteenth-century Ireland, nor did they monopolise (though they dominated) the historiography of the 1990s. The exploration of the politics of labour and of class struggle, industrial organisation and challenge, sustained by the journal *Saothar*, saw noteworthy publications in the 1990s. On the one hand, Emmet O'Connor's *A Labour History of Ireland 1824–1960* (1992) offered a survey of modern Irish history in which labour and social class is installed as the presiding idea, the central organising perspective, of the narrative. Commemorative essays on trade union anniversaries, histories of individual unions, a series of stocktaking reviews of the historiography of labour in Irish history, and a larger number of articles on specific sites of industrial and political conflict, constitute a substantial contribution.[98] Moreover, local studies of labour history continued to be published in the 1990s – though at a modest pace and with an uneven geographical spread. Again, for a particular local case-study that addresses a range of important historiographical issues one may turn for an exemplar to Cork, and to Maura Cronin's *Country, Class or Craft? The Politicization of the Skilled Artisan in Nineteenth-Century Cork*.[99] The exploration of political agendas of different groups in urban Ireland in the later nineteenth century – class, confessional or communal politics – needs further local studies of this kind.[100]

However, it may well be that the most significant new contribution of the 1990s to the political history of nineteenth-century Ireland came in the flourishing area of studies of Irish Unionism: both in terms of the publications specifically concerned with the study of Irish – and, with understandable emphasis, Ulster – Unionism, and also in terms of general histories of Ireland under the Union in which the Unionist position and perspective are given more extensive and sympathetic discussion than was the case in earlier general histories.[101]

This growth in the number of publications on Irish Unionism, in its various dimensions, is, no doubt, the outcome of a number of factors operating in Irish society and among historians of Ireland during the past two decades or more. There is the increase in the number of leading scholars (including historians) born in, shaped by and sensitive to the complex political culture of Northern Ireland. Then there is the increasing desire for new historical analyses, at a time when a 'solution' to the conflict was deemed by all reasonable, moderate people to require the avoidance of any talk of victory or of any side 'prevailing' and, instead, an endorsement of 'parity of esteem' in devising the frameworks of accommodation to which all parties to the conflict might assent. Achieving parity of esteem, in turn, seemed to require at least some level of mutual understanding. In particular, and prob-ably in compensation for the historic neglect of scholarly attention to it, the origins and political character of popular Unionism demanded urgent exami-nation. Moreover, the number of conferences and publishing houses anxious to serve their market, and the fact that Northern Ireland became in many academic institutions throughout the world a key case-study of societies in conflict, no doubt provided a further stimulus to the flow of publications dealing with the origins and development of Unionism as a political idea in Ireland, and as a popular ideology in Ulster.

At a deeper level than these, as it were, opportunistic stimuli towards publication, there is the acceptance by a significant number of historians and other scholars writing on Ireland that the certainties and myths which sustain political activists in any movement, and which become codified in the rhetoric (and in the educational systems) of states and political regimes of the kind established in Ireland in 1920–2, need to be interrogated closely in the light of the historical evidence; and that, whatever the immediate political outcome, some of the uncertainty and complexity which was present in any given moment in the past needs to be recovered and re-presented. This anti-determinist reflex – which for a time was simplified and denounced as 'revisionism' – carried with it certain dangers, not least the temptation to indulge the counter-factual or to discuss the actual outcomes (and actors) of the historical process in dismissive or excessively cynical terms.[102] But the dominant intellectual temper of those historians who have been most prominent in offering a critique of Irish nationalism's tenets (and its 'version' of history), and, more recently, in exploring Irish Unionism, has been described by Alvin Jackson (himself a distinguished representative of the new direction) as 'empirical and sceptical' in approach, rejecting the definitive 'story' of Ireland narrative, or the Whiggish view of political and general historical forces 'culminating' in what was settled in Ireland in 1920–2.[103] Jackson's own remarkable general history, *Ireland 1798–1998* has been described as 'analytical, sceptical and humane',[104] and these virtues are well represented (though their relative weighting varies between different authors and works) in the best of the general histories, of Ireland and specifically of Ulster, and in a good proportion of the academic studies of Irish Unionism written during the past two decades.[105]

The shadow of contemporary political preoccupations invariably lies across historiographical directions and trends. Thus, in a political climate in which 'frameworks of accommodation' is a banner of virtue for most people anxious to see an end to bloodshed and conflict in Northern Ireland, it is only natural that earlier attempts at devising such frameworks should be looked at sympathetically. The Union arrangement of 1801 was one such framework, and Unionist ideas and political opinions throughout the nineteenth century covered a broad spectrum of positions on this framework: some seeing it, in liberal terms, as an enabling framework for accommodation between Britain and Ireland and within Ireland itself; others seeing it as a framework devised (and accordingly deserving of support) in order to guarantee the primacy (in power, influence, and symbolic esteem) of one confessional identity over another.[106]

The historiography which emerged in the 1990s, in terms of its tone and intellectual temper (whatever the precise political position of its practitioners) may be described as largely an historiography of liberal unionism, in which a continuing critique of the ideology (and, more particularly, the strategic political aims and internal inconsistencies and contradictions) of Irish nation-alism, is joined by a more sympathetic investigation than has hitherto been available of various aspects of Irish Unionist sentiment and argument during the nineteenth century, and, specifically, by an exploration of the complexity and vitality of popular Unionism in Ulster. The sheer range and variety of the contributions to this historiography can only be emphasised rather than illustrated here, covering as it does publications relating to Unionism and empire, agrarian tension, urban class politics, evangelicalism, popular ritual, together with a long list of specialist and local studies and of biographies.[107] Of the latter, Jackson's study of Colonel Saunderson is especially interesting, seeing him, as it were, as Parnell's Northern Unionist 'marker', and thereby underlining the indigenous strength of Ulster Unionist sentiment (as distinct from its function as political capital for outsiders such as Randolph Churchill, or indeed Edward Carson).[108] It would, perhaps, be appropriate to leave the last word on this recent flowering of historical scholarship on Irish Unionism to Alvin Jackson, in a passage from his general history of Ireland published in 1999:

> The history of Unionism in Ireland is a history of simplification, of retreat and retrenchment. Through much of the nineteenth century Unionism – defined very broadly as a belief in the constitutional connection between Britain and Ireland – was the normative condition of Irish politics. Unionism was a luxuriant intellectual growth, which entwined itself around mainstream Liberal and Tory politics and which pollinated even those more popular movements that have been seen exclusively within the history of nationalist development and progression: O'Connellite repeal and Parnellite Home Rule were, stripped of their patriotic ebullience, campaigns for a more workable relationship with Britain – for a more refined Union – rather than for absolute separation. Even when the definition is tightened and when Unionism is seen in a more conventional light (as the movement upholding the Act of Union), its ideological grip upon a wide and diverse section of Irish society, whether northern or southern, was still astonishing.[109]

In tone and poise it is difficult to think of a passage written during the 1990s by an Irish historian of Irish nationalism which combines emotional detachment with intellectual sympathy in a manner similar to this profile of Irish Unionism by Alvin Jackson.

⋆　⋆　⋆

The employment of a comparative dimension in the discussion of nineteenth-century Irish political developments has been generated from several different sources of interest and analytical approaches. Firstly, in studies on international relations, and specifically on conflict case-studies, the Irish, and specifically the Northern Ireland experience attracts attention: here the formidable, if frequently impenetrable, study of Ian Lustick must be mentioned.[110] The work of Tom Fraser has, more lucidly, used comparative frameworks, principally looking at partition settlements, with India and Palestine as cases for comparison with Ireland.[111] Ireland's ambiguous position within the British empire has been the subject of a fine collection of essays, many of them prompting a comparative perspective.[112] In particular, comparisons between Ireland and India in the nineteenth century have informed a number of publications. Some, but by no means all, of the authors making this comparison with India draw on the colonialist discourse, explicitly in terms of dependency theory and economic retardation, but also in terms of strategies of social control, elite management, and cultural hegemony.[113]

Closer to home, one of the more interesting developments of the recent past has been the increasing habit of comparing aspects of Ireland's historical experience with the experience of Scotland and, more recently, of Wales. Not surprisingly, both parallels and differences have emerged from these comparisons. The Irish–Scottish comparison has been in progress, at an academic level, for some time, encouraged by the periodic Irish–Scottish symposia of historians, the proceedings of which have produced a number of excellent volumes.[114] More recently, a more demonstrably political agenda has come into play, stressing the historic links, affinities and cultural continuities between Scotland and Ulster, as part of the contemporary cultural politics of cultivating a pan-British identity among loyalists as a counter to the perceived pan-nationalist agenda of celebrating 'varieties of Irishness'.[115]

But the debate (and more recently the political reality) of devolved government within the United Kingdom has relevance for the attractions of the comparative approach, together with the case made by some historians in recent years for adopting a British history perspective for the analysis of the relationships between all the peoples of the islands of Britain and Ireland. It has been argued that taking the archipelago as a whole as the key site or context of reference permits a fruitful examination of the common predicaments as well as the differences in circumstance of the English, the Scottish, the Welsh and the Irish, in all their cultural particularity, and their economic, social and political distinctiveness and interrelatedness.[116] While, as we have said, the Irish–Scottish comparative lens has been in use for some time, it is encouraging to see the beginnings of some meaningful Welsh–Irish comparisons.[117] Needless to say, a key site for investigating these interactions between the peoples of Ireland and Britain is the study of the immigrants of the different peoples: their fate in their new host society and their relationship to the politics of their host society as well as to the fate and politics of their native land.[118]

Turning, in conclusion, to a summary of what the 1990s produced in writings on Irish politics under the Union, I have sought in this essay to emphasise a number of key features of this body of writing. The increasing presence of ideology (its construction, its deployment, the conflicts over the 'meaning' of historical episodes or events) has been a striking feature of these writings. Postcolonialist discourse and, within limits, gender discourse have been important points of departure and of conjunction for scholars coming from different academic disciplines. Local studies – increasingly professional and increasingly organised in special series of publications – have illumined and clarified the local contours of political action (social forces, local leadership, the particularity of local issues) in ways which permit, indeed require, us to test all received generalisations about national issues and movements. A growing use of comparative models in the discussion of Ireland's historical experience has been noted. Finally, the 1990s saw the maturing of a strong and sympathetic historiography of Irish Unionism. This decade saw new and interesting questions posed for the writing of nineteenth-century Irish political history; and, significantly for the future, it also saw the emergence of new ways of posing such historical questions.

# CHAPTER 2

# Social History

❋

*Gary Owens*

The current state of writing on the social history of nineteenth-century Ireland could be summarised in two ways.

1.  The quantity of work being produced on nineteenth-century Irish social history has never been greater and its quality has never been higher. Historians in larger numbers than ever before are asking new questions about familiar topics such as popular protest, the Great Famine, and landlord–tenant relations. They are also experimenting with novel methodologies, many of them borrowed from other disciplines, and they are exploring a range of new and exciting subjects. The latter includes everything from popular medicine and newspaper cartoons to gender studies, reading and prostitution. Evidence of change and expansion is everywhere. Measured by the annual bibliography appearing in *Irish Economic and Social History*, the number of historical books and articles relating to social topics more than doubled in the 1990s.[1] The decade also saw new periodicals launched that brought the fruits of this research to an ever-expanding audience.[2] Even the journal that once seemed an impregnable bastion of high politics and empiricism, *Irish Historical Studies*, appeared to shake off its traditional image. It published a number of provocative essays on social and cultural themes and, by way of review articles, introduced its readers to current trends in postcolonial scholarship, critical theory, cultural studies, and works on gender and sexuality.[3] By the close of the decade, older attitudes and preoccupations seemed to be giving way to new ones; historians of nineteenth-century Ireland had, along with their counterparts in other countries, taken an unmistakable social and cultural turn.

2.  While the quantity of work being produced on nineteenth-century Irish social history has never been greater and its quality has never been higher, the gaps in our knowledge have never appeared wider. Research on many familiar topics has been uneven and in some cases it has apparently come to a

standstill. Areas that have long needed investigation remain virtually untouched; our knowledge of certain subjects is almost non-existent. Despite a willingness on the part of many historians to experiment with new techniques and cross-disciplinary approaches, they have not done so in anywhere near the same proportions as their counterparts in other countries. Elsewhere, for example, methodologies that, for want of a better term, go by the name of the 'new history' appear to have become the predominant mode of discourse. Patrick Joyce's observation about the current state of British history is simply not applicable to the study of nineteenth-century Ireland, namely: 'If once we were all social historians, now we are beginning to be all cultural historians. "Cultural history" seems to be the new disciplinary identity, which is increasingly organising the formats of scholarly activity.'[4] For all of the work that has been undertaken on Irish social history over the past decade or so, the field remains comparatively underdeveloped. It is still perceived as subordinate to political history of the traditional kind whose empiricist methodologies, positivist suppositions, and 'top-down' perspectives continue to hold sway among the majority of Irish historians. If certain of them have taken a social/cultural turn, most of their colleagues continue to follow straight, narrow and well-trodden paths.

Anyone who is familiar with the historiography of nineteenth-century Ireland will likely read each of those statements with varying degrees of approbation, disagreement, ambivalence, bemusement, or complete indifference, depending upon their interest in such matters and their notions of what the study of history is all about. Nevertheless, both assessments might be combined to form a broadly acceptable summary of certain trends. The essay that follows examines a selection of topics related to these trends that have engaged the attention of historians over the past decade and that will probably do so in the foreseeable future. It also discusses some anomalies in the historiographical landscape: fields of research once heavily cultivated that have lain fallow for years, fields that have never been worked with the intensity they deserve, and in some cases fields that have never been worked at all.

A brief article that surveys scholarly terrain as sprawling and diverse as social history cannot hope to be all-inclusive, nor can it help but reflect some personal research interests. Besides surveying familiar historiographical landmarks such as the Great Famine, this chapter discusses a few topics that up to now have not figured prominently in the literature on nineteenth-century Ireland or that are not commonly associated with 'social history' as that term is usually understood. Some of these are indicative of developments in what is commonly called the 'new history' or the 'new cultural history' that currently informs the work of historians of other countries. With its preference for examining past cultures 'from the bottom up', its enthusiastic borrowing of methodologies from other disciplines, its assumption that the production of 'value-free' history is impossible if not undesirable, and its fascination with a seemingly limitless range of subjects, the new history offers exciting possibilities for the study of nineteenth-century Ireland. Above all, it suggests a myriad of fresh alternatives to the assumptions, tastes, and orthodoxies that once dominated Irish historiography.[5]

★   ★   ★

Twenty years ago, a book roughly similar to this one brought together a group of scholars who surveyed what had been published during the 1970s on particular periods and sub-fields of Irish history. Remarkable as it now might seem, the Great Famine barely figured in any of their discussions. The reason was obvious: very little had appeared on the subject during that decade or, for that matter, during most of the preceding ones.[6] Although there was a stirring of interest in the Famine during the next ten years with the publication of such important works as Joel Mokyr's cliometric *tour de force*, *Why Ireland Starved*, James S. Donnelly's comprehensive chapters in the *New History of Ireland*, and the stimulating analyses of Mary E. Daly and Cormac Ó Gráda, relatively few items appeared until the mid-1990s.[7] Then, to put it mildly, came the deluge.

The decade of the 1990s – particularly the sesquicentenary of the Famine in 1995–7 – witnessed a flood of books, articles, and related matters that was unprecedented in Irish historiography. So intense was the outpouring that by 1997 Christine Kinealy could observe that 'more has been written to commemorate the 150th anniversary of the Great Famine than was written in the whole period since 1850'.[8] The inundation eased considerably by the close of the decade, but it showed no signs of ever abating completely. After years of virtual neglect, the Famine seemed to have emerged as a separate field of study in its own right.[9] As such, it produced a discernable historiography whose general structure has been likened to that of a modern war. We have, for example, a core of general works constructed mainly from the official records of central agencies that provide a view of events as seen from 'command headquarters' – that is, from the cabinet, the treasury, Dublin Castle and the like. These have often provoked controversy because they have necessarily addressed the question of culpability.[10] By the close of the 1990s, in fact, it had become almost obligatory for Famine scholars to point reproachful fingers at policy makers, intellectuals and bureaucrats in much the same way that military historians apportion blame among politicians and field commanders for disastrous or misguided strategies. At the same time, these works have sharply delineated the general features of the Famine and the efforts made, or not made, to combat its ravages and relieve its victims. Alongside these general works there has emerged a rich array of studies of specific problems and localities – the equivalents of regimental histories, analyses of battle tactics and weapons, records of specific campaigns, and accounts of life and death on the front lines.

From the perspective of the social historian, however, there are certain places where the comparisons between military and Famine historiography do not seem to be exact. One of these is the first-person narrative, the counterpart of the memoirs, diaries, and personal letters of rank-and-file soldiers that are now the stock-in-trade of military history. Until recently, the Famine equivalents of such items appeared to be scarce or non-existent. As David Fitzpatrick notes:

> From Black '47 to the present, the personal experience of suffering has eluded interpreters of the Irish Famine, largely dependent upon the attempts of contemporary analysts to generalise and simplify the chaotic reality. The reports of outsiders such as travel writers, journalists, philanthropists and government officials provide moving but often conventional evocations of suffering, which typically reveal more about the assumptions of the observer than the experience of those observed.[11]

Over the past decade or so, Fitzpatrick, Kerby Miller, and others have revealed the riches that can be found in letters to and from Irish emigrants during the nineteenth century.[12] In particular, they have shown how the letters of Irish people during the 1840s and 1850s to friends and relations abroad can yield remarkably vivid glimpses of the day-to-day experiences of individuals living through the Famine. The obvious challenge now confronting historians is to locate and utilise even more of this type of evidence, a process that Fitzpatrick observes is barely in its infancy. The task promises to be an arduous one, given the disparate and far-flung nature of these collections and considering that perhaps a million such letters were sent out of Ireland during the Famine years alone, but the rewards are potentially great.[13] Are there somewhere caches of correspondence between Irish people during the crisis years and immediately after that are comparable to, say, the invaluable epistolary accounts of life in the trenches and the home front during the Great War? Is there sufficient material of this kind to point up the vast diversity of individual and group experiences during the Famine, a diversity that Fitzpatrick reminds us is necessary to bear in mind if we are to escape the trap of perceiving the event as starkly uniform in its horror and devastation?[14] The answers to such questions might well be in the negative but they are nevertheless worth seeking.

The diversity of the Famine's impact is one of the main themes of Líam Kennedy, Paul S. Ell, E. M. Crawford and L. A. Clarkson's important

*Mapping the Great Irish Famine: A Survey of the Famine Decades* (Dublin, 1999), a book whose title masks its ultimate achievement of providing the first comprehensive single-volume social history of the event.[15] Drawing upon more than three decades of evidence (*c.*1841–71) in order to analyse conditions before, during and after the Famine, it also presents a vivid portrait of Irish society in the middle years of the nineteenth century.

*Mapping the Great Irish Famine* grows out of the database of Irish historical statistics, a monumental project launched in the early 1990s through the efforts of Kennedy and Max Goldstrom in the Department of Economic and Social History in Queen's University, Belfast.[16] The depth and comprehensiveness of the database allow the authors to analyse a variety of subjects from a regional perspective, something that previous studies had been unable to do in a systematic way. Thanks to their use of hundreds of maps and scores of charts and diagrams, it is now possible literally to see patterns and changes over time and space. In certain categories, including population decline, houseful sizes, types of houses, religious affiliation, and illiteracy rates, they are able to give visual form to their data at the level of Ireland's 320 or so baronies. Other topics are treated by way of counties and poor law unions. All of the material is grouped together in five large sections (population, social conditions, and the like) and nearly two-dozen sub-categories (e.g., the drolly entitled 'Adam and Aoife: gazing at gender ratios', '*An béal bocht*: the decline of the Gaelic language', etc.), and each of them is accompanied by a lively introduction that analyses the maps and charts that follow. Though the book does not provide a bibliography – a sorely needed resource for the social history of these years – its authors liberally season their text with helpful footnotes that steer the reader to a range of primary and secondary sources. Many of the latter reflect the most advanced Famine scholarship of recent years.

The database sharpens many familiar features of Irish society in these decades and revises others. It comes as no surprise, for example, to see graphic evidence that people in the west of Ireland were less literate than their eastern counterparts (women more so than men); that they married younger, spoke Irish in larger numbers, lived in worse houses, were more commonly engaged in agriculture than manufacturing, and suffered higher proportions of sickness, death, eviction and emigration during the Famine. But when it is finely tuned, the data can also disclose the complexities that lay beneath these general patterns. A good example is literacy whose advance from east to west, though inexorable, was halting and uneven: for at least three decades the population of several County Waterford baronies proved exceptionally resistant to reading and writing; illiteracy was especially tenacious among females in Connemara, west Mayo, and parts of west Donegal. Demographic trends are another case in point. The database shows that fertility rates were dropping in certain counties in Leinster before the Famine and this, combined with other forces such as a rise in emigration, helped to put the brakes on overall population growth well before the crisis years. The decline in fertility rates stemmed from a number of demonstrable causes, among them a rise in the mean age of marriage (and contrary to conventional wisdom, Irish people in the early nineteenth century did not marry at an unusually young age) and a trend towards celibacy in both sexes. These are features long associated with Irish society in the *late* nineteenth century but, as the database shows, they were clearly discernable before 1841 and the Famine did little to alter the general patterns of marriage and family formation.

Topics such as these, chosen from the wealth of material on display in *Mapping the Great Irish Famine*, reflect the continuities and discontinuities that ran through Irish society in the nineteenth century and underscore the central place of the Famine in the history of modern Ireland. With regard to the latter, the database lays firmly to rest the once-current notion that the Famine was not a watershed, but that it merely accelerated social and economic changes that had long been at work. As the authors conclude:

> The bulk of the evidence suggests that the Great Famine did mark a fundamental divide in Irish history. It was a dark chasm, partly bridged by stepping-stones, between two epochs . . . the Great Irish Famine convulsed society at all levels, with consequences for virtually every sphere of life from the religious to the economic, and the cultural to the political. The nature and form of the relationships which connected the effects of the Famine to the phenomenon itself varied, as did the timing. Some of the relationships were indirect or worked with a time lag, but were no less important for all that. Viewed from the mirror of late Victorian society, pre-Famine Ireland must have appeared a strange, even foreign country.[17]

As helpful as it might be to see Irish society during the Famine era through the wide-angle lenses that the database provides, it is the close-range perspective – the 'personal experience of suffering' in Fitzpatrick's words – that holds a special fascination for scholars and general readers alike. This partly accounts for the upsurge in the number of Famine studies of specific localities that appeared in such large numbers during the 1990s that they might now be said to constitute an historiographic sub-category all their own. Among the more well-known of these is Robert Scally's study of the community of Ballykilcline, County Roscommon before and during the Famine, a book that tries to look beyond the boundaries of that small town-land and explore wider social and cultural matters.[18] It is, in other words, an experiment in microhistory. Similar works by historians of other countries, particularly France and Italy, have shown that small can be, if not always beautiful, at least highly illuminating.[19] Scally's book, which is notable for being one of the few examples of an Irish microhistory,[20] is illuminating as

well, even if it leaves certain questions unanswered and stretches for conclusions that are not always within reach of the evidence.

Like many microhistories, *The End of Hidden Ireland* is constructed around
a corpus of legal documents, in this case the records generated by a decade-
long dispute between the tenants of Ballykilcline and Crown Commissioners
over unpaid rents. The tenants lost, and in 1847 the majority of them were
evicted. Scally works outward from this tangled affair to discuss the social
and cultural environment of the inhabitants of Ballykilcline. He argues, for
example, that theirs was a closed, traditional, timeless world – the 'Hidden
Ireland' of Daniel Corkery's classic account – crushed by the might of a
modernising, colonial, market-driven system. In reality, the 'traditional' world
that Ballykilcline supposedly represented was, at least in economic terms, a
recent phenomenon: its population (bi-lingual or monoglot English-speakers)
engaged in subsistence arable farming only from the mid-eighteenth century
onwards. Nor were they particularly isolated and inward-looking: they had
the knowledge and wherewithal to hire prominent legal counsel in their
dispute with the Crown; they won the support of none other than the eminent
MP, the O'Conor Don; and recent archaeological excavations in the area
indicate that they participated in a far-flung market network.[21]

Despite these and certain methodological issues that the book raises,[22]
*The End of Hidden Ireland* represents a significant contribution to nineteenth-
century historiography. It is unquestionably the most ambitious, if not the
best-written, example we have of a study that links events in a tiny community
to macrohistorical trends. That it sometimes falls short of the mark set by
practitioners of microhistory in other fields does not detract from its achievement. Above all, it should encourage others to undertake similar projects.
Nineteenth-century Ireland abounds in well-documented subjects – trials,
violent incidents, everyday events and rituals, small groups and communities –
that might be used to open windows onto larger, unexamined vistas or give a
fresh perspective to long-familiar landscapes. They require only discovery,
spadework and imagination.

A handful of works that took a broader view of the Famine have appeared
more recently, testifying to an enduring – if not an expanding – interest in the
subject. Chief among them is James S. Donnelly's masterful *The Great Irish
Potato Famine*.[23] His book is built around the valuable chapters on the Famine
that he contributed to volume five of the *New History of Ireland*,[24] an exceptional compilation of historical scholarship that, alas, carries an exceptional
price tag. Donnelly's analysis is now available in a reasonably priced edition
that also contains his more recent research on Famine clearances, emigration,
and the poor law. To these have been added lengthy chapters that explore
historiography and the ways that nationalists constructed the Famine in the
late nineteenth century. As well, the book contains more than a hundred

well-produced illustrations, maps, and charts – each of them with helpful captions – which in themselves constitute an important visual record of the catastrophe and its aftermath. Donnelly has provided social historians and others with a much-needed, comprehensive account that will be a boon to scholars and general readers for decades to come.

★   ★   ★

Death and its supposed pre-eminent place in the Irish imagination is a good example of a subject that awaits investigation at both the micro and macro level. To many observers, Irish people in the nineteenth century appeared to be obsessively preoccupied with the rituals of death and mourning. Typical was the German visitor Johann Kohl who commented in the 1840s that, whereas public mourning was more widespread in the United Kingdom than any place that he knew in Europe, nowhere did it seem more pervasive than in Ireland.[25] More recent observers have discussed a culture of death that developed in Ireland during the nineteenth century, a veritable *thanatophilia* that permeated literature, the arts, social institutions, and nationalist politics. One writer, in fact, uses the term *theatrum mortis* or 'theatre of the dead', as a metaphor for the funerary culture that is said to have blossomed in Ireland over the course of the nineteenth century and that persists to the present day.[26]

The extent to which this term is appropriate, however, remains an open question since the subject has generated so little research. There is nothing in nineteenth-century Irish historiography to compare with the recent work of British, American and, above all, French scholars who have emphasised the central place of death and bereavement in their respective cultures.[27] 'Every society', writes the French historian Michel Vovelle, 'gauges and assesses itself in some way by its system of death'.[28] This is a central assumption of recent work on attitudes toward death and the afterlife in nineteenth-century France, a society that bore obvious similarities to Ireland. Not only were both countries predominantly Roman Catholic, but they each experienced social, religious, economic and political changes in the century or so before the Great War that were, if not identical, certainly profound in their respective effects. In the case of France, these changes generated new attitudes towards death that were expressed in folk religion, clerical teaching and conduct, the disposal of the dead, funeral rites, and the commerce of death.[29]

Presumably there were equivalent alterations in Irish thought and behaviour during the nineteenth century. But what were they? Gearóid Ó Crualaoich's short but useful investigation of the 'merry wake' – one of the few studies of Irish mortuary rituals to have appeared in recent years – offers a couple of suggestions that could serve as the starting point for further work.[30] Wakes, like other traditional activities such as pattern-festivities and pilgrimages, became contested practices in eighteenth- and nineteenth-century Ireland. Religious and civil authorities denounced these rituals for a host of reasons, but they especially disliked the licentiousness, high-spirits, and emotional displays of public mourning that accompanied them. Nevertheless, the merry wake persisted and became, as Ó Crualaoich suggests, 'a central social mechanism for the articulation of resistance – or at least reaction – on the part of the Irish peasantry to new forms of civil and clerical control in Irish society'.[31] He also points to the differences between wakes associated with 'timely' deaths (usually of elderly people 'whose time had come') and those for 'untimely' deaths (typically the young or healthy). These he relates to 'two separate cosmological mechanisms or agencies of death' that co-existed in the folk mentality, one of them Christian, the other pre-Christian. There was, in other words, a remarkable complexity inherent in this unique mortuary ritual that reflected wider cultural realities.

The largely unexplored urban face of death in nineteenth-century Ireland also offers a wide array of research opportunities. Starting in the 1820s, public cemeteries were established in Dublin, Cork, Belfast, Limerick and other places that were open to Catholics and Protestants alike. For the first time in Irish history, the kinds of funerals, tombs, and interments that had hitherto been available only to a small portion of the population became a possibility for the majority. In Dublin as elsewhere, there was a steady commerce in death that developed to support the new burial practices. For example, the number of city firms listed as undertakers doubled between the mid-1850s and 1870; there was a corresponding expansion of establishments specialising in the accoutrements of bereavement (e.g., crape, paramatta, jewellery made from Whitby jet) for middle- and upper-class mourners. However, we know next to nothing about this phenomenon and a host of related topics. These include possible differences between Catholic and Protestant mortuary rituals and sentiments about death, as well as regional and class variations; the effects of the 1832 Anatomy Act which, as Ruth Richardson has shown, brought substantial changes in English attitudes toward burials, especially among the poor;[32] the impact of cholera and the other deadly epidemics of the nineteenth century – not to mention the Great Famine – on popular conceptions of death, burial and the afterlife; the design and social function of urban cemeteries; and the structural changes in funerary culture that took place in Ireland from the late eighteenth century down to the Great War.

The spectre of death haunts the pages of Jacinta Prunty's prize-winning *Dublin Slums 1800–1925: A Study in Urban Geography*, and for good reason: Dublin's mortality rates in the nineteenth century were unquestionably the highest of any city in the United Kingdom. The capital was literally a death trap for its poorer inhabitants. As her subtitle suggests, however, Prunty is less concerned with the culture of death than with its social and physical environment. Her study is notable on a number of grounds, not the least of them being its focus upon urban poverty, a topic that historians have hitherto passed over in favour of research on rural distress. Their comparative lack of interest in Dublin's poor is surprising, considering that about half the capital's inhabitants were slum-dwellers and that they lived in conditions more appalling than anywhere in western Europe. The city's poor were also inescapable: they were most heavily concentrated in the squalid tenements of the Liberties on the south side and those on the former Gardiner estate on the north side (Prunty makes the latter the subject of a meticulous case-study). At the same time, there was hardly an area of Dublin where the destitute could not be found: Prunty shows them living literally in the shadows of the finest Georgian homes, in cramped courts behind the better shops, and in the dark cellars of houses on both sides of the Liffey. Unlike their British counterparts, they were not the victims of industrialisation but of the *absence* of industry and of the general economic malaise that gripped the country from the early 1800s onward. Those who profited from their misery were not so much villainous British or ascendancy landlords but middle-class Dubliners, Catholic as well as Protestant, who speculated in city property.

Prunty, a geographer, delineates the gloomy features of Dublin's slum problem, illustrating through scores of maps and charts precisely where the poor lived, where deadly diseases thrived, and where housing was the worst. Above all, she details the various schemes that generations of reformers, politicians, charitable bodies and others undertook to improve conditions. Their progress was painfully slow and their victories were invariably piecemeal but, considering the enormity and complexity of the difficulties confronting them, it is a wonder that they accomplished anything at all. As Prunty notes, Dublin's slum problem consisted of a tangle of discernible but tightly interwoven threads:

> contagious disease, poor sanitation . . . multiple occupancy and overcrowding of old building fabric, moral and physical 'degradation', vagrancy, begging, homelessness, and the policing, control and relief of the poor by state and charity organisations, all set against a backdrop of (initially) worthless local government and endemic poverty.[33]

Her book suggests what might be achieved for other Irish cities. How did slum conditions in the capital compare with similar districts in Cork and Limerick and with the working-class areas of Belfast? It might also be instructive to see Dublin's slums set even more directly against those of Britain and the continent. Further work on urban poverty might, as with the Famine, seek to understand the subject from the perspective of its victims rather than those who observed it from the outside. As Prunty herself notes, what is missing from the masses of official and private records are the voices of the urban dispossessed themselves. First-hand information about everyday life, customs and experiences relating to Dublin's slums prior to 1900 is thin on the ground but it does exist. Literary sources and travellers' accounts, however distanced from the subject, might be mined for information and used in innovative ways. So, presumably, could emigrants' letters and newspapers, the latter source having only recently become the subject of serious analysis.[34]

Much of Prunty's book is necessarily concerned with questions of public health and sanitation. As such, it adds to our knowledge of the history of medicine in nineteenth-century Ireland, an immense territory that historians have hardly begun to chart. It is indicative of the status of work on the subject that a collection of articles billed as 'the first substantial modern history of medicine in Ireland' did not appear until 1999. As its editors Greta Jones and Elizabeth Malcolm note, the essays that comprise the volume – most of which deal with nineteenth-century subjects – 'are in effect a collection of spotlights illuminating a small number of points in a vast sea of darkness'.[35] While there are many histories of hospitals, medical schools, biographies of doctors, and studies of state assistance to medicine, as Jones and Malcolm remark, in words that could easily be applied to other areas of Irish social history: 'the approach taken to these topics has in the main been positivistic, factual and descriptive rather than analytical and contextual'.[36] Their volume offers a corrective to these traditional approaches and gives ample evidence of how new paths might be carved out of familiar terrain. Certain articles – among them Laurence M. Geary's study of a priest-healer in the 1820s, Peter Froggatt's investigation of medical education, and Maria Luddy's look at nursing in late nineteenth-century workhouses – reveal the pervasiveness of sectarianism and politics in areas that have typically been considered free of such influences.[37] Other essays such as Markus Reuber's 'Moral management and the "unseen eye"', suggest how the history of particular institutions, and not merely medical ones, might be illuminated through innovative techniques borrowed from other disciplines. He examines Ireland's lunatic asylums in the early nineteenth century through their architecture and discloses how social attitudes toward the insane were mirrored in the very shape and structure of the buildings that were erected to contain them.[38]

Joseph Robins's *The Miasma: Epidemic and Panic in Nineteenth-Century Ireland* adds another perspective to the history of medicine.[39] His highly readable account of the impact of infectious disease (chiefly typhus and cholera) contains a wealth of information drawn from an impressive array of sources. Ranging widely both in time and space (about a quarter of the book deals with the spread of disease through Irish emigrants to Britain and North America), it offers a useful guide for those who would undertake the much-needed task of investigating the social and cultural impact of the great epidemics of the nineteenth century in greater depth.

★   ★   ★

'Vast' is an adjective that does not begin to describe another subject that is closely associated with nineteenth-century Ireland: that of public violence, particularly the public violence associated with mass protest. Back in the 1970s, Irish historians developed a keen interest in one facet of this pheno-menon: namely, rural unrest as expressed in the activities of agrarian secret societies, or whiteboyism, especially in the pre-Famine period. The work of these scholars produced a rich yield of books and articles and by the early 1980s, it seemed destined to generate even more fruitful results. Writing in 1983, for example, Samuel Clark and James S. Donnelly outlined the kinds of work that had been carried out on pre-Famine agrarian secret societies up to that time.[40] It appeared to them that the more historians learned about whiteboyism, the more they began to comprehend its complexity, magnitude and importance. There was, they wrote, 'an inseparable link' between this collective activity and the very structure of rural society to the extent that 'an appreciation of the one is impossible without an understanding of the other'. It was important, therefore, for scholars to undertake a systematic analysis of the various movements, from lengthy, large-scale protests extending over vast regions to more geographically restricted, short-lived disturbances and the forces that gave rise to them. 'Only when historians have accumulated a much wider range of such studies', Clark and Donnelly concluded on a note of positivist optimism, 'will they be able to make general statements with some measure of confidence and to provide tests for many of the hypotheses . . . with which they have been working'.[41]

A number of important studies of rural violence appeared over the next few years, among them contributions from M. R. Beames, Tom Garvin, and Donnelly himself, but with the 1990s scholarly interest in the problem all but vanished.[42] The only substantial work of the past decade to focus on secret society activity of this kind was Kevin Kenny's masterful analysis of the Molly Maguires, a book that is mainly concerned with the activities of that group in the United States during the late nineteenth century.[43]

If publication on this subject came to a near standstill during the 1990s, it was not because the work of the 1970s and 1980s had left nothing more to say. If anything, the research of those years merely delineated the problem and suggested new paths to follow. We still lack full-scale analyses of various nineteenth-century disturbances, among them the immense Rockite insur-rection that disrupted Munster and parts of Leinster (1822–4), the Terry Alt agitation that was rooted in County Clare (1829–31) and the Whitefeet disorders that spread across various midland counties (1830–4), to name some of the more well known. Historians have shown comparatively little interest in these and similar phenomena despite their prominence in the contemporary imagination and despite a rich store of information about them that exists in such locations as the National Archives of Ireland, the reports of parliamentary commissions, contemporary newspapers, and the folklore archives in University College Dublin and the Ulster Folk and Transport Museum.[44]

We need more studies of agrarian protest for essentially the same reasons that Clark and Donnelly offered two decades ago, but they should be studies that do more than relate the highlights of specific insurrections and analyse the social composition and economic motivations of secret societies. They might also probe more deeply into the mentalities and cultural milieux of the people who participated in them, areas that previous works did not investigate in depth. This would not be an easy task, but one approach that offers some guidance is that of Peter Sahlins who has analysed a similar rural protest movement, the 'Demoiselles' in France in the 1830s, from a cultural perspective; that is, through the value systems, perceptions, rituals, and symbolic expressions of its participants.[45]

Luke Gibbons and David Lloyd, two non-historians who have written extensively on nineteenth-century Ireland, have also offered some fresh ways of thinking about popular protest. They have each emphasised how the mental and symbolic worlds of agrarian groups contrasted with those of mainstream nationalist movements. Lloyd notes, for example, that the rhetoric of Daniel O'Connell's nationalist project emphasised abstract national symbols such as Kathleen Ni Houlihan which, like other metaphoric constructions, aimed to subsume the particular into the universal; in this case, to inspire good nationalists 'to subordinate their private interests into the greater will of the nation'. By contrast, agrarian secret societies expressed themselves allegorically and metonymically through such figures as 'Terry Alt's Mother' or 'Queen Sive' and in so doing stressed the local, the particular, the tangible. These qualities contributed to 'a language of personal acquaintance', as Gibbons puts it, that was incompatible with the transcendent, totalising aspirations of mainstream nationalist movements.[46] Theirs was a coherent (if sometimes muted) political language that deserves to be listened to as closely and taken as seriously as the hegemonic rhetoric of contemporary writers, party leaders and MPs. Customarily, popular movements have been treated as political aberrations or, at best, as curious specimens of 'proto-nationalism'. When viewed from the perspective of traditional historiography, notes Lloyd, they appear as shadowy confederacies 'whose lines of force are interrupted, inconsequential, peripheral to the main line of historical development'.[47]

He suggests an alternative perspective for Irish historians in the work that students of popular movements in India have pioneered over the past two decades. Under the rubric 'subaltern studies', they approach the history of colonial India from the point of view of the mass of the population who developed strategies of resistance that often differed from those of nationalist political leaders and their parties but that were no less effective. Examining these strategies often requires them to rely heavily upon unconventional sources: oral testimony, popular memory, folklore and visual artefacts among others.[48]

Another form of rural violence that was endemic to certain areas of Ireland, particularly in the pre-Famine years, was that of faction fighting. Again, Clark and Donnelly raised pertinent questions about this phenomenon in the early 1980s that still require answers, namely:

> What were the reasons for the transformation of factions after 1800 into especially violent collectivities? . . . What were the special characteristics of Irish society and of the relationship between Irish country people and the state that made faction fighting so much more prevalent in early nineteenth-century Ireland than in most other western European countries?[49]

The activities of fighting factions have rarely been treated with the seriousness or the thoroughness that they deserve and that historians of other countries have devoted to their counterparts.[50] Irish factional warfare is too often dismissed as a kind of primitivist recreation – ritual head-bashing among country lads with a perverse sense of fun who lacked for other amusements.[51] This does not do justice to the earnestness and deadliness with which these groups conducted their vendettas or the extent to which factions were imbedded in the day-to-day life of their communities. As with agrarian secret societies whose fringes often blended imperceptibly into those of fighting factions, information about these groups too often comes from people who held them in contempt: the constabulary, newspapers, and mainstream politicians of all descriptions. But the biases and omissions inherent in much of the evidence need not deter historians from using these sources in different and more creative ways and from drawing upon records that have been under-utilised (the huge amount of material in the folklore archives comes once again to mind). Until we have a clearer, more comprehensive picture of factions, secret societies, and the perceptions of those who constituted, supported, and opposed them, our knowledge of nineteenth-century Irish rural society will remain incomplete. The same holds true of the sectarian violence that developed and grew to maturity in Ulster prior to 1914.[52]

Factions and secret societies did not have a monopoly on public violence in the nineteenth century. The state exercised its fair share as well, chiefly in the form of public executions. This is a subject that historians of Britain, Germany and elsewhere explored in some depth during the 1990s but it has generated little interest among Irish scholars.[53] We know little about the working of the capital code in Ireland prior to the abolition of public hangings in 1868, though it would seem to have operated with greater ferocity than we have perhaps realised. It has been suggested, for example, that Ireland in the mid-nineteenth century was relatively innocent of the noose when compared with the rest of the United Kingdom.[54] In reality, the proportion of Irish executions to its population was probably not that much different from its larger neighbour – the nation that led the rest of Europe in its use of the public gallows. There were, for example, just over 500 people executed in England, Wales and Ireland during the three decades leading up to the elimination of public hangings. Nearly a third of these (some 150) took place in Ireland whose population varied between one fifth and two fifths of England and Wales. These figures would suggest that the gibbet was as familiar a sight to Irish people in the first half of the nineteenth century as to their English and Welsh neighbours. Newspapers sometimes described crowds in the tens of thousands turning out for hangings in larger towns and the common practice of executing convicted felons at the sites of their alleged crimes (often on portable gallows) could bring the grim spectacle to smaller places in more remote districts. The Dublin and provincial press regularly carried detailed accounts of executions – often with the final words of the condemned and gruesome descriptions of their deaths – suggesting the existence of an interested readership. Needless to say, hangings also featured prominently in popular poems and ballads.

But how did Irish people in the nineteenth century regard executions and how, if at all, did their perceptions change over time? Is it possible to speak of a uniquely Irish scaffold crowd, one that was comparable to the English version that Victor Gatrell tells us 'touched the deepest anxieties of the polite classes . . . [and] takes us to the heart of popular mentalities as well'?[55] Was there a movement afoot in Ireland, as in other countries from at least the 1820s, to abolish public executions? If so, who took part in it and what forms did their campaigns take? These are but a few obvious questions that need to be answered concerning this large and woefully neglected topic.

⋆ ⋆ ⋆

For every book, article, and topic mentioned above, dozens more beg for discussion. This examination of selected writings on selected subjects – the Famine, death and bereavement, urban poverty, medicine, rural protest and public violence – has merely hinted at the kinds of questions that have engaged social historians in recent years. The many challenges and opportunities that these topics offer have their counterparts in countless other areas that are ripe for further investigation. These include the study of popular and material culture; rural and urban class relations; the social dimensions of sport; perceptions of childhood, old age, and sexuality; the family; social memory and commemoration – the list could be extended indefinitely.

The wider field of social history is increasingly being discussed in terms of 'total history', a phrase suggesting that every aspect of human activity now seems open to examination. Historians are currently investigating problems that were unheard of even a decade ago and they are producing histories of topics that once were thought not to have a history. It is not uncommon these days to encounter full-length studies of such matters as gestures, public fears, smells, sounds, silences, shoplifting, dreams, reading, gossip, and even the meaning of black clothing in the nineteenth century. Underpinning this activity is the notion that, in Peter Burke's words, 'what had previously been considered as unchanging is now viewed as a "cultural construction", subject to variation over time and space'. [56]

If Irish historians have been more reluctant than others to follow these trends, they will almost certainly do so in greater numbers over the coming years as the horizons of social history continue to expand. At some point in the twenty-first century – and we can only hope that it occurs sooner rather than later – someone will publish a monumental synthesis of research in the field that does for the social history of nineteenth-century Ireland what Cormac Ó Gráda and Alvin Jackson have recently done for Irish economic and political history respectively.[57] Given the quality of scholarship that is now being produced and the prospect of more creative work yet to come, it will rest upon substantial foundations indeed. Being the first work of its kind, its appearance will also signal the coming of age of modern Irish social history.

# CHAPTER 3

# Women's History

❋

*Maria Luddy*

My focus on women's history is deliberate, although literature surveys in the field of women's history almost always include a substantial discussion of gender history. Debates about the value and meanings of gender history as opposed to women's history have waged in the wider historical community but have received little attention from historians of Ireland. Gender history is often considered, because of its promise of inclusiveness and theoretical possibility, a more 'appropriate' way to study women in history.[1] Gender analysis, however, has not been a principal concern of any Irish historian, a sign perhaps of our lack of engagement with international historical debates in this area. Indeed, we have hardly managed to get to grips with women's history.

It was in the 1970s that the first modern treatments of Irish women came to be written. The landmark was the broadcast, between October and December 1975, of a Thomas Davis lecture series on the position of women in Irish society. This series was published in 1978 as *Women in Irish Society* edited by Margaret MacCurtain and Donncha Ó Corráin.[2] It contained survey articles on topics ranging from 'Women in early Irish society' to 'Women and the family'. The end of the 1980s boasted three edited collections and three monographs directly concerned with women in Ireland in the nineteenth century. By the end of the 1990s there were in the region of sixty articles and some forty books dealing either with, or, at least containing substantial information on, women in Ireland in this period. The more substantial published studies have focused predominantly on five particular areas: religion, work, emigration, education and politics. Other subjects such as crime, sexuality, illness and poverty have received relatively little attention from historians. From the limited work currently available it is already clear that historians of women in Ireland have made a critical contribution to the study of nineteenth-century Ireland.

*Maria Luddy*

RELIGION

Religious communities of nuns have received particular attention from historians. Since the 1980s the emphasis has moved away from finding heroines and models of piety among nuns to an analysis of the general membership of religious communities, women's reasons for choosing a convent life, the charitable, educational and welfare work of the community, the internal structure of these communities and nuns' relationships with each other, with church authorities and the public generally. Recent discussion of convents and nuns has revolved around issues of autonomy and control, of the practical impact of female religious communities on the social and cultural development of Irish society since the late eighteenth century. Caitriona Clear's 1987 monograph, *Nuns in Nineteenth-Century Ireland*,[3] was the first attempt to examine the role of nuns as women in Irish society, and investigated the social composition of these communities along with the work they carried out, their financial arrangements and, importantly, the attractions they offered young women in society.[4] In Clear's work nuns played an auxiliary role in the modernising Catholic church emerging in Ireland from the late eighteenth century. Because of their subordinate position and subjugation by the church hierarchy nuns could not develop a clear sense of their power and place in Irish society.

A more recent study of nuns delves deeper. Mary Peckham Magray's *The Transforming Power of the Nuns: Women, Religion, and Cultural Change in Ireland, 1750–1900* (1998)[5] adds considerably to our knowledge of the attraction of religious life for women in this period. Her insights differ considerably from those revealed in Clear's work. Women, Magray argues, were central to the emergence of convents from the late eighteenth century in spite of the credit for this expansion often being given to clerics. It was women themselves who generated the momentum for convent foundation, providing financial support for these communities. While social, demographic and cultural changes have been given as reasons for convent expansion, Magray argues that it was also the nature of convent life itself which proved a powerful attracting force for many women. Communal life offered them not only a spiritual but also an emotional and material experience. Magray also focuses attention upon the personal relations that existed within religious communities where loyalty to the community was often encouraged through personal devotion to the leadership. She makes a strong case for the role of nuns in revitalising the Catholic Church as allies of the reforming bishops appointed from the 1830s. Here Magray, at odds with Clear, argues convincingly that it was the development of women's religious communities and the work they carried through that made possible the transformation of the Irish church and Irish society in the nineteenth century. One of the major strengths of the work is to show that women religious were central to the evolution of social and

44

cultural life in nineteenth-century Ireland; to ignore their influence is to misunderstand a major historical force in Irish society.[6]

The studies completed on convents have laid bare the internal hierarchical structure of religious communities that rested on the distinction between lay nuns and choir nuns, distinctions essentially of class. The division between lay and choir nuns was not just a customary or traditional one but was consciously institutionalised in the rules and regulations of the community. Internal convent hierarchies provide a microcosm for the study of class relations in the nineteenth century. Class and wealth decided leadership issues within convents as much as they did in the wider community outside the convent walls. What these works show is that religious life could be liberating for many women. Once within the convent, some women used that life as a vehicle for advancement and self-expression. Some women could also achieve positions of authority and power that were unavailable to lay women.

Other recent work on nuns includes the publication of a biography of Margaret Aylward, founder of the Sisters of the Holy Faith.[7] Indeed, the most popular form in which women's history has been presented in Ireland is through the biographical study. It is a genre beloved of publishers who see a ready market for such work. Biographies can of course provide important insights into individual women's lives for this period but their quality varies. Biographies tend to focus on the achievements of individual women, often without fully exploring the context in which these women lived and their relationships and alliances with other women and men. While there are numerous hagiographical accounts of the lives of convent founders it is essential that more objective studies of individual women's lives be undertaken in order that such women can be restored to their historical significance. Prunty's life of Margaret Aylward begins that process. Like many other religious founders Aylward was a formidable individual. Her story reveals the difficulties some Irish women had in coming to terms with convent life. She attempted to enter religious life on two occasions before eventually forming her own religious community. Aylward's work was in a sense reactive and strongly motivated by the proselytising efforts of the Irish Church Missions; indeed there is a sense of triumphalism in the title of the congregation she established. Prunty had copious source material to work with, not least the papers of the charitable work engaged in by Aylward and her assistants in the Ladies of Charity and St Brigid's Orphanage, a boarding-out institution. Prunty also provides details of the charitable work of these organisations in her 1998 book on Dublin slums.[8]

Scholarship on the impact of religion on women's lives has not been confined to the study of nuns. P. J. Corish has been one of the few historians to explore the influence of Irish mothers on the religious practices of their families. It seems clear that in peasant and middle-class households women ensured that children were baptised, taught their prayers and attended the necessary religious ceremonies required of them. This was a 'duty' which came to them as mothers.[9] Corish focuses attention on the Catholic religious experiences of women at a time when many of the Catholic rituals surrounding birth, marriage and death centred on the home rather than the Church, which became the case after the Famine. Women of the stature and class of Mary O'Connell, the wife of Daniel O'Connell, played such a role in her family.[10] The work of S. J. Connolly reveals the strong communal nature of pre-Famine Catholicism where the important rituals allowed for emotional and spiritual displays of behaviour not approved of by the Church.[11] Despite these studies we still have little idea of how women understood themselves as spiritual beings or how they viewed their place within the Church as lay women. We need to explore further how laywomen related to male clerics, and how they were guided by them.

Whilst some attention has focused on the role of women in Irish Catholicism, much less work has been carried out on the impact of religion on Protestant laywomen. Hempton and Hill in their book *Evangelical Protestantism in Ulster Society, 1740–1890*[12] devote a chapter to the place of women in evangelical religion. They discuss the reasons why women were attracted to evangelicalism and how women's role in evangelical sects changed over time. By the early nineteenth century, women who had preached and led meetings found themselves deprived of these functions through the imposition of strong male control over these various denominations. Women's energies were, instead, as in many other denominations, guided into domesticity, charity and philanthropic work. Holmes, examining the Ulster revival of 1859,[13] looks specifically at working-class women's ecstatic religious behaviour in this revival. She argues that it was during a time of religious upheaval and emotional chaos that women were able to transcend the limited gender roles defined for them by society. Conversion was possible for anyone and allowed for a spiritual equality that transcended class and gender roles. Women converts also encouraged others to convert and developed leadership roles within the revival. Holmes suggests a continuing female presence in revivalism after 1859, a presence which readily adapted to changing social conditions.

The work of Andrea Ebel Brożyna provides a textual analysis of a range of moral, educational, temperance and missionary literature that shaped the construction of gender and piety in both Catholic and Protestant literary texts in the years between 1850 and 1914. In her 1999 book *Labour, Love and Prayer: Female Piety in Ulster Religious Literature, 1850–1914*,[14] she argues that in the creation of the 'ideal' Christian woman both Catholic and Protestant literature espoused similar values. Their view of the Christian woman was essentially the same. For Catholic and Protestant women, female piety was viewed as domestic, and women's place was seen as being firmly in the home;

for Ulster Catholics and Protestants the piety of their womenfolk was an essential part of their religious cultures. It is of course a literature written and available to women of the middle classes and the similarity of this pious literature may be a consequence and expression of similar class allegiances and aspirations rather than actual religious beliefs. What is needed to expand on Brożyna's study is an examination of the devotional practices and beliefs of rural women of the lower classes throughout the period. An investigation of Irish language sources would undoubtedly also add to our understanding of the experience of religious agency.

Brożyna also refers to the place of the Virgin Mary within religious imagery. The late eighteenth century onwards saw a revitalisation in the presentation of the Virgin Mary as a role model for women. Mary was not an image specific to Catholicism, where she provided an obvious role model for the nun, her modesty, purity and chastity being the hallmarks of contemporary female decency. As Magray and others have shown, confraternities and sodalities devoted to the Virgin proliferated from the 1840s, as did the celebration of the month of May from 1830.[15] The clergy encouraged this popular Mariolatry. The veneration of the Virgin Mary was in effect symbolic of a larger transformation in the nature of popular piety in the nineteenth century. The apparition of the Blessed Virgin Mary at Knock in 1879 was symptomatic of the status the Virgin had acquired within the realm of popular devotion.[16] Throughout the nineteenth century, the Catholic Church used Mary, and a host of female saints, which appealed to women and brought them into the Church. These are aspects of religious adherence that still await further exploration by historians of Ireland.[17]

The impact of religion on women's lives can also be seen in their propensity for charity work. While women were to remain inferior within the Church, their work in convents or as lay philanthropists was essential to the Church in the spread of its mission. Philanthropy has won the attention of a number of historians. Luddy's work on charity has attempted to explore two strands in nineteenth-century women's philanthropy, a benevolent strand which attempted to alleviate the symptoms of poverty without questioning the underlying causes of that poverty, and a reformist tradition which attempted to initiate legislative measures to improve the lot of the poor.[18] Her work confirms the sectarian nature of philanthropic involvement. She also argues that among Catholic women most charitable work was left to nuns and the dominance of women religious in such work relegated lay Catholic women primarily to a fund-raising role. In consequence lay Catholic women were less likely to become active in campaigns for social change in comparison with their Protestant or Nonconformist counterparts.[19] Protestant and Nonconformist women, who had direct experience of active charity work, were most moved to engage in political campaigns to alter the position of women in society.

Securing the vote at local and national level was seen by many activists as one significant way of bringing about change in Irish society. Once women had secured these franchises they would fight for the poor, and particularly for women and children. Margaret Preston has further explored women's benevolence through the language used by philanthropists and charity workers in Dublin in the nineteenth century. She argues that essentialist notions of race were applied to the poor as characteristics of class. The concern of most philanthropists was to create loyal and useful subjects of the British Empire.[20] While Preston's work concentrates on the latter part of the century, it is clear that throughout the period, creating a docile peasantry, particularly through the influence of poor women as mothers, was a principal and stated aim of many philanthropists and philanthropic organisations.[21] Despite the extensive nature of private philanthropic activity in the nineteenth century it remains an under-researched area of study. We are still unaware, for instance, how female charities differed from male charities. How did Catholic charity networks, especially those managed by nuns, foreshadow the services that would be provided in twentieth-century Ireland? What impact did more 'scientific' approaches to poverty, emerging from mid-century, have on the role of women involved in such work?

WORK

The participation of women in the Irish workforce, and the economic significance of their labour, has been obscured in historical inquiry until relatively recently though there is, as yet, little sustained analysis of women's working lives in the nineteenth century. Mary E. Daly has written a useful general history on *Women and Work in Ireland* that devotes two sections to the nineteenth century.[22] While we have some sense of the variety of work undertaken by women we still have little insight into their occupational mobility. Nor do we know much about the impact of gender roles on women's employment or the factors – economic, regional or personal – that affected women's working lives. There are a small number of articles on women workers in the pre-Famine era but our knowledge of general working practices for women in this period is hazy. It seems clear that a woman's domestic contribution was not then confined to cooking, cleaning, and child-rearing alone; they also made a vital contribution to the family economy by working alongside men. Mary Cullen has estimated that labourers' wives' earnings from spinning, and – when times were really difficult – begging, accounted for at least 15 per cent of the families' income and this percentage could rise to 35 per cent at times.[23]

The role of women in the textile trades has received relatively substantial treatment. Anne McKernan has explored the recruitment of women weavers during the Napoleonic Wars.[24] Marilyn Cohen, in a 'micro-history' of the parish of Tullylish, surveys the development of the linen industry over two centuries, in part by exploring the intersections between gender and class.[25] Much of the detail relating to women's textile work deals with the last decades of the century. Brenda Collins, for instance, reveals the extent of women's employment in the sewing trades.[26] Collins, in her various articles, has completed the most sustained analysis of the sewing trade in Ireland, linking outwork and homework with women's domestic work, social and domestic organisation and migration. The issue of homeworking is also explored by Margaret Neill.[27] The strengths of these works lie in the fact that they are regionally based, charting the changing relationships between family members and the world of paid work. They acknowledge the variety of employment opportunities that went into family survival and reveal new insights into the cultural understanding of work and gender which operated in the sewing and textile industries. What has not been explored are the identities ascribed to women workers, whether they are engaged in paid or unpaid work, or the links that existed, for instance, between the sexual division of labour and social change. A sustained analysis of women's involvement in the textile industry through the century and on a countrywide basis also requires exploration.

Joanna Bourke, in a number of publications, has contributed significantly and controversially to the subject of women's work in the later decades of the nineteenth century.[28] She attributes the decline in women's employment in the last decades of the century to a boom in the rural economy that allowed women to opt out of paid work in favour of unpaid domestic duties within the family. Women, she argues, thus made a choice to return to domestic work. The idea that this was a choice or a strategy on the part of women is difficult to sustain, however, in the light of the fact that employment opportunities for women were declining and emigration was a substantial feature of the life cycle of young Irish women by the end of the century. The number of women in employment fell steadily from 29 per cent in 1861 to 19.5 per cent by 1911.[29] This controversial argument has not received the attention it deserves from historians of women's work in Ireland. Bourke's various studies concentrate on the period between 1890 and 1914 and so we get little sense of the development of women's attitudes to, or their participation in, work prior to 1890. It is also the case that part-time and occasional paid work by women was a widely practised strategy in many rural households. However, Bourke's research is especially strong in revealing the vital role of women in household agriculture, particularly through poultry rearing. She also shows how the spread of creameries affected women's role in dairying. This was an example of the way in which the introduction of technology often resulted in women workers being displaced by men. Similarly the co-operative movement, which was responsible for encouraging creameries, attempted, without success, to encourage women to organise poultry rearing on a co-operative rather than on an individual basis. It was also the case that most of the efficiency schemes, like those advocated by the co-operative movement, tended to transfer managerial power to the male members of the family or to male organisers. Women objected to selling eggs to creameries because the money was added to the milk account, which was paid to the man, rather than coming directly to the woman.[30]

An area of constant employment for women was domestic service. This was the only sector of female employment to expand significantly in post-Famine Ireland. By 1911 one working woman in three was in service. Despite the significance of domestic service for women, and indeed for its impact on the middle-class family, the literature is almost non-existent. Mona Hearn's pioneering work on this subject explores, through documentary sources and oral history, the experiences of those who worked as domestic servants in Ireland from the end of the nineteenth century.[31] Servants were crucial to the smooth running of middle-class and aristocratic homes and Hearn's work concentrates on the urban servant or the servant of the 'big house'. We still need to explore the world of the rural servant, the nature of the work they did and their relationships with their employers and with each other. By the 1890s there was a fall in the number of female servants and by the end of the nineteenth century other opportunities were emerging for women. For example, they could become nurses, clerical workers or shop assistants. Also, an increasing number of young women apparently preferred to emigrate rather than work in service. The commercial and manufacturing sectors expanded from the 1860s and, after a period of stagnation, revived in the 1890s. By the end of the nineteenth century trades such as millinery, drapery and retail services were important occupational sectors for women. The increase in labour-saving devices may have also reduced demand for servants. Hearn concludes, in her study of servants, that we cannot see the decline solely in terms of economic factors. 'Change', she argues, 'came because the inferior, dependent position of the servant became unacceptable in a more democratic world.'[32] Women were involved in all kinds of paid work. They opened huckster shops or engaged in street selling, others ran public houses, grocery shops, and other retail businesses either on their own or with family members. Some worked as charwomen, washerwomen, or took in lodgers. A significant number throughout the century were engaged as wet nurses or cared for boarded-out children from the workhouses. Other women begged or worked as prostitutes. These are all aspects of Irish women's work that still require investigation.

While there is still much to be discovered in the area of women's work we have also to recover women's trade union history in Ireland. Theresa Moriarty has made a substantial contribution to the early history of women's trade unionism, revealing how working women, who were notoriously difficult to organise, were able to organise themselves.[33] Moriarty's work exposes the roots of women's trade union activism as lying in the late nineteenth century, rather than the early twentieth century where they have often been placed by Irish historians. Historians of Irish women's work have used a wide range of sources to reveal some of the patterns in women's work in the nineteenth century. But there are still many unanswered questions and many aspects of women's working lives that require investigation. How, for example, did women's standing within households differ between rural and urban families? How did rural women adapt to urban life? How were the changes that occurred in women's work dictated by expectations of women's place in society? How did working opportunities for women differ in the post-Famine period from those available in the preceding half century? We need a detailed regional study of women's employment opportunities that will allow comparisons to be made. While we still have much to learn about women's work in nineteenth-century Ireland, what is obvious is that many Irish women found that in order to engage in remunerative and rewarding work they had to leave the country.

## EMIGRATION

While there has been a substantial amount of research published on Irish women generally for the nineteenth century, relatively little has been published on women as migrants or emigrants despite the fact that in the post-Famine period historians have noted that emigration from Ireland was markedly different from that of other countries. While families and young men emigrated from other European countries, almost equal numbers of men and women emigrated from Ireland. Some women emigrated through sponsored migration schemes, like those outlined in Dympna McLoughlin's work.[34] Transportation, of course, also forced many Irish men and women to leave the country. Between 1787 and 1853, the British and Irish courts transported thousands of convicted criminals to the Australian colonies. Of the almost 40,000 convicts who sailed from Ireland, 9,104 were women.[35] Recent work on women transported to Australia moves beyond common assumptions about the criminality of transportees; women are instead viewed as individuals who were skilled, often literate, nearly all young and healthy and consequently these qualities made them 'exceptional' migrants. Many, it has been shown, adapted well to their new environment.[36] They made calculated decisions about their lives, many securing their social and financial futures by marrying well. Others entered the labour market and made a successful transition to society. Such scholarship restores agency to women and explores how contemporary middle-class sexual and cultural anxieties shaped the perception of convict women.

Despite the numbers of Irish who migrated from Ireland there is still no substantial study of Irish women in nineteenth-century Britain. Women migrants have also tended to be marginalised in important studies of Irish migration to America in the last century.[37] Hasia Diner's monograph, *Erin's Daughters in America,* which appeared in 1983, remains the most useful treatment of Irish women in the United States. Since the appearance of that work a number of important articles on Irish women migrants have been published. The most substantial collection has been edited by Patrick O'Sullivan as *Irish Women and Irish Migration* which forms part of a multi-volume series entitled *The Irish World Wide.*[38] Interestingly, the series is made up of six volumes, only one of which is devoted to women. Should women have a separate volume or is there something to be said for including aspects of women's migration in all of the other volumes? There is still no agreement among historians on which motives were most important in encouraging women to migrate.[39] Was it a lack of employment opportunities, poor marriage prospects, an expectation within the family that emigration was inevitable? Were Irish women knowingly prepared for emigration through the educational system?[40] A number of the 'pull' factors associated with women's emigration, such as the wish to marry, have been recently queried.[41] Much detailed archival and statistical work needs to be completed before some of these questions can be adequately answered.

Work on emigration focuses on the number who emigrated, their final destinations, and the 'push' and 'pull' factors that shaped the migratory pattern. Through the studies that have been completed on women and emigration, we have some idea of how single women in particular managed their new environments and we have some understanding of how they conducted their family lives. We know of the successes and also of the tribulations of some emigrant women. David Fitzpatrick, for instance, in his book *Oceans of Consolation,* reveals the insurmountable problems that faced some migrants.[42] In relation to Britain, Kanya-Forstner has explored Irish women's use of Catholic charity networks in Liverpool. But the experiences of Irish women in nineteenth-century Britain have still to be systematically examined.[43] While emigration offered women opportunities, it also brought disappointments.[44] We still need to know what became of those Irish women whose emigration 'failed'. What can we learn of those who ended up in prison or as prostitutes in those far away cities?

EDUCATION

Perhaps the most under-researched aspect of Irish women's history is that of education. Historians have only begun to explore the educational experiences of girls and women in Ireland. John Logan has charted the attendance of boys and girls at educational establishments throughout the century. His statistical work reveals that men dominated the teaching profession until the 1870s and that the increasing numbers of girls attending schools from mid-century may have been a consequence of the feminisation of teaching.[45] While teaching as a career offered financial independence to women, few held school principalships. As Logan shows, while women accounted for 55 per cent of teachers by 1900 they held only 28 per cent of school principalships, and in many of these schools they were the sole teacher. We still need, however, to explore the power relationships that existed within schools, particularly those between principals and staff, especially where men were principals. In those schools where women were principals, how did they relate to school managers and school inspectors? How similar was the status of male and female teachers in nineteenth-century Ireland? We still have almost no insight into how women national schoolteachers were 'formed'. The ethos of training colleges and their impact on the cultural life of nineteenth-century Ireland deserve exploration.

Anne O'Connor has completed the most extensive research into the education of girls in the nineteenth century.[46] Her work, dating from the 1980s, remains the only published investigation of secondary education for girls in Ireland in this period. O'Connor argues that the introduction of the Intermediate Education (Ireland) Act of 1878 'revolutionised' girls' secondary education. It was, as O'Connor shows, religious as well as academic rivalry that increased the numbers of females studying at second and third level. Catholic middle-class parents urged for changes to the education their daughters were receiving in the convent schools. Competition among lay and convent schools also forced convent schools to meet the new demands.[47] While activists had to fight to have girls included in the benefits of the Intermediate Act they also had to fight for access to university education. Again it was women of Protestant and Nonconformist backgrounds who led the campaign for access to universities in Ireland. Many activists argued that education would make women better wives and mothers, and enable them better to fulfil their social and moral duties. But it was these newly educated middle-class women who were to be an important shaping force in early twentieth-century Ireland.[48] What can we make of the paucity of published work on women and education in Ireland? As with much of the research on women in nineteenth-century Ireland, many studies remain unpublished in theses which are not generally accessible and of course it is also true that the number of researchers in nineteenth-century Irish women's history is small and that students often seem more attracted to twentieth-century history.

While much of what we know of girls' and women's education throughout the century centres on campaigns for the extension of educational rights, there is still much work to be done in the area. It would be interesting, for example, to explore the experience of convent boarding school life for girls at this time. The changing institutional nature of women's education might also be viewed in the context of the social and cultural changes occurring in this period. We know little of the aspirations of the young women who attended these schools and colleges. What expectations had they of using their education? How were Irish women taught to form relationships with those in authority? Did extra-curricular activities, even religious devotions, allow students to develop ways of organising together for a specific end and purpose? Were Irish women trained to be dependent or independent beings? An exploration of women's education along these lines might go some way to explaining their political participation in the twentieth century.

POLITICS

The fight for suffrage in the twentieth century has received most attention from historians interested in Irish women's political activities but surprisingly little has appeared on that subject for the nineteenth century. Generally the nineteenth century saw women engage in a myriad of campaigns that broadened their political participation to an unprecedented level.[49] Carmel Quinlan's recent work, *Genteel Revolutionaries: Anna and Thomas Haslam and the Irish Women's Movement*, adds considerably to our knowledge of the early suffrage movement in Ireland. Quinlan makes it evident that the women's movement was not solely a single issue movement – the fight to acquire the parliamentary franchise for women – but that it involved campaigns for the education of girls and women, against the Contagious Diseases Acts, and for women's place in local government, all struggles in which the Haslams played a significant role. Quinlan also identifies a Miss Robertson, of whom little is known, as the probable first organiser of suffrage in Ireland in the 1860s, allowing the campaign for suffrage earlier origins in Ireland than have noted by historians to date.[50] However, we still lack any sustained analysis of the motives and aspirations of these early women activists, nor do we know much about their links with English-based suffrage groups.[51] So much attention has been paid to suffragism and the debates around nationalism and unionism in the early twentieth century that the campaigns of the late nineteenth century have been forgotten. Substantial legislative progress was made by women before the turn of the twentieth century.[52] For instance, from 1838 women who had the required property qualifications could vote for poor law guardians, a fact completely ignored by historians. Luddy has also put forward the view that while there were significant issues that garnered the public support of women in the nineteenth century, it was amongst Unionist women, campaigning against Home Rule, that organised mass protest could be witnessed.[53]

Many of the issues around which women campaigned have been discussed by Luddy.[54] At local level women played a role in informal activity, much of which was based on issues of relevance to the community in which they lived. National politics and issues such as anti-slavery and temperance also won their attention. Within nationalist organisations women were particularly important for their writings, but they also played a practical role in these organisations, such as the Young Irelanders.[55] The Ladies' Land League has received attention mainly through analysing the work of Anna Parnell in that organisation. The reprint of Parnell's *Tale of a Great Sham* is an important contribution to understanding Parnell's expectations of both the Ladies' Land League and the Land League.[56] There are also a number of biographies of Parnell.[57] However, there has been little work examining the Ladies' Land League as an organisation distinct from Anna Parnell. The work of TeBrake makes an attempt to understand the appeal of the Ladies' Land League to peasant women in the west of Ireland.[58] Yet, while arguments have been made about how the Ladies' Land League was undermined by the male run Land League, almost no attention has been paid to the political activism that developed amongst both peasant and middle-class women through their involvement in the League in the early 1880s. Studies of the Ladies' Land League have also encompassed how women were represented during this period.[59] Much emphasis has been placed on the nationalism of Anna Parnell, a subject that needs to be more deeply investigated with regard to other women in this period. Attitudes to republicanism and women's involvement in the centenary celebrations of 1798 have received attention from Crossman who explores these issues through the pages of the *Shan Van Vocht*.[60] Crossman examines the ways in which republicanism was represented in the paper and the role envisaged for women in the 1798 celebrations. Further exploration of the significance and understanding amongst Irish women of concepts such as republicanism must be undertaken before we can write accurately about women's participation in nationalism in this century.

## WOMEN AND THE FAMINE

The cataclysmic event of the nineteenth century was of course the Great Famine. Numerous publications have appeared on this event but no historical work has dealt specifically or at any length with the position of women during the Great Famine. Patricia Lysaght has used folklore sources to understand the Famine as a human tragedy, and as a means of exploring how women's roles were fundamentally altered during that period.[61] The reprint of a contemporary narrative by Asenath Nicholson, throws light on one woman's attempts to relieve distress and reveals how one particular individual responded to the suffering encountered.[62] Both Mary E. Daly and Cormac Ó Gráda cover aspects of women's survival during the famine period and show that women were more likely to survive the catastrophe than men.[63] David Fitzpatrick, in one of the few articles devoted to the subject of women and the Famine, further explores this theme through an analysis of statistical data to confirm that women did in fact survive the Great Famine better than men.[64] They were physiologically better able to withstand the hardship encountered and he argues that the allocation of relief through the workhouse also favoured women among young adults. His argument is marred somewhat by the context in which he places his evidence and his comment that the 'intention of [his] essay is to provoke discussion of the evidence for discrimination against women in Irish history'.[65] Historians of women in Ireland have not investigated the issues of women's history as matters of 'discrimination', a point I will return to later. Among the aims of women's history is to understand the ways in which society has been structured to privilege either sex.

INSTITUTIONS

One of the significant features to emerge from a study of Irish women in the nineteenth century is the level of institutional care that developed to assist or confine women. Women appear to have been more vulnerable to destitution than men. Lack of employment opportunities, poor pay, lack of skills or the chance to acquire them, life crises such as death or illness of a husband, pregnancy, and the number of dependent children all affected a woman's ability to support herself and her family. Since women's work was often seasonal or irregular, their capacity to remain economically independent was limited. The result was that they were much more likely than men to enter state institutions such as workhouses, and to use charitable services. McLoughlin, Burke, Luddy and others have explored how women used certain types of institutions to meet their economic and welfare needs. While the workhouse regime was very bleak, women became adept at using the system for their own ends. McLoughlin has shown how female paupers used emigration schemes organised by some boards of guardians to make their way to America and other countries.[66] Burke's study of workhouses also explores generally how women fared in these institutions.[67] Irish women also used the refuges of the Salvation Army when they were distressed through pregnancy, or 'at risk' in some way.[68] Luddy has explored the use made by women of Magdalen Asylums as places of refuge and has argued that women's decision to both enter and leave these institutions was, for most of the nineteenth century at least, a matter of choice. Frances Finnegan has written a sustained critique of the role of the Catholic church, and especially that of the Good Shepherd Sisters in running Magdalen asylums.[69] While addressing the confinement of women in these institutions and the harsh conditions under which these women were held, particularly in the twentieth century, Finnegan fails to investigate how these institutions changed over the period, or how they were shaped by the society in which they operated. The figures she provides on those who entered and left these asylums, together with figures of length of stay and the ages of those held in the institutions are interpreted in a more negative way than Luddy who sees the entrance and departure of the women in these asylums as a sign of the permeability of these institutions in the nineteenth century.[70] By the end of the nineteenth century, and certainly by the early decades of the twentieth century, many such institutions had become places of confinement rather than refuge. The presence of Magdalen Asylums offered the Irish public a place of confinement for their 'wayward' daughters, placing them away from the public gaze. What is it about Irish society, and attitudes to sexuality that allows such confinement to occur? What role do families and the Catholic Church play in arranging such confinement? What impact did ideas of shame and respectability have on women's status in Irish society? What was being 'hidden' in these institutions?

Other institutions in which women were to be found were mental asylums. Published work on the nature, extent and regimes of these institutions has recently emerged. Elizabeth Malcolm, using a small sample relating to female patients in St Patrick's Hospital, argues that family breakdown resulting in financial hardship was a significant feature in the admission of female patients in the 1840s. She also contends that a failure to emigrate may also have been a reason many older individuals ended up in asylums.[71] The family context appears to have been a crucial factor in the admittance of women to mental asylums. The findings of Oonagh Walsh, relating to the Connaught Lunatic Asylum, provide a revealing picture of women within that institution. Women were more likely than men to be admitted on what she terms 'moral' grounds, which, rather than corresponding to sexual immorality, included illness resulting from grief or poverty. Walsh also argues that women fared better than men within these institutions.[72]

Issues of crime, sexuality and intimate relationships are now beginning to be explored. Luddy has analysed the lives of women who worked as prostitutes and also examined the ways in which society attempted to rehabilitate 'fallen' women in the nineteenth century.[73] Sexuality was expressed in behaviour and language and configured by political, social and cultural forces at work in society. Behaviour and reputation also shaped the treatment of women before the courts. The nature of crimes against women has come under investigation from a number of historians.[74] Conley argues that Irish judges were surprisingly 'gender blind' when it came to cases presented before them, though one would need strong statistical evidence to support such a claim. Steiner-Scott, examining the issue of domestic violence and the penalties imposed on offenders, argues that many men beat their wives with impunity, an argument

that contrasts sharply with Conley's findings. We still know too little about
the informal systems of regulation that existed within communities to come to
any real understanding of how violence against women was viewed in Irish
society in the nineteenth century. Did communities take the law into their
own hands? And if so, how and under what circumstances did they do this?
What, for instance, was the power of gossip within communities? The impact
of traditional beliefs on a community and a particular family is revealed in the
killing of Bridget Cleary by her husband in 1895. In her 1999 book, *The
Burning of Bridget Cleary: A True Story,* Angela Bourke has intertwined history,
folklore, oral culture and literature to reveal the complexities of life in rural
Ireland at the end of the nineteenth century. This interdisciplinary work is
unique in the study of women in Irish society and encourages a greater use of
other disciplines in our work. We still need to develop a sustained analysis of
the forces that shaped sexuality and its expression in nineteenth-century
Ireland. We need to know what expectations women and men had of marriage,
what moral norms pertained in the pre-Famine period and how these might
have altered in the period after 1850. Police, court and church records,
together with poor law records, offer sources to begin those studies.

SOURCES

The significant feature of the works reviewed above is their basis in primary
source material. For many years it was believed that the sources for women's
history did not exist in sufficient quantity to justify research in the area. The
works cited above belie this view. Knowledge of sources has also been made
more accessible through the work of the Women's History Project. This
Project, which was initiated in 1997, undertook a survey of sources relating to
women's history in Ireland. The findings of that survey were published in
CD-ROM format and are also available on the World Wide Web. This
*Directory of Sources for the History of Women in Ireland*[15] contains the records of
262 repositories and has information and descriptions of over 14,000
collections and sources with over 100,000 pieces of information. Much of the
material relates to women in nineteenth-century Irish society. The sources
include convent archives, county council records, the records of psychiatric
hospitals, libraries, museums and public and private institutions and organisations. It contains listings for all known poor law records. It is clear from
these sources that women were to be found in almost all official, public and
private documents. They are spoken of in institutional records such as the
minutes of a poor law board or the committal forms of a nineteenth-century
lunatic asylum; they recorded the functionings of their convents, institutions
and landed estates in finance ledgers, reports and correspondence; they were

affected by the financial constraints imposed by local authorities such as county councils; they were tenants whose payments were noted in thousands of rentals. Women also recorded their personal lives in letters, diaries, journals and common place books; they painted, stitched, embroidered and wrote music, plays, poems and novels. Serious scholarly activity is totally dependent on access to primary sources. That these sources exist is without question, and the recent work of the Women's History Project has made those sources more accessible to researchers.

### CONCLUSION

We have a growing catalogue of articles on the history of Irish women in the nineteenth century. There have also been some notable reprints of edited and annotated letters and diaries that provide essential material for researchers.[76] Perhaps one of the most interesting and inclusive works on women to emerge is the *Field Day Anthology of Irish Writing*, vols 4 and 5, *Irish Women's Writing and Traditions.* The production of these volumes was a vast undertaking and includes contributions from literary critics, historians, folklorists, Irish language specialists and many others. It covers the history, literature and language of Irish women from about 600 to 2000. Much of the material relates to the nineteenth century and the work will undoubtedly encourage further research into many areas of Irish women's lives. What is necessary to further develop Irish women's history is the monograph that provides in-depth coverage of a particular area of study. We have barely a handful of such works. Neither do we have any general texts that delineate Irish women's historical experience. A very long list could be constructed of the areas of women's history that still require investigation. For instance, we have no study of landed women in nineteenth-century Ireland. Did they play any role in the management of estates? How did they manage their households? How significant was their political role, as patrons of parliamentary constituencies, as canvassers for votes? We know little about the intimate life of women, how they viewed husbands and children, how they dealt with maternity, friendships, love and sexuality. We need also to ask questions about women at the bottom of the social spectrum. We have no published work on women within the Irish prison system; we have little information on the criminality of Irish women. We know little of the lives of women hawkers and agricultural labourers.

Many historians, and not just male historians, are uncomfortable with the term 'women's history'. It is a term that we are often asked to defend because of its apparent exclusiveness. Often the first question put to practitioners of women's history relates to the inclusion of men, as opposed to any assessment of the work that is actually being done. Often women's history and historians of women are pilloried for carrying the baggage of a political agenda. Some claim that women's history is emotive, or concerned with women as 'victims'. In Ireland in the 1990s it was primarily women who remained the principal proponents of women's history. Should we be concerned by this? Does it matter that it is mainly women who write Irish women's history? Perhaps not. Ultimately, historical inquiry is about confrontation and discussion with the past and with other historians. The construction of history depends on open inquiry and honest debate in which historians listen to each other, are prepared to accept the significance of historical research, and are persuaded by evidence and debate.

One way of recognising a serious acceptance of the work already done on women's history is its incorporation into general historical studies. It is disappointing to see that only general reference is made to women's history in the textbooks that have appeared recently.[77] The majority of practitioners continue to focus on men's activities and to marginalise, or exclude, even the obvious intersections with women's lives. Has the legitimacy of the field of women's history been accepted by historians of Ireland generally? Has women's history become a 'permanent' feature of university history courses? Without doubt the works already published on women's history have extended our knowledge and understanding of Irish history generally, particularly in areas associated with religion, politics, the workforce and welfare. For the area to grow further, students need to be encouraged into researching aspects of women's history. Reclaiming the past of Irish women and integrating that work into Irish history is a significant challenge that we all face as historians.

# CHAPTER 4

# Religious History

✾

*David W. Miller*

## INTRODUCTION

The period from 1801 to 1921, which I take to be Ireland's 'long' nineteenth century, has an obvious unity. It is, for Ireland, the lifetime of a single polity, the United Kingdom of Great Britain and Ireland. The polity which bore the formal name of 'the Kingdom of Ireland' collapsed in the 1790s,[1] and the polity created in 1801 was supplanted in Ireland in 1921–2 by two new polities – the Irish Free State (later renamed 'Éire' and then 'the Republic of Ireland' without ceasing to be the same polity) on the one hand and Northern Ireland on the other. So this periodisation does look like an exercise of cutting history at its joints. But does it work for religion?

Churches also think of themselves as being, or having, polities, and indeed sometimes conceive their sphere as transcending ordinary human experience. In the study of *this* world, however, it is often useful to think about the relationship of ecclesiastical polities to power within the (civil) polity. In eighteenth-century Britain the established churches played a vital role in sacralising the polity, thereby enhancing the power for which those inside it (sometimes called 'the governing classes') were competing, vis-à-vis the relative powerlessness of those outside it.[2] In the Irish polity in the same period the established church was manifestly unable to play this role. Although the 1800 Act of Union contained a guarantee of the established status of the Church of Ireland, in fact from the 1830s that status became very much a matter of contention within the new polity. Disestablishment in 1869 marked the real end of the ecclesiastical arrangements associated with the Irish polity which had collapsed seven decades earlier. So in an important sense the periodisation of religious history in modern Ireland seems to be out of step with that of political history, a major terminus of the former falling approximately midway between two major termini of the latter.

The historiography of the 1990s turns out to be a good vantage point from which to consider issues arising out of this periodisation problem: is the seemingly untimely discontinuity in the churches' political history reflected in other aspects of religious history? And does such a discontinuity in religious history occur in the next macro-division of Irish political history, in which, presumably, we are now living? To address such questions I must divide the literature which I have been assigned into rough-and-ready categories, though the boundaries between the categories are quite fuzzy. Because civil polities and churches are inherently complex organisations which both make sweeping claims on human loyalty, it makes sense to me to consider their interaction under a single heading: 'Church history as political history'. Given that heading, I need another under which to consider relationships between churches and social formations which are not organisationally complex and do not ordinarily claim transcendent loyalty, such as gender, ethnicity and class; I call that category 'Religious history as social history'. Between 'state' and 'society', so to speak, the churches carry on a lot of business under rubrics such as 'spirituality' and 'theology' which they may conceive as internal to themselves; though that conception may well be flawed, it is useful, at least provisionally, to place some studies of such business in a third category, 'Religion as cultural phenomenon'.

## CHURCH HISTORY AS POLITICAL HISTORY

A generation ago, when I myself was entering the Irish historical profession, very little nineteenth-century Irish religious history had been written, and the questions about religion that begged for answers all seemed to concern the relations between ecclesiastics and secular politicians. Why did the political role of churchmen loom so large for Irish historians at that time? Part of the answer, of course, is that political history still dominated the historical profession and that the role of churchmen in that history still fascinated both consumers and producers of Irish history as it had the guests at the Dedalus Christmas dinner. Furthermore the sources – a dozen or so well-preserved archives of correspondence of bishops with statesmen, with their agents in Rome and with each other – constituted a closed universe of discourse which virtually cried out to be assembled into a coherent story. The fact that the hierarchy since the 1850s had generally conducted its political business behind closed doors added to the fascination of the subject, and it is perhaps significant that the first layperson with the temerity to ask to see not just the odd letter but the entire contents of these archives was an American, Emmet Larkin.

The appearance in 1996 of Larkin's *The Roman Catholic Church and the Emergence of the Modern Irish Political System, 1874–1878* completes a monumental seven-volume political history of the Irish Catholic hierarchy from the rise of Cullen to the fall of Parnell. Given the publication two years earlier of Donal Kerr's *'A Nation of Beggars'? Priests, People, and Politics in Famine Ireland, 1846–1852*, the second of his two volumes on Catholic ecclesiastical politics during the administrations of Peel and Russell, it is now possible to read a continuous, detailed and authoritative account of the subject from 1841 to 1891. So in the course of one generation the dearth of historical literature on the politics of Irish churchmen has been supplanted by abundance.

Despite its dense narrative style, Larkin's seven-volume work has a strong and overarching analytic structure, for which the fourth volume – which appeared last – provides the keystone. The origins of his analysis lie in an early fascination with constitutional history: the efforts of several generations of British historians to explicate that mother of all social constructions, the British constitution. He discerned in late nineteenth-century Ireland the evolution of a political system, with well-understood but uncodified rules, in which the players were not king, lords and commons, but the leader, the bishops and the party. This analysis led him to a bolder claim – that the role of ecclesiastics in the late nineteenth-century Irish political system endured beyond independence and contributed crucially to the preservation of Irish democracy in the age of dictatorship in western Europe. Implicitly he proposed a new periodisation at variance with the traditional treatment of the Union as a coherent era (and with the rationale for this volume). Jim Smyth has observed that recent reconceptualisation of eighteenth-century Ireland as a (Protestant) confessional state calls for moving its termination forward to 1829–30.[3] Larkin is in effect suggesting that a (Catholic) confessional state created between 1878 and 1886 continued until some unspecified time well after 1922. The principal critic of this argument, J. J. Lee, acknowledges the brilliance and power of Larkin's 'constitutional' metaphor in making sense of the events which he narrates but challenges his claim of decisive ecclesiastical influence in the post-1921 polity.[4] It is easier to see the force of Lee's argument in these post-Eamonn Casey days than it would have been in the era of John Charles McQuaid when Larkin formulated his thesis. Even if Larkin's claims for the Church's 'constitutional' powers are overstated, it does seem that seven decades after the formation of the present (southern) Irish polity the religious system from which the latter gained much of its identity has undergone a crisis as serious as that which overtook the late established church seven decades after the Act of Union.

Although the mere existence of a 'gap' is never a sufficient reason to undertake any historical project, it is instructive to note what has not been covered by Kerr or Larkin. No general account of the Irish Catholic Church's high politics yet exists for the period from 1801 to 1841. A similar hiatus exists for the period from 1891 to 1898, and eventually Miller's account for

1898–1921, which was researched before the opening of the episcopal archives, will no doubt be supplanted. Recent biographical studies of four important prelates – John Thomas Troy (Archbishop of Dublin, 1787–1824) by Vincent J. McNally, James Doyle (Bishop of Kildare and Leighlin, 1819–34) by Thomas McGrath, and William Crolly (Bishop of Down and Connor, 1825–35, and Archbishop of Armagh, 1835–49) by Ambrose Macaulay – give us a clearer understanding of ecclesiastical politics in the early part of the century. C. D. A. Leighton's article on Gallicanism and the veto controversy adds an important dimension to our understanding of the period.[5] For the period after 1891 the most important recent contributions are Mary Harris's monograph on the Catholic Church and the formation of Northern Ireland and Thomas Morrissey's biography of William Walsh (Archbishop of Dublin, 1885–1921). Within the period covered by Kerr and Larkin there have been three recent books on high ecclesiastical politics. Oliver Rafferty's study of the Church and Fenianism will be discussed below. In a monograph documenting Paul Cullen's opposition to the Independent Irish Party, S. R. Knowlton contests the late John Whyte's contention that that Party would have failed even without that opposition. The most recent volume of Evelyn Bolster's history of the Diocese of Cork contains substantial material on the role of William Delany, Bishop of Cork, 1847–86, in ecclesiastical politics.[6]

Perhaps because Catholic high ecclesiastical politics are becoming so thoroughly covered, there has been a recent shift of attention to popular politics and the lower clergy. Gerard Moran has contributed a full-length biography of Father Patrick Lavelle and edited a volume on radical priests which includes contributions on Father Thaddeus O'Malley by Fergus A. D'Arcy, on Canon James MacFadden by Breandán Mac Suibhne and on the novelist Canon P. A. Sheehan by Lawrence W. McBride. In *Unusual Suspects*, Denis Carroll presents biographical sketches of Fathers John Kenyon, Thomas O'Shea, Matthew O'Keefe, and Michael O'Flanagan. John Quinn analyses Father Theobald Mathew's difficulties with the bishops.[7] As a companion volume to a reprint of Father Anthony Cogan's history of the diocese of Meath, Alfred Smyth has written a perceptive biography of Cogan himself. Father Patrick Kavanagh, author of *The Wexford Rebellion*, is the subject of an article by Anna Kinsella.[8] The Irish-Ireland priest, Gerald O'Donovan, who became an anti-clerical novelist, is treated in an article by John Ryan, and the conflict between Irish-Ireland and the Church is the subject of an article by Frank Biletz. Donal Kerr has contributed a survey of the Church's stance toward political violence from the Whiteboys to the Fenians and Thomas Morrissey an essay on the relationship between the papal social encyclicals as interpreted by Irish clergy and the ideological stance of James Connolly.[9]

Protestant ecclesiastical politics has received less attention than its Catholic counterpart. Alan Acheson's *A History of the Church of Ireland, 1691–1996*, is an excellent example of denominational history comparable to Finlay Holmes's survey of Irish Presbyterian history, a revised version of which has recently been published under the title *The Presbyterian Church in Ireland: A Popular History*. Irish Methodism receives a general treatment in English by Dudley Cooney and in Irish by Risteárd Ó Glaisne. Again, clergy who caused trouble within their particular denominations come in for special attention. We have accounts of the careers of two Protestant clerical gadflies – Classon Porter, Non-Subscribing Presbyterian minister of Larne, and Augustus B. R. Young, ritualist and pro-Home Rule rector of Ballybay[10] – and Denis Carroll includes two ministers of the mainstream Presbyterian church, Isaac Nelson and J. B. Armour, in his gallery of radical clergy.

The high politics of Protestantism are addressed in a challenge to the traditional view that the Church of Ireland was especially resistant to high-church teachings, in an analysis of the critical appointment of Richard Whatley to be archbishop of Dublin, and in a case study of disendowment focusing on Christ Church Cathedral.[11] Perhaps the most serious gap in our knowledge of Protestant ecclesiastical politics is the absence of a thorough treatment of the attempted rapprochement between the Presbyterian Church and the Church of Ireland proposed during the 1830s by Henry Cooke. That initiative, far from being a mere demagogic ploy, was a serious attempt to salvage an established church by enlisting the Tory party in an imaginative reconceptualisation of the nature and purpose of religious establishment. Ultimately it fell victim not so much to Irish politics as to Peel's shabby treatment of Thomas Chalmers and the Evangelical majority in the Church of Scotland.

A good deal had already, by 1990, been written about the history of education, the area of public policy which most engaged ecclesiastical attention; much of the recent scholarship mainly adds detail to familiar landscape. Kenneth Milne explores the educational policies advocated by Charles Brodrick, who served as coadjutor to the Church of Ireland arch-bishop of Dublin in the second decade of the century. Two articles by Sean Griffin augment our knowledge of the early development of curriculum materials for the national education system. Paul Connell and Francis Duffy analyse the transition to that system in Counties Meath and Cavan respectively. A case study of a Donaghadee national school by George Beale illustrates the *reductio ad absurdum* of the board's growing acquiescence to clerical claims: its difficulty in securing the amalgamation of two Presbyterian schools in a single small town.[12]

Several important pieces of educational history have been occasioned by particular celebrations. The bicentennial of Maynooth College, the national seminary, and the sesquicentennial of one of the 'godless' colleges, Queen's (afterwards University) College Cork, both in 1995, were marked by the pub-lication of solid institutional histories by Patrick Corish and John A. Murphy respectively. The beatification of Edmund Rice, founder of the Christian Brothers, called forth both an excellent popular biography by Dáire Keogh and a collection of commemorative essays on the Brothers' schools.[13]

Perhaps the most refreshing example of educational history, however, is Senia Pašeta's *Before the Revolution: Nationalism, Social Change and Ireland's Catholic Elite, 1879–1922*. Her subject is the generation of middle-class Irish Catholics educated in University College Dublin before independence. She addresses much more than the conventional topics of the political origins and curriculum of UCD and of the secondary school system which provided its students. In a short compass she provides a rich evocation of the mind of a remarkable cohort of students and an understanding of the formation of a Catholic intelligentsia.

## RELIGION AS CULTURAL PHENOMENON

In a decade in which a journalist could write a book entitled *Goodbye to Catholic Ireland*,[14] historians have been attentive to just how and when the Catholic Ireland we once knew said 'Hello'. In a 1972 article Larkin argued that in the third quarter of the nineteenth century Ireland underwent a 'devotional revolution' in which the discharge of religious obligations increased decisively and continental styles of devotion became widespread.[15] The most searching critique of this thesis is a 1990 essay by Thomas McGrath, who maintains that the increasing compliance with canonical norms during the generation after the Famine was not revolutionary, but part of an evolutionary process by which determined churchmen, over the course of four centuries, gradually overcame obstacles to the implementation of the decrees of the Council of Trent. McGrath makes this argument the theme of *Religious Renewal and Reform in the Pastoral Ministry of Bishop James Doyle of Kildare and Leighlin, 1786–1834*, one of his two volumes on that remarkable prelate. Both McGrath's critique and Larkin's provocative original characterisation of the devotional revolution as 'making practising Catholics of the Irish people in a generation'[16] are examples of what Raymond Gillespie characterises as the 'view of religion as a set of power relationships'. Both seem to conceive of religious beliefs and practices as something imposed upon the populace by an elite. Gillespie's alternative view – that religious ideas result from 'a dialogue between the doctrinal positions offered as coherent intellectual systems by the various churches on the one hand, and the religious needs of the inhabitants of Ireland on the other'[17] – seems to define the current direction of research on devotional change by Irish historians including, significantly, Larkin himself.

The claim that devotional change in nineteenth-century Ireland was 'revolutionary' rests on the premise that the mid-twentieth-century pattern of nearly universal compliance with canonical norms of religious practice was not present in pre-Famine Catholic Ireland. Quantitative evidence for this premise was first published in 1975 by David W. Miller.[19] On the basis of mass attendance data in the 1835 *First Report of the Commissioners of Public Instruction, Ireland,* he suggested that the extremely high levels of mass attendance throughout Ireland in, say, the 1950s, were found only in a few major towns and prosperous eastern rural areas during the 1830s. In western Irish-speaking areas, mass attendance was much lower. In a recent article Miller has returned to the data with mapping technology which was not available to him in the 1970s to address various criticisms of the original article. He demonstrates that, despite much seemingly random variation, the data support the generalisation that mass attendance was nearly universal in the southeast corner of the country in the 1830s and tapered off gradually to twenty per cent or less of Catholic population in scattered areas of the north and west.[20] Based as it is on nearly 2,000 data-points, this generalisation is robust.

Given the controversy over the crucial quantitative evidence, it is remarkable how much consensus there is over how to characterise, if not to explain, the development of Catholic religious practice in the decades before and after the Famine. Patrick Corish, sketching in 1985 the 'tridentine evolution' theory which McGrath would later elaborate, wrote of post-Famine mass attendance as 'everywhere . . . pushing toward the full attendance already the norm in the towns in the 1830s'.[21] The late Ignatius Murphy, in his monumental history of the diocese of Killaloe, recognised the dramatic rise in mass going during the second half of the nineteenth century, but attributed it to the decline of poverty and such improvements as the construction of chapels in remote areas rather than any change in the disposition to attend mass.[22] Miller has recognised the importance of such hypotheses, indicating his intention to use the 1834 data to test the explanatory power of such variables as social class, church resources and walking distances to account for variations in mass attendance. It seems clear enough that the ratio of poor to non-poor in rural Ireland was much greater in the 1830s than in the 1870s and that the poor were less likely than the non-poor to attend mass. The question whether poverty caused negligence or sufficiency prompted observance, however, may not be so easy to answer as Murphy supposed.

So, at this point the assertion that Catholic devotional practice underwent remarkable changes between the pre-Famine decades and the end of the century is scarcely disputed. However, some scholars are reluctant to adopt the label 'devotional revolution' with its implication that the majority of nominal Catholics had previously been somehow in default upon clearly specified religious duties. Larkin's reference to 'making practising Catholics of the Irish people' invited the equally ahistorical exercise of itemising the bases for 'excusation' of absences implied by the 1834 data[23] – as if, for example, a Catholic whose priest routinely visited his townland twice a year to hear confessions and say mass felt he needed an excuse for failing to go to mass on the other 50 weeks of the year. At this point the differences over pre-Famine canonical practice represent not so much disagreement about the facts as divergence between (equally legitimate) social scientific and pastoral concerns – between explaining human behaviour and judging it.

Early reaction to the devotional revolution hypothesis included a claim that most innovations in devotion happened before 1850, and, in an article on Archbishop Troy, Dáire Keogh has restated this claim in a more guarded form.[24] In general, however, the evidence for devotional innovation before mid-century relates mainly to Dublin and other major towns.[25] Murphy, for example, finds that liturgical innovation in Holy Week in the diocese of Killaloe probably started only in the mid-1840s and then only in the larger towns.[26] The parish mission was clearly a major agent of devotional change, and Murphy indicates that only a small number of such missions were held anywhere in Ireland before 1850, whereas some 43 were held in Killaloe diocese during 1852–75 and 16 more during 1876–1904.[27]

What we need is an understanding of religious practice which takes seriously what Gillespie calls the 'dialogue' between clerical prescription and lay religious needs. In other words we need to pay attention to folk practices and beliefs which offered access to the supernatural through channels not specified in the Tridentine Decrees. Traditional events such as wakes, patterns and pilgrimages have tended hitherto to be conceptualised by historians much as they were by contemporary clergy: as practices to be either stamped out or taken over by the church. Happily, the past decade has seen significant historical work, such as Desmond Mooney's 'Popular Religion and Clerical Influence in Pre-Famine Meath', aimed at incorporating these phenomena into our understanding of the totality of religious experience.[28] Similarly, the late Daniel Gallogly's article on priests and people in the diocese of Kilmore juxtaposes the canonical functions of the clergy with the popular understanding of the powers of those same clergy.[29]

There has been considerable work on pilgrimages and those features of the landscape which are objects of pilgrimage, notably holy wells. Three very interesting recent books by Peter Harbison, by Michael Dames and by Walter and Mary Brenneman deal with pilgrimage over the past millenium or so without directly engaging the specific questions which interest nineteenth-century historians.[30] All three take for granted that the landscape provides a secure basis for some sort of continuity between ancient and modern pilgrimage ritual. That assumption is unceremoniously rejected by Michael P. Carroll in his *Irish Pilgrimage: Holy Wells and Popular Catholic Devotion*. According to Carroll, the elite of seventeenth-century Gaelic society undertook their own 'devotional revolution' by inventing the practices which would be mistakenly regarded, two centuries later, as survivals of pagan Celtic ritual. This new system of patterns and pilgrimages was syncretised with just enough tridentine devotion to appease the clergy while ensuring that the vital business of feuding would not suffer the inconvenience of different kin groups having to gather peaceably in a parish chapel each Sunday for mass. This devotional regime persisted until the merchants and commercial farmers of a new Catholic elite which emerged during the eighteenth century were able, through their clerical cousins, to suppress it because the faction fights and sexual licence accompanying patterns threatened their interests in social stability and the integrity of agricultural holdings across generations. The presence of a huge agrarian underclass masked the effects of this 'second' devotional revolution until the Famine.

There is much to admire in Carroll's ingenious argument. His determination to look for the meaning of practices in their particular historical setting rather than in their remote origins is sensible. A similar determination prompted Gearóid Ó Crualaoich, for example, to move beyond the ahistorical thinking which sometimes characterises the explanations of folklorists and tease out of folklore data a richly nuanced account of how the 'merry wake' functioned within the pattern of social relationships in nineteenth-century counties Cork and Galway.[31] Moreover, Carroll is certainly correct to connect the huge impact of the Famine upon class structure with the timing of devotional change in the nineteenth century. Nineteenth-century historians will, however, probably await a verdict upon Carroll's lightly documented account of seventeenth-century developments from their colleagues who specialise in early modern Ireland.

Whereas some historians will be troubled by the extent of the sociologist Carroll's reliance on theory where empirical evidence is wanting, many find the work of anthropologist Lawrence J. Taylor very illuminating – no doubt because history and anthropology are kindred sciences of the particular. In his *Occasions of Faith* Taylor builds what he subtitles 'an anthropology of Irish Catholics' upon ethnographic fieldwork in southwest Donegal supplemented by research in archival and other nineteenth-century sources. He takes the devotional revolution as a given, but the devotional regime which it brings does not so much supplant popular religion as create new opportunities for the syncretism of popular and official religion. A central metaphor in that process is 'healing', which in Taylor's analysis can range from the miraculous cure of a physical ailment to feelings of wholeness which would not seem out of place in an American new age setting. Of course, tridentine Catholicism had always had processes for recognising miraculous healings, which Laurence Geary describes in his article on the Irish healings in the 1820s of Alexander von Hohenlohe, a German priest who was also a prince of the Holy Roman Empire.[32] It is not such a notable, however, but the 'drunken priest' – i.e. the priest who has been suspended from ministry for misconduct – that Taylor identifies as a typical agent of miraculous healing in the post-revolution devotional regime. Such a figure has special curative powers which priests in good standing lack, for popular religion continues to regard religious careerism as a path away from direct contact with the supernatural. Modern 'charismatic' prayer meetings offer new ways to seek 'healing' in social interaction alongside the older reliance on the holy well.

But perhaps the most pervasive syncretism of popular and official religion after the devotional revolution is found in Marianism. It is interesting that James S. Donnelly, Jr, who began investigating popular religion around 1990 with a study of Lough Derg, perhaps the most celebrated of traditional Irish pilgrimage sites,[33] quickly found himself drawn into the huge topic of Marian devotions on which he has published two substantial articles and projected a major book. The Marian apparition at Knock in 1879 has received attention not only from Donnelly but also from Paul Bew, who has explored the connections between the celebrated vision and the Land War and from John White who reports the discovery of significant new archival material on the episode. The Brennemans have noted the development of complex relationships between the Virgin Mary and St Brigid as objects of devotions at various holy wells.[34] It would be quite useful to have a study comparable to William Christian's work on local shrines in early modern Spain[35] which would systematically track the changes in devotions at particular Irish sites from the pre-Famine Ordnance Survey materials, through the Folklore Commission archives, to current ethnographic observation.

The 'devotional revolution' concept was originally advanced as an hypothesis specifically about Roman Catholicism. However, the central issue raised by the research which it has prompted – the relationship between official and popular religion – is equally germane to the study of Protestantism. In *Evangelical Protestantism in Ulster Society, 1740–1890* by David Hempton and Myrtle Hill we learn that the same Methodist preacher who condemned as superstitious the folk practices of Catholics might be quite prepared to traffic in 'special providences' which played upon similar credulities in his Protestant audience.[36] Hempton and Hill's pioneering work is extremely ambitious, addressing the dominant socio-theological theme in transatlantic Protestant history over the 150-year period which it covers as that theme impinged on all the Protestant denominations represented in Ulster. It is the starting-point for all further study of popular Protestantism in nineteenth-century Ireland.

One direction which that further study should take is the deconstruction of the highly ambiguous term 'evangelical', which had very different histories for the two principal Protestant communities in Ulster – the Anglican community of mainly English origins and the largely Scottish community which adhered to Presbyterianism. Among nineteenth-century Anglicans, in Ireland as in England, 'Evangelicals' were members of the religious party which took its lead from the conversionist preaching of John Wesley in the eighteenth century. But in Presbyterian discourse the term 'Evangelical' was used to describe the opponents of the dominant 'Moderates' in the eighteenth-century Scottish General Assembly over issues of doctrine and polity which had little to do with individual conversion. Furthermore, Wesleyan initiatives in eighteenth-century Ulster made their main impact in areas of Church of Ireland rather than Presbyterian settlement.[37] It was not until 1859 that the Presbyterian clergy confronted a similar phenomenon which was having effects on their adherents comparable to those which the established church encountered two generations earlier.

So the conversionist version of evangelicalism in which Hempton and Hill are most interested is a type of popular religion which found a following in the two Ulster Protestant communities at two very discrete moments in their respective histories: in the late eighteenth century in the Anglican case, and in 1859 and thereafter in the Presbyterian case. The withdrawal of a Methodist society from the Church of Ireland in 1816 was paralleled in the decades following the 1859 revival by the drift of many converts out of the Presbyterian Church.[38] This discontinuity raises the question of how the Presbyterian churches avoided for so long the popular challenge which the established church had faced at the beginning of the century. The appearance of Ian McBride's path-breaking analysis of eighteenth century Ulster Presbyterianism[39] gives us a firmer basis for understanding the popular side of the dialogue posited by Gillespie between clerical prescription and popular needs in this particular community. Recent publications on the 1859 revival include the 1962 doctoral thesis of Alfred Russell Scott – a mine of useful information – as well as important articles by Myrtle Hill, Janice Holmes and Stewart J. Brown.[40] Holmes has met an important need in her book on revivalism in both Ireland and Britain from 1859 until 1905. I am of the opinion, however, that we will not really understand the Revival until we know why it happened so late – in other words until we understand the functions and dysfunctions of Irish Presbyterianism in the two or three generations *before* the Revival.

RELIGIOUS HISTORY AS SOCIAL HISTORY

At this point in the history of the field, our need for further analysis of high ecclesiastical politics is quite modest. Further research on religion as a cultural phenomenon – embracing both official and popular dimensions – is certainly desirable. But our most urgent need, I would argue, is for better *explanations* of what we already know. I believe that that end will best be served by writing religious history as social history, by which I mean focusing on relationships between religion and social formations *other than* the polity: principally gender, class, family, local community and ethnicity. I have deliberately listed ethnicity last because I would assign it the lowest priority in this agenda. Because religious divisions were so central to Irish politics in the nineteenth century, and because with the growth of democracy the polity was rapidly expanding, connections between ethnic solidarities and religion have received a good deal of attention.[41] Both Larkin and Taylor, for example, have much to say about Catholicism's role in the formation of Irish nationalism (as indeed I have myself). Similarly, for Hempton and Hill the rise of evangelicalism is a crucial factor in the creation of a pan-Protestant identity overriding denominational differences by the late nineteenth century.

One of the benefits of looking at the relationship between religion and social formations other than ethnicity is that it offers opportunities for comparative insights across the Catholic–Protestant divide. Pašeta's finding that educated female Catholics in the generation before independence sought out contacts with Protestant women at the same time that their male counterparts were erecting religious difference into the main component of their identity alerts us to the possibility that gender can yield such insights. In her *Labour, Love, and Prayer: Female Piety in Ulster Religious Literature, 1850–1914* Andrea Ebel Brożyna takes advantage of just that possibility. By examining a wide range of denominational periodicals and other devotional literature she discerns significant parallels between the experience of Protestant and Catholic women. Most strikingly, she argues that despite the obvious anxiety of Protestant writers to distance themselves from Catholic doctrine when discussing the Virgin Mary, Catholic and Protestant accounts of her life sent virtually identical messages about the proper role of women in Victorian Ulster. Performance of the religious duty of charity is another subject area in which comparative studies across the Catholic–Protestant divide can yield important new insights. Maria Luddy's *Women and Philanthropy in Nineteenth-Century Ireland* suggests that both religious systems tended to limit the development of an understanding of the social origins of poverty.[42] In both her study of Dublin slums and her biography of Margaret Aylward, foundress of the Sisters of the Holy Faith, Jacinta Prunty illuminates the intertwined charitable and sectarian motives on the part of activists and their supporters in both Catholic and Protestant camps.[43]

Feminist scholars often see philanthropy as an endeavour in which middle-class women were able during the nineteenth century to escape the domestic sphere to some degree. For middle-class Irish Catholic women the tremendous growth of female religious orders, it is argued, offered wealthy, assertive women opportunities to exercise agency in the public sphere. The most fully developed version of this argument is Mary Peckham Magray's *The Transforming Power of the Nuns*, which maintains, however, that the special advantage enjoyed by such women was largely lost after the mid-nineteenth century as bishops gained the upper hand over the female religious in their dioceses. On the other hand, Luddy's study of nuns as workhouse nurses demonstrates that those males who sat on poor law boards of guardians were still finding the mothers superior to be formidable contenders in the public sphere at the end of the century. Nevertheless, Luddy's observation that from the 1850s the extraordinary growth of female religious orders virtually monopolised Catholic female organising of charitable activity[44] suggests that middle-class Catholic laywomen may have been disadvantaged vis-à-vis their Protestant counterparts in this respect. It probably also helps to explain the finding of the late Alison Jordan that the Belfast Catholic community, which presumably had relatively few middle- and upper-class women in any event, tended to leave charitable initiatives to the clergy.[45]

There is, of course, a second gender, though men's history is not yet a well-developed field in Ireland. The spectacular growth of religious orders of women in the nineteenth century was paralleled by a similar growth of men's orders, which also presents opportunities for shedding light from a gender perspective on religious developments. Lay confraternities and, indeed, such para-religious phenomena as Orange and Hibernian orders would also bear investigation from this angle. But perhaps the most promising arena for gender-based analysis in Irish religion is the great nineteenth-century adventure of overseas missions, for which Edmund Hogan has laid the groundwork in *The Irish Missionary Movement*.

One way to characterise the devotional change in the nineteenth century is as a shift from household-centred to a chapel-centred religious practice. For that reason alone we need a better understanding of the interaction between family and church in all aspects of religious behaviour in the various denominations. For example, Timothy W. Guinnane, in his impressive study of demographic change in post-Famine Ireland, points out that simply invoking official Catholic objections to contraception is insufficient to explain the unusual Irish fertility patterns. He calls for a more refined understanding of both the teaching and the authority of the Catholic Church in Ireland in this period.[46]

Local community is another social formation whose relationship to religion merits attention. The pamphlet series, Maynooth Studies in Local History, which publishes master's theses from that university's programme in local history has issued several relevant case studies, including one on religion in Celbridge by Desmond O'Dowd and another on a Dublin Church of Ireland parish by John Crawford. In another of the Maynooth Studies, Proinnsíos Ó Duigneáin places the celebrated 1827 trial of the Catholic controversialist Rev. Thomas Maguire for seduction into the context of the County Leitrim village in which Maguire was parish priest. In an article on the 'Callan

Controversy' Patrick Hogan similarly explores the local context of a dispute which attracted national attention at the time. When Father Robert O'Keefe tried to introduce bold innovations in a national school, he not only found himself at odds with his ecclesiastical superiors, but also became the centre of intense and violent local conflict. It is a fascinating story in which a popular priest known for his knowledge and expertise in natural science ends his career the object – like Taylor's 'drunken priest' – of belief on the part of his remnant of followers that he possesses miraculous thaumaturgical powers.[47]

As I have indicated, I regard the 'imagined community' of nationality to be a relatively unhelpful object of analysis at this stage of our study of religion in Ireland. However, there are some manifestations of 'community' which lie between the conventional, face-to-face relationships of the parish and the imaginary relationships of nationality which can usefully be investigated. The Catholics of Ulster constitute an especially good example of such a community, and it has been subjected to the keen interpretive scrutiny of two distinguished historians, Marianne Elliott and Oliver Rafferty. Similar studies on the other side of the sectarian divide include Kennedy, Miller and Graham's study of the decline of the Protestant community in County Longford, Miriam Moffit's study of the dwindling Church of Ireland population scattered over the landscape of northern Connaught, Lindsay Brown's articles on Monaghan Presbyterians, studies by John Tunney and Ian d'Alton on the respective Protestant communities of Donegal and Cork, and Rafferty's and Hill's essays on the Catholic and Protestant communities respectively in County Down.[48]

However, it is the relationship of the churches to changes in social class that, at the moment, holds the greatest promise for giving us new insights into Irish religious history in the nineteenth century.[49] During the past generation Irish historians have come to understand the growing political and social importance of the relatively well-off tenant farmers in Catholic society in the decades after the Famine. Eugene Hynes was the first to point out that a good deal of the change in mass attendance associated with the devotional revolution might be explained by the loss, through death and emigration, of a huge proportion of the underclass of cottiers and labourers if, as seems plausible, they were less likely than their betters to comply with canonical norms.[50] How exactly the demographic impact on religious and other cultural behaviors worked remains to be empirically explored,[51] but that there was a massive and fairly sudden change in social stratification is indisputable. In a 1990 article Hynes offers a more developed explanation for how the resulting class arrangements and their Catholic culture were socially constructed.[52]

In *Catholic Fiction and Social Reality in Ireland, 1873–1922*, James H. Murphy divides late nineteenth-century Catholic Ireland into six social classes, three of which are 'middle': a Catholic upper middle class which envisaged a contented Ireland under the leadership of themselves and the Catholic gentry within the United Kingdom, a Catholic lower middle class consisting of the comfortable farmers who in fact became the backbone of Irish nationalism, and a Catholic intelligentsia. He then offers a brilliant two-part analysis of how Catholic fiction reflected the needs and aspirations of these three classes. Between 1873 and 1890 a series of upper middle-class Catholic writers produced novels which represent Irish Catholicism in ways intended to win over an English readership to sympathy for an Ireland led by these writers' own class. By 1900, however, that class has clearly lost out to the 'lower middle class' – i.e. the farmers who are beneficiaries of land reform. Members of that class did not tend to be novelists, and their tastes in fiction are difficult to determine, but Charles Kickham's *Knocknagow* is identified as a likely favourite of theirs. The most important Catholic fiction written between 1900 and 1922, however, is written by the Catholic intelligentsia who are embarrassed and distressed by the narrow-minded Catholicism and nationalism of the lower middle class who have already won hegemony in the new Ireland which is coming into being.

Murphy's Catholic upper middle class, recharacterised as 'the Catholic *arriviste* middle classes', become central figures in Oliver P. Rafferty's *The Church, the State and the Fenian Threat, 1861–75*. [53] It is a mistake, Rafferty believes, to conceptualise Catholic clergy primarily as reflecting their social backgrounds and therefore ultimately advancing a nationalist agenda. In the 1860s the agenda which mattered to Cullen and the hierarchy was consolidation of the economic and social position which the Catholic middle classes had been gaining since the 1840s. By threatening that agenda, Fenianism put at risk ecclesiastical hopes for a Catholic political order in Ireland dominated by that class but within the polity of the United Kingdom. [54] One might go a step further than Rafferty does to point out that this emerging middle class in Dublin and other major towns was the Catholic grouping which came closest to Cullen's devotional standard at the time of his succession to the primacy.

In the work of Murphy and Rafferty we can discern the beginnings of a new conceptualisation in which processes of class development supplant the simplistic and ultimately circular invocation of ethnicity to explain major developments in the religious history of nineteenth-century Ireland. Similar work is needed on the Protestant side, and Miller's suggestion that we rethink the Presbyterian Church's experience in the nineteenth century in terms of a shift from a communal to class-based religious system is a step in that direction. Such reconceptualisations bring us back to the problem of periodisation with which we started. In a number of ways, religion in Ireland underwent dramatic change in the middle decades of the nineteenth century. The obvious candidate for an underlying cause for the discontinuity of this process, if not for the process itself, is the Famine. The sesquicentennial Famine observances prompted a number of works which touch on role of religion in that terrible calamity. Kerr's popular account of the Catholic Church's role, Helen Hatton's study of Quaker relief, and the articles by David Sheehy on Archbishop Murray and the Famine in Mayo, by Christine Kinealy on the role of private charity, by Peter Gray on the government's role and by David W. Miller on the Presbyterians and the Famine address religious issues especially directly. The two main points of contact between religion and the Famine on which these works focus are a religious duty – charity – and a religious explanation – providence. Both charity and providential thinking are responses to the Famine as an immediate conjuncture. What is needed now is attention to how the longer-term social processes which were initiated or hastened by that conjuncture affected and were affected by religion. The most obvious of those processes was sweeping change in class structure and the ensuing social constructions by which Irish people made sense of their place in society and in the cosmos.

# CHAPTER 5

# Historical Geography

❉

*Matthew Stout*

## INTRODUCTION

This essay seeks to assess recent works in historical geography. Like the founders of the *Journal of Historical Geography* I have made no attempt to define the parameters of the subject.[1] Instead, as an historian with a background in historical geography and cartography, I present a review of publications that fall within the wide parameters of landscape archaeology, landscape history *and* historical geography. The range of materials consulted is not confined to the work of historical geographers writing within geography departments because practitioners of place-based history in Ireland have increasingly found themselves harboured within history departments and beyond. It is instructive to those who study the nineteenth century to see the wide array of sources that are being used to illuminate the past, including economic and local history, archaeology, folklore, and even literary criticism.

The review begins with two studies that established a baseline for the discipline at the beginning of the period under consideration: roughly 1988 to 2003. It then examines subsequent work, highlighting especially innovative research. For convenience, it looks at studies that examine Ireland before the Famine, work specifically about the Famine, its aftermath, urban studies and finally the legacy of the nineteenth century. Nineteenth-century historical geography was long dominated by T. W. Freeman,[2] and his influence can be felt into the 1980s. The focus of this essay is the degree to which historical geography has contributed to our understanding of the past since the publication of the study provided in *A New History of Ireland V* (1989).

When the 'official' history of the nineteenth century was published in 1989 it featured an essay by T. W. Freeman that was itself an historical document.[3] Freeman offered a welcome source-driven counterbalance to Estyn Evans's landscape-dominated historical geography,[4] but the work in the *New History* (which was published a year after Freeman's death) arrived over four decades after it was first realised in his classic *Pre-Famine Ireland* published in 1957.[5] His chapter, 'Land and people', provided a description of Ireland as it was recorded in the first census of Ireland in 1841, which was 'a social survey, not a bare enumeration'.[6] Thus Freeman's paper mirrors the agenda if not the tone of more recent research that concentrates on finding meaning in the landslide of official statistics. Of primary importance was the issue of rising population, where it was located and the appalling conditions in which the mass of people lived. The total number living in Ireland in 1841 was 8,175,124.[7] Just as staggering, this population was essentially rural with only twenty per cent living in settlements with more than twenty houses.[8] But whether rural or urban (Belfast stood out as the one exception to an otherwise squalid urban landscape),[9] the people were overwhelmingly poor. Forty per cent of Irish families lived in fourth-class houses – one-roomed, mud-walled cabins with no windows. Correspondingly, 45 per cent of farm holdings were between one and five acres.[10] Only seven per cent of land holdings were over 30 acres – what emerged as the viable farm size in post-Famine Ireland.[11] Freeman fully accepted the Malthusian interpretation of the disaster that was to strike those individuals enumerated in the 1841 census: 'the conclusion is inescapable and simple: there were too many people on the land.'[12]

This short article offered a glimpse of the vast body of official quantitative and qualitative data that came in torrents as Britain struggled with the 'Irish problem' after the Act of Union in 1801. Freeman exploited the rich vein of unpublished Valuations archives, the Devon Commission and other reports on industry, transport, markets and fairs, etc., an explosion of sources for nineteenth-century historical geography matched only by the explosion in population.

Freeman makes it clear that, despite impending disaster, the historical geography of that troubled century in Ireland is often the story of progress and innovation, most notably in the development of public transport on the roads, canals and railways. It was a time also of administrative innovation. An act of 1838 divided the country into 130 poor law unions,[13] thrusting aside the medieval legacies of parish, barony and county while affirming the sanctity of the townland. Here we had a reorganisation of the island on a scale worthy of the French Directory. It was this type of 'progress' that led many contemporary observers into the overly optimistic view that Ireland could become an industrial nation on the model of its more powerful neighbour. Freeman highlights the misguided notion, held by many in the nineteenth century, that a developing infrastructure would bring to light, and to market, as yet untapped resources like the chimerical Munster coalfields; 'the most extensive in the British empire' according to one misguided observer in 1844.[14]

Scholarship had already progressed considerably when the Freeman article was posthumously published, including, most notably, Cormac Ó Gráda's

1988 answer to Freeman's 1957 study.[15] *Ireland Before and After the Famine* offers a more nuanced view of Ireland in the run-up to the catastrophe, to say nothing of its aftermath. This rigorous economic history (written in the cliometric tradition of Joel Mokyr)[16] points out that population pressure might have been 'adjusting downwards' even in the west where population increase was fastest.[17] The potato, far from being the 'root' of all evil, was in fact a mechanism to avoid famine as it was predominantly used as animal feed during good times. An Irish economist, praising the potato in 1834, noted that 'potatoes cannot be easily hoarded or exported, yet pigs can and potatoes may be considered as the raw materials of which pigs are manufactured'.[18]

According to Ó Gráda, the poor were unlucky in the timing of the Famine: a failure one generation later and the starving population would have been more easily incorporated into expanding American and British economies without the huge death toll.[19] Ó Gráda makes it clear, however, that the 'what ifs' of history don't amount to a whole lot, as the Famine did come aided and abetted by the Irish landowning class; only two Irish MPs voted against the Gregory clause, an infamous act that forced people to give up their land before they could receive Famine relief.[20] The tragedy persisted until at least 1851, a longer famine than most contemporary observers or later historians allow.[21] 'Donor fatigue' set in well before the tragedy ended.[22]

Ó Gráda highlights not just the poverty of those dependent on the potato but also how that poverty existed against a backdrop of increased inequality.[23] Banking flourished in the nineteenth century driven by middle-class Catholics.[24] The politics of the middle class (emancipation and repeal) took central place in history and in subsequent historiography only because the poor had no voice in the political system. Away from the small farm, potato-dependent west, farmers managed to increase production in the pre-famine years with output perhaps doubling in the economic export-driven end of Irish agriculture.[25] Ó Gráda rightly complains about historians and many historical geographers, who focus exclusively on the land issue and questions of land tenure when writing on the years after the Famine. If the focus were instead concentrated on changing farming methods and transformations that take place at the all-important family farm level,[26] the continuous occupation of families on the same plots of land in the pre- and post-Famine landscape becomes manifest.

What these writers – one a historical geographer, the other an economic historian – have in common in their statistical studies is the relegation of the importance of place. Geography was critical in shaping the variety of historical experience, and the landscape itself is a rich source for the past. This neglect may be acceptable in the work of Ó Gráda, an economic historian, but Freeman's summary must be regarded as a failure to engage with the spatial element of the past. He does use a number of choropleth maps[27] and other statistical mapping to illustrate wealth, population density, etc. (for that matter Ó Gráda reproduces a fine map of population change), but Freeman confines his historical geography to the brief but essential point that there were two Irelands at the time of the Famine: east and west, either side of a line from Derry to Cork.[28] These divisions were explicitly acknowledged by the 1841 census enumerators.[29] Freeman is never truly engaged with the process of historical settlement: he laments the destruction of rural housing and the evidence for the once ubiquitous fourth-class house, but he rarely discusses how the nineteenth century survives in the landscape today or, more importantly, how the landscape and other spatial issues (like international trade) shaped the geography of nineteenth-century Ireland.

BEFORE THE FAMINE

In recent years, the best (and most widely read) depiction of nineteenth-century historical geography has been Kevin Whelan's 1997 contribution to the *Atlas of the Irish Rural Landscape*.[30] After establishing the importance of the eighteenth century in providing the foundations for the developing landscape, Whelan, following in the tradition of Tom Jones Hughes,[31] is at pains to detail the complex geography of pre-Famine Ireland. The island was roughly divided into five regions (not just the two that contemporary Famine commentators detected) whose settlement patterns differed largely owing to the underpinning agricultural economy of the respective zones: the dairying zone based around the Cork provisions trade; the cattle fattening region of the east midlands; the tillage region of the southeast; the proto-industrialised northeast whose dense population was made possible by the linen trade; and the small farming regions of the west.[32] Ireland was a complex mosaic; grazier landscapes featured huge fields and farms and few people. The linen zone held Ireland's densest population, but one that was relatively prosperous and Protestant. W. J. Smyth has cautioned that within regions, and even counties, the topography is complex and settlement forms vary widely.[33] Whelan's summary and other detailed studies discussed in this chapter similarly highlight the error inherent in seeing pre-Famine Ireland merely as place of poverty and over population.

It is only the last of these five regions, the small farm West, that is easily recognised in most written histories of 'Ireland before the Famine'. In the *Atlas of the Irish Rural Landscape*, Kevin Whelan concentrates on the western small farm zone explaining by means of a simplified model the development and demise of the widespread clachan and rundale form of settlement.[34] Contemporary evidence attests to the fact that clachans began as partnership leases on poor land in the eighteenth century. As population grew, shares in the land were subdivided, leading to fragmented holdings and the rapid expansion of the clachan. Clachans continued to expand up to the eve of the Famine.[35]

In his ongoing work on the transformation of seventeenth- to nineteenth-century landscapes, Smyth notes that the whole process by which families proliferated, subdivided land, and colonised new frontier lands still remains to be documented at local level in areas throughout Ireland.[36] But Nolan, for one, in an essay stemming from the same geographical tradition as Smyth, has shown that the relentless surge of population into the uplands was not only a western phenomenon. On the upper slopes of Glenasmole in the Dublin Mountains, the productive area of townlands increased as much as fifty per cent. Rentals doubled as a result of these improvements.[37] Similar trends were identified in County Waterford. Growth in population and the spread into unprofitable land are reflected in an increase in road mileage, from 227 to 507 miles, and in the number of limekilns, from three in 1773 to 107 in 1840.[38] Penetration into the Knockmealdown Uplands raised the limit of settlement from 610 feet to 710 feet.[39] House clusters (University College Dublin speak for clachans)[40] are clearly shown to be, for the most part, the result of late population growth in the more remote parts of Waterford county. The vast majority were located adjacent to unprofitable lands above the 450 feet contour.[41] In Smyth's study of County Cork the spread of population was shown to have been facilitated by kinship structures which permitted the sub-division of land, landlord initiatives (or the lack thereof), corn/potato rotations, early marriage among those practising this non-capital intensive potato economy and lastly, the widespread availability of underutilised land.[42]

None of the above cited work on the clachan and rundale settlement phenomenon has found it to have pre-early modern antecedents. Smyth writes:

> Some of these territorial arrangements in the working of the land may have been quite old, but a comparison of partnership farming areas with the zones of Ireland's population increase from the second half of the eighteenth century would suggest that many of these partnership groups developed as a product of the excessive population pressure on limited land resources over this exceptional period.[43]

Nonetheless, the anthropologist Tom Yager recently revived the controversy about the basis of this settlement form in a somewhat idealised examination of Erris in County Mayo.[44] The wiping out of the system of communal farming that Yager describes was indeed about capitalism but not in the sense that it was replacing communism. It was untrammelled population expansion into unsettled areas that led to the creation of this system, not ideology, and it was purely the profit motive, to bring land back within the financial reckoning of the landlords, that led to its demise. Yager does point out that the system of redistribution which survived in some areas of Ireland prevented the fragmentation of holdings that was the *bête noire* of the Congested Districts Board (CDB).[45] The widespread fragmentation that the CDB struggled with must mean that the practice of redistribution, as it survived in Erris, was an anomaly.[46]

Despite Whelan's compelling scenario regarding the rise and precipitous fall of clachan and rundale, historical geographers continue to search for their origins (a tradition in the profession that is almost as old as the clachans themselves). Yager revives the notion, largely based on folklore of the Erris area, that its origins are medieval and its distribution at one time widespread in Ireland.[47] This is manifestly not so. It would be just as valid to hold the view, also based on folklore, that the chaotic clachan and rundale system was created by 'Lord Rundale' to ensure that the Irish would 'be always fighting among themselves'.[48] The Medieval three-field system and the two field system are not the same, culturally or economically, and the medieval origins of other systems in Ireland that have a superficial resemblance to that found in the West do not prove an early origin for clachan and rundale.[49]

Whelan has provided more detailed analysis of landscape and society in the West and, more specifically, life on Clare Island, off the coast of Mayo.[50] Contemporary observers were aware both of the great expansion of population in the west of Ireland and how it had become possible through potato and lazy-bed cultivation. He quotes Edward Wakefield who wrote in 1812 about the potato's importance:

> Throughout a great part of the west of Ireland, the culture of the land is in so infantile a state that the earth is rendered productive rather by the accumulation of labour than by the assistance of skill or capital. There, the crop of potatoes is everything, a crop cultivated chiefly with the spade, on it depends the subsistence of the cultivator and his whole family.[51]

'Infantile' perhaps, but spade cultivation was an extremely effective way of surviving on these marginal lands. Just as farming technologies adapted to conditions so too did settlement patterns. On Clare Island, clachans grew up across the whole island which was 'undivided and held by the inhabitants in common'. The rent was paid 'by the bulk',[52] that is in one payment to the landlords leaving the tenants to determine both the amount of money owed and who got what land, a remarkable display of community living.[53]

In writing on Clare Island Whelan acknowledges the difficulty in obtaining sources relating to pre-Famine Ireland and the earlier in the century one tries, the more rare these sources become. As a result, few have attempted an analysis of the early decades of the nineteenth century. Smyth notes that the Famine acts as both an historical and historiographical hinge, because of the abundance and ubiquity of sources from the 1840s in contrast to the 'limited range and areal incompleteness of the source materials used' prior to the 1840s. 'There is still much hidden of the reactions, activities and experiences of the great majority.'[54] There are, therefore, still many 'geographies' to be explored.

Undaunted by source deficiencies, Smyth has identified the main forces at work at the beginning of the nineteenth century in County Cork that may apply to the rest of the island: a shift in market prices favouring tillage and dairying; expansion in brewing and distilling; growth of estate bureaucracy and elimination of the middlemen where possible; phenomenal population growth; the development of the Catholic middle class seen both in the growing confidence of farmers and in the expansion of the Cork suburbs.[55]

A great deal of ingenuity has been necessary to chart the historical geography of the early nineteenth century. Kevin Whelan's 1988 study on the development of Catholic Church institutions established a model for the use of these sources.[56] Four early sources were interrogated to establish that the chief social and economic division in pre-Famine Ireland was not simply an east–west one but more accurately a south–east/north–west division and that it was in mid Munster and south Leinster that the modern Irish nation – Catholic, conservative and middle class – emerged.[57] Charting the distribution of the first surviving Catholic register in each parish, Whelan established a modernising south-east region where registers were mainly established prior to 1800 and an underdeveloped north-west region where most first registers post-date 1870.[58] The southeast was the area of greatest Catholic wealth. This is indicated by a list of the valuation of Catholic parishes in 1800 contained in the Castlereagh *Memoirs*.[59] The early development of the southeast has its origins in the distribution of priests trained on the continent (as listed in the 1704 *List of Registered Clergy*) who would have been exposed to modern Catholic thinking.[60] The ultimate expression of the success of the southeastern region was the preponderance of donations from the area in support of Daniel O'Connell's Emancipation project as revealed in the *O'Connell Annual Annuity Rolls*.[61] The zone of radical conservatism identified by Whelan also figures prominently in the origins of hurling as it is played today.[62]

W. J. Smyth, who also has a well-established pedigree in the creative use of pre-'official' source material, ingeniously uses the tenant tree planting records to trace the expansion of rural wealth in the early nineteenth century (figure 1). Trees are a long-term investment and their planting is a product of innovating farming societies.[63] Their planting was also contingent on a high population of landless labourers to do the work and it echoes other activities of the Catholic middle class such as liming and crop rotation.[64] Smyth uses the creation of parish registers and church construction in a similar fashion. The number of registers expanded rapidly in the early years of the century, indicating both an advancing church and congregation.[65] In Cork, 53 per cent of parishes organised registers between 1825 and 1845. Seventy per cent of

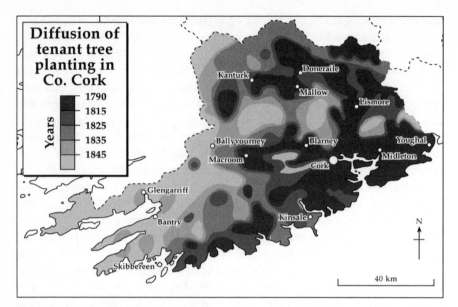

Figure 1. W. J. Smyth's map shows the spread of tenant tree planting, 1790–1845. At first sight, the record of tenants who planted trees does not seem too promising an historical source, but Smyth's isopleth map uses the spread of this phenomenon as a surrogate for charting the growing wealth and confidence of the Catholic middle class in pre-Famine County Cork.

*Source:* After W. J. Smyth, 'Social, economic and landscape transformations in County Cork from the mid-eighteenth to the mid-nineteenth century', in Patrick O'Flanagan and C. G. Buttimer (eds), *Cork: History and Society* (Dublin: Geography Publications, 1993), pp. 655–98, see p. 677, fig. 16.6.

parish churches were built or rebuilt during this period.[66] Modernising economies in Cork saw to it that the middle-man class was all but eliminated by 1820, in a period described by James S. Donnelly, Jr (in *Land and People*) as an era of reform in estate administration.[67]

The rise of the Catholic middle class was an unequivocal challenge to Protestant landlords. Nonetheless, L. J. Proudfoot has focused on the varied social composition of landlords and tenants and challenged the commonly held perception of these groups as homogeneous and directly opposed groupings.[68] Proudfoot detects a continuity of ownership in Waterford estates (for example) with the survival of both Old English and Gaelic surnames; a critical qualification of the consensus view that the Protestant landlord class were necessarily regarded as being 'foreign' or 'outsiders'. Proudfoot does so, however, without assessing the religious affiliation of those landlords from long-established families. The fact that they were overwhelmingly Anglican means that we should not reject the notion that they were culturally and ethnically 'alien', however simplistic it may be to draw conclusions from an analysis of their surnames.[69] Proudfoot's branding of the results of much careful research as 'stereotype' is an unhelpful form of revisionism. L. M. Cullen has also suggested that the background of Protestant landlords families counted for more than did their religion when he controversially stated that 'converts retained links with Catholic relatives and other Catholic families, and their outlook almost invariably remained sympathetic to their former co-religionists'.[70] One example (at least) from County Meath challenges this view. In Dunsany, in County Meath, the change of religion by the Dunsany family led to a Protestant revolution in the landscape with the construction of a gothic village and demesne as late as the 1830s. This demonstrates that the ethnic and cultural origins of landlords were not a decisive factor in shaping nineteenth-century geographies, but their religion was.

Showing a similar creativity in the innovative use of source material as that demonstrated by W. J. Smyth, the historian David Miller analysed mass attendance: an index of modernity, the proximity of towns and the degree to which patterns had been suppressed (figure 2).[71] The public instruction committee was established in 1834 to assess the numbers of Catholics and Protestants in Ireland and the level of mass attendance was calculated as a by-product of this activity. Miller was able to map this data through the use of Geographical Information Systems (GIS) and some sophisticated areal statistics. Critically, a map of the devotional revolution in 1834 was the end result and the area south and east of a line from Dundalk to Killarney is revealed as the zone of main mass attendance.[72] Mass going was, therefore, primarily a question of class, with the better-off farmers dominating religious practice, a pre-Famine pattern accentuated in the Famine's aftermath.

Kevin Whelan used Miller's map as the basis for significant observations about Daniel O'Connell and the repeal movement.[73] The historical geography of this political campaign had been overlooked until Whelan revealed it to be a movement of the Catholic middle class pursued largely in the zone of their greatest influence: Munster and Leinster. The poor were again abandoned by O'Connell who had previously secured 'emancipation' only for those with land valued at over forty shillings, a rarity in the West. Similarly, the Protestant North was excluded from the emerging Catholic Irish nationalism which negated the campaign of the United Irishmen and lies at the foundation of the sectarian states set up after 1922. The origins of the Christian Brothers can also be better understood as a result of Miller's analysis.[74]

THE FAMINE

The mid 1990s commemoration of the Great Irish Famine should have been, but was not, the basis for significant advances in the understanding of the geography of Ireland's greatest tragedy. Numerous works examined the

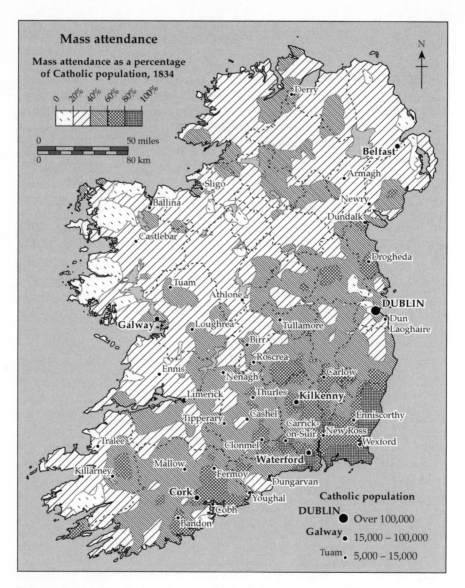

Figure 2. David Miller's map of mass attendance (as reproduced in K. Whelan, *Daniel O'Connell*) was made possible through a highly sophisticated process involving the latest Geographical Information Systems (GIS) and complex statistical analysis. The map has been used subsequently to explain the development of Daniel O'Connell's repeal movement and the origins of the Christian Brothers.

*Source:* After Kevin Whelan, 'Daniel O'Connell: the Kerry proteus', in Kevin Whelan (ed.), *Daniel O'Connell* (Dublin: Keough Notre Dame Centre, 2002), pp. 22–9, see p. 25; based on a map in D. W. Miller, 'Mass attendance in Ireland in 1834', in S. J. Brown and D. W. Miller (eds), *Piety and Power in Ireland 1760–1960: Essays in Honour of Emmet Larkin* (Belfast: Institute of Irish Studies, 2000), pp 158–79, see p. 173, fig 7.5.

decline in population at local level, and the efforts to deal with the great calamity, in particular through the scrutiny of poor law records. Most of the resulting statistical analysis did not truly engage with the landscape or individual processes at work.[75] One measure of the missed opportunities was *Mapping the Great Irish Famine*.[76] This well-funded and well-staffed project did not develop the means of expressing census statistics in a meaningful or creative manner. Indeed, whole series of computer generated county maps use equal but coarse class intervals to show, in effect, nothing.[77] Maps based on barony and poor law union units are better, but often confusing and would have benefited from the use of simplified isopleth maps[78] (in the manner, for example, of W. J. Smyth and David Miller) to accentuate meaningful geographical boundaries.

A great exception to the general disengagement was Brian MacDonald's *A Time of Desolation*.[79] An appendix at the rear of this book blandly states that the population of the Clones, County Monaghan poor law union declined by almost 15,000 individuals (35 per cent);[80] as close as much other analysis came to an understanding of the Famine. But MacDonald uses this statistic merely as a springboard for a much more exhaustive regional study amalgamating the widest possible range of sources. Critical geographical insights are garnered from a series of Civil Parish maps that examine population decline on a townland by townland basis. MacDonald's analysis discovered disease and death to have been particularly acute along rivers and roads where the passing traffic of the destitute infected the roadside homes of the poor. Proximity to Famine burial grounds also contributed to a higher death toll.[81] One of the key features of high death rates was the misfortune to be on an estate that lacked a resident landlord.[82] In contrast, townlands where soup kitchens were set up recorded lower declines or even increases in population, suggesting the means of surviving the Famine attracted a population who remained *in situ* after the Famine years.[83] Two things stand out in MacDonald's study: firstly, the coroner's reports as reported in the local papers show the individual horror behind the statistics:

> William Marshall Thompson, surgeon, examined [the body of George Graham]. From the stomach to the rectum was perfectly empty; not even a particle of matter in them. He conceived that the deceased had died from want of food.[84]

The second outstanding feature of the Clones study are the appeals from poor law union officials, workhouse boards, relief committees, and parish priests to the authorities in Dublin for increased aid; The Reverend Charles Welsh wrote to the Lord Lieutenant 'For the sake of God, let something be done for us.'[85] The official responsibility for deaths during the Famine has rarely been shown in such stark relief.

The historical geography of the Famine, when viewed up close, becomes its archaeology and one scholar has highlighted this material aspect of the nineteenth century. Charles Orser is an American archaeologist with a background in the archaeology of slavery. He represents a new trend in historical archaeology that has its origins in the United States. For Orser, archaeology provides a voice for those speechless individuals who appear only in the debit column of official statistics.[86] His work has focused on Strokestown in County Roscommon, building on Robert Scally's history of the area,[87] and the attention drawn to Strokestown House following the foundation of the Famine museum in 1995.[88] Orser's work is in its infancy but early results showed how locally manufactured pottery survived alongside higher quality wares from England, and uncovered improvements made to the land once unproductive tenants had been removed through a notorious series of evictions.[89] Further excavation will provide a 'thrilling potential and unbounded opportunity' for recreating the ordinary lives of Famine-era peoples.[90]

Burtchaell's analysis of the Famine in County Waterford determined that the death toll and emigration did not blight the county evenly or predictably. Curiously, the most heavily populated and poorest townlands were not those hit hardest during the years of hardship.[91] The impact of the Famine was, instead, explained by two factors: the degree to which aid was delivered and the abilities of the local landlords, large farmers and the government to maintain this assistance to the poor to the end of the decade; and the degree to which landlords resorted to the draconian measures made possible by the Gregory clause and the operation of the poor law.[92]

AFTER THE FAMINE

While this review focuses mainly on work published in the last decade, it is impossible to neglect Smyth's groundbreaking work on Clogheen/Burncourt that described pre- and post-Famine landscape change in the varied environment of south Tipperary (figure 3).[93] This outstanding study combined estate records, official statistical sources and a detailed survey of the modern landscape to portray the origins and evolution of just one Catholic parish in unprecedented detail. By 1840, the crowded landscape reflected the population growth and settlement expansion charted by Smyth though estate records and official sources. On the long-settled valley floor, a new landlord demesne had been carved out and the commercialisation of the pastoral economy consolidated substantial grazier farms. The mountain slopes attracted intensive potato-based colonisation, and a dense network of small farms. The Famine exposed the fragility of these small farm and landless families. The collapse was most notable on the northern Galtee slopes, where there was ruthless landlord clearance of small holdings. The more economically diversified small farm zone to the south on the Knockmealdowns survived better owing to its proximity to the village of Clogheen and access to Clonmel. In the decades following the Famine, both small farm zones were wiped out. Over the next half century the number of farms below thirty acres fell from 400 to 86. The number of farms of 30 acres and above remained virtually the same but they became larger (the number of farms over a hundred acres doubled).[94]

The landless class in Clogheen/Burncourt and elsewhere was eclipsed by the Famine and emigration. They left behind an empty lowland, but with its big farm structure intact and strengthened. Smyth describes the far-reaching effects this had on Irish society. At local level the control of the land, marriage and inheritance were closely guarded. Surplus sons and daughters either emigrated (in the case of the less well off) or were provided for in other farms

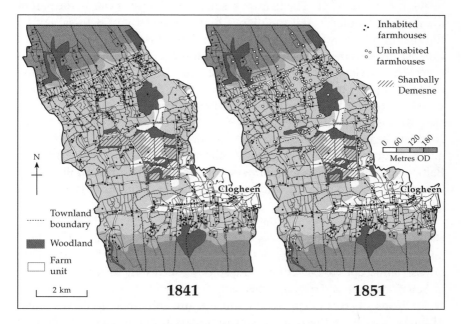

Figure 3. W. J. Smyth's maps of Clogheen/Burncourt before and after the Famine. These maps (as reproduced in the *Atlas of the Irish Rural Landscape*) show how surviving the Famine was a question of class and, to a certain extent, location. The small farmers dependent on the potato were hit hardest but those near the village of Clogheen had a better chance of surviving, at least in the short term. Continuity of land holdings and dwellings was a feature of the larger farms in the lowlands.

*Source:* After Kevin Whelan, 'The modern landscape: from plantation to present', in F. H. A. Aalen, Kevin Whelan and Matthew Stout (eds), *Atlas of the Irish Rural Landscape* (Cork: Cork University Press, 1997), pp 67–103, see p. 90, fig. 48; based on maps in W. J. Smyth, 'Landholding changes, kinship networks and class transformation in rural Ireland: a case study from County Tipperary', *Irish Geography* 16 (1983), pp. 16–35, see pp. 20, 23, figs 2–3.

or places within the legal profession, the church, journalism and trade.[95] Indeed, marriage was controlled to so great an extent that Ireland, in 1871, had the lowest marriage rate of any European country.[96] Once entrenched, the rural mindset expanded outwards into towns and cities creating the strangling conservatism that characterised Irish society in the last half of the nineteenth century and the first half of the twentieth.

My own modest local analysis of the historical geography of the Famine and its aftermath, attempted in one townland what Smyth's landmark study had achieved in an entire parish.[97] Taking advantage of the extraordinary diaries of Elizabeth Smith,[98] I related her contemporary observations with the statistical sources available from the Famine period and after. It was possible, for the first time in this study, to locate precisely individuals and their homes within the small estate and to chart the decline of both people and buildings between 1841 and 1881. The Famine resulted in a failure of will on the part of the resident landlords and the diaries hint at the sense of betrayal felt by Elizabeth Smith towards her tenants when there was a low level of agrarian violence towards the end of the Famine. This must have influenced her decision to leave Ireland in 1850. The subsequent loss in patronage meant that the hardest hit portion of the population were those living and working on the Baltyboys estate. Two fifths of the population decline experienced between 1851–81 was related to the removal of estate labourers and their families.[99] In contrast, the large tenant farmers remained on their farms (albeit with smaller numbers of labourers) and literally inherited the post-Famine earth. In Baltyboys today the big house survives, but the houses *and* the families of the larger farmers dominate the landscape. The homes of the small farmers and labourers lie in ruins.

Every ruined cottage in the Irish landscape, every individual whose absence is implicit in the statistics of nineteenth-century population decline, tells of other historical geographies. The Irish diaspora created mirror images or Irish landscapes in Newfoundland; starkly contrasting urban geographies in American cities; and remote settlements in the mining towns of the American Great Plains and Australian deserts. The literature on the subject is vast: John Mannion's work on the Irish in Newfoundland is rich in landscape history and serves as a model for the historical geography of the emigrant experience.[100] The historiography of the diaspora is conveniently detailed in a recent study by Kevin Kenny.[101]

The importance of the landlord in shaping the landscape and developing the local economy remained undimmed through the first half of the nineteenth century and survived in some places into the post-Famine years. And, while the Famine rightly draws our attention towards the tragic and stark break with the past, Duffy has provided a corrective with his study of the Shirley estate in county Monaghan where significant improvements were pushed through during the 1840s.[102] He rightly focuses on the landlords as agents of change and the estate as the unit of that change.[103] In the case of the Shirley estate, 'Estate improvement books' provide details of activities at individual farm level. These record everything from the construction of houses to the provision of a crowbar for removing field stones.[104] Investment in farm improvements began at two per cent of income in 1842, rising to ten per cent (right through the Famine years) to 1850.[105] Huge quantities of thorn quicks provided by the Shirley estate are further testimony to the landlord's role in creating the tightly enclosed field patterns of the Monaghan drumlins.[106] The amount of money injected into the economy by landlords could be huge; £20,000 was spent on rebuilding Lismore castle, the heart of the Devonshire estate, between 1811–14 and £48,000 was spent between 1851 and 1858 on rebuilding it yet again.[107]

These late and massive investments stand out as an anomaly in the otherwise depressed world of post-Famine estate management. More typical was the collapse of rental income that led ultimately to the demise of the land-lord system. The Encumbered Estates Courts made possible the sale of many properties whose owners faced incremental legal entanglements including entailed wills that prevented the sale of many properties prior to the passing of this new legislation. Proudfoot has shown that, in County Waterford, 190 estates were processed by the Encumbered Estate courts, most of these prior to 1864.[108] In a parallel study, Lane has shown how the purchase of the encumbered estates could often prove to be a profitable financial speculation. Rents in Galway, for example, rose steeply in the years 1852–60 and this was often accompanied by a harsh eviction policy carried out by the new owners. The influx of land onto the market did not depress prices as landlords shifted from intensive tillage to extensive grazing.[109] A good practical point about the causes of estate failure has been made by Proudfoot; he pointed out that the large demesnes dedicated to uninterrupted pasture and exotic trees required cattle and sheep to maintain their verdure.[110] They were not, therefore, a feature of the unproductive expenditure which is often identified as a source of the ultimate failure of landlordism in Ireland.

The early nineteenth century was still a period of substantial landlord investment in towns and villages: £71,000 was spent by the Dukes of Devonshire on Dungarvan between 1801 and 1820, and £20,000 between 1820–30 in Lismore.[111] But the relationship between urban development and estate management lessened in the post-Famine years. Improved transport, especially the spread of the railway network, lessened the need for a dense urban matrix. In Waterford, the focus of work by Lindsay Proudfoot, the waning importance of town and village building led to a re-ordering of the urban hierarchy. Waterford city became the focus of investment and trade while the urban centres of Lismore, Dungarvan and Tallow became surplus to requirement and stagnated.[112]

While Duffy and Proudfoot focused on estate records, the post-Famine period has also been examined through the forensic examination of Griffith's valuation, OS maps and extensive fieldwork.[113] From these sources,[114] Jack Burtchaell has developed a classification of settlement based on the value of land holdings: landlords (and middlemen), strong farmers, small farmers and cottiers.[115] His work mirrors contemporary perceptions of farming and the most recent division of nineteenth-century society based on house values.[116] For Geraldine Stout, the nineteenth century speaks to us through its documents (most notably Griffith's Valuation and the first edition OS maps) but more eloquently through its buildings. In some cases the absence of structures speaks with even greater fluency of post-Famine Irish society: 'In many places, the sole trace of these houses is a weed-entangled gateway with everlasting sweet pea pushing up through the undergrowth.'[117] The vertical structure of a society still dominated by landlords and larger farmers is shown to have a horizontal expression, graphically detailed by Geraldine Stout (figure 4).[118]

The Famine and its aftermath in County Mayo was also the subject of detailed statistical analysis by Donald Jordan.[119] This study confirmed that the inequalities in society did not end with the Famine and the wholesale removal of the destitute during the Famine years. The richest land still supported fewer persons and population decline between 1851-81 was most marked in the richer agricultural lands of central and south-east Mayo.[120] There, even before the Famine, marriages occurred later and were economically motivated. This tendency became even more marked in the post-Famine years.[121] By the end of the century, however, even the poor small farm fringe adopted the marriage practices of the better off regions.[122]

All historical geographers, writing in a post-revisionist consensus, agree that *Phytophtora infestans* put an end to that which underpinned a way of life and an entire settlement form in the West of Ireland. The area came to be seen as a problem, neatly and geographically detailed in an item for the *Illustrated London News*:

> There are two sides of Ireland. The western side of the country is always in a deplorable condition. If you take a map of the whole island and strike a tolerably straight line from the town of Londonderry in the north to Skibbereen near Cape Clear, the most southerly point, you divide the region of comparative prosperity from nearly all the districts suffering from chronic misery.[123]

Maps of land valuation and famine severity graphically depict this Western poverty.[124]

Decades later, in the wake of the land acts which began the process of turning more prosperous tenant farmers into landowners, the 'backwardness' of the area became an even more obvious reality. This grinding poverty

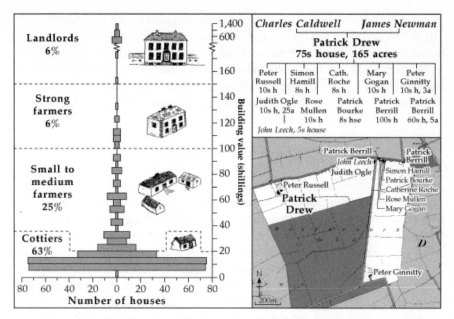

Figure 4. Geraldine Stout demonstrated the pyramid-like structure of nineteenth-century society by concentrating on its buildings as recorded in *Griffith's Valuation*. The vertical stratigraphy was typically played out horizontally with the strong farmers' houses being located in the middle of townlands while poorer labourers occupied the figurative and actual margins of society.

*Source:* After Geraldine Stout, *Newgrange and the Bend of the Boyne* (Cork: Cork University Press, 2002), pp. 148, 160 figs 4, 31.

became entwined with Home Rule politics and became a preoccupation of the British authorities wishing to counter both the poverty and the popularity of the Home Rule movement.[125] As a result, the *laissez faire* policies of the Famine years yielded to far reaching state interventions.[126] The greatest expression of this new policy was the Congested Districts Board (CDB) that was founded as a response to near famine conditions that again struck the 'West' in 1889–90.[127] By the time of its dissolution in 1923, the CDB had purchased over 1,000 estates, restructured 30,000 plus holdings and redistributed of 300,000 hectares of land.[128] Much of the pre-Famine landscape was erased in the process.

Historical geographers in Ireland have an affection for the Congested Districts Board that might outweigh its importance. It produced many far-reaching changes including the development of the western infrastructure and agriculture, but most notably in its *tabula rasa* approach to what remained of clachan and rundale landscapes. One of the CDB's most dramatic projects was on Clare Island. The entire island was purchased in 1895 and completely remodelled. A stone wall six feet high and seven miles long was constructed to divide the common land from more productive agricultural lands. The latter were divided up evenly into 76 individual farms; clachans were dispersed and even townland boundaries, the most enduring feature of the Irish landscape, were redrawn.[129] The Congested Districts Board rivals the poor law union as a subject crying out for a major historical geographical monograph.

In international terms, the lion's share of recent work in historical geography has focused on metropolitan centres.[130] But the opposite is true in Ireland where the impending disaster, the disaster and the long-term effects of that disaster inevitably lead Irish scholars to examine the rural landscape, where, after all, the majority of the population lived. Nonetheless, town and village construction, primarily a feature associated with eighteenth-century landlord improvements, continued into the nineteenth century in the west of Ireland accompanied by road building into previously unserviced areas.[131]

Urban issues have been the focus of some notable studies, however. Whelan's research has shown that the most notable 'urban' expansion in the Irish countryside was a feature of the post-Famine years.[132] It was a characteristic of planned estate towns and villages to have the Catholic chapel on the outskirts or at further remove to major crossroads. Throughout the century the isolated chapels attracted an alternate set of central place functions – national schools, pubs, parish halls, GAA pitches – and ultimately the emergence of 400 'chapel villages'.[133] This explains why throughout the countryside we often find distinct villages beside one another, often inadequately serviced. A good example of this is the chapel village of Oldtown in County Dublin with its post office, library and dispensary (in 1937) adjacent to Clonmethan with its 'stunted' Church of Ireland parish centre.[134]

The historical geography of Irish cities has also received some attention in recent years, overturning the widely held concept that post-Union Ireland brought in a century-long period of urban stasis. Louis Cullen has shown that in Dublin the stunning developments of the eighteenth century 'continued to expand effortlessly'.[135] In the south of the city much of what is thought of as Georgian housing was in fact built in the nineteenth century: Fitzwilliam Square, and developments along the Grand Canal, for example.[136] The magnificently planned Pembroke estate pushed beyond the confines of the Grand Canal after the 1820s and reached Ballsbridge by the end of the century. However, there was a decline in the quality of housing on the north side of the Liffey as fashionable living shifted southwards. Sackville Street, Mountjoy Square and other residential areas comprising the Gardiner estate became important traffic arteries and gradually lost their residential status. The proximity to industry contributed to the decline in housing standards.[137]

The Gardiner estate was selected as a case study in Jacinta Prunty's groundbreaking study of the historical geography of Dublin slums (figure 5).[138] From 1800 the decline in its status was precipitous and the Encumbered Estates Court sold off the area to individuals during the Famine. The decline of the existing housing stock and infilling of vacant lots with 'lowly dwellings' followed.[139] The Census of 1841 recorded 16.5 persons per house, making this area more congested than the most populated district in London (11 persons per dwelling): 'the stench and disgusting filth of these places are inconceivable, unless to those whose harrowing duty obliges them to witness such scenes of wretchedness'.[140]

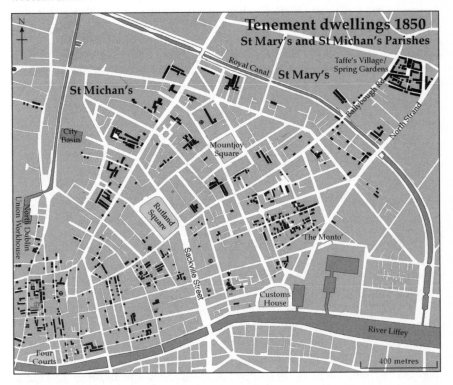

Figure 5. Jacinta Prunty's map of tenement dwellings in Dublin's northside in 1850. Prunty's work single-handedly addressed what had previously been one of the lacunae of nineteenth-century historical geography – the tendency to overlook urban spaces. The concentration of tenements north of the Customs House clearly indicates the location of the 'Monto' made world famous as 'Nighttown' in James Joyce's *Ulysses*, and in Sean O'Casey's Dublin trilogy.

*Source:* After Jacinta Prunty, *Dublin Slums, 1800–1925: A Study in Urban Geography* (Dublin: Irish Academic Press, 1998), pp. 290–1, fig. 8.3.

Prunty lays bare the underbelly of Dublin's vast slums that made it the unhealthiest major city in Britain or Ireland.[141] It was disease and the threat of it spreading amongst the more prosperous that first made slums an issue for Dubliners. In 1818 the two most intractable areas of poverty were identified: the old medieval core in the southwest of the city and extensive areas north of the Liffey.[142] This poverty and poor housing conditions lay at the foundation of disease and the high mortality rates experienced in the city, but little was accomplished by way of remedy until the model housing schemes of the last quarter of the nineteenth century. Before the end of century, public housing was established as the only means by which Dublin's slums could be eradicated.[143] Until that occurred, the poor of Dublin had some support from a network of religious charities and, as a last resort, the system of poor law workhouses to fall back on. The rivalry between Catholic and Established Church schools, asylums and other charitable institutions is one of the more unseemly stories recounted in Prunty's opus.[144] For the poor, however, the competition focused greater attention on the slum problem and contributed to their receiving some alleviation in their sufferings.[145]

Nothing on this scale has been attempted elsewhere in Ireland but Des Cowman has examined some aspects of pre-Famine Waterford.[146] The Napoleonic war years saw a huge increase in manufacturing, especially distilling, a growing prosperity that continued for a time after the war in Waterford. Curiously, in the years preceding 1831 the town declined in population from 40,000 to 28,000, accounted for by emigration to North America and Australia.[147] Here is an example of pre-Famine emigration on an unexpected scale. This is a truer index of the poverty and economic decline experienced in the city. Cowman controversially attributes the decline in the city's fortune to a failure on the part of the local business people to adapt to changing circumstances.[148]

Additional work on Irish towns and cities has featured in recent popular publications that are largely the work of historical geographers. *Irish Towns* and *Irish Cities* are popular books based on radio series.[149] *The Irish Historic Towns Atlas* is a project that relies heavily on OS maps and mid-century official sources to provide impeccable overviews of the nineteenth-century urban landscape (figure 7, p. 102). Further research, no doubt inspired by Prunty's landmark study, will be facilitated by Nolan and Simms's indispensable guide to sources relating to Irish towns.[150]

## THE NINETEENTH-CENTURY LEGACY

For the historical geographer (or landscape archaeologist, call them what you will), the greatest legacy left us is the stock of nineteenth-century houses and farms. Duffy has lamented the neglect of this rich resource and is correct in attributing the disregard of post-1700 landscape components to 'an official reluctance to attribute significance to more recent "modern" accretions'.[151] Who is at fault? Surely not the archaeologists whose surveys have focused on their area of expertise, the compilation of a database listing all features pre-dating 1700. Their success has thrown into sharp relief the consequent failure of architectural historians to treat seriously the decline of nineteenth-century buildings, in particular vernacular housing. For example, only 37 of 181 'fourth class houses' in the Boyne valley survive.[152] And while recent developments to preserve big houses must be applauded, they are not as threatened as are the once ubiquitous homes of the cottier class. This may be about to be corrected with the architectural survey of Ireland now in the hands of Willie Cumming, a committed socialist, and which may at last look beyond the big-houses to the more threatened homes of the poor.[153]

In terms of documents, our greatest legacy from the nineteenth century is the Ordnance Survey Archive and the OS maps are the most extensive primary source for the historical geography of nineteenth-century Ireland. The Ordnance Survey first edition maps were completed at a scale of six inches to a mile (1: 10,560) on the eve of the Famine. This series was followed by the 'third edition' completed at the turn of the twentieth century at a scale of twenty-five inches to a mile (1: 2,500). Numerous town and city surveys were also completed at even larger scales.[154] Fate and British imperialism saw to it that historians today have a detailed portrait of the landscape before and after the century's cataclysmic events. Historians in Ireland are also extremely fortunate that our greatest historical geographer turned his attention to the detailed study of the motivations and means by which this great mapping project came about.[155] John Andrews' landmark study of the Ordnance Survey was published prior to the period here reviewed, but its recent, and much welcomed paperback edition justifies renewed attention to this monumental work.[156]

The story of the nineteenth-century mapping enterprise is told by Andrews in *Shapes of Ireland* (dealing with the period prior to the foundation of the Ordnance Survey)[157] and *A Paper Landscape*. He shows how a Herculean task of mapping Ireland at an unprecedented level of accuracy was accomplished through the genius and dedication of William Colby and Thomas Larcom. The mapping was accompanied by a team of scholars who examined the geology, placenames and archaeology of the island. The vast Ordnance Survey archive, so successfully mined by Andrews, almost equals the maps themselves in providing an understanding of the nineteenth-century landscape. Two recent publishing enterprises have made this archive more accessible to the public. The Institute of Irish Studies has published all the 'Statistical remarks' compiled between 1830–7 in their Memoirs of Ireland series (figure 7, p. 102). Researchers in Ulster will find the *Memoirs Index* of inestimable value.[158] Four Masters Press has begun to publish the Ordnance Survey 'letters', until now available only in typescript in a few depositories.[159]

In Andrews's masterful monographs he also demonstrates how the Ordnance Survey was very much a product of the British colonial enterprise in Ireland, a cartographic tradition stretching back to Elizabethan times. The maps were needed to measure the land as a precursor to its valuation, which in turn facilitated its effective taxation. The maps harmonised a cacophony of land divisions and provided standardised English placenames for the now standardised townland matrix. The Anglicisation of the Irish landscape was complete and Andrews's depiction of the process inspired *Translations*, the 1981 play by Brian Friel.[160]

The effects of the work of the Ordnance Survey were also long lasting: the de-Anglicisation process cannot take place until we are at last provided with an Irish-language version of the indispensable *Townland Index*. The link between mapping and political and cultural imperialism is a powerful theme running through Andrews's history; it is manifest in a quotation from Lord Salisbury, who observed in 1883 that 'The most disagreeable part of the three kingdoms is Ireland, and therefore Ireland has a splendid map'.[161]

Threats to the nineteenth-century fabric can come from unexpected directions. The post office in Northern Ireland has tried, but not without stiff resistance, to eliminate the use of townland names from postal addresses. Local historians rallied to the townlands' defence, maintaining that the Irish landscape can often only be understood on a townland by townland basis.[162] Studies of eight individual townlands were published as part of that campaign and by so doing they provided a practical template for the study of nineteenth-century historical geography at a micro scale. The format asks nine questions of a townland's makeup, many of which can be answered through an analysis of official sources and Ordnance Survey maps. Crawford also makes an eloquent appeal for the study of townlands now before rural decline and sub-urbanisation change them out of all recognition from the farming communities they have traditionally been.

Another legacy with roots deep in the nineteenth century is the rich collection of folklore, especially that preserved in the Department of Folklore at University College Dublin. The importance of the landscape in shaping perceptions and behaviour has been dramatically brought to life in Angela Bourke's *The Burning of Bridget Cleary*.[163] Bourke utilises the folklore archive and police records to recreate a masterful description of a minor if horrible event. The importance of the story lies in the complicated forces that influenced the killing of a woman thought to be a 'changeling'. Among these forces were jealousies created by an invisible hierarchy within the lower class, the undeserved occupation of a state-funded labourer's cottage and the proximity to a ringfort. The book turns a bright light on the lives of the working class in Ireland, a neglected group prior to Bourke's study. *Bridget Cleary* reminds us that ancient beliefs and modes of behaviour survived long into post-Famine Ireland. A poltergeist forced a family to emigrate to America in the Clogher Valley in the nineteenth century.[164] On the Hook Peninsula a Catholic priest became a major middleman on the lands of a notoriously sectarian Protestant landlord. This was permitted because the priest had exorcised a ghost from the landlord's mansion of Loftus Hall.[165] Human behaviour is complex and it is not always determined by economics or politics. Historical geographers, and historians in general, should bear these complications in mind when making generalisations about the past.

It has been observed that the legacy of the nineteenth century was not reflected in the Irish literary revival at the dawn of the twentieth century.[166] But Kevin Whelan has demonstrated how the historical geography of the Famine in Ireland was in fact embedded in James Joyce's 1907 short story 'The Dead'. In the dramatic passage from the end of the story we are transported to the west of Ireland where the passionate pre-Famine countryside had vanished beneath the snows. This is, in Whelan's interpretation, a metaphor for the sterilisation of Gaelic culture beneath the stifling blankets of Roman Catholicism and British imperialism.[167] In this breathtakingly original article, Whelan goes on to demonstrate that the geography of the short story mirrors the history, geography and economy of Dublin at the end of the nineteenth century (figure 6). The aunts in the story are unmarried, mirroring post-Famine trends of lowering marriage rates. They are down-at heel and inhabit the old run-down medieval core of the city. The upwardly mobile couple live in the Protestant suburbs of south County Dublin.[168] The railway, the great infrastructural leap forward in nineteenth-century Ireland, facilitates the abandonment of the inner city in the same way that it facilitated rural depopulation. As Whelan shows, the historical geography of late nineteenth-century Ireland inspired and informed one of the greatest short stories in the English language. Quoting the American author William Faulkner, Whelan summarises the Famine legacy: 'The past is not dead. It is not even past.'[169]

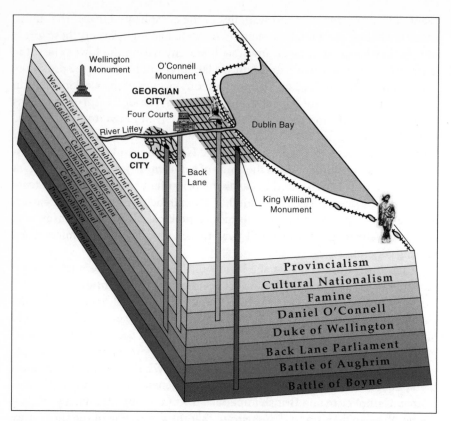

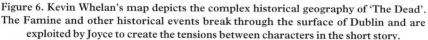

Figure 6. Kevin Whelan's map depicts the complex historical geography of 'The Dead'. The Famine and other historical events break through the surface of Dublin and are exploited by Joyce to create the tensions between characters in the short story.

*Source:* After Kevin Whelan, 'The memories of "The Dead"', *Yale Journal of Criticism*, 15 (2002), p. 86, fig. 6.

## CONCLUSION

Recent studies into the historical geography of the nineteenth century have made some significant strides. This has been most notable in the field of urban studies under the guidance of Professor Anngret Simms. Her ongoing *Towns Atlas* project keeps urban issues to the fore and inspired Prunty's work on the Dublin slums; it continues to be a model for future research. Lindsay Proudfoot must also be credited with placing urban issues at the heart of historical investigations. The study of rural Ireland in the nineteenth century remains dominated by the school of geographers established by Professor Tom Jones Hughes of University College Dublin. Most notable among these are Kevin Whelan, W. J. Smyth and P. J. Duffy, all of whose work figures prominently in this review. Another disciple of Hughes, William Nolan, has also contributed indispensable works of scholarship. Much of recent research in historical geography rests on the foundations of his seminal 1975 monograph on the historical geography of Fassadinin, in County Kilkenny.[170] As important, however, was Nolan's establishing a venue for the research of others. The county by county History and Society series is a massive and continuing labour of love that has inspired and motivated vast amounts of material, much of it touching on nineteenth-century subjects and featuring at least one essay based on the key mid-nineteenth century primary sources (figure 7). Geography Publications, Nolan's publishing house, continues to produce a wide range of useful material.

There is much work to be done. The process of land transfer facilitated by the land acts, and the resulting landscape change, needs to be examined at farm, townland and estate level. The development of agriculture through the century should receive renewed attention.[171] More specifically, progress in agricultural implements and techniques needs to be charted. The significance of spades and ploughs to rural peoples is manifest, but only Jonathan Bell seems to give the subject the attention it deserves.[172] The recent foundation of the Irish Agricultural History Society may foster work in this direction. More work on the geographies of the encumbered estates, poor law unions and Congested Districts Board needs to be attempted, alongside the more intimate geographies of prison, school and workhouse.

What the historical geographies discussed in this essay have in common is the use of landscape and maps not merely as illustrations but as fully fledged components in the heuristic process. The making of maps can draw the historian's attention to developments often obscured by the avalanche of nineteenth-century statistical sources. But the shading of counties in grey tones – the production of statistical maps based on inappropriately large and deceptively homogeneous territorial units – will not necessarily provide insight into the lives of the individuals and communities who shaped the geographies of the past. Historical geographers working in nineteenth-century studies must be more conscious of the humanity behind the official statistical sources compiled from mid-century. The landscape remains a powerful record of the past and a key to understanding these historic forces. Historical geographers, who traditionally admit to few limitations, may also have to accept the discipline's inability to reckon fully with the human suffering – 'the line which says woodland and cries hunger' – that characterised the nineteenth century in Ireland.

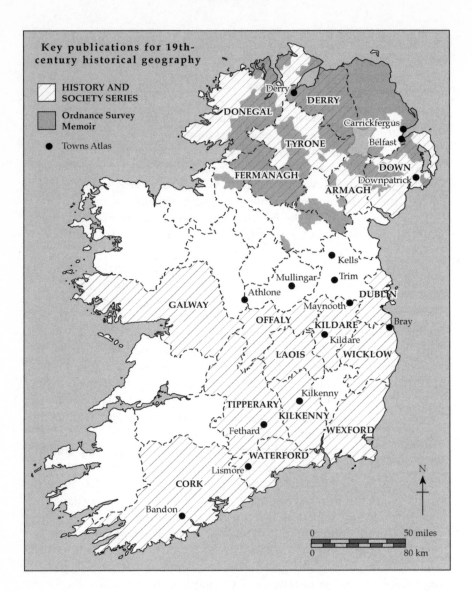

**Key publications for 19th-century historical geography**

HISTORY AND
SOCIETY SERIES

Ordnance Survey
Memoir

● Towns Atlas

Derry

DERRY

DONEGAL

Carrickfergus

TYRONE

Belfast

DOWN

FERMANAGH

Downpatrick

ARMAGH

Kells

Mullingar

Trim

Athlone

DUBLIN

GALWAY

Maynooth

OFFALY

KILDARE

Bray

Kildare

LAOIS

WICKLOW

Kilkenny

TIPPERARY

KILKENNY

Fethard

WEXFORD

WATERFORD

Lismore

CORK

Bandon

N

0            50 miles
0            80 km

Figure 7. The distribution of key publications containing extensive analysis of
nineteenth-century historical geography.

*Source:* Original map

*That the Science of Cartography is Limited*[173]

– and not simply by the fact that this shading of
forest cannot show the fragrance of balsam,
the gloom of cypresses
is what I wish to prove.

When you and I were first in love we drove
to the borders of Connacht
and entered a wood there.

Look down you said: this was once a famine road.

I looked down at ivy and the scutch grass
rough-cast stone had
disappeared into as you told me
in the second winter of their ordeal, in

1847, when the crop had failed twice,
Relief Committees gave
the starving Irish such roads to build.

Where they died, there the road ended

and ends still and when I take down
the map of this island, it is never so
I can say here is
the masterful, the apt rendering of

the spherical as flat, nor
an ingenious design which persuades a curve
into a plane,
but to tell myself again that

the line which says woodland and cries hunger
and gives out among sweet pine and cypress,
and finds no horizon

will not be there.

# CHAPTER 6

# Anthropological and Sociological Studies

✳

## Marilyn Cohen and Joan Vincent

As disciplines, both anthropology and sociology have long had an historical component. A dualism between natural science and the humanities (particularly science and history) entered modern American anthropology as early as 1897 with Franz Boas's *The Study of Geography*, at just about the time that Alfred Cort Haddon was bringing his field research on the Aran Islands to a close.[1] Derived from its nineteenth-century origins, anthropology's hybrid nature invites both qualitative and quantitative research. Its humanities dimension is reflected in the Irish historical studies of those who, like Eric Wolf, view anthropology as 'less subject matter than a bond between subject matters'. In Wolf's words, anthropology, like history, 'thrives on its peculiar combination of its interest in particular cases with a most general perspective on the course of human development. . . . Hence, the anthropologist will always pay tribute to true skill in observing detail and eliciting meaning'. In this 'emphasis on the particular' and in its search for the 'vibrancy of particular life', anthropology also resembles literature: 'What is worth studying', Wolf concludes, is 'human experience understood as the experience of life'.[2]

The historical ethnography of Ireland owes a great deal to the nineteenth-century bureaucratic records: censuses, reports, commissions of inquiry, and institutional records, as well as the flurry of newspapers that emerged at this time. For the anthropologist, these are cultural texts calling for the exploration of subjugated local knowledges or of cultural hegemony. These may take the form of 'folk' and 'orthodox' views of Catholicism as discussed by Lawrence Taylor or the commentaries of poor law guardians and commissioners as described by Joan Vincent.[3] Field anthropologists tend to use the Irish archives, whether national or local, in a somewhat distinctive way. The immense detail recorded in the nineteenth century offers opportunities for cultural and social reconstructions akin to the field experience. Anthropology as a discipline involves 'working among people' and, indeed, the lure of 'turn of the century' manuscript censuses, in particular – replete as they are with persons born in the 1840s and the three-generational families that they established – has led historical ethnographers to a somewhat Braudelian view of a 'long nineteenth century'. This, and access to the private and public memories of the people among whom they live and work (the 'archive-in-the-field') renders such transgressions rewarding.

Sociologists (again according to Eric Wolf) are more 'tough-minded'.[4] Sociology, as a science of society, seeks to understand and rationally explain the revolutionary social transformations associated with the development of capitalism in the West. Its scientific approach to social transformations and social problems shapes the methods and perspectives of those engaged in nineteenth-century Irish research. The historiography presented here reflects the recognition (now shared by anthropologists) that social relations, structures and processes of change are the consequences of historically generated human agency. Although sociology has a qualitative side based in fieldwork and in-depth interviews, the ethnography – a written account focusing on a particular population, place and time – has not been its signature method, as it has been for anthropology. Most sociologists favour quantitative approaches, although, as we shall see, the work of both Jane Gray and Eamonn Slater, to be discussed shortly, suggests important exceptions.

During the 1990s the anthropological and sociological study of nineteenth-century Ireland flourished, encouraged, in part, by a sustained academic interest in interdisciplinary projects and their institutionalisation within Irish studies.[5] No previous decade has seen such a comprehensive and coherent body of publications. The bibliographic search for this chapter elicited over 100 English-language items, gleaned from published bibliographic sources, the worldwide web, and networking with scholars in academic departments and Irish studies. At the beginning of the twenty-first century, Irish historical sociology and anthropology address a wider audience than ever before, and also have increased visibility within their own disciplines.

As a means of further surveying and analysing these trends, this essay is divided into three parts. The first section centres on the most sustained contribution that anthropology and sociology have made to a subject in which both disciplines are grounded: the great conceptual arch that historian Karl Polanyi in his classic 1957 study called *The Great Transformation*:[6] the advent of modernity in nineteenth-century Ireland. Recent publications have returned to this subject with a focus on the structural transformations in the transition to capitalism, the rise of the nation state, racism, identity and the Irish diaspora. In the second section, under the conceptual arc of 'Knowledge as Culture', the review focuses on 'situated knowledges': socially constructed ways of contesting the Irish landscape, land as property and symbol, and the new, purposeful 'civilising' institutions introduced into the nineteenth-century Irish landscape. The review concludes with a discussion of trends and lacunae.

'THE GREAT TRANSFORMATION'

Significant transdisciplinary themes emerged in the social sciences in the 1990s. Two, singled out by David Lloyd and Paul Thomas, were the securing and consolidation of capitalism in Great Britain and Ireland along with the hegemony of the 'ethical state' characterised by institutional differentiation and the regulation of social space by new centralised bureaucratic institutions.[7] With their disciplined recognition both of holistic interconnections and of the need for contextualisation, anthropologists and sociologists made significant theoretical and empirical contributions to both themes.

Although debates within political economy surrounding the development of capitalism have spawned a sophisticated theoretical literature, the Irish case study has been largely overlooked. For example, Eamon Slater and Terrence McDonough in their 'Bulwark of landlordism and capitalism' (1994) conceptualised the system of production in rural nineteenth-century Ireland as feudal rather than capitalist, arguing that a surplus was extracted from the Irish peasantry through extra economic coercion.[8] Whereas English tenants were protected by Common Law, Irish tenants were subjected to the arbitrary power of the landed class and its agents who increased rental charges while turning a blind eye to subletting and family subdivision. Thus, for Slater and McDonough, the demise of the feudal mode of production was due not to the dynamics of the international capitalist market, as most classical political economists have argued, but rather, in Ireland, to developing class struggle between landlords and tenants.

While it has long been recognised by historians that Ireland's economic transformation was determined by political dependence on England, world systems theory provides a powerful macro-level framework for exploring global power relationships and their effects on Irish economy and society. Historical sociologists have fruitfully applied this perspective to the nineteenth-century Irish cotton and linen industries. Denis O'Hearn, in his 1994 article on the British subjugation of the Irish cotton industry, published in the *American Journal of Sociology*, demonstrates how a global perspective reveals processes by which economic 'cores' are created in countries like England while 'peripherialisation' results in colonies like Ireland.[9] O'Hearn combines Immanuel Wallerstein's world systems concepts of core, semi-periphery and periphery with economist Joseph Schumpeter's notions of innovation, leading sectors, and creative and adaptive responses. In doing so, he shows that terms such as 'core, semi-periphery and periphery' have been under theorised: the Irish cotton industry clarifies their distinctions and interrelations. Despite cotton's promise in the late eighteenth century, it was not a leading sector industry as in England. Ireland's cheap labour and waterpower could not compete with England's localised innovations in spinning. The vulnerable Irish cotton industry collapsed after the removal of tariffs on yarn and cloth. In his contribution to the volume *The Warp of Ulster's Past* (1997), O'Hearn extends these insights to the Irish linen industry which was semi-peripheral and dependent.[10] The replacement of Irish cotton by linen, he reveals, was not an exchange of like industries but rather the replacement of a potential leading sector industry by a dependent one.

Sociologist Jane Gray also applies world systems theory to link gender with uneven development in the Ulster linen industry. She integrates a regional perspective with gender theory in an article published in *Journal of Peasant Studies* (1993) and in her 1996 chapter in the volume *Gender and Class in Modern Europe*. Combining Wallerstein's concepts with Hans Medick's proto-industrial model, she finds gender fundamental to explaining divergent regional trajectories in capitalist development. An asymmetrical division of labour at the household level, with men weaving cloth while women and children spun yarn, generated the logic for unequal exchange relations between core eastern linen weaving and peripheral western yarn spinning districts.[11] The availability of cheap yarn spun by women and children in peripheral households facilitated class differentiation and capital accumulation in the core districts. Gray expands these insights in a comparison of Irish and Scottish rural industry in *The Warp of Ulster's Past*.[12] Since women as spinners of linen yarn were important to the political economies of both countries, the different ways that gender constructed labour allocation in households and unequal exchange across households partially explain the differing trajectories of the Irish and Scottish linen industries.

Both Gray and the anthropologist Marilyn Cohen evaluate Medick's proto-industrial model, through their focus on Irish case studies. While Gray focuses on the unequal gendered division of labour in households where self-exploitation defines the prevailing economic logic, Cohen, in her 1990 article on peasant differentiation and proto-industrialisation in the *Journal of Peasant Studies*, addresses 'agency'. She argues that linen producers along the River Bann in north-west County Down played an active and, at times, entrepreneurial role in capitalist development, along with merchants and bleachers.[13] These contributions of historical anthropologists to the analysis of capitalist development characteristically focus on one locale. Locality-based research and political economy perspectives find staunch advocates in Philip Gulliver and Marilyn Silverman as exemplified by their 1996 article in *Focaal*.[14] Their research on social transformations in Thomastown, County Kilkenny spans the *longue durée* from the twelfth century to the present using the specifics of this locale to re-evaluate and develop several theoretical problematics. [15] The corpus of their publications, some of which are published in local journals, makes visible the agency of categories of Irish people who are silenced by macro-level historiography. [16]

Thomastown was and remains a market town and Silverman and Gulliver's publications, particularly their book *Merchants and Shopkeepers* (1995), highlights non-agricultural labourers and the commercial middle class. [17] Although there has been a growth of studies on urban cultures in Ireland, this book stands alone as an intensive historical ethnography of middle-class retailing and shopkeeping. [18] Instead of world systems theory, which marginalises small towns like Thomastown, Silverman and Gulliver offer the comparative tool of a 'gateway locality'. A gateway locality lies on the geographical periphery of a larger area, in this case Europe, but is a centre for commercial colonial expansion through regional, national and international trade.

Silverman deepens her analysis of non-agricultural labourers in Thomastown in *An Irish Working Class* (2001). As concerns with the 'conditions' of labouring people increased over the nineteenth century, so too did 'common-sense' understandings of the nature of poverty, charity, paternalism, and deference. This led to changes in working-class consciousness as well as forms of political organisation and resistance. Most distinctive in Silverman's contribution to nineteenth-century studies is her exploration of fishing rights on the River Nore, accomplished through detailed analysis of court records and newspaper coverage. [19] There are no other studies of inland salmon fisherman in the British Isles and few references to the role of salmon in local political economies. Labourers seeking to supplement their earnings claimed customary or common law rights to engage in salmon fishing which led to confrontations with the landed gentry who then sought to deny them access by privatising fishing resources.

Marilyn Cohen's historical ethnography of Tullylish parish in northwest County Down also extends over a long period. In her chapter in *Down: History and Society* and in her book *Linen, Family and Community in Tullylish County Down* (1997), she compares paths of rural industrial development and their attendant urban settlements in Down with those of Belfast. [20] She argues that there was no simple linear process of capitalist development; rather, rates and paths of class formation and mechanisation diverged along sub-regional, occupational and gender lines. The specific challenges faced by early Victorian capitalists in securing sources of labour and capital bore the heavy imprint of paternalism. As a managerial strategy, paternalism reproduced patriarchal familial deference and extended female dependence to male factory owners and supervisors in the workplace. Cohen also argues in *Irish Urban Cultures* (1993) that the neglect of smaller urban centres (such as Gilford/Dunbarton, County Down) and of their distinctive problems, reduces our understanding of the complexity and diversity of urbanisation and urbanism in nineteenth-century Ireland.[21]

In political economy generally, the consolidation of private property and the concomitant elimination of customary rights and relations are important themes in the development of capitalism. Like Slater and McDonough, anthropologists Vincent and Jonathan Bell suggest that the concepts offered by political economy are inadequate for understanding this process.[22] They offer a supplementary focus on customary entitlement to habitation and seasonal migration. Bell's article in *Folk Life* (1995) focuses on the habitations of rural labourers to reveal changing relationships between farmers and labourers. In his 1991 article in the *Review of Scottish Culture*,[23] he writes of squads of young women from northwest Donegal who worked as fish curers and 'tattie hokers' or potato harvesters in Scotland. Vincent's study of conacre rights in *Articulating Hidden Histories* (1994) roots the conacre truck system in the customary entitlement of families to secure habitation and work within a locality. The conacre custom contributed to their survival throughout capitalism's recurrent crises. Conacre, combined with household strategies such as the seasonal migration of menfolk, saw potato-fed Irish men harvesting the fields that supplied the grain-fed Scottish urban poor. (Ironically, some competed with poor Highland Scots women to do so.)[24]

It is impossible to write about capitalist transformations in nineteenth-century Ireland without addressing class. Again, deconstruction has been the order of the day for recent historical anthropologists and sociologists who have combined class with religion and gender. Cohen in the *Journal of Interdisciplinary History* (1994) argues that owing to the close articulation between religious affiliation and all aspects of social life in Gilford/Dunbarton, religion both designated and reproduced power relations.[25] She also explores how class intersects with gender in her 1992 article in the *Journal of Family History* where she focuses on the survival strategies of female-headed households, a sizeable minority of working-class households in all Irish linen-producing regions.[26] In female-headed households ideological norms associated with respectable feminine domesticity were necessarily modified by re-entry into the workforce or continuous employment to 'make ends meet'.

The publications of the sociologist Mary Hickman, including her 1995 book *Religion, Class and Identity*, view Irish migration to Britain as the coercive circulation of labour driven by the need for cheap labour and new markets.[27] The global division of labour that emerged in the nineteenth century rendered surplus Irish labour important to the industrial development of Britain and the United States. A highly visible immigrant group in Britain, distinguished by their occupations, religion, and national identity, the Irish were feared as a threat in terms of contagious disease and public disorder. For this reason, the English Catholic Church was given the task of de-nationalising the Irish. The state viewed the Catholic Church, dominated by elite families who survived the penal laws, as the only agency able to restrain and incorporate the Irish working class into the British body politic. Hickman argues that the history of Roman Catholic state schools in Britain illuminates the significance of anti-Catholic and anti-Irish hostility in shaping the development of elementary education both in Britain, and Ireland. [28] Thus, the integration of the Irish and their incorporation into British society as political subjects were founded upon their segregation and differentiation from the rest of the working class.

Although migration has been viewed as integral to Ireland's 'cultural ethos', most studies have focused on migration from the poor post-Famine rural west. Cohen, in her chapters on migration in *The Irish World Wide: Irish Women and Irish Migration* (1995) and *Reclaiming Gender* (1999), argues that the depiction of the typical Irish female migrant as rural and western reinforces a stereotypical and dichotomous image of women's migration as a transition from traditional to modern life. In some regions employment opportunities in industry provided an alternative to migration. The stereotypic 'modernisation' model lacks historicity, denies women's agency and has little relevance to the industrialised northeast of Ireland, where 'modernised' women did not migrate in the nineteenth century but stayed at home as the backbone of the labour force in the linen industry. [29]

Against the backdrop of structural transformations and human agency, anthropologists and sociologists have explored the contested formation of Irish identities. The poetry of rhyming weavers allowed Jane Gray to examine gender and plebian culture among linen producers in the early nineteenth century. She found that after the introduction of mill-based spinning in 1825, working-class identity was founded as much on difference as on similarity.[30] Her 1993 analysis of weaver James Orr's poem 'The Penitent' in the *Journal of Historical Sociology* furthers the growing linkage of sociology with literary studies. Here Gray shows that independent weavers, by stressing the cultural values of sobriety, respectability and dignity, sought to distance themselves from others who had become impoverished or dependent. In a second analysis published in the *Journal of Interdisciplinary History* (1993), tea drinking provides Gray with a gendered lens through which to view class formation and lived experience.[31] At the peak of prosperity in the late eighteenth century, men's consumption of tobacco and women's consumption of tea and other colonial luxury commodities signified autonomy and well-being. Tea drinking, a symbol of the successful household, was associated with a woman's world of respectable sober domesticity. When the rural industrial way of life became threatened with the spread of mill-based spinning in the early nineteenth century, tea drinking became associated with its addictive qualities. By the mid-nineteenth century, tea and tobacco were no longer symbols of artisan independence but negative stimulants used for survival within a rigorous factory system.

Marilyn Cohen's 1997 analysis of the gendered subjectivities of linen industry workers in *The Warp of Ulster's Past* continues this exploration of respectability.[32] Working-class men could maintain respectable masculinity by supporting families at home and through gendered discrimination in the workplace where men filled all managerial and skilled occupations. For married men, who expected to be breadwinners, waged work outside the home was the foundation of their social identity, whereas for married women, given the intermittent nature of women's waged work and the rigid sexual division of labour in the household, identity was determined more by unwaged domestic work and household roles.

Silverman's monograph *An Irish Working Class* provides a sustained description of an 'all-pervasive socio-cultural map' that has existed in Thomastown since the early nineteenth century. With class at its core, it separates categories of people into hierarchies, fundamentally shaping their social interactions and networks. [33] She explores working-class awareness, experience, collective actions and the materiality of their working lives, their cultural codes and their social world – a *metissage* made up of the multiple languages, categories, experiences, networks and identities accumulating over time.

Not unexpectedly, religion is central to the socio-cultural maps of the Irish in the nineteenth century. Indeed, in a 1996 article in the *Southwest Atlantic Quarterly*, Lawrence Taylor suggested that 'nineteenth century Ireland was imagined as a [proto-national] community . . . in and through a religious idiom'.[34] This is problematic. In 'Peter's pence', a fine article discussing nationalism and official Catholic discourse in mid-nineteenth century Ireland, and published in *History of European Ideas* (1993), he questioned the uncritical assumption that the majority of poor and oppressed Irish peasants were loyal to a church that was increasingly rich, powerful, ultramontane and anti-pathetic to peasant culture and religious practices. [35] Taylor's work seeks to redress the privileging of ritual performances over discourse and narrative in the anthropology of religion.[36] Another essay on 'The languages of belief' illustrates how Catholic narrative discourse played an important role in defining and expressing worldviews. Specific forms of religious narratives (folk story, magazine piece, redemptionist sermon) contribute to defining different and competing ways of being religious as the increasingly hier-archical social world of the Irish countrymen becomes expressed both in class and supernatural terms. Taylor thus discerns a dialogical relation between social and cultural formations wherein religious discourse played a vital role in the reinforcement of meaning and power. Freedom from the restrictions of the authoritarian hierarchical church was frequently sought in drink. Drunken priest stories analysed by Taylor in several publications, including his chapter in *Religious Orthodoxy and Popular Faith in Europe*, describe the shamanic power of priests who drink. Such stories were framed by the idiom of opposition: Gael/Gall; drunken priests/bishops; political/spiritual; worldly/natural.[37]

Approaching Irish Catholicism from a higher level of abstraction, the sociologist Eugene Hynes traces interconnections between ecclesiastical policy and social institutions in the volume *Sociological Studies of Roman Catholicism: Studies in Religion and Societies* (1989).[38] Hynes seeks specifically to understand the 'devotional revolution' that occurred after the Famine. Like Taylor, he focuses attention on the 'flock' rather than the Church hierarchy. For the tenant farmer class that became dominant in Irish society after the Famine, Catholicism reinforced a need for family unity, discipline, control over sexuality and order. This rural class provided the church with most of its clergy, its staunchest followers and its most committed believers. The 'devotional revolution' thus saw priests becoming increasingly influential as they represented the interests of the tenant farmers, shopkeepers, and merchants.

KNOWLEDGE AS CULTURE

It is now generally understood that 'culture' no longer refers to *shared meanings*. Rather, culture is contested. Many institutions, classes, and groups compete in the articulation of the social meaning of things. Ideas and knowledges are developed at many sites and positions, producing what Donna Haraway has termed 'situated knowledges'.[39] The State's construction of knowledge, local knowledge, and subaltern knowledge (especially working class and gendered knowledge) are all examples of 'situated knowledges' that have engaged Irish anthropology and sociology in the 1990s and since.

Thus in her book *An Irish Working Class*, Marilyn Silverman explores forms of bureaucratic and administrative 'categorisation, codification, rule articulation and system building' that constrained the development of any popular discourse concerning labour, including the parliamentary inquiries being made into the condition of 'the poorer classes'. She conducts a thorough investigation of the part played by the working classes in south Kilkenny's urban politics and the manner in which their very presence was demeaned. Its opening section entitled 'Encountering labour in the field, archives and theory', provides an informative demonstration of how she, as an anthropologist, operates in the field.

Irish ethnography has, by and large, followed the fieldwork tradition established by Arthur Cort Haddon a century ago. Haddon himself enjoyed quite an interdisciplinary revival in the 1990s, featuring in cultural geography, as shown by the *Atlas of the Irish Rural Landscape*, and in Taylor's essay on 'The anthropology of Ireland and the Irish view of anthropology' (1996).[40] More comprehensively, historian Greta Jones addresses situated knowledge as cultural code in her essay 'Contested territories' (1998) where she pits Haddon's scientific address to the Belfast Field Club against the literary romantic conservatism of Synge, Yeats and, most vehemently, the Gaelic League.[41] At issue, she argues, is the nature of the 'modern' Irish landscape.

Landscape as a cultural code in Ireland has long perpetuated contested domains between Planter and Gael, Protestant and Catholic. In his essay 'Contested terrains: differing interpretations of County Wicklow's landscape' (1993), Eamonn Slater reconstructs Mr and Mrs S. C. Hall's famous tourist handbook. Its English authors view the landscape through eyes trained to recognise the romantic and the picturesque. They contrast Wicklow's beautiful (and settled) fertile valleys with its sublime (and barren) mountain peaks. Local guides challenge the tourists' 'superior gaze' from their own lived experience of dispossession. In his discussion, Slater usefully identifies a series of interpretive oppositions: coloniser/native; walked in/worked on; consumer/ producer; transient/belonging; and the like.[42]

A new topographical trend to emerge in the 1990s focused on the 'civilising' institutions introduced into the nineteenth-century landscape and their post-Famine transformations. These include workhouses, mental hospitals, and national schools. Three articles by Jamie Saris provide an excellent example. Based on field research in County Sligo, these are: 'Mad kings, proper houses, and an asylum in rural Ireland' (1996); 'The asylum in Ireland: a brief institutional history and some local effects' in the edited volume *Sociology of Health and Illness in Ireland* (1997); and 'Producing persons and developing institutions in rural Ireland' (1998).[43] Saris explores the designs and moral discourse surrounding the imposition of these institutions, their relative success in achieving their framers' transgressive goals, and the impact on them, in turn, of those whose passage to a specific rationality, enlightenment and modernity they attempt to channel. He attributes their transformations to increasing bureaucratisation within the centralising British state and also within the context of emergent specialised modes of treating the insane throughout the world.[44] These specialised nineteenth-century bureaucratic institutions were constructed, Saris suggests, so as to bring about 'the transformation of social persons, the social and natural environments, and, indeed, an entire moral order'. The transformative impact of Sligo's large mental hospital on its inmates and on those who encountered it as 'a local presence' was part of 'an ongoing multilevel process of historical agents confronting a developing world system of market and political relationships within a colonial (later independent) state structure'.[45] The periodisation Saris adopts correlates well with changes in other public institutions studied by ethnographers.[46]

Tanya M. Cassidy also features sites in the Irish northwest in her study of Irish asylums and inebriate reformatories from the nineteenth century to the present.[47] In 'Irish drinking worlds: a socio-cultural reinterpretation of ambivalence' (1996), Cassidy relates how insanity was frequently attributed to 'intemperance and whiskey', an issue she develops further in her review of 'Alcoholism in Ireland' in the edited volume *The Sociology of Health and Illness in Ireland* (1997). In one intriguing passage (p. 178), Cassidy suggests that sectarian commercial politics played a part in the medicalisation of spirit consumption and the institutionalisation of those categorised as ill. Legislation restricted whiskey distilling, which was dominated by Catholics, and fostered the prosperity of commercial beer brewing by wealthy Protestants. It is to be hoped that work of this calibre will help lay to rest the unfortunate impact of Nancy Scheper-Hughes's *Saints, Scholars and Schizophrenics: Mental Illness in Rural Ireland* (1982).[48]

Paradoxically, the centralising state's drive to 'modernisation' gave new life to the subjugated knowledge contained within *dinnseanchas*, the Irish poetic tradition that relates the original meaning of place names to local mythico-historical events. 'The place name', Seamus Heaney observes in his classic essay 'The sense of place' 'succinctly marries the legendary and the local'.[49] Memory and dialogue continue to constitute place and history to this day but rarely in an uncontested way as Vincent shows in an essay on 'The Land War in the Irish northwest' (1999). Land League meetings were identified and recalled by the places – even the fields – where they were held and, in recollection, formed a litany of 'agitation' throughout the region.[50] Similarly, for those residing in the vicinity of St Columba's hospital in Sligo, Saris reports that the landscape was 'a story mediated by place-name boundaries'.[51]

Not only landscape and the out-of-doors feature in the topographical tradition; the transformations wrought by colonisation have also been read in Irish house design and family forms. The cultural meaning of the 'west room' and the 'stem family', first discussed in two classic ethnographies – Conrad Arensberg's *The Irish Countryman* (1937) and anthropologist–folklorist Henry Glassie's *Passing the Time in Ballymenone* (1982) – were revisited in the 1990s by Taylor in his essay 'Re-entering the West Room' and by Donna Birdwell-Pheasant in a series of essays based on her fieldwork in County Kerry.[52]

Birdwell-Pheasant sets out to construct a developmental model of the Irish family to set alongside those of Arensberg and historian David Fitzpatrick. While keeping the name on the land was a consistent goal, the three-generation family was less a reality in the nineteenth century than an ideal. A suggestion that the ruling symbol in Irish reality was not land, but rather the idea of family and place, underwrites Birdwell-Pheasant's analysis of settlement patterns in rural Ireland from earliest times to the present. Land as property, she argues, is an English conceit. The key Irish concept is 'home place', a term she first heard during field research in Kerry. Reading the landscape, she identifies a model whereby the 'home place' and most of the family land went to one heir while the rest of the land was shared among siblings who lived around it. Although the heir occupied a substantial farm-house, had relatively secure tenure, and a high probability of supplying the next generation of heirs to the 'home place', this inheritance system, she argues, works against the development of class (unlike primogeniture in England). During the transformation of the rural landscape between 1750 and 1850 the home place became more ornate, but as population rose, the quality of peripheral houses declined. The number of home places remained remarkably constant.[53]

Birdwell-Pheasant's analysis of the interrelationship of family, house and land settlement contributed to Timothy W. Guinnane's demographic study, *The Vanishing Irish*.[54] Demographers and economic historians have frequently called for greater recognition of regional comparisons in Irish historiography and this has found anthropology and sociology well placed to make a distinctive contribution. The best example of this is their work on the Irish Famine.

Unlike scholars from other disciplines, field-working ethnographers view the Great Famine as an event that may be recognised as striking a locality at a specific time but which may be understood only in terms of the prior social, political and economic structuring of that place. Ethnography focuses on a particular population, place and time with the deliberate goal of describing it to others. Thus far, few anthropologists have actually entered upon their field research in Ireland with the specific intention of studying the Famine. An exception, of course, is Charles Orser whose archaeological dig at Strokestown, County Roscommon, promises a unique material contribution to the histor-iographical record.[55] Yet in the 1990s it became almost requisite for the long-term fieldworker to reconstruct the lived experience of the Great Famine in her/his local research site. Three steps were usually involved: first, the use of evidence gleaned from local and national archives, public and private; second, comparison with other localised Irish famine accounts; third, a contextualising of variations in experience of famine within regional, national and global frames. Throughout, interpretation rested on prior cultural knowledge of a particular population and of a place, and what both were like at the specific time.[56] The following types of questions may be asked: how the Famine unfolded developmentally over time; how public relief measures were received; how newspapers 'spun' the Famine story locally; to what extent government demands for statistics were obeyed and how its instructions were carried out; how various families, schools, workhouses, land agents, clerics and the like affected and reflected the lived experience of disease, hunger and flight for different sectors of the population.

By coincidence, the regions in which most Famine research has been carried out are the Irish northwest, County Down in the northeast, and south Kilkenny in the southeast.[57] A comparison of published findings to date suggests some of the social and cultural factors involved in the Great Famine.

These include landlord and newspaper recognition of the extent of suffering as the Famine progressed, topographical differences in the distribution of public relief measures, the degree of 'collusion' between local gentry and the state, popular resistance to rising poor law taxes, the use of 'desertion of wives and children' as a family strategy, and – inevitably – those in each locality who actually profited from the Famine. As measures of famine, the answers are different for each of the three locations, contributing, it may be suggested, a more nuanced social and cultural historiography of the Famine to supplement existing administrative and political historiography.

★  ★  ★

In conclusion, we focus briefly on trends and lacunae. An explicit reference to Irish Studies as a genre emerged in the 1990s and Irish historiography's growing receptivity to theoretical approaches in the social sciences has brought historical sociologists closer to their colleagues in economic and social history, especially those whose methodologies include a significant quantitative or statistical component. Similarly, cultural theory and the 'literary turn' in anthropology have brought Irish ethnographers closer to colleagues in social history and literary studies. At the same time, there has been a clear thrust towards formulating a new sociology of Ireland reflected in the publications of Anne Byrne, Ronit Lentin and Hilary Tovey.[58] With the superb example before us of Anne Byrne, Ricca Edmondson and Tony Varley revisiting the County Clare of Arensberg and Kimball, exploring its family life and its politics, we may hope for more such re-evaluations and re-workings of the ethnography that has shaped our understanding of Irish rural society in the past.[59]

The blurring of disciplinary boundaries reflects the redefining of national historiography in Ireland and the deconstruction of meta-concepts and narratives in the academy. Historical anthropologists and sociologists are becoming increasingly visible in debates surrounding significant themes in Irish Studies. We hope that this review essay will enable the reader to appreciate commonality and the breadth of topics and knowledge they explore. We hope to encourage cross-disciplinary research and citations among scholars engaged in research on nineteenth-century Ireland.

The importance of regional differentiation, locality, and the specificity of Ireland's historical transformations has shaped the trajectory of Irish historical anthropology and sociology as its practitioners focus on issues related to the transition of capitalism, the rise of the nation state, sectarianism, identity and the Irish diaspora. Increasingly, they focus on the intersections between places and broader processes of change as well as between concepts themselves – most notably, class, nationalism, race/ethnicity and, above all, gender.

Gender theory has always invited linkages since its symbolism is omnirelevant in social life and a clear movement beyond 'herstory' is well under way. Thus, as the reconstruction of Irish historiography from the rubble of deconstruction continues, our attention shifts to discontinuity, differentiation, contextualisation and the inclusion of neglected, silent or silenced categories of actors. This will certainly continue. Changes in cultural and social life over time and lived experience of them are assuredly complex phenomena. We hope, therefore, that this review goes some way to encourage further dialogue among researchers in both the sciences and the humanities over the great transformations of nineteenth-century Ireland.

# CHAPTER 7

# Literature in English

✾

*Sean Ryder*

The nature and extent of current interest in nineteenth-century Irish literature in English makes a striking contrast to earlier decades, when critical discussions of nineteenth-century Irish writing tended to focus on a relatively narrow range of writers, and students and scholars were inclined to view the period as far less interesting than the early twentieth century. Attention normally centred on those late nineteenth-century writers associated with the Literary Revival, notably W. B. Yeats, Augusta Gregory and George Moore. The canon was sometimes stretched to include mid-century predecessors like Samuel Ferguson and James Clarence Mangan, particularly insofar as they could be read as the Revivalists' artistic antecedents. Critical works on the pre-Revival period were scarce by comparison with works on the Revivalists themselves, and those studies that did appear, like Thomas Flanagan's *The Irish Novelists 1800–1850* (1959), remained standard works for many years. Even a major historical critical study like Malcolm Brown's *Politics of Irish Literature* (1972), which paid relatively ample attention to the wide cast of nineteenth-century writers, still approached pre-1880s writing as a curtain-raiser for the work of Yeats, Synge, Joyce and O'Casey.

Not only did the prevailing canon privilege particular writers; it also privileged certain genres. Poetry and poetic drama were the most prominent genres of the Revival, and it was poetry that received most critical attention when critics looked back into the nineteenth century. Although the novelists Maria Edgeworth and Somerville and Ross were given some attention (often as examples of a regional trend within the tradition of the English novel), the vast body of Irish fiction was generally neglected by critics. Pre-Revival theatre was also deemed unworthy of consideration, with the exception of Boucicault, whose work was made significant by Sean O'Casey's backward glance.

There were a number of reasons why the Revival overshadowed the critical response to Irish writing earlier in the nineteenth century. Firstly, there were the pronouncements of the Revivalists themselves, especially Yeats, who had an aesthetic and psychological need to distinguish himself from his precursors. In the late 1880s Yeats energetically set about anthologising, eulogising and tabulating his nineteenth-century predecessors – largely in order to construct a role for himself as both the inheritor of a tradition and as someone who would radically extend and improve upon that tradition. Thomas Kinsella, writing as late as 1980 (in his introduction to *The New Oxford Book of Irish Verse*), illustrates how powerful and pervasive Yeats's views were. In his anthology, Kinsella simply repackaged Yeats's perspective for readers of the late twentieth century, casting his own cold eye over what he calls the 'ill-starred enthusiasms and miscellaneous activities' of Yeats's predecessors.[1] Writing as an Irish poet in search of a usable past, Kinsella dismisses the nineteenth century almost in its entirety:

> I believe that silence, on the whole, is the real condition of Irish literature in the nineteenth century – certainly of poetry. There are enough hideous anthologies to bear me out: collections in which one falls with relief on anything that shows mere competence.[2]

Not only did Yeats's views determine the literary canon; they also shaped the way literary critics viewed the whole history of the nineteenth century. As W. J. Mc Cormack has pointed out, critics of Anglo-Irish literature have almost inevitably derived their historiography from W. B. Yeats.[3] Yeats, again for his own reasons, divided nineteenth-century nationalist politics into a conflict between an aristocratic, tragic, Protestant Parnell, and a distastefully populist, pragmatic and Catholic O'Connell – with John O'Leary being an almost unique bridge between both sides. This polarised version of the Irish nineteenth century was essentially a way for Yeats to justify his own aesthetic and his class interests. For Yeats, the Catholic, nationalist, populist culture which had become central to post-Famine Irish politics could not, on its own, produce a modern Irish literature. Such a development would require the aesthetic values of the rapidly declining Ascendancy, hence Yeats's valorisation of authors like Standish O'Grady whose work meant little to Irish popular culture, but a great deal to disaffected Protestant intellectuals. Literary critics, following this lead, have paid scant attention to the reading and writing of that Catholic middle-class and rural populace who comprised the majority popu-lation throughout the century.

A second force that shaped the twentieth-century view of nineteenth-century literature was a version of nationalist cultural criticism that emerged in the new Free State, demonstrated most famously in the critical writings of Daniel Corkery. In general, Corkery's cultural nationalism valued writing that reflected the 'Irish national being', which for him was primarily Catholic, nationalist and rural.[4] For Corkery, the literature of the Ascendancy in the nineteenth century was simply a 'Colonial' literature – which meant that however well-crafted the work of Edgeworth or Somerville and Ross might be, it was less significant than the clumsier prose of Charles Kickham, which at least attempted to represent and speak to 'the people'.[5] Corkery was particularly harsh on what he called 'the shameful literary tradition of the Prout, Maginn, Lever, Lover school of writers', who, like Shaw and Wilde, were essentially 'servants of the English people'.[6] Corkery's project had no place for novelists like Sheridan Le Fanu or Bram Stoker either: not only because of their class impediment, but also because their work did not usually address 'Ireland' as a subject. Corkery's argument implied that it was not sufficient for a writer to be Irish to be 'canonised'. He or she must also write *about* Ireland, and write authentically and nationalistically at that. Interestingly, the English literature syllabi of Irish universities in the 1940s and 1950s seem to combine Yeats's aesthetic canon with Corkery's nationalist one. A mid-century BA course at University College Dublin entitled 'Anglo-Irish literature 1800–1880', for example, focused on Thomas Moore, George Darley, the de Veres, James Clarence Mangan, Samuel Ferguson, Thomas Davis, Denis Florence McCarthy, Edward Fitzgerald, William Allingham, Gerald Griffin, William Carleton, John Mitchel and W. E. H. Lecky – all writers who would have been largely acceptable to both Yeats and Corkery. A contemporaneous MA course examined Ferguson, Mangan, Edgeworth's *Irish Stories* and Carleton's *Traits and Stories*.[7]

A third force shaping the canon of nineteenth-century literature was the impact of international modernism on literary scholarship. Modernist aesthetics, with its emphasis on detachment and self-reflexivity, suited the formalist 'New Criticism'. Students and critics were taught to favour the 'well-wrought urn', an internally coherent and self-sufficient object. 'New Criticism' abhorred cliché, narrative loose ends, and conflicting registers of voice and discourse, except in cases where these might be read as forms of 'ambiguity' that are ultimately resolved at a psychological or emotional level. 'New critics' tended to read poems as acts of private meditation rather than as public and historical interventions. It tended to privilege metaphoric forms over metonymic ones, poems over novels, and content over context. The 'New Critical' style of reading, in other words, was poorly qualified to recognise or appreciate the achievement of a great deal of nineteenth-century Irish writing. It was also unhelpful that the study of fiction from the 1950s to the 1970s was dominated by the 'moral formalism' of F. R. Leavis, whose insistence on establishing the narrow parameters of the 'Great Tradition' meant that a great deal of nineteenth-century fiction simply dropped out of view. The qualities singled out by Leavis in his description of the achievements of the English nineteenth-century novel – the qualities of 'moral sanity', of 'felt life' and so on – were noticeably absent in Irish fiction of the same century, dealing as it did with quite a different set of contexts and demands from those of Jane Austen and George Eliot.

For these reasons, the bulk of nineteenth-century Irish writing remained unexamined by critics, or was judged merely as historical background to the twentieth century. Pre-Revival nineteenth-century literature became less readable, less interesting, less critically significant than it had been for many of its original readers. This critical orthodoxy has been given its most sustained challenge in recent years: partly in response to a changing inter-national critical scene, and partly because of changing conditions in Ireland itself. The changing critical context has been marked by the emergence of methodologies such as feminism, post-structuralism, postcolonial theory, new forms of historicism that are distrustful of hierarchical discriminations between high and popular art, and new interest in the history of publishing and the book.

The new work on the Irish nineteenth century has been engaged in a twofold process. One is largely a bibliographical and historicist task: to recover texts and authors obscured by twentieth-century criticism, thus providing a fuller and more complex view of the period. The second task is methodolo-gical, and often accompanies the first (but not always). It involves subjecting both canonical and non-canonical writings to new readings, informed by the insights of late twentieth-century critical theory. A new attention to the importance of gender as a theme and as a context is one example of such a development. So too is the new valorisation of characteristics previously considered to be marks of aesthetic 'failure' – for instance, contradiction, linguistic instability, stylistic hybridity, and lack of narrative closure. A new kind of historicism has also been in evidence, though of course Irish literary criticism has almost always been historicist in some fashion (even Yeats and Corkery refused to separate literary significance from historical context). The new focus on the materiality of texts has enabled more detailed attention to the social and political contexts of writing and publishing, which are no longer seen as merely secondary to literary interpretation. Finally, there has been an emergence of meta-critical writing which has begun to historicise Irish literary criticism itself, drawing attention to the ideological forces which have shaped all critical responses to nineteenth-century writing (including, of course, those of the present day).

The changes in Irish cultural politics in general have also had an impact on the direction of Irish literary criticism. Political developments North and South, changing relationships between Ireland and Britain, and ideological and economic changes within Irish society, have been accompanied by various forms of revisionary thinking. The literary critical equivalent of this has involved questioning the parameters of the national canon, adopting a more capacious definition of literary Irishness, and counteracting what is sometimes construed as politically motivated neglect. 'Big House' fiction and Ulster Protestant writing, for instance, have been re-examined in ways that reflect wider debates about the politics of Irish culture in the late twentieth century. And it has not been merely minority or unionist Irish traditions that have been given new attention; the nationalist tradition itself has been re-examined by critics, and newer, more complex models of Irish nationalism have emphasised its variegated and conflicted nature.

★   ★   ★

Several critical studies from the 1990s have offered generalising overviews of the nineteenth century. For the most part these studies have continued the traditional focus on the relationship between nineteenth-century literature and the history of Irish nationality; that is, they continue to define the significance of nineteenth-century literature primarily in terms of its role in the construction of a national culture. Unlike F. R. Leavis's 'great traditions' of nineteenth-century fiction and poetry, which were canons ostensibly constructed on moral and aesthetic grounds, Irish literary historians have usually based their claims for the value of nineteenth-century texts on their historical or political importance. This evidently remains the case, although recent versions of Irish cultural history have largely been more complex or iconoclastic than their predecessors.

One of the most important and path-breaking of these recent nineteenth-century overviews has been Joep Leerssen's *Remembrance and Imagination* (1996). Following on from his wide-ranging study of pre-nineteenth century ideas of nationality, *Mere Irish and Fíor-Ghael* (2nd edn, 1996), this work charts the nineteenth century's construction of images of Irishness, including the 'creation of an Irish self-image'. Leerssen especially focuses on the phenomenon of 'Celtic exoticism', which in the nineteenth century is a feature of both national and externally generated discourses on Ireland. The development of the 'auto-exotic' becomes for Leerssen a way of explaining the Irish preoccupation with cultural self-analysis in both the nineteenth and twentieth centuries. In its very self-conscious adoption of European theory and methodology (particularly from the work of Bakhtin and Genette), the book is almost unique in Irish studies.

Leerssen's theoretical frame allows him to concentrate on the mechanics of discourse. As a result he offers a very clear and useful description of the distinctive features of nineteenth-century literary discourse, especially the novel. He identifies what earlier critics may have seen as aesthetic failure in less censorious terms as a form of heteroglossia, or multiplicity of register; he argues, for instance, that the Irish novel tends to comprise an amalgam of the discourses of travel description, antiquarianism, and sentimental comedy.

The resulting stylistic vacillation and uncertainty of voice mean that an Irish novel like Lady Morgan's *The Wild Irish Girl* becomes a 'novel which pretends to be about Ireland [but] in fact is about other texts about Ireland'.[8]

This focus on discursive instability is part of Leerssen's general argument about the formation of national self-images, and helps him to explain why Ireland found it so difficult to develop stable modes of self-representation such as the realist novel or positivist historiography. His main thesis, however, has to do with the debates over the status of historical truth and methodology, taking as a special case study the debates about round towers. Here Leerssen sees a battle being waged between the discourses of 'historical fact' and 'historical imagination', a conflict that characterises a great deal of literary, political and scholarly discourse in the nineteenth century.[9] Leerssen seems to accept the validity of such a distinction, and ultimately to lament the fact that the latter discourse – 'historical imagination', with its auto-exoticist strain and 'poetics of anachronism' – prevailed in nineteenth-century Ireland. The result, according to Leerssen, was the production of a debilitating version of history that was morbid, cyclical and 'uncanny' rather than amenable to rational explanation.[10] What made this process unique within the context of other European nationalisms was that the Irish version of remembrancing was tied to a project of revival and renewal, rather than just preservation or resistance.

Leerssen's methodology allows him to move usefully from literature, to antiquarian writing, to historiography – demonstrating the common discursive underpinning of all of these discourses. This is a particularly welcome strategy, and one that should continue to prove illuminating for scholars and critics. Such an interdisciplinary approach is not entirely new: the nineteenth century itself did not always make significant distinctions between genres, and, as we have seen, the UCD English syllabus in the mid-twentieth century required students to read historian Lecky alongside the poet Mangan and polemicist Mitchel. What makes the new interdisciplinarity different is its attitude to language, which it tends to assume is the very material of culture rather than a mere tool for the expression of ideas.

Although he claims to be avoiding the established canon, Leerssen does in fact tend to write about familiar authors: Brooke, Moore, Morgan, Maturin, Banim, Lever, Lover, Edgeworth, Kickham, Boucicault, and so on.[11] It is not the canon that he has challenged as much as the way of reading the canon. A more radical challenge to the canon would involve a more detailed look at the realm of popular culture – not merely as a remnant of a disappearing Gaelic world (as it tends to be in Leerssen's work) but also as a site of modernising, hybrid, English- or dual-language texts that may actually prefigure the Joycean openness Leerssen celebrates in the conclusion to *Remembrance and Imagination*. This is a line of inquiry, as we shall see, that has been opened up by the work of critics like Niall Ó Ciosáin and David Lloyd.

The attention to national 'representation' as found in Leerssen's book, and the resulting attention to the constructedness of discourse, is a feature of a great deal of writing about the nineteenth century. Seamus Deane's *Strange Country: Modernity and Nationhood in Irish Writing since 1790* (1997), like Leerssen's work, offers something of an overview of the nineteenth century, and like Leerssen he seeks to explain the function and character of much nineteenth-century writing by reference to its ideological function. Deane's argument has to do with the construction of national character, a well-worn theme but here approached in new ways, and in Deane's distinctively concentrated and deconstructive style. Beginning with Burke, Deane explores the ideological manoeuvres and contradictions that lay at the heart of the attempt by the Anglo-Irish to represent Ireland in the nineteenth century. Bound up with this are the issues of modernity, improvement and nationality, and the interrelationship of these issues. What Leerssen's book describes as 'exoticism', Deane sees as an inevitable consequence of a deeply contra-dictory ideological project that could not reconcile its own foundational ideas with the economic realities of a colonial condition. Deane argues that much nineteenth-century literature, and fiction especially, can be read as an attempt to negotiate and understand a basic ambiguity between the 'representation of a country that is foreign and unknown, in which the conditions are phantas-mogoric, especially to the English reader, and a country that is, at the same time, part of the British system, perfectly recognisable and part of the traditional world that the French Revolution had overthrown'.[12] This is also a struggle between imperial capital on the one hand, with its rhetoric of progress and modernisation, and national character on the other, which is necessary to the narrative of modernity, but which in Ireland has tended to be associated with recalcitrance or hostility to modernity. Problems arise in Ireland because national character, understood in the nineteenth century to be the basis for nationality, tended to function in a Burkean fashion as a sign of Irish exclusivity and uniqueness; at the same time nationality had to be linked to modernity (as was the case with English 'national character') if it was to be renovated for the present and future. Deane proceeds to read a number of nineteenth-century texts in order to trace the stratagems for reconciliation of these apparent binaries, including Edgeworth's *Castle Rackrent*, Griffin's *The Collegians* and Moore's *Melodies*.

Deane's project resembles Leerssen's in its attempt to trace the meaning of 'normalcy' in discourses on Irish culture and identity. However, Deane gives much more attention than does Leerssen to political and economic discourse (a discussion of the meaning of 'land' and 'soil' in Davis, Mitchel, O'Grady and Stoker, for example, forms a central section of Deane's book). He argues that since the time of Burke, Ireland has been defined as a 'strange country', resistant to the supposed 'normalisation' offered to it by the 'objective' historian (or the progressive spectator or the rational political discourse, all of whose self-defined difference from 'strangeness' can be deconstructed). 'Normality', argues Deane, 'is an economic condition; strangeness a cultural one. Since Burke, there has been a series of strenuous efforts to effect the convergence of the twain, even though the very premise of their separation has been powerful in assuring that the twain will never meet.'[13] Those efforts at integration had been largely abandoned by apologists for the Union after the Famine; subsequently, such efforts became the project of nationalism. 'The pursuit of such a reconciliation', Deane argues, 'provides a paradigm for Irish writing in the nineteenth century; one of the discursive formations that paradigm produces is a renovated version of a national character that must, by a variety of procedures, political and cultural, be disciplined into such sobriety of behaviour as would be in accord with the requirements of economic progress and development.'[14]

Repositioning canonical texts within a new or revised narrative frame is also a characteristic of Declan Kiberd's *Inventing Ireland: The Literature of the Modern Nation* (1995). Although Kiberd's chief focus is on twentieth-century Irish literature, he provides fresh insights into the writings of nineteenth-century figures Oscar Wilde, Somerville and Ross, and Augusta Gregory by reading them as significant exemplars in the long process of decolonisation and national reconstruction. Like many earlier studies of Irish writing and nationality, Kiberd's primary interest is in the twentieth century; however, his approach is especially innovative because of its explicit use of postcolonial theorists such as Said, Fanon, Nandy, Achebe and Ngugi. Kiberd uses them to derive a model of postcolonial, deconstructive hybridity that undermines hierarchical binary distinctions between Irish and English identity and culture, between masculinity and femininity, and between tradition and modernity. The writings that are most interesting for Kiberd's argument are those that encourage or manifest this liberating turn. Thus Wilde becomes a challenging and creative figure of multiple identity, his work a continual rejection of antithetical thinking: 'the Wildean moment', argues Kiberd, 'is that at which all polar opposites are transcended'.[15] Somerville and Ross are valued for their own attempts to transcend the restrictive vision of their class without abandoning the special insights their class position might offer on a changing Ireland. As with Lady Gregory, whom Kiberd shows to have bravely faced up to the challenge of fundamentally rethinking the values and contradictions of her Anglo-Irish inheritance, the gender position of these writers is assumed to have given them a certain critical vantage point on the dominant ideological norms of their day.

The volumes of Terry Eagleton's Irish trilogy published in the 1990s – *Heathcliff and the Great Hunger* (1995), *Crazy Jane and the Bishop* (1998) and *Scholars and Rebels in Nineteenth-Century Ireland* (1999) – contain several important essays on nineteenth-century Irish culture and like the previous works amount to something of an overview of the century. Some of the essays provide new readings of canonical figures like Yeats, Moore and Oscar Wilde, but perhaps the most valuable are those that respond to, in Eagleton's own words, 'two kinds of narrowness in contemporary Irish cultural studies'.[16] The first is a narrowness of canon, which Eagleton counters by recovering nineteenth-century figures like Fr Prout, W. E. H. Lecky, Isaac Butt, George Sigerson, John E. Cairnes, William Wilde and John Mitchel, thus, ironically, reinstating a canon that might have been quite recognisable to nineteenth-century critics. The second narrowness is one of approach: '[m]uch in Irish cultural studies is shaped nowadays by what one might loosely call a postmodern agenda, which brings into play some vital topics but in doing so tends to sideline other questions of equal importance . . . religion and education, for example'.[17] It is this breadth of focus that makes Eagleton's work most valuable, especially for the student or critic coming to the nineteenth-century culture for the first time. Essays like 'Form and ideology in the Anglo-Irish novel' and 'Culture and politics from Davis to Joyce' provide elegant and immensely useful exercises in synthesis and coverage, and interpretative frames that have a welcome clarity.[18] Eagleton's depiction of the nineteenth century as 'a peculiarly shocking collision of the customary and contemporary'[19] does not represent methodological innovation or a fundamentally new view of the century, but does offer a memorable and pithy starting point. In particular, the essays in *Scholars and Rebels*, like the work of Leerssen and Deane, fill out the intellectual context for nineteenth-century writing for an audience of students and critics who may simply be unaware of the importance of many of the figures discussed and of the fascinating 'intellectual ferment' of the time.[20]

Some of the issues raised by Eagleton in his essay 'Form and ideology in the Anglo-Irish novel' have also been taken up by David Lloyd, whose remarkable work on Mangan, nationalism and minor literature in 1987 offered a challenging new paradigm for considering Irish writing in the nineteenth century, based upon the application of poststructuralist and Marxist arguments.[21] Lloyd's chief work in the 1990s on the nineteenth century consisted of two closely argued essays from his collection *Anomalous States* (1993). One of these, 'Violence and the constitution of the novel', re-examines the oft-repeated observation that the nineteenth-century Irish novel is formally a heteroglossic, self-reflexive, incoherent mode of expression when compared to the English novel of the same period, an issue addressed not only by contemporary critics like Leerssen and Eagleton, but also by nineteenth-century novelists themselves. Reacting against the common explanation of this phenomenon in terms of the incoherence and instability of Irish society itself in the nineteenth century, Lloyd argues that assuming a simple correlation between social instability and formal instability in fiction depends on misleading assumptions about the nature of fiction itself. Lloyd describes the task of the novel as not merely one of representing society – a simple 'reflection model' of fiction – but rather of assisting in the ideological work of producing ethical national subjects along the lines demanded by bourgeois political economy (a project common to both imperialism and bourgeois nationalism). Viewed in this light, the atypicality of the Irish novel is chiefly a matter of the alternative moral economy of agrarian Ireland resisting incorporation into a particular ideological project. It is not simply that Irish society and its material base are backward or endemically violent, and therefore unsuitable for novelistic treatment. It is rather that the kind of binary categories through which the novel performs its task of bourgeois reformist education (distinguishing modern *vs* primitive, individual *vs* social, progressive *vs* regressive) could not convincingly be applied to Irish agrarian culture, any more than such culture could easily be assimilated into the structures of the bourgeois state. Lloyd's arguments point to the crucial fact that fiction has a regulative, political function that is not always admitted by literary critics; the failure to recognise this is a major problem: 'what is certain is that the tendency in literary criticism to understand the Irish novel and its conditions of emergence in binary terms, such that Irish society is read principally in terms of what it lacks *vis-à-vis* England or Europe, has seriously hampered the understanding of the phenomenon'.[22]

Lloyd's work on the novel, and his exploration of popular balladry in the essay 'Adulteration and the nation', also from *Anomalous States*, point to a glaring and surprising absence in each of the previously discussed overviews of the nineteenth century; that is, the field of Irish popular culture. Leerssen's work deals with the culture of the élite: antiquarians, historians and middle and upper-class writers whose work shaped the historical imagination of their own class, at least in the first instance. The work of Deane, Kiberd and Eagleton similarly deals with figures working within a middle-class and ascendancy sphere. Lloyd's 'Adulteration and the nation' however turns its attention to nineteenth-century street ballads in order to continue his exploration of the function of literature in the construction of the state. Describing the form and function of street ballads on the one hand, and more 'refined' and poetic nationalist effusions that appeared in the pages of *The Nation* and in various anthologies on the other, Lloyd makes the connection between Irish popular culture and subaltern, non-bourgeois forms of nationalism. His argument depends on a crucial distinction between bourgeois nationalism, which aims at the capture of the state, and is socially conservative, and subaltern, insurgent modes of anti-colonial resistance; the latter, unlike bourgeois nationalism, are not organised in the image of imperialism itself, but offer less centralised and more flexible structures. These latter forms are characterised in the cultural sphere by hybridity of form and content – they are 'adulterated' mixtures of

English words and Irish airs, burlesque style and political message – and therefore offer a more liberating aesthetic than conventional and selective 'high culture'. Lloyd thus sees a continuity between the nineteenth-century street ballads and the work of Joyce, both of which defied the demands of bourgeois taste.

Luke Gibbons, in his seminal essay 'Identity without a centre: allegory, history and Irish nationalism' (1992; reprinted in *Transformations in Irish Culture*, 1996), similarly draws attention to the culture of agrarian movements and the challenge they posed to the systems and aesthetic values of both the state and mainstream nationalism. Like Lloyd, he sketches out a rough picture of an alternative social, political and representational system operating in the nineteenth century, and in doing so reminds us of the frustrating lacunae in our knowledge of nineteenth-century popular culture. Georges-Denis Zimmerman's *Songs of Irish Rebellion* (1967, reprinted 2001) remains exemplary of the kind of retrieval of popular culture that is still needed. Scholars of eighteenth-century popular culture like Kevin Whelan (1996) and Mary Helen Thuente (1994) have provided recent models for such work in their studies of the mobilisation of popular culture in the United Irish movement. The challenge remains, however, to push this exploration further into the nineteenth century.

The most extensive and ground-breaking exception to the relative neglect of nineteenth-century popular culture is Niall Ó Ciosáin's *Print and Popular Culture in Ireland 1750–1850* (1997), which offers a welcome and detailed analysis of the popular printed material of the early nineteenth century, including chapbooks, popular histories and religious texts. Ó Ciosáin extends the almost exclusively political focus of the preceding studies by situating popular reading and publishing practices within the sociological contexts of literacy, language change, education and social stratification. He reminds us to beware of simplistic assumptions about the effects of such issues; he shows, for instance, that oral tradition frequently absorbed elements of print culture, rather than vice versa, and that the growth of literacy is related to the shift from Irish to English in quite complex and varied ways.

The issue of language change is itself remarkably absent from many of the recent writings on the nineteenth century, perhaps because many of the critics and literary historians are not confident or competent in dealing with Irish language material, and also perhaps from an unwillingness to challenge the view that the two languages were mutually exclusive. Robert Welch is, like Kiberd, one of the few Irish literary critics who writes with ease about both language traditions. Welch's book *Changing States* (1993) is valuable to the reader of English-language material for outlining the dual-language context for nineteenth-century Irish writing. His conclusion about the effect of language change, however, lacks the subtlety of Ó Ciosáin's argument, and largely reiterates the traditional nationalist view (as found in Corkery) that the loss of the Irish language set Irish culture irredeemably adrift. Welch's approach imagines nineteenth-century Ireland as a fallen place, lacking the coherence imposed by a Gaelic social and cultural order which had allegedly found expression through the Irish language. The loss of this system of representation is seen to have caused a literary crisis, which Welch describes ultimately in terms that sound extraordinarily romantic and Yeatsian: 'This is the world of absence that gives us so much vapid verse in the nineteenth century . . . Ireland had no language, no established way of life, no set of representations: it was a mood, a cloudy intimation, a dream.'[23]

The work discussed so far has generally viewed the nineteenth century in relation to the development of nationalism, or nationalisms. However, the work of two major literary historians has offered an alternative perspective: that of Protestant and unionist culture. W. J. Mc Cormack's ambitious and somewhat eccentric *From Burke to Beckett*, a reworking of his *Ascendancy and Tradition* book, appeared in 1994. Three of its chapters deal in some detail with the nineteenth century: 'Ascendancy and cabal 1800–1840', 'Mid-century perspectives' and 'Tribulations of the intelligentsia'. In writing 'literary history', which he distinguishes from 'critical appreciation', Mc Cormack continually moves among different forms of textuality, including canonical literature, historiography, and political and evangelical pamphlets, in an interdisciplinary spirit we have already noted in Leerssen and Eagleton. His particular attention is upon the nature and meaning of Protestant 'Ascendancy' in Irish culture, and he effectively argues that the notion of Ascendancy as an exclusivist social group (or cabal or coterie) only emerges after the Famine. This provides him with a way of reassessing those earlier Protestant writers who do not fit this character, and also allows him to connect later Ascendancy culture to the practices of literary modernism. Through his reading of Le Fanu and Lever, Mc Cormack also provides a provocative challenge to the Yeatsian view of the nineteenth century: 'The mid-nineteenth century is not a degeneration of romanticism as much as it is the early manifestation of modernist anxieties. And Ireland is less a backward and marginal culture than it is a central if repressed area of British modernism.'[24] In an interesting way this parallels arguments that have been made by Deane, Kiberd, Lloyd and Gibbons in recent years concerning the anomalously 'modernist' character of much Irish writing in the eighteenth and nineteenth centuries – a feature usually explained by reference to Ireland's colonial condition. Mc Cormack's often surprising paths through the culture of the Ascendancy give a strong flavour of the nineteenth century from the inside. To encounter, as one does in Mc Cormack's work, not one but two W. B. Yeatses (grandfather and grandson), and not one but two John Mitchels (father and son) is no mere gimmick; it is a striking reminder that individual creativity never exists in a vacuum, and that historical context comprises personal and familial forces in addition to the more impersonal forces of economics and ideology.

Norman Vance's *Irish Literature: A Social History* (1990) is the second major work to deal explicitly with Protestant culture and writing in the nineteenth century. In his wide-ranging study Vance deals with three nineteenth-century writers: Thomas Moore, William Carleton and Thomas D'Arcy McGee. Vance make his agenda clear. He opens the book by praising the recent revisionism in Irish historiography, and in the same spirit seeks to recover figures whose work has been either buried or manipulated by what he calls the selectivity of 'extreme' and 'moderate' versions of nationalism. Thus Thomas Moore is invoked in order to be set beside the neglected radical Presbyterian William Drennan. The latter's rationalist, sceptical, progressive vision, Vance argues, was unacceptable to a nineteenth-century nationalist canon based on romantic melancholy, and therefore disappeared. Thomas Moore's work, on the other hand, though it actually contains much of the same strain of European enlightenment thought to be found in Drennan, has been erroneously read by nationalism only for its dreamy elegiac character. Carleton and D'Arcy McGee are read as later victims of the confused and conflicted Irish condition, the more progressive aspects of whose writing could never be properly sustained: they both 'drew strength from, reinforced and [were] intellectually hampered by an atavistic sense of tradition'.[25] Although the retrieval and re-reading of these figures is valuable, it could be argued that Vance's own method depends upon the very discriminations that he wishes to see transcended; his continually implied opposition between nationalist 'atavism' and liberal pluralism, for example, may itself be read as a reductive binarism in need of deconstruction.

In terms of opening up the canon, and providing methodological challenges, the issue of gender in relation to nineteenth-century Irish writing has proved a highly productive focal point for recent criticism. This has taken two main forms: one is the recovery or reassessment of women writers; a second is the investigation of the ideologies or representations of sexuality, femininity and, to a lesser extent, masculinity, in nineteenth-century literature. Several works stand out. The first is the volume of essays entitled *Gender Perspectives in Nineteenth-Century Ireland*, edited by Margaret Kelleher and James H. Murphy (1997). Siobhán Kilfeather's essay 'Sex and sensation in the nineteenth-century novel' has a wider remit than the other literature essays, and offers (like Lloyd's essay discussed above) optimistic understanding of the supposed 'failure' of realism in Irish fiction. For Kilfeather, what is construed by critics like Eagleton and his predecessors as 'failed realism' may be precisely the source of these novels' potential for critique. The affectivity of the representation of 'sensation' and 'sex' in nineteenth-century fiction may, she argues, have served as a mode of resistance to the intrusion of bourgeois and colonial law into the space of public sexuality. In Kilfeather's words,

> Nineteenth-century novels have as much trouble representing bodies and sexuality as in representing famine, dispossession and emigration. This is not because sex is simply an unspeakable subject in nineteenth-century Ireland, but because Irish writers reject the domestication of sexuality in ways that disrupt and depose the conventions of realist fiction.[26]

Other essays in the same volume illustrate further varieties of gender-based criticism with a mixture of textual analysis and historical work. It is significant that Maria Edgeworth's work is the focus of three of the essays in the volume, a fact that confirms her status as one of the most interesting Irish novelists for contemporary critics, as evidenced by recent work elsewhere by Claire Connolly, Clíona Ó Gallchoir and others.[27] In *Gender Perspectives*, there are also essays on women's education, the role of women writers in nationalism, and the historiographical project of recovering neglected figures like Rosa Mulholland (a mainstay of the vastly influential *Irish Monthly*), and the 500 women writers identified by Anne Colman (many of whom are given bio-bibliographical treatments in her *Dictionary of Nineteenth-Century Irish Women Poets* [1996]).

Other contributions to the analysis of gender in the 1990s include this author's discussion of gender discourse in early nineteenth-century Irish nationalism,[28] and the more extended treatment of the same issue in C. L. Innes's *Woman and Nation in Irish Literature and Society 1880–1930* (1993). These studies show how images of femininity and masculinity functioned in nationalist writing (usually in forms that replicated the bourgeois doctrine of 'separate spheres'). Innes's work also describes the contributions to nationalism by figures like the Parnell sisters and Lady Gregory. Further biographical accounts of such women include helpful articles by Jan Cannavan and Brigitte Anton, and a full-scale biography of Jane Elgee, Lady Wilde (the Young Ireland poet 'Speranza') by Joy Melville.[29] Speranza's significance for Irish literature and nationalism is spelled out further in an important essay by Marjorie Howes.[30] Margaret Kelleher's *The Feminization of Famine* (1997) is a strikingly original study that demonstrates the centrality of the feminine in representations of famine in both Irish and Bengal literature. For the nineteenth-century scholar, Kelleher gives valuable accounts of Carleton's and Trollope's representations of the Famine, then examines a number of famine accounts written by women, concluding that while certain issues are foregrounded by some women – such as the subject of philanthropy (in which many women were engaged) – in general women writers 'share many of the fears and dilemmas expressed by their male contemporaries'.[31]

Volumes 4 and 5 of the *Field Day Anthology of Irish Writing* (2002) provide a rich resource for the study of gender in nineteenth-century Ireland. The volumes are organised in categories that cut across traditional generic boundaries such as 'literature' and 'historiography', and instead invite a different kind of reading that makes one aware of the inescapable historicity of texts, just as it forces one to be aware of the inescapable textuality of history. Volume 4's thematic headings include titles as diverse as 'Hymns and Hymn-Writers 1850–1930', 'Sexual expression and genre 1801–1917', 'Infanticide in nineteenth-century Ireland' and 'Writing for children 1791–1979'. Such categories enable the recovery of many literary texts (such as hymns or children's literature) that clearly played a major role in the everyday lives of nineteenth-century women and men, but have never been allotted a place in mainstream Literary Studies. Other acts of recovery include a section on oral traditions, and in volume 5 of the anthology the works of some thirty nineteenth-century women writers are reprinted. The nineteenth-century specialist will find fascinating and useful material throughout the anthology, including a valuable archive of nineteenth-century discourses on sexuality, crime, philanthropy, education, labour and so on.

Not surprisingly, a major preoccupation of Irish literary criticism in the 1990s was the Great Famine. Margaret Kelleher provided a foundational survey of literary representation of the Famine in her essay 'Irish Famine in literature', one of the RTÉ Thomas Davis lectures (1995). Chris Morash's monograph, *Writing the Irish Famine* (1995), provided a more comprehensive survey, and valuably drew attention to the methodological issues raised by the material, arguing that an analysis of the literature of the Famine makes one aware how much the meaning of the object of representation cannot be easily separated from the mode of representation itself. The overviews discussed above by Deane and Eagleton also contained discussion of the meaning and representation of the Famine, as did an interdisciplinary volume of essays edited by Chris Morash and Richard Hayes, *Fearful Realities* (1996) which contains several essays on the representation of the Famine in nineteenth-century writings by John Mitchel, Asenath Nicholson, John de Jean Frazer and *The Nation* newspaper.

A quick glance through the invaluable IASIL (International Association for the Study of Irish Literatures) bibliographies published annually in the *Irish University Review* gives an idea of the range of canonical authors whose work has been revisited in the past decade. Among novelists, Maria Edgeworth, Sydney Owenson/Lady Morgan, Sheridan Le Fanu and Bram Stoker figure most frequently. The work of the first two, poised in interesting ways between the eighteenth and nineteenth centuries, and between enlightenment and romantic sensibilities – has been newly assessed in the light of feminist as well as other politicised perspectives, often with special attention to their dialogic and multi-valenced forms. Sheridan Le Fanu and Bram Stoker have also become newly interesting because of the recent tendency to read the Irish Gothic as a register of crisis in Ascendancy culture. The Irish Gothic also offers possibilities for feminist readings of Victorian Irish sexuality. Mid-century novelists like the Banims, Carleton, Lover and Lever have received less attention, though a recent collection of essays on Lever suggests that his work may be subject to increasing scrutiny in the future.[32] The work of later novelists has been largely subsumed into larger critical studies and overviews, though James H. Murphy's valuable study of Catholic fiction fills a genuine gap in our knowledge of the reading and writing of fiction in the later part of the century.[33] An important exception is the canonical figure of George Moore who has been subject to a highly impressive biography by Adrian Frazier that illuminates a great deal of Moore's nineteenth-century background.[34]

Among poets, Thomas Moore has become a new figure of interest, a transitional figure whose work is not only important for its content, but also for the effects it produced. The past decade has also discovered Moore as a prose writer, with *Memoirs of Captain Rock* (1824) in particular serving as an important resource to critics like Luke Gibbons and Terry Eagleton. One of the most interesting scholarly publications during the 1990s was James Flannery's book and CD version of Moore's *Melodies* which at least partly overcomes one of the most obvious limitations to our contemporary encounter with nineteenth-century verse – the fact that we now read rather than *hear* the songs in the way that much of the nineteenth century did.[35] Similar multimedia projects would in fact make a major contribution to our understanding by enabling critics to assess the importance of music and performativity in a very great deal of the nineteenth-century poetic tradition.

Other poets who have been subject to recent attention are James Clarence Mangan, whose work is at last available in a comprehensive collected edition edited by the late Augustine Martin and others, and in a selected edition by the author. Ellen Shannon-Mangan has also published a useful biography of the poet, and Jacques Chuto a remarkable bibliography of the poet's vast output.[36] Samuel Ferguson's achievement too has been re-examined in a major monograph by Peter Denman, and as part of a study of Victorian epic poetry by Colin Graham.[37] The latter work is a valuable reminder of the wider, cross-channel context for the work of so many Irish writers in the nineteenth century: not simply in terms of markets and publishers but also in terms of shared ideological projects, both at a pro-imperial level, as with Ferguson, and at a more subversive level, as with radical popular verse. The figure of W. B. Yeats still looms over the poetic achievement of the nineteenth century, and the 1990s saw the publication of more indispensable volumes of the OUP *Collected Letters*, as well as two biographies (Roy Foster's and Terence Brown's), all of which offer exciting new resources for thinking of

Yeats as a nineteenth-century poet.[38] Oscar Wilde too has now been firmly incorporated into nineteenth-century Irish literary history. As recently as 1982, Roger McHugh and Maurice Harmon could uncontroversially state that 'The plays of Oscar Wilde . . . properly belong to English theatrical history'[39] – a position no longer secure in the wake of the arguments made in the 1990s by Kiberd, Eagleton and others.

Along with this critical work on nineteenth-century authors and issues have come welcome bibliographical and publishing developments, which promise to assist scholars of the future. The initial three volumes of the *Field Day Anthology of Irish Writing* which appeared at the beginning of the decade, were criticised for neglecting women writers and for omitting writings that might problematise its supposedly nationalist bias. Even so, the anthology does provide students of the nineteenth century with a vast array of texts, many not reprinted since the nineteenth century itself. Seamus Deane's selection of nineteenth-century English-language poems and songs, and writings on the Famine, is perhaps too brief to satisfy the specialist but remains a useful introduction. His category of 'Political writings and speeches 1850–1918' attempts to demonstrate the often quite direct link between literature and politics by unexpectedly including extracts from Boucicualt's *Arrah-na-Pogue* and Kickham's *Knocknagow*. A further, burgeoning bibliographical resource has been the World Wide Web: electronic archives such as those provided by the CELT project at UCC and the EIRdata project associated with the Princess Grace Library contain both texts and information about texts and authors.[40] One of the most astonishing internet resources is the Bodleian Library's Broadside Ballads Website, which has made thousands of photographically reproduced and fully searchable nineteenth-century ballads available freely on the web, linked to playable music files and annotations.[41]

⋆   ⋆   ⋆

What is to be done next? From a theoretical point of view, 'postcolonial' theories are likely to continue to shape the study of Irish literature in the nineteenth century. The complex meanings of colonialism and imperialism within an Irish cultural frame have not by any means been sufficiently explored. So, too, the application of feminist insights to Irish writing and culture needs to be extended, in order, for instance, to examine the construction and ideologies of 'masculinity' as well as 'femininity' during the century. Even the definition of the 'nineteenth century' is likely to be revised, a process already begun by critics like Leerssen and Gibbons, who have challenged the rigid distinction between eighteenth and nineteenth-century cultures. And just as critical attention has begun to focus on the distinctive meanings of 'Protestant culture', critical work needs to be done on delineating and understanding the nature of 'Catholic' culture in the period 1798 to 1900. This is a twofold task, demanding better understanding of the literate middle-class culture of the later century, and a deeper investigation of popular culture right through the century. This would include examining not just 'literary texts' but broadsheets, chapbooks, devotional reading and newspapers. Gary Owens has valuably shown how even the rituals and symbols of O'Connell's monster meetings can be read as popular 'texts'.[42] The signifying practices of popular periodicals – the chief means of literary transmission for most of the Irish nineteenth century – is in fact a vast area demanding new research. Inroads have begun to be made by recent work on the *Dublin University Magazine*, and the Irish elements of *Illustrated London News*. But publications like Cox's *Irish Magazine*, the numerous penny journals, *Duffy's Irish Catholic Magazine*, *The Nation* and the *Irish Monthly* need to be explored in more detail.[43] Pre-Revival dramatic practices largely remain hidden to critics and students, having been for so long overshadowed by the monumental presence of the Irish Literary Theatre.

Even within the more conventional parameters of 'literature', an expanding canon will involve paying new attention to writers whose work may look more intriguing to contemporary critical preoccupations than it has to critics of the past. Emily Lawless, Dion Boucicualt, Charles Kickham, Charles Maturin and Aubrey de Vere are all examples (by no means exhaustive) of figures who are much more interesting than the scarcity of criticism would suggest.

The recent work sketched out here has provided new answers to the question: why study the nineteenth century? In the past, that question might have been formulated as follows: why would one want to study the nineteenth century, given its apparent under-achievement, and given the obvious richness of the writing that succeeded it? The scholarship of recent years has shown that to be a misguided question. Thanks to the efforts of the scholars and critics described above, and building upon the pioneering work of earlier decades by critics like Tom Dunne, James Cahalan, Robert Tracy, John Wilson Foster and Terence Brown, the literature and literary culture of the Irish nineteenth century has begun to look like a fascinating and essential field for any understanding of Ireland's difficult and remarkable cultural history.

# CHAPTER 8

# Gaelic Culture and Language Shift

✳

*Niall Ó Ciosáin*

In 1960, Seán De Fréine pointed to the paucity of discussion in historiography and cultural commentary of the language shift in nineteenth-century Ireland.[1] While the intervening years have seen some research in the area, the observation still holds considerable truth. This is particularly the case when the extraordinary speed and scale of the shift are taken into account. In the barony of Barrett's in mid County Cork, for example, 80 per cent of those born in the 1820s could speak Irish. Just thirty years later, that figure was down to 20 per cent.[2] There can have been few social or cultural practices which were so rapidly and radically transformed, and which have attracted so little extended commentary. A similar observation can be made about the culture of Irish-speaking communities in general, of the politics, religion and overall worldview of about half the population before the Famine and a quarter afterwards. There is no equivalent in Ireland of the multi-volume *Social History of the Welsh Language* being produced by the Centre for Advanced Welsh and Celtic Studies in Aberystwyth, which devotes no fewer than four volumes to the nineteenth century.[3]

In the historical surveys published in the 1990s, those of Boyce and Jackson for example, Irish is mentioned only in passing, if at all.[4] This is understandable enough, given that these are narratives of conventional politics. The absence is more surprising in other spheres. With some exceptions, scholars of Irish literature have ignored the nineteenth century. An example is volume 21 (1990) of the journal *Celtica*, which is a *festschrift* for Brian Ó Cuív, who wrote the standard account of Irish language and literature in the nineteenth century. In this volume, only two items out of fifty-nine were about topics after 1800, despite the expertise of its dedicatee. This neglect is the result of literary scholars' valorisation of creativity, originality and technical achievement, which are less characteristic of the literary production in the nineteenth century, even though literate culture was widespread, and more manuscripts were produced than in any other century.

There is also a striking lack of attention devoted to Irish in new forms of social and cultural history, particularly those influenced by forms of post-colonial theory, which discuss histories and experiences which are said to be 'hidden', 'occluded' and 'subaltern'. If we define a subordinate language as 'one restricted to domains from which power in general societal terms is absent',[5] then Irish was a subordinate language, a subaltern discourse *par excellence*. Yet it is a very muted presence in the work of a commentator such as David Lloyd, who discusses subalternity and the disjunctions between elite and peasant society and consciousness without much discussion of material in Irish. Another example is Robert Scally's 'view from within' of Ballykilcline, a small County Roscommon community before the Famine, located in a region which was substantially Irish-speaking. Scally mentions general questions of language only in passing, does not at any point make clear what language was actually spoken by that community, and uses no Irish language sources whatsoever, although his title is borrowed from a classic study of Gaelic culture. In other words, despite their desire to 'recover subterranean or marginalised practices', these writers merely re-enact the same processes of marginalisation.[6]

This anomalous nature of much commentary on the culture of nineteenth-century Ireland is best illustrated by the way Irish is dealt with in the major canonical statement of literary approaches to Irish history, one which functions essentially within a postcolonial paradigm, the three-volume *Field Day Anthology of Irish Writing*, published in 1991.[7] The anthology is scrupulously multilingual, and contains texts in middle and modern English, old, middle and modern Irish, Latin, and Norman French. The reader who is looking for texts in Irish from the nineteenth century, however, discovers something very curious – there is no section in the anthology for such texts. There is a section on writing in Irish from 1600 to 1800, edited by Alan Harrison, and one on writing in Irish after 1900, edited by Eoghan Ó hAnluain. Between these two, however, there is a gap, with no section called 'writing in Irish 1800–1900'. This is not to make the usual criticism of anthologies, that of balance and selection, whether too much Joyce or not enough Swift has been included, but to point out that there is in fact no place at all for a particular type of text, no category corresponding to it. This suggests that the difficulty lies with the overall conception of the anthology, a hypothesis that is strengthened by the fact that the nineteenth-century sections are mainly contributed by the general editor of the anthology, and presumably its chief architect, Seamus Deane.

Examination of these sections on the nineteenth century, moreover, deepens the anomaly. Although they are concerned with writing in English, they do in fact contain some texts in Irish, introduced in an extraordinary way. 'Poetry and song 1800–1890', while mostly devoted to Mangan,

Ferguson and Davis, contains some 'traditional folk songs', beginning with 'The Lament for Richard Cantillon', given in Irish and also in Petrie's translation into English in the 1850s. But Petrie's gloss on the original song, also given, states that it was written a century earlier, in 1750. The second, 'An raibh tú ar an gCarraig' is likewise dated to the early eighteenth century. Another section edited by Deane, entitled 'The Famine and Young Ireland', consisting largely of political and economic commentary on the Famine published between 1846 and 1870, also has two texts in Irish. These are excerpts from the archives of the Irish Folklore Commission, that is to say, oral accounts collected on the centenary of the Famine in 1945.

In other words, the absent section on writing in Irish from the nineteenth century has been replaced with some songs from the previous century and some folklore (not 'writing' at all, some would argue) from the following century. Five sections further on, something equally curious happens, when the only genuine pieces of nineteenth-century composition in Irish in the anthology, six poems or songs by Raftery, whose dates are given as *c.*1784–1835, find their place in a section called 'Poetry 1890-1930', also edited by Deane.

There is no discussion of these editorial decisions within the anthology, but some explanations can be suggested. The implications of the chronological transposition of the poetry and songs are fairly clear. The eighteenth-century songs are moved to 1800–90 and Raftery to 1890–1930 because that was when their English-language translations were published. In other words, they are included not as writing in Irish, but as writing in English, entailing a complete subordination of the culture of the subaltern language to that of the hegemonic language. A similar observation can be made about the use of the oral accounts of the Famine. Moreover, both types of chronological transposition have the even clearer implication that Irish language culture was static and unchanging, despite the enormous social changes of the two-century span in question (partly brought about by the Famine, which the anthology itself simultaneously treats as a central event).

In contrast, the absence in the first place of any category corresponding to nineteenth-century writing in Irish tells a slightly different story, one that is well illustrated by the overall physical layout of the anthology. The section on writing in Irish 1600–1800 comes early in volume 1, while that on the twentieth century is almost at the end of volume 3, over three thousand pages (and two volumes) away. The clear suggestion is that there is no continuity at all between the two, with the first representing a tradition that was as good as dead by 1800, and the second being the production of a very self-consciously revivalist literary culture. One would hardly guess from this that the first half of the nineteenth century saw a quantitatively greater production of manuscripts and printed books in Irish than any earlier period, and a greater readership.

Nineteenth-century writing in Irish is therefore displaced and occluded, while the culture which produced it is marginalised and exoticised, and that in a prestigious anthology which set out to take account of a variety of cultural traditions. The *Field Day Anthology* has become a standard resource for research and teaching, and yet this omission does not appear to have been noticed by reviewers or commentators. All of this illustrates the difficulties involved in approaching nineteenth-century Gaelic culture through the available literature. There are many other such anomalies to be found in commentary on the subject – for instance, the most informative, aware and acute analysis by far of language shift in nineteenth-century Ireland occurs in a book which is not about nineteenth-century Ireland at all. This is J. J. Lee's *Ireland 1912–1985*.[8] It is hard to think of a phenomenon of comparable scale of which such an observation could be made.

★   ★   ★

Before looking at the Irish language in the nineteenth century, it is necessary to separate two distinct, though linked, questions. On the one hand, there is the culture, or cultures, to which Irish speakers belonged, and on the other, there is the process of language shift which was so marked in the period. Indeed, it is probably fair to say that much of the occlusion and confusion described above arises from a failure to make this distinction, a failure which results in teleological anachronism. The process of language shift was inevitable and irreversible, the argument goes; it had started by 1800; therefore Irish culture was effectively finished by 1800 as well, and could be ignored in the nineteenth century, to the extent that it existed at all. This certainly seems the view of Deane, who in an earlier survey described Gaelic culture as 'well and truly dead by the end of the eighteenth century', and in this he is followed by others such as Leerssen, according to whom 'the native tradition in the nineteenth century is almost silent, having been pauperised into virtual illiteracy'.[9] This may have been true of aristocratic culture, but it is unjustifiably elitist to expand the judgement to Gaelic culture as a whole.[10] This article will observe this distinction between the process of language shift and the culture of Irish, looking first at general treatments of one or both areas, then at the historiography of shift and finally at analyses of Gaelic culture.

The 1990s saw one superb general view of the second half of the century, the late Brian Ó Cuív's chapter on 'Irish language and literature 1845–1921' in the *New History of Ireland*, volume 6. Ó Cuív had covered the first half of the century with equal authority in his contribution to volume 4 in 1986.[11] These two chapters, substantial in content and containing much original research, could well be issued as a separate book along with his account of an earlier period in Vol. 3 . This would be not simply the best general account

139

of the subject available, but the only one. An account of the nineteenth century is given by Cathal Ó hÁinle as part of his contribution to the multi-authored *Stair na Gaeilge*. His focus is on literacy, literature and education, and his conclusions are authoritative if perhaps a little pessimistic for the pre-Famine period.[12]

An overview of a different kind is found in *1782–1881: Beathaisnéis* by Máire Ní Mhurchú and Diarmuid Breathnach. In this volume the authors have extended back in time their project of a comprehensive biographical dictionary of the twentieth-century world of Irish. It contains over 160 biographies, many of them substantial and all of them fascinating, making it an indispensable reference work.[13]

Tony Crowley's *The Politics of Language in Ireland* (2000) is a useful collection of primary texts, with a nineteenth-century section which focuses on Bible societies, *The Nation* and Revivalism.[14] The texts form the basis of a chapter in the same author's *Language in History* (1996). The potential of the collection as a resource for either teaching or research is limited, however, by a number of features. It is a 'sourcebook', but does not specify the sources of any of the texts it contains. O'Connell's often-quoted remark about 'witnessing without a sigh the gradual demise of Irish', for example, is placed in the 1830s in the sequence of the book although it first occurs in O'Neill Daunt's *Recollections*, published in 1848. More importantly, the conception of 'politics' underlying the selection is a narrow one, and both the collection and the chapter deal for the most part with programmatic statements about language by public figures which appeared in print – about Irish as an issue in public debate, rather than about the relations of power which obtained in practice between languages. The overall effect is old fashioned and heavily reminiscent of similar collections published seventy years ago by T. J. Corcoran.

Turning to questions of language shift, the 1990s saw some original research, but most commentators seem content to repeat the classic analyses of Maureen Wall, Máirtín Ó Murchú and Oliver MacDonagh, with little account being taken of the scathing critique recently offered by Lee.[15] Some features of the resulting consensus are worth dwelling on. First there is the use of a 'natural' terminology. Karen Corrigan quotes Wall to the effect that 'it was naturally to the advantage' of emigrants to know English, while Brighid Ní Mhóráin cites Ó Murchú's statement that 'it was only natural that language change would follow social advancement'. Liam De Paor refers to the 'ebb' of Irish, while several writers on Donegal quote Charles McGlinchey's description of Irish 'melting away like snow off the ditches'.[16]

Language shift is presented as natural, but also cultural or psychological, and many commentators are at pains to emphasise the voluntary nature of the process. Donald Akenson, for example, quotes MacDonagh's statement that 'the essential reason for the decline of Gaelic was the popular will', and Reg

Hindley refers to a 'collective decision' to change. This analysis (originating, again, with Wall) was a necessary and a healthy corrective to an earlier misplaced emphasis on coercion, tally sticks and the like, and Líam Kennedy has gone thoroughly over the arguments against the existence of a conscious and deliberate state policy of eradicating Irish. As an explanation in itself, however, it is vacuous. The 'collective decision' turns out in practice to be a 'natural' recognition of the utility of English, and reduces to a description of some structural features of nineteenth-century Irish economy and society, usually without relating them in any detail to language use in practice. As Akenson puts it, 'the Irish peasantry was shrewd enough to read the economic signs of the times' and therefore switched to English.[17]

Another feature of this line of reasoning is that it is not reversible. Material circumstances explain a shift from Irish to English, but the reverse is apparently inconceivable. The shift could only be halted or slowed down through an act of political will, through agency rather than through material circumstance, and, as Hindley points out, 'it cannot be overemphasised that there was in effect no language question in Ireland . . . in the early nineteenth century'. Unless someone deliberately decided to revive Irish, in other words, language shift was irreversible. This line of argument could be countered by reference to the favourable impact of the early industrial revolution on the fortunes of the Welsh language, as Brinley Thomas and Lee have done, but this has not found an echo in the wider historiography.[18]

The fundamental structural cause of shift in most accounts is economic. The market operated in English, and therefore any involvement in commercial transactions was bound to lead to the acquisition of English. The extent and frequency of market involvement is never specified, however, and the chronology of language shift is not compared explicitly with that of commercialisation or monetisation. For the pre-Famine period in particular, when, as Joel Mokyr and Cormac Ó Gráda point out, most of the population 'grew their own food, provided their own fuel, and often were close to self-sufficiency in clothing and housing', there appears to be a disproportion between the force of the economic motive and the speed of language shift. Moreover, the issue is not purely economic, and questions of power and status cannot be entirely removed from this process. If language shift is a way of reducing transaction costs, for example, why does it not also operate the other way around? Would it not be more rational for one cattle dealer to learn Irish than for thirty farmers to learn English? This may well have happened, but we need a far more detailed ethnography of language use before we can decide whether it did or not. Moreover, Lee has provided an effective criticism of this line of argument by pointing out that participation in the market can explain the acquisition of English but not the rapid loss of Irish.[19]

★   ★   ★

The starting point for a social history of language in the nineteenth century is the censuses, which from 1851 onwards recorded people's declared ability to speak English and Irish. Age cohort figures from the four censuses of 1851, 1861, 1871 and 1881 were used to project the findings back as far as the late eighteenth century in an already classic paper by Garret Fitzgerald, published in its full form in 1986 and in a shorter version in 1990. He was primarily concerned with the reliability of the reported figures and with establishing a chronology of shift in different regions rather than with the causes and mechanisms of that shift.[20]

Most studies move on from figures to explanatory frameworks and examine shift as shown in census figures on a larger scale. Two ambitious book-length surveys appeared in the 1990s, both concerning Munster: Mairéad Nic Craith's study of County Cork during the nineteenth century and Bríd Ní Mhóráin's of the barony of Iveragh, County Kerry, from the eighteenth to the twentieth century.[21] Both place language shift within a context of broader social change, as illustrated for the most part in censuses and other official reports. Ní Mhóráin's is the more successful of the two, and indeed can be read as a fine piece of social history, independent altogether of language. This strength is also part of its weakness, however, as the relationship between social change and language use tends to be treated as self-evident rather than as requiring to be elucidated (however, as noted above, she is not alone in this). A good example is chapter 6, 'An dátheangachas aistritheach ag teacht chun cinn, 1851–1921' (The growth of transitional bilingualism, 1851–1921), where out of a total of 39 pages language is only discussed on 14, and two of those are passing references. When language is explicitly addressed, the result is always penetrating, and there is for example on pp. 152–5 an intriguing discussion of the gender distribution of language, something rarely referred to elsewhere. Ní Mhóráin also makes brief but telling use of the household returns from the 1901 and 1911 censuses, the first for which they survive, to show the relationship between occupation, literacy and language use. Nic Craith's book, on the other hand, is less satisfactory, partly because of the larger coverage attempted. The patterns of shift in the various baronies of a huge county (population in 1841 was three-quarters of a million) differ markedly, but no attempt is made to explain this variation. Patterns of marriage and emigration are discussed at length, but their relationship with patterns of language use is not made at all clear. Census figures are also the basis for the chapter on the nineteenth century in Reg Hindley's *The Death of the Irish Language*. The main focus of the book is on the twentieth century, however, and the earlier sections contain little that is new.[22]

Some noteworthy general articles have appeared since 1990. Máirtín Ó Murchú's survey of language shift in the nineteenth century focuses on the use of Irish in political activity and organisation; Sean Connolly's longer-term examination of patterns of change in popular culture very effectively places language shift in a much broader context; and De Fréine examines in a comparative framework the role of the Great Famine in the process of language shift.[23] Two articles from a conference on 'L'Irlande et ses langues' held in Rennes in 1992 discuss and describe the relationship between languages in everyday use in Ireland. Michel Flot analyses episodes of shift and conflict in the writing of Gerald Griffin, while the material in the archives of the Irish Folklore Commission describing language use is surveyed by Grace Neville. Although the latter sources come from the mid-twentieth century, many or most of their conclusions can be extended back well into the nineteenth, and the discussion of linguistic domains and code-switching is very illuminating.[24]

Other studies concentrate on specific causes of language shift or on particular regions. The role of emigration is considered by Karen Corrigan in a study which marshals much recent writing in sociolinguistics. The substantive discussion is , however, inconclusive, even contradictory, and the reader is left uncertain about the causal relationships between emigration and language shift. In this respect the title of the article ('For God's sake teach the children English') is emblematic. It comes from a letter written in Irish from New York to Donegal in the later nineteenth century. It shows that learning English was perceived as a necessary prelude to emigration, but its very next phrase ('and don't be blind like the donkeys who come out here') shows that in practice monoglottism was no obstacle to emigration. Máirín Nic Eoin's study of County Kilkenny discusses literary production in Irish as well as language shift, and traces, in the author's words, 'a shift in the status of Irish from a living language among the general population to that of a symbolic code to be collected, studied and treated as a subject of antiquarian interest by a growing body of well-to-do scholars'.[25]

The census household returns from 1901 and 1911 have been used in a small number of studies to produce a more detailed and less conventional picture of language use and shift. Mary E. Daly's comparison between three electoral divisions in County Donegal and three in County Galway shows that in the former English was acquired independently of literacy, whereas in the latter the two were learnt together. This was due to the importance of seasonal migration in Donegal.[26] In his introduction to Cosslett Ó Cuinn's *Scian a Caitheadh le Toinn*, a collection of folklore from Inishowen, County Donegal, Aodh Ó Canainn uses the returns to pinpoint the precise moment at which different families stopped transmitting Irish to their children, a decision for the most part taken after one or more children had been born, rather than at marriage.[27] His data also question easy links between emigration and language use, and show that the houses nearest a Royal Artillery base, a presumed source of English, were in fact more rather than less likely to speak Irish.

Three articles, all on language shift in Inishowen, appeared in the *Donegal Annual* in the 1990s, all inspired by Ó Cuinn and by Charles McGlinchey's *The Last of the Name*, but they are more general and conventional in their findings than Ó Canainn.[28] Finally, a bizarre case is discussed by Ciaran Devine, who examines the 1901 returns for County Down, and finds major discrepancies between them and the published report. On the individual household forms, to cite one example, 196 monoglot Irish speakers are recorded in Banbridge, whereas the printed tabulations convert these into 56 bilinguals and no monoglots![29]

\*  \*  \*

The subject of literacy offers a link between the question of language shift and that of the general culture of Irish speakers. On the one hand, our most immediate knowledge of that culture is through its written documents; on the other hand, the desire for reading and writing, and the rapid growth in education consequent on it, has been seen as the main force behind shift, an argument made with some force in 1981 in L. M. Cullen's influential *The Emergence of Modern Ireland*. It is true that the literacy desired was overwhelmingly in English. However, as Máirín Ní Dhonnchadha has argued, this did not mean that popular literacy in the nineteenth century was exclusively in that language, and that Irish-speakers were by definition illiterate. In a review of a 1990 collection of articles, *The Origins of Popular Literacy in Ireland: Language Change and Educational Development*, she discerned this belief among some of its contributors, as well as being implicit in its title.[30]

The literacy that did exist in Irish, in its manuscript and its print forms, was the subject of substantial discussion in the 1990s. A major contribution was made by Dermot McGuinne in his learned and beautifully produced *Irish Type Design*, a history of the different fonts produced for printing in Irish, which also contains useful discussions of bookselling and reading.[31] I have also explored Irish-language print culture in *Print and Popular Culture* and in a number of articles. These distinguished different types of print literacy in Irish, compared printed production with that in Welsh and Breton, and examined the most frequently printed text in the nineteenth century, O'Sullivan's *Pious Miscellany*, and its reception.[32]

Also worth noting in this context is a study by Malachy McKenna of a short religious text which had four editions in Monaghan between 1800 and 1835. The article contains an invaluable (if also incomplete) list of books in Irish printed in the nineteenth century.[33] Two printing projects from the end of the century were the subjects of books. Fionnuala Uí Fhlannagáin's *Mícheál Ó Lócháin agus An Gaodhal* discusses the first periodical of any duration printed in Irish, a newspaper published in New York from 1881 to

1904, and the first Irish-language newspaper to appear in Ireland, *Fáinne an Lae*, which appeared between 1898 and 1900, received a definitive treatment by Caoilfhionn Nic Pháidín.[34]

The more challenging area of manuscript culture also advanced substantially in the 1990s. Catalogues were published of the Murphy collection in Cork, which contains seventy-six manuscripts, mainly nineteenth century, by Breandán Ó Conchúir, and of the Mount Melleray collection, with four nineteenth-century manuscripts, and then six later additions, by Pádraig Ó Macháin. Four other manuscripts, which belonged to John O'Daly and which appeared in Norway in 1990, were described by Ronald Black.[35] The transatlantic destination of many manuscripts is highlighted in two articles: Kenneth Nilsen's intriguing study of Michael O'Byrne, a teacher of Irish and a collector of manuscripts in New York between 1878, when he arrived from Waterford, and his death in 1928, and Edgar Slotkin's description of two manuscripts.[36]

The main overview of pre-Famine manuscript literacy which appeared in the 1990s was L. M. Cullen's magisterial survey of production from 1700 to 1850. This provides the most comprehensive study yet of the changing patterns of education, writing and reading among literate Irish-speakers. Some notable explorations of regional manuscript cultures in the eighteenth and nineteenth centuries have appeared in the Geography Publications series of county histories. Éamon Ó hÓgáin has studied County Kilkenny, in the form of a biographical catalogue of 25 scribes, 15 of whom were active in the nineteenth century. Ó Súilleabháin has done likewise for County Waterford where the figures are 33 and 13, or, in terms of manuscripts, 137 of which 114 are from the nineteenth century.[37]

William Mahon discusses County Galway, where manuscript production was far smaller and less learned than in the south, predominantly from the nineteenth century and often in phonetic English spelling. These manuscripts, and Connaught manuscripts as a whole, have been the subject of a pathbreaking article by Cullen, who argues that the disdain felt for these productions by scholars such as Hyde, and a consequent failure to collect and preserve them, has led to an exaggerated emphasis on the orality of popular Gaelic culture in the later nineteenth century. Moreover, as Cathal Ó hÁinle has pointed out, Hyde was also inclined to see the songs as anonymous folk songs rather than as compositions by recognised poets. The result was a primitivism which suited both revivalists and denigrators of Irish, then and later, but which gave a distorted picture of Gaelic culture[38]

The most substantial study of individual scribes and their production to appear in recent years was Meidhbhín Ní Úrdail's *The Scribe in Eighteenth and Nineteenth Century Ireland*. This surveys three generations of the Ó Longáin family, from Mícheál mac Peattair, born in the 1690s and initially a land agent in County Limerick, to Seosamh who in 1865 became scribe to the Royal Irish

Academy. The family is followed from rural Limerick to urban Cork and Dublin, and a parallel process is shown in the manuscripts, which show the gradual influence of print culture and antiquarianism. The latter stages of this process are visible in a very attractive appendix of 28 reproductions of manuscript pages. The best known member of the dynasty was of course Mícheál Óg (1766–1837), poet and United Irishman. This book offers by far the most complete account of his life, and is well complemented by Rónán Ó Donnchadha's earlier edition of a selection of his poetry, and by Tom Dunne's re-assessment of the poems written by Ó Longáin during and about the 1790s.[39]

A scribe from a very different milieu is the subject of Ciarán Dawson's *Peadar Ó Gealacáin*. Ó Gealacáin was active in north Leinster, County Meath in particular, and worked for a period with the evangelical Irish Society. Little is known about Ó Gealacáin outside his manuscripts, and the book therefore consists essentially of a well-annotated catalogue of these, with many texts given in their entirety. The scribal milieu in this area was a bilingual one, and Ó Gealacáin himself published verse in English and associated with poets who, while they were Irish speakers, wrote mainly in English. One of these, Michael Clarke, was discussed by Séamus Mac Gabhann, another of whose articles presents Ó Gealacáin (or Peter Gallegan) in English.[40] Other useful articles on scribes included Eilís Ní Dheá's three short accounts of west County Clare scribes which together constitute a survey of a regional manuscript culture, and Nessa Ní Shéaghdha's list of the occupation of 43 scribes, over half of them active in the nineteenth century.[41]

Some individual texts or groups of texts were also edited and discussed. Prominent here is Neil Buttimer, whose project of contextualising manuscript material continued during the 1990s. His chapter on Gaelic culture in the Cork county history, while covering the period 1700–1840, features a large proportion of nineteenth-century material and shows a vibrant and politically aware scribal culture.[42] Buttimer has also surveyed perceptions of France in the same manuscript material, and presented a series of early nineteenth-century texts dealing with such topics as the Napoleonic wars, Emmet's rebellion and the cholera epidemic of 1832.[43] Other short texts from manuscripts, mainly dealing with O'Connell and electoral politics, were published by Diarmaid Ó Muirithe and Pádraig Breatnach.[44]

More ambitious interpretative or synthetic treatments of Gaelic culture concentrate on political songs. Tom Dunne's survey of what he calls 'a significant corpus of political songs and poems' from the first half of the century shows a continuing engagement with and commentary on the process of popular political mobilisation associated with Daniel O'Connell. O'Connell was, in Dunne's words, 'the great folk hero of this volatile bilingual world', and Ríonach Uí Ógáin's *Immortal Dan* makes available in English a great deal of material relating to him. Gearóid Denvir has made an eloquent case for Raftery as a 'file pobail', a public poet who embodies and expresses the attitudes of the society to which he belongs, while there are also some suggestive comments in Maura Cronin's examination of early nineteenth-century song, in both Irish and English, relating to the 1798 rebellion. Proinsias Ó Drisceoil's book-length study of Amhlaoibh Ó Súilleabháin, schoolmaster, merchant, politician and diarist, gives by far the fullest and most complex picture yet of a member of the Irish-speaking O'Connellite middle class who were the élite of Gaelic society before the Famine. Cullen's sketch of life in nineteenth-century Callan also contains a brief but highly suggestive re-evaluation of Ó Súilleabháin.[45]

Among the studies devoted to the Great Famine are two articles presenting Irish-language material relating to that catastrophe. Antain Mac Lochlainn discusses texts which are fairly well known and which had already appeared in print, notably poems by Peatsaí Ó Callanáin and Aodh Mac Domhnaill, arguing that Gaelic culture had 'a distinct reaction to the Famine', while Buttimer, in a more adventurous exploration of a range of previously unpublished verse and scribal colophons, arrives at a similar conclusion.[46]

One aspect of Gaelic culture which has been surprisingly under-researched is the area of religion and the churches, particularly the Catholic Church. Religion (not necessarily orthodox) was fundamental to the worldview of Irish speakers, and churches were crucial in determining the speed and character of the language shift, but the historiography in this area has been variable. This is all the more remarkable given the prominence of religion and churches in discussions of other Celtic language areas. Victor Durkacz's *Decline of the Celtic Languages*, the principal comparative account, concentrated almost exclusively on religious organisations and their educational projects, while there has been no shortage of analysis of the relationship between Catholicism and the Breton language. One Breton specialist, the late Michel Lagrée, even produced a masterly short comparative survey of religion and language in Brittany and Ireland in the nineteenth century.[47] In Ireland, by contrast, most writers seem content to echo the misleading analysis contained in Maureen Wall's classic article of 1969, according to which the Catholic Church as an institution actively promoted Irish, at least in the eighteenth century, a view which should not survive a reading of Gearóid Ó Tuathaigh's classic article of 1986.[48]

The most comprehensive account dealing with any one denomination is Roger Blaney's *Presbyterians and the Irish Language*, almost half of which is devoted to the nineteenth century. Its title is to be taken literally, and its predominant focus is on individuals rather than on the church. There are extensive sections on the Rev. William Neilson, also the subject of a short pamphlet by Séamus Ó Saothraí, and Robert McAdam, where Blaney brings an anglophone public over some of the ground first explored by Breandán Ó Buachalla in his 1968 book *I mBéal Feirste Cois Cuain*. Blaney discusses the Bible Societies and their activities in Irish in places like the Glens of Antrim in the 1840s, an episode also described by Anthony Buckley.[49]

For the Church of Ireland, Risteárd Giltrap's short book *An Ghaeilge in Eaglais na hÉireann* is a useful introduction, though its format is that of a popular text rather than an original work. The early 1990s also saw the completion of Pádraig de Brún's mammoth survey of teachers employed from the 1820s onwards by the Irish Society to teach scripture reading in Irish. This is probably the most comprehensive listing of Irish scribes and readers in Leinster and south Ulster, and is a resource of inestimable value.[50]

As regards the Catholic Church, to which the vast majority of Irish-speakers belonged, its relationship with the language still remains something of an untold story, the best guide to which is still Ó Tuathaigh's article of 1986 referred to above, which covers the period up to 1850. The same author's study of Maynooth makes clear just how little Irish, even for simple cate-chetical purposes, was taught or used in the church's chief seminary. Two articles focus on the first professor of Irish in Maynooth, Paul O'Brien. Both Séamus Mac Gabhann and Diarmuid Ó Muirithe concentrate on the man rather than the institution, and explore his background in the folk culture of north Leinster. Two essays about the role of Irish in the early years of the Christian Brothers, by Liam P. Ó Caithnia and A.P. Caomhánach, can, in the absence of source material, offer little more than speculation.[51]

The most substantial and suggestive contribution relating to Irish in the Catholic Church is Tadhg Ó Dúshláine's survey of manuscript sermons, which discusses well over 120 examples from the nineteenth century.[52] This makes the sermon by far the most popular genre of prose composition as well as the type of formal discourse in Irish most frequently encountered by the general population (outside the very poorest), and many avenues of explora-tion are suggested by this material. They are relevant not only to Gaelic culture, but to the social history of Catholicism in general in this period. Debate on the so-called 'Devotional Revolution' has tended to concentrate on measurement of attendance at church services, ignoring for the most part the basic diffi-culties of a quantitative sociology of religion, and has consequently paid less attention to the content of those services. Also worth noting in this context are some studies of the religious material printed in Irish in large amounts during the first half of the nineteenth century. As well as the works by Malachy McKenna and myself cited above, William Mahon reproduces the entire text of a catechism used in Connaught, and supplies an excellent introduction. Elegies on two Munster priests were edited within a festschrift for Seán Ó Tuama, one from 1819 by Breandán Ó Buachalla, the other from 1864 by Seán Ua Súilleabháin.[53]

The present survey will not include studies of either antiquarian scholarship on Irish or individuals and organisations dedicated to its revival. The former is best seen as part of a broader English-language scholarship, while the latter, particularly the Gaelic League, belong more to the twentieth century. An exception has to be made, however, for an excellent collection of essays published to mark the bicentenary of the birth of Eugene O'Curry, an antiquarian scholar who was at the same time a product of west Clare Gaelic culture. There are studies of his song collecting by Breandán Ó Madagáin, his scholarly work in the Ordnance Survey and the Catholic University by Pádraig De Barra, Pádraig Ó Riain, Tadhg Ó Dúshláine and Art Ó Maolfabhail, and a lengthy poem in praise of Charles II by O'Curry edited by Liam P. Ó Murchú.[54] Some of this work has been summarised elsewhere in English by Nollaig Ó Muraíle.[55] Another great antiquarian scholar, John O'Donovan, was also the subject of a substantial article by Ó Muraíle, which presents an invaluable survey of all previous biographical treatments, as well as copious quotation from hitherto unused material.[56] Other works worth noting include Joep Leerssen's survey of early language revival organisations and fascinating portraits of two early revivalists, Thomas Swanton in west Cork and Patrick Carmody in Waterford.[57]

★   ★   ★

In conclusion, instead of attempting to sum up a historiography which in any case may not be a well-bounded, coherent unit of analysis, either in its content or in its chronological limits, it may be more useful to suggest a few directions for future research.

While the issue of the causes of language shift has been the subject of continuous discussion, this is much less true of the effects of the shift. With the principal exception of Lee, whose powerful short survey has been repeatedly referred to, writers tend not to discuss the subject explicitly, and it is not always clear whether they regard a particular language as a transparent window on a 'real' world – in which case language shift is not problematic but merely involves relabelling things – or as fundamental to the construction and understanding of that world – in which case it might constitute a radical reordering of perception - or have some intermediate position between these extremes. There has been no attempt in the 1990s, for example, to emulate the attempt of Miller, Boling and Doyle to characterise languages in nineteenth-century Ireland from the point of view of the Sapir–Whorf hypothesis, and to deduce worldview from syntax and verbal categories. That approach, while open to charges of circularity of argument, at least suggested a cultural characterisation of language shift.[58]

If there is an orthodox approach to this question, it is a tendency to equate the process of language shift with that of a more general acculturation or even to make the former a cause of the latter. Angela Bourke, for example, writes that 'rich resources of imagination, memory, creativity and commemoration were jettisoned when the Irish language and its traditions were denigrated and discarded'.[59] Similarly Declan Kiberd, in his discussion of Hyde's *Love Songs of Connaught*, presents the songs, and by extension the Irish language, as expressive of a direct sexuality as opposed to the 'Victorian prudery' of the English language. Consequently, when Fr Peter O'Leary and others objected to the content of the songs, this is treated as part of O'Leary's attempt at 'a translation of Victorian values into the Irish language'.[60] These types of polarities and explanatory schemas, while suggestive, do less than justice to the variety of Irish-language cultures. The printed religious literature and manuscript sermons of pre-Famine Munster were inculcating attitudes that were extremely 'respectable', even puritanical, and it would be more accurate to see the objections of O'Leary as the expression of a difference within Gaelic culture itself, between the attitudes of comfortable Irish-speaking Munster farmers and those of far poorer Connaught smallholders. Sexual discipline could and did exist in Irish, along with organised and orthodox religion, literacy, print culture, social welfare categories and other aspects of modernity.[61]

The challenge, in other words, is to give due causal weight to the process of language shift in nineteenth-century Ireland without making it equivalent to other forms of change that were intimately linked with it. A more satisfactory approach to the subject could proceed along at least two lines of inquiry, both of which would shed much light on the culture of nineteenth-century Ireland more generally. The first would focus, not on two separate languages, but on the ways in which they were both used simultaneously by individuals and groups. In sociolinguistic terms this involves an 'ethnography of speaking' in a profoundly, if momentarily, bilingual and diglossic society. (The main examples of such ethnography which appeared in the 1990s were by Flot and Neville, discussed above, while Dawson and Mac Gabhann gave a highly suggestive picture of a bilingual poetic and scribal culture.) To give an example, one central issue which has not yet been explored in detail is the use of Irish in law courts, particularly after the 1820s when, with the establishment of the Petty Sessions courts, access to litigation became widespread. While the language of the courts was English, plaintiffs, defendants and witnesses were allowed give evidence in Irish through an interpreter, even when they were not stricly monoglot, a right confirmed by the Queen's Bench in 1856. Moreover, in contrast to Wales, interpreters in Ireland were paid by the court rather than by the witness. Thus, the hegemony of English did not always hold sway. At the Galway Petty Sessions in April 1837, for example, a woman called Mary Flaherty, who sold cabbages in the town market, successfully prosecuted two men for abduction. She gave her evidence in Irish through an interpreter, successfully overcoming the double disadvantage of language and gender, and possibly that of social class as well.[62] At the other extreme, was the trial for the Maamtrasna murders in the 1880s, in which interpreting difficulties may well have contributed to a celebrated miscarriage of justice and the execution of a monolingual Irish-speaking defendant, Myles Joyce, who was probably innocent.[63]

The other line of inquiry would be to consider the impact of language shift in areas and phenomena which were not strictly linguistic. To illustrate this, we can consider one of the principal popular religious manifestations of the later part of the century, the Marian apparition in Knock, County Mayo, in 1879. Historians writing about the apparition have tended to focus on its coincidence with local famine and the early stages of the Land War, and on the reaction of the Catholic Church to it.[64] Looking at the dramaturgy of the event itself, however, something of an oddity appears. Irish Catholicism in this period was heavily influenced by France, with new religious orders in Ireland being often branches of French orders and with churches and convents importing their devotional objects and decor overwhelmingly from French manufacturers. Marian apparitions were also a strong feature of French devotion, with Lourdes in 1858 and La Salette in 1846 being among the best known and most influential. Both these apparitions followed a classic pattern, taking place in mountainous areas, with the Virgin Mary appearing to children, delivering a brief message and then disappearing. Most importantly, for our purposes, that message was delivered in the local language, Occitan (more precisely, Béarnais) and Franco-Provencal respectively.[65] In Knock, by contrast, the apparition was in a town, seen by a large group consisting mainly of adults, lasted for a few hours and was entirely silent. There was no message, either in Irish or English.

This peculiarity could well be explained, at least in part, by the linguistic situation. At a time of rapid language shift, it is likely that a group of visionaries who ranged in age from 6 to 75 would have had a variety of linguistic competences, making a common message unlikely. Moreover, while official Catholicism in France was often supportive of local languages, seeing them as barriers to the French-speaking secularism of the state, the Catholic Church in Ireland was much more hostile to Irish.[66] Indeed, some clerical supporters of La Salette and Lourdes took the fact that messages were given in a local language as proof of their authenticity. It is hard to imagine the Catholic clergy in Ireland, engaged in consolidating a form of orthodoxy in English at the expense of a range of frequently Irish-language local practices, reacting in the same way.

These are some of the ways in which a more satisfactory historiography of language in nineteenth-century Ireland might be written, one which would contain a more detailed and grounded exploration of language use and attitudes in practice, while at the same time enriched by comparative study of linguistic situations in Europe and elsewhere. Such a historiography would do justice to a society and a culture which, in its bilingualism and diglossia, contained a complex and rich range of cultural practices.

# CHAPTER 9

# Art History: Using the Visual

✳

*Fintan Cullen*

The nineteenth century has had a hard time gaining academic attention in Irish art historiography. Studies on the twentieth century and the contemporary lead in terms of the volume of material published,[1] while the eighteenth century has always attracted attention owing to the popularity of the Georgian phenomenon,[2] but it will perhaps come as a surprise to those outside art history that the nineteenth century has only recently been reassessed in terms of visual production. This was the century that fostered some of Ireland's most successful painters and sculptors, figures such as Daniel Maclise, John Henry Foley and the ever-popular Walter Osborne who travelled to France and embraced the *plein air* tendencies of the avant garde. The century also saw the establishment of Ireland's leading art institutions, most of which are still with us: the Royal Hibernian Academy and National Gallery of Ireland, both in Dublin, the Crawford Gallery in Cork and the Belfast City Art Gallery which later became the Ulster Museum.[3] The National College of Art and Design, although originally established in the eighteenth century, was, as John Turpin has shown,[4] extensively reorganised in the nineteenth century into the multi-layered entity that now occupies the site of a former distillery on Dublin's Thomas Street.

All the same, in recent decades the nineteenth century as a whole has been the subject of only one exhibition, a large survey curated by Cyril Barrett in Cork as part of Rosc 1971.[5] Incorporating Irish art productivity from the Romantic landscapes of James Arthur O'Connor to the genre watercolours of Jack Yeats, the show also included sculpture, medals, furniture and a section on Cork artists. As Barrett pointed out in the accompanying catalogue, this Cork display was the first exhibition on nineteenth-century Irish art since Hugh Lane's Irish art show at the London Guildhall in 1904[6] and nothing comparable has been put on in the ensuing thirty years. Is this a case of neglect or of changing interest?

An answer may be found in the change of emphasis from overall general views to specific studies on individual artists and, more recently, to thematic and/or contextual studies that have finally placed the study of art in the nineteenth century on something resembling a level playing field with other areas in cultural studies, most especially literature. This is not to bemoan the lack of survey-like exhibitions on Irish nineteenth-century material but to indicate where the work has been done, work that will be discussed in the following pages. But given the developments in the historiography, perhaps the time has come for another major exhibition of Irish nineteenth-century visual material so that we can critically reassess the productions of that period on the walls of public galleries.

As will be shown, the old certainties of the past, still trumpeted in that Cork Rosc exhibition of 1971, are no longer acceptable. A canon of great male artists who sought success in London and played significant roles in such august institutions as the Royal Academy of Arts, or of others who followed the avant garde trail to Grez-sur-Loing or Brittany: these are not the only narratives we have of Irish nineteenth-century achievement in the visual arts. Popular visual material, cartoons, reportage, portrait engravings, emblemata, etc., as well as exhibition histories, theoretical writings and arts and crafts initiatives, are all now gaining ground as legitimate areas for study. Just as Barrett's exhibition catalogue is no longer a satisfactory guide to the century, so too Anne Crookshank and the Knight of Glin's seminal survey of Irish painting, first published in 1978 and recently updated as *Ireland's Painters*, casts a rather conventional eye over the first hundred years of Union.[7] Their approach is artist-based and although revealing much needed biographical detail and informed views on authorship, *Ireland's Painters* leaves us with an incomplete view of how art survived the post 1801 constitutional situation.

## 'A NATIONALISTIC ART'

Ironically, it was the late Cyril Barrett who offered a new agenda four years after the Cork Rosc. In an important article in *Studies* in 1975,[8] he asked a vital question: was there 'a nationalistic art' in the nineteenth century? No longer were we asked to consider a litany of names and a catalogue of key works but rather we were asked to consider what actually was produced and why. On re-reading Barrett's article, one is frustrated by the often unanswered questions and the wild generalisations, but it has to be acknowledged that he showed that there was an alternative history to that of the successful Irish artists in London, as well as a cultural flip side to the production of myriad portraits of Lords Lieutenant and members of the aristocracy as revealed in Anne Crookshank and the Knight of Glin's 1969–70 exhibition *Irish Portraits 1660–1860*.[9] Concluding that there was a distinct absence of Irish 'nationalistic art' in the nineteenth century, Barrett offers an important explanation, courtesy of Charles Gavan Duffy, when he writes that 'it is safe to say that the failure to produce a body of extreme nationalistic art was . . . because there was no public demand for it'.[10] Barrett's article is short on in-depth analysis and rich on leading questions, but for the first time in recent Irish art historiography, vital issues regarding the relationship between the visual and the historical were being aired. A quarter of a century after Barrett's article, the key theme of a missing audience for Irish art in the nineteenth century is still in need of serious attention. In searching for an explanation for this missing audience, the literary theorist David Lloyd's discussion of the crisis of representation for the Irish novel in the early- to mid-nineteenth century offers some explanation for this missing audience and, more generally, for the absence of a 'national art'.[11] Ireland's unstable middle class, he claims, did not 'furnish representative figures', a vital ingredient of so many realistic novels in the century, and a 'struggle for hegemony' resulted amongst the people likely to form the novel's reading public. Lloyd's definition of the 'complex and shifting affiliations' of this class allows us to see parallels in the art-viewing public of the period.

It would be wrong to imply that Barrett's article did not have an immediate influence. One art historian did take up his challenge. In 1980, the late Jeanne Sheehy published her still invaluable *The Rediscovery of Ireland's Past: The Celtic Revival, 1830–1920*.[12] Inspired, as she says in the notes to that book, by Barrett's essay, her monograph on the Celtic Revival as illustrated in the visual arts and architecture, is a rich collection of blind alleys and unfulfilled dreams by a range of artists and patrons. The book casts a wide net over a hundred years of production and revealed for many, especially non-Irish Studies readers, the wealth of material pertaining to a nationalist ethos. Unfortunately, the book does not sufficiently establish connections between its material and the political and cultural preoccupations of the time. Empirical observations and wry comments mixed with colourful anecdotes often prevent us from fully engaging with the art and artefacts discussed.

Despite its shortcomings, Sheehy's book released the study of Irish art in the nineteenth century from the iron grip of the artist monograph. Although individual artists are discussed, *The Rediscovery of Ireland's Past* offered a healthy alternative to the concentration on artists' lives and the establishment of their œuvre which is still the main stay of far too many art historical studies. Moving on from Barrett's *Studies* article, Sheehy examined the connection between art production and national aspirations. This was a far cry from the grand survey of Irish art contemporaneously published by Crookshank and Glin in *Painters of Ireland*, which is basically an illustrated dictionary of Irish artists. Granted Crookshank and Glin's study goes beyond earlier reference material such as Walter Strickland's two-volume *Dictionary*,[13] by dividing the artists according to the traditional genres of landscape, portraiture, etc., but

*Painters of Ireland* is fundamentally driven by artists' lives and a chronological arrangement. It is thus not surprising to notice how studies of individual Irish artists, published in recent decades, still dominate Irish nineteenth-century art historiography. In the last quarter of a century, all of the following have been the subject of monographs or exhibition catalogues: Francis Danby, William Mulready, Daniel Maclise, James Arthur O'Connor, Roderic O'Conor, John Butler Yeats and Walter Osborne.[14]

Sheehy's study of the relationship between art and national fervour was a lone voice for much of the 1980s. One of the main reasons for that was the state of art historical education in Ireland, particularly at university level. The major changes occurring elsewhere in the study of art history took their time in reaching Ireland or in affecting the work of those active in the study of Irish visual material. The 'new' art history as it came to be called was a strongly Anglo-American affair that encouraged interdisciplinarity and a contextualisation of the discipline so as to go beyond the preciosity associated with connoisseurship.[15] The cautious approach to the discipline that dominated the study of art history in Ireland was perhaps not helped by the small number of academics in the field. The subject is only taught in three of the seven universities in the Republic (two in Dublin and the other in Cork) while of the various art colleges, Dublin's National College of Art and Design is the only one that teaches the history of art to degree level. In Northern Ireland, the subject is taught at the University of Ulster while encouraging signs emanate from the Queen's University at Belfast which recently appointed its first full-time art historian. Although most of these institutions include scholars active in nineteenth-century Irish studies, the productivity is still small. Equally, the study of historical material is not adequately assisted by the major art galleries that house the main collections of nineteenth-century Irish art. The National Gallery of Ireland prides itself on its rich display of Irish paintings and its incomparable collection of material relating to the Yeats family, but as an institution it needs to do far more to encourage the study of the Irish visual tradition. This may change with the opening of the new wing to house the Irish collection and with the eventual publication of the long awaited scholarly catalogues of the Irish paintings. Well-researched and instructive exhibitions have been mounted in the last 15 years or so on such themes as *The Irish Impressionists* (a misnomer but a useful pulling together of Irish artists who travelled to France in the late nineteenth century) and individual monographic shows have occurred on such painters as Nathaniel Hone, Frank O'Meara and Walter Osborne.[16] But the focus of too many of these shows has been on demonstrating, for blatant popular reasons, that Irish art and Irish artists were in touch with mainstream French avant garde developments. None of these exhibitions and their catalogues sufficiently addressed the home situation: themes such as the role of the visual in a country divided by land agitation and national preoccupations. This is in startling comparison with a country like Scotland whose National Galleries have, in recent years, mounted a number of important thematic exhibitions that have discussed the cultural history of the nation in a fashion seriously absent in Ireland.[17]

We had to wait until the turn of the Millennium to get a taste of the possibilities inherent in a well worked out and politically provocative exhibition on an Irish artist who can also be placed amidst the canon of artists who worked in France from the 1870s to well into the twentieth century. Niamh O'Sullivan's ground-breaking exhibition and catalogue on Aloysius O'Kelly (1853–1940s?), mounted at the Hugh Lane Municipal Gallery of Modern Art in Dublin from November 1999 to January 2000, indicates where the study of Irish nineteenth-century art history should be going.[18] Its subtitle informs us of its concerns: *Re-Orientations. Painting, Politics and Popular Culture.* O'Sullivan painstakingly pulled together a hitherto uncatalogued œuvre that ranges from drawings of evictions for the *Illustrated London News*, to oil paintings of robust Connemara peasants on the Atlantic seaboard to images of back street Cairo and later urban views of New York's East River. The full picture of a late nineteenth-century Irish artist is revealed, from hard-hitting commentary on the colonial condition to the artist as wanderer, a victim of the inevitable diaspora.

The recent exhibition on Aloysius O'Kelly is an exception. Political issues relating to the nineteenth century do not receive sufficient curatorial treatment in the national collections of Irish visual material. Recent commemorations such as the passing of the Act of Union and the Famine could all have occasioned thorough examinations of the visual dimensions to these events but unfortunately temporary exhibitions and accompanying catalogues have been few and far between.[19]

## VISUAL CULTURE *VS* ART HISTORY

Sheehy's *The Rediscovery of Ireland's Past* indicated the potential for cross-disciplinary study of Ireland in the nineteenth century. The challenge was not taken up again until 1990 when Trinity College, Dublin hosted the annual conference of the British Association of Art Historians. The conference demonstrated the potential within Irish art historiography for exploring such themes as colonialism, church control on art production, the denial of women and the inevitable preoccupations with national identity. The success of the conference was partly due to the fact that nothing like it had ever taken place before in the realm of art history in Ireland. Within a short period of time further challenges to the traditional art historiography began to appear. Texts such as Belinda Loftus's *Mirrors: William III and Mother Ireland* (1990), the late Adele Dalsimer's *Visualizing Ireland: National Identity and the Pictorial*

*Tradition* (1993) and Raymond Gillespie and Brian P. Kennedy's *Ireland. Art into History* (1994)[20] offered new ways of examining the nineteenth century. Some succeeded more than others. *Mirrors: William III and Mother Ireland* is, we are told on the back cover, the result of 15 years' research 'conducted both at street level, and in libraries, museums and galleries and archives stretching across Ireland and Britain'. The book has the appearance of having been written for the general reader and avoids, in the text at any rate, an over-abundance of distracting erudition. It should be read by all concerned with the representation of conflict, for what we have here is a revealing discussion of a much under-analysed subject.[21] The result is a readable, abundantly illustrated and challenging account of how the two sides of the Irish political divide have created icons and perpetuated mythologies of and about themselves since at least the seventeenth century.

The title of Loftus's book, however, is obscure and is not explained until the very end: 'Are William III and Mother Ireland' as representations of the two traditions 'condemned to be forever mirror-images locked into opposition'? Or 'can we gaze in the mirror together, and imagine our future faces'? Loftus suggests that if each side were to attempt to understand each other's traditions and respect the sense of difference, the divide may be weakened. Yet, divided in two, the book deals with each tradition separately. Loftus points out that 'nowhere in the Western world can one find a historical figure [such as William of Orange] playing such an important role in a current conflict'.[22] Her task is to ask why William lives on to this day. The second section is a study of how nationalist, and to a lesser extent loyalist, communities in Northern Ireland use female political symbols and why they do so in such different ways. The nineteenth century is revealed as a key period for the consolidation of the visual imagery associated with each tradition. It was during that century that the equestrian imagery of King Billy, what Loftus calls 'Horseback Heroes', came into its own after much dilution from such eighteenth-century originals as the former lead sculpture in Dublin's College Green (1701) or the oil painting by Benjamin West (1778). Equally, Mother Ireland, as a nationalist trope comes to full maturity in the statuary (for example John Hogan's marble monument to James Doyle, Bishop of Kildare and Leighlin, 1837–9, Carlow Cathedral) and popular imagery of the nineteenth century as she is represented as Hibernia and/or the Submissive Female. Here, Loftus tackles the nature of symbolic female representation in a way that goes beyond the mere listing of types and in a more demanding and precise fashion than Marina Warner in *Monuments and Maidens*.[23] She makes a good point about the irony of Ireland being dependent upon English visual culture in its creation in the nineteenth century of a nationalist image such as Maclise's *The Origins of the Harp* (1845).[24] The importance of Loftus's work and her follow-up volume on emblemata is that she convincingly conveys to the alert reader the importance of a total view of visual culture of the nineteenth or any other century.

The other two interdisciplinary books mentioned, Dalsimer's collection of essays and Gillespie and Kennedy's edited volume, are less successful but do suggest new areas for investigation. In their introductory essay, Adele Dalsimer and Vera Kreilkamp call for a more 'ambitious' analysis of the visual but it is a call frustrated by the lack of art historical skill in the assembled essays. Published as the outcome of an exhibition of Irish watercolours from the National Gallery of Ireland at Boston College, the essays offer an impressive line up. We have Margaret MacCurtain on the representation of the Irish colleen, Kevin O'Neill on 'the relationship between literary and visual forms of cultural and political expression', the late Maire de Paor on antiquarian artists and Nancy Netzer on drawings illustrating the Irish Industrial Exhibition of 1853. But the problem with the book is that the visual is not analysed in terms of its own discipline, too often it is discussed as an illustrative aid to history. This is also a problem in Gillespie and Kennedy's collection. Both books are ostensibly far more interesting ventures in Irish visual historiography than the factually inclined survey. However, neither lives up to the somewhat ambitious introductions. In *Art into History* the editors write as if they themselves have discovered the potential of visual culture for historical insight and wish now to reveal their discovery to the world of Irish Studies. Although reference is made in the notes to Simon Schama and Francis Haskell, the problem with this compilation is that it lacks any unifying theoretical approach. The range of material discussed is wide, with the nineteenth century dominating much of the focus of the 13 chapters. The editors erroneously claim that the book looks to wider areas than traditional art history has heretofore; the best essays are by art historians whom one could truthfully place in the traditionalist camp, while the less successful essays demonstrate a serious misuse of visual material. As an example of the former, Alistair Rowan, an architectural historian, offers us a well-informed discussion of denominational distinctions that differentiate Irish church buildings in the Victorian period. A far weaker essay by the historian Fergus O'Ferrall discusses the representation of Daniel O'Connell. In many ways this piece points out the failures of the enterprise. O'Ferrall's essay does little to extend our knowledge of the power of visual imagery to influence social or political thinking. It is quite probable that many of the portraits of the Liberator did just that, but O'Ferrall is so unable to express how an image 'works' that his essay becomes a mere listing of portraits that leaves us still indebted to the National Library of Ireland's dry but unanecdotal *Catalogue of Irish Portraits*.[25] Context may be everything to the two editors, but, one has to ask, what context? Certainly not the context of visual language.

The use by historians of visual material relating to the nineteenth century has increased dramatically in the last decade but not always to the point of furthering our understanding of the imagery concerned. A quick overview of its use since 1989 will suffice. That year saw the publication of *The Oxford Illustrated History of Ireland* and volume 5 in the series *A New History of Ireland*, also from Oxford, dealing with the period 1801–70; volume 6, which covers 1870–1921, appeared in 1996.[26] Other publications in recent years which give prominence to Irish imagery as a resource are Peter Gray's *The Irish Famine* and the highly successful journal *History Ireland*.[27] Roy Foster's well chosen selection of paintings and drawings, magazine illustration, cartoons and architectural photography in his chapter on 'Ascendancy and Union' in *The Oxford Illustrated History of Ireland* conveys a welcome sensitivity to appearance and purpose. Although the images are rarely discussed in the text, Foster supplies each one with a thoughtful caption that integrates them into the narrative. It is important to be told that Haverty's full length portrait of O'Connell as the great liberal statesman 'hangs in the Reform Club, London', while the superb photographs of Portlaw, County Waterford from the collection of the National Library of Ireland tell us a great deal about 'planning' and local economies.[28]

The two relevant volumes of *A New History of Ireland* are accompanied by over a hundred pages of illustrations. Again, cartoons, paintings, photographs of buildings and popular illustrations are asked to comment on the period but the interpretation is left largely to the reader. Apart from a group of paintings by the likes of Maclise, Osborne and O'Meara and buildings by such architects as William Burgess (St Finn Barre's Cathedral, Cork) and E. W. Pugin and G. C. Ashlin (St Colman's Cathedral, Cobh), which are discussed by Cyril Barrett and Jeanne Sheehy in two excellent chapters in vol. 6,[29] the vast majority of illustrations act as a silent resource. Surprisingly this works. Unlike what occurs in Peter Gray's book on the Famine, the reader is allowed to consider the 'state' of nineteenth-century Ireland by comparing, on the same page, an *Illustrated London News* sketch of a wretched Connemara cabin (1846) with an engraving of a decade earlier showing the over-the-top gothic gateway to the demesne of Markree, County Sligo.[30] Having earlier read Cormac Ó Gráda's densely written chapter on 'Poverty, population and agriculture, 1801–45',[31] one is fully equipped to make much of this intriguing juxtaposition.

Turning to Peter Gray's *The Irish Famine* one is faced with a frequent problem bemoaned by art historians: the uncommented use of art as illustration. Gray's profusely illustrated book is aimed at the popular market and again a vast array of 'Irish' imagery is used. We jump from *Punch* vignettes to the inevitable *Illustrated London News* to more considered works by such painters as Erskine Nicol, George Frederic Watts and Daniel MacDonald, but we are never asked to analyse the artistic or cultural significance of these images. This lazy misuse of art and popular imagery as mere illustration is understandable in the context of the Thames and Hudson series of which

Gray's text is part: it appears in a series that offers comparable, pocket-size accounts of *D-Day*, *Ancient Rome* and *The Incas*. But if Irish imagery of the nineteenth century is to be taken seriously it has to be allowed to rise above this type of treatment. [32] Historians, in particular, need to confront the visual in a more considerate fashion and accept that it is as much part of the cultural mix of a period as contemporary diaries and other text-based sources. Part of the blame for the misuse or silent abuse of Irish visual material in studies of the nineteenth century may also lie with art historians. As a discipline, art history within Irish studies needs to be more imaginative in showing how images can be discussed contextually; it needs to move beyond the preoccupation with artists' lives and the identification of a corpus of works; it needs to explore more challenging methodologies. [33]

In a word, what the study of art history in Irish Studies needs is 'debate'. An example of a recent scholarly disagreement will indicate my point and may suggest ways in which the study of Irish nineteenth-century imagery can enter the mainstream of Irish scholarship. The example is the interpretation of *Punch* cartoons by Lewis Perry Curtis, in his seminal studies on the subject, *Anglo-Saxons and Celts: A Study of Anti-Irish Prejudice in Victorian England* (1968), followed a few years later by *Apes and Angels: The Irishman in Victorian Caricature* and the ensuing criticisms of his views by such fellow historians as Sheridan Gilley and Roy Foster. [34]

Since their appearance nearly thirty years ago, Curtis's two books have greatly influenced the general view of the Irish in the Victorian period to the extent that a highly negative image is dominant. Others have followed his line[35] and Curtis's analysis of the development of a simianised Celt within the pages of London journals such as *Punch* and *The Tomahawk*, as well as in such American publications as *Puck* and *Harper's Weekly*, has become an invaluable guide to an episode in the history of prejudice. A counter attack in 1978 by Sheridan Gilley questioned Curtis's dependence on racial prejudice as the key to the negative representation of the Irish, claiming that anti-Irishness came to the fore only in relation to specific religious and political issues. [36] Roy Foster concurred with Gilley and the latter's opinion of Curtis that he was the product of a misguided 1960s Kennedy liberalism. Foster argues that *Punch* did not single out the Irish for racial abuse but mocked all: 'its representations of the Irish [were not] very pronouncedly different in physiognomy from the representations of English plebians'. [37] Foster then goes on to supply us with a well argued insight into the individuals behind *Punch*.

Counter-reactions to Gilley and Foster's revisionist critiques of Curtis were soon to follow. Luke Gibbons in *The Field Day Anthology of Irish Writing* suggested that Gilley's criticisms of Curtis were 'hampered by an assumption that racial stereotyping necessarily entails hostility and repulsion: "benevolent" stereotypes that depicted the imaginative Celt as complementary to

Anglo-Saxon rationality served colonial domination far more effectively than crude forms of debasement, since they justified the continuation of "the Union" between Britain and Ireland'.[38] More recently, Curtis himself has replied at length to both Gilley and Foster. His 1997 revised edition of *Apes and Angels* not only makes his book available to a new generation but allows him space to fully confront his critics. Responding to what he calls his 'Anglocentric or revisionist' critics, Curtis claims that a full refutation of their opinion on his work 'would run to too many pages and sound much too defensive'. Yet what we get is a formidable twelve pages of text and over forty endnotes that deal almost exclusively with Gilley and Foster's comments![39]

One might think that Curtis's defence, which, despite his claim, is exactly what those twelve pages are all about, would bring this quarter of a century old discussion to a conclusion. But no, Curtis's enthusiasm for his subject is such that in his revised edition, we get a fascinating array of new material as well as an extension of his discussion into the twentieth century. Looking back over Curtis's work, one has to credit him with releasing a vital subject for study. As listed in my accompanying endnotes many have followed him in studying racially motivated cartoons in *Punch*, while others such as Niamh O'Sullivan have expanded the subject by examining in depth the works of one illustrator, Aloysius O'Kelly, who features briefly in Curtis's book.[40] *Apes and Angels* legitimised the study of popular illustration in relation to nineteenth-century Ireland and we must be grateful for that.[41] What now needs to be done is to integrate the study of this popular form of illustration with other visual imagery such as high art painting and develop a more rounded picture of how nineteenth-century Ireland was represented.[42]

THE FUTURE

It is through such spats that art history in the context of Irish nineteenth-century studies will strengthen. At present there is not enough of a dialogue going on between those who work on visual material and those in other areas of research. Equally, there is still too much of a division between those art historians concerned with fact and those exploring new methodologies with which to examine the past.[43] The Society for the Study of Nineteenth-Century Ireland, the much celebrated colonialism conferences hosted by the National University of Ireland at Galway and similar academic groups need to encourage more art historical involvement just as art historians need to move beyond the secure boundaries of their own subject organisations. The nineteenth century is a mine of still under-explored areas for visual examination. One major area in need of attention is the relationship between artistic production and Ireland's colonial situation in the nineteenth century. With the exclusion of my own work and the recent publications on Aloysius O'Kelly by Niamh O'Sullivan, this area of investigation has been the preserve of literary and social historians. We now need more art historians or visual culturalists involving themselves in this area. The work of a theorised interdisciplinarian like Luke Gibbons is instructive in this regard. From the late 1980s with his perceptive comments on the relationship between landscape and Irish romanticism in the nineteenth century (all a prelude to a discussion of Irish cinema) to his 1998 analysis of Maclise's *The Installation of Captain Rock*, Gibbons has seriously radicalised the examination of Irish visual imagery.[44] In the immediate context of art history, Gibbons's gift is to refuse to accept the standardised definitions of such pillars of the academic visual tradition as classical landscape or history painting; instead he subjects them to the peculiar circumstances of colonial Ireland and thus challenges the reader to interrogate the nature of those genres.

Other areas in need of extensive exploration include the cultural politics of exhibitions and display[45] as well as Irish theoretical writings on art. Some years ago, Adele Dalsimer and Vera Kreilkamp rightly lamented the lack of a penetrating sociological analysis of Irish art production as Andrew Hemingway had supplied for London in *Landscape Imagery and Urban Culture in Early Nineteenth-Century Britain*, but at least the raw materials are now becoming available.[46] My own *Sources in Irish Art: A Reader* will hopefully remind readers of the writings of an array of individuals such as Sydney Owenson (Lady Morgan) and Thomas Davis which still need careful analysis.[47] Many aspects of Ireland's nineteenth-century visual history have not been touched on in this essay, the most obvious are architecture, photography, craft and design as well as sculpture. Architectural studies are in a relatively healthy state, greatly aided by the excellent work of the Irish Architectural Archive.[48] The shameful lack of critical studies on Irish photography in the nineteenth century will hopefully decrease now that that medium has its own dedicated archive in Dublin.[49] The history of nineteenth-century design is dominated by studies on the Celtic Revival/Arts and Crafts Movement and thanks to the work of such scholars as Nicola Gordon Bowe it is one of the few areas in Irish visual studies that has shown the way in making important intellectual connections with other neighbouring cultures such as Scotland.[50] The history of sculpture is also slowly gaining ground in research, in particular the role of public sculpture and the politics of memorials.[51] An important aspect of some of the work being done on sculpture is an examination of the plethora of nineteenth-century feminine representations of Ireland, be it in such prominent sites as around the drum of Foley's O'Connell Monument in Dublin or in the domestic sentimentality of Belleek pottery.[52]

Despite the hive of activity in diaspora studies, the migration of Irish artists demands closer attention. Niamh O'Sullivan's work on Aloysius O'Kelly indicates the large reservoir of material that exists about Irish artists abroad.

Too often the concentration has been on artists who succeeded in London or immersed themselves in avant-garde circles in France but in the light of the O'Kelly revelations, more is needed on Irish-born artists who emigrated to the United States or elsewhere.[53] We need to know more about the creative diaspora and the possibility of a lingering Irish identity among such success stories in American nineteenth-century art as, for example the *trompe l'œil* painter, William Michael Harnett (1848–92). Hartnett's family emigrated from Clonakilty, Co. Cork in 1849 but almost forty years later, his *Still Life – Violin and Music (Music and Good Luck)* (1888, Metropolitan Museum of Art, New York), shows a violin with a sheet of music from Moore's fourth volume of *Irish Melodies*, 'By That Lake, Whose Gloomy Shore'.[54]

The only thing that will improve and develop the study of nineteenth-century Irish art is dialogue, but that dialogue needs to extend beyond the obvious interdisciplinary demands of the academy. It is all very simple. First of all we need increased dialogue between university-based scholars from art history with colleagues from such disciplines as literature, history and critical theory. Secondly, we need increased dialogue between all such university-based scholars and museum and gallery curators. Only then will we get the books, articles and exhibitions that will examine the nineteenth century in a mature and challenging way.

# CHAPTER 10

# Musicology

✳

*Harry White*

## INTRODUCTION

Since its inception as a formal mode of scholarly discourse in the mid-nineteenth century, musicology has been characterised by successive transformations of style, technique and focus. These transformations are themselves expressive of the habitual (and fruitful) dependence of musicology on a host of neighbouring discourses, many of which have shaped and even pre-determined its ability to countenance and absorb the phenomenon of music itself. The reception of music in European culture, for example, certainly insofar as its systematic investigation and recovery are concerned, depended in the first instance on models of German philology and art history which imbued the processes of *Musikwissenschaft* with the spirit and demeanour of scholarly positivism. The main business of German musicology in the nineteenth century was in fact the scientific recovery of music itself, in which problems of transmission, archival investigation and editorial recension almost completely eclipsed other considerations, such as reception history and criticism. While German musicology gave every appearance of excluding such considerations from its purview (if only because these concerns were simultaneously addressed in aesthetics and the philosophy of history), the pursuit of musicology in other European countries and in North America sustained this commitment to archival recovery and notational exactitude, at least in the first instance.[1]

It is not my purpose here to explain the dependence of musicology on philological and archival models of investigation, but rather to emphasise that such models can only flourish where a plenitude of actual music survives. Put plainly, the prior existence of music as a central expression of European culture, or even as an 'imaginary museum of musical works', has determined the models of thought by which it has been received and understood.[2] North American musicology, which until recently has sustained this preoccupation with the European musical art work, represents a confirmation that 'the music historian focuses first and foremost on works of music: these are what he surveys'.[3]

This formulation, however, is unlikely to work in a context where the musical work is in scant supply, or where the definition of what constitutes such a work is a permanent cause for dispute. There are essentially five dominant modes of musicological discourse which prevail in the reception of European art music at the beginning of the twenty-first century, but not all of them are easily applied to music in Ireland. I have already identified the first of these as philological: the others may with equal brevity be nominated as generic, narrative, critical and cultural.

If the recovery and transmission of the musical work in European musicology depends on philology, the study and classification of individual works in terms of genre and style likewise depend on art history. Art history also provides a model of thought for narrative modes of music history, in which the genesis and evolution of style are more or less integrated into a wider context which takes account (sometimes cautiously) of the history of music as a history of ideas originating not in the music itself, but in the political, social and even cultural circumstances which bring this music into being. Anglo-American musicology has more recently argued the case for moving beyond these three models in favour of a critical re-engagement with the musical work itself in terms which respond to the work as a self-standing object and as a matrix of extra-musical ideas.[4]

What all of these models share is an underlying assumption about the substantive presence of the musical work. At one extreme, the hermetic condition of analysis removes the musical work from any consideration of history, so that the autonomy of the musical object (itself a nineteenth-century construct) remains absolute. At the other extreme, the musical work is subsumed to the point where it becomes either an object of deconstruction or a metanarrative of social and cultural history. But in either case, the claims of music remain paramount, simply because the music itself is there.[5]

When the music is not 'there', when music is an elusive or fragmentary phenomenon, another model of musicological discourse is required. In oral (or non-literate) musical cultures, even when these are very strong, the resolution of music into incomplete notational forms will not necessarily accommodate such music to modes of discourse devised in the first place for the art music tradition. In any case the history of such music requires a fundamentally different approach.[6]

So too does the history of music in Ireland. It is a striking feature of much (if not all) of the work to be surveyed in this chapter that it is in the main preoccupied with aspects of music history other than the music itself: music education, organology (the history of musical instruments), music and the

Roman Catholic church, music and nationalism, and so on. Even within the domain of so-called 'folk' music, the emphasis is on the provenance of sources, rather than on any intrinsic assessment of or aesthetic engagement with the musical work. In short, the model of musicological discourse which most sensitively accommodates music in Ireland is a cultural model. By 'cultural model' I mean an integrated discourse which apprehends music in Ireland in terms of Irish culture generally, or more narrowly defined, in terms of the immediate context in which music functioned (as in: the use of music in Irish education, the quest for sources of folk music, the phenomenon of music as an expression of nationalism, and so on).

Some years ago, writing about music in Ireland in the nineteenth century, I observed that a defining feature of that music was that it could 'nourish every condition except its own'.[7] I meant by that remark that the symbolic resonances of music in Irish culture were much richer than the thing itself. Music could and did act as a powerful agent of political change, as a symbol of dispossession, as an unmistakable expression of colonial and nationalist ideologies and as a brilliantly deployed image of cultural regeneration, above all in the Celtic Revival. But the contrast between this symbolic fecundity and the impoverished state of musical infrastructures (to say nothing of the repeated aesthetic failure to create a durable mode of art music) was drastic indeed during the same period. To understand this contrast is to understand the complex reception history of music in Ireland after the Act of Union. One could say that in the nineteenth century the *idea* of music was a vital element in the protean condition of Irish culture, whereas the *expression* of music was not. But even this generalisation is prone to serious modification, especially given the recovery of the ethnic tradition after the Famine, even as art music lapsed into silence.

In the survey of research which follows here, I have not attempted to impose this reading of Irish cultural history (and the place of music therein) on the work of individual authors, other than to draw directly from their findings in support of my own conclusions. In a country where *any* kind of systematic musicology was extremely rare before the mid-1980s, it is astonishing and immensely encouraging to find that within the past ten years so much work has been undertaken on the music of this period.

Writing about the state of musicology in Ireland in 1988, I remarked that a significant showing had yet to be made in nineteenth-century studies, a remark that required radical amendment as of 2001.[8] The monographs, series, edited volumes and collections devoted to music in Ireland which have appeared since the late 1980s not only permit musicology to figure for the first time in a publication such as this, but prove beyond doubt that the practice of musicology itself is now a securely established part of Irish studies in the early twenty-first century.

## SERIES, EDITED VOLUMES AND COLLECTIONS

The series of books, Irish Musical Studies, was established in 1990 with a volume entitled *Musicology in Ireland*, edited by Gerard Gillen and Harry White.[9] This book, along with the others which followed it, was intended to provide for the first time a venue for the presentation of musical scholarship which had begun to engage musicologists throughout the 1980s. Although its address on nineteenth-century Ireland was initially tentative, the series as a whole and *Musicology in Ireland* as an individual publication reflect the growth of research in this area over the past decade. Two essays from the first volume, Hugh Shields's 'The history of *The Lass of Aughrim*' and Barra Boydell's 'The flageolet in Ireland', attest to that interdependent condition of music in Ireland to which I have alluded here. The Shields essay is (partly) an exercise in textual criticism which traces the sources of *The Lass of Aughrim* from its origins in eighteenth-century Scotland, through the ballad tradition in nineteenth-century Ireland, to its 'transposition' in James Joyce's story, 'The Dead'. The process by which a Scottish ballad, re-texted and re-contextualised in nineteenth-century Ireland, is absorbed into Joyce's fiction (where it functions both musically and verbally as an iconic agent of remembrance and felt life), is emblematic of a more general movement discernible in Irish cultural history. The pattern by which music in Ireland in the nineteenth century is rehoused and creatively re-deployed in Irish fiction, poetry and drama, is in striking contrast to the afterlife of traditional music in other European countries. We do not find *The Lass of Aughrim* re-emerging as the slow movement of a romantic symphony, but as a vital trope of regret in modernist fiction.[10]

Barra Boydell's scrutiny of the Dublin music trade in the first three decades of the nineteenth century directs our attention towards that vast undergrowth of amateur music making which still awaits research (and not just in Ireland). Boydell restricts himself to a technical description of the flageolet and examines its repertory by means of the collections and arrangements published for the instrument in Dublin and London. The instrument makers, publishers and extant repertory identified by Boydell represent 'only the smallest fraction of the music published at the time'. This being the case, we are prompted to think about the sheer proliferation of music publishers, tutors, collections, instrument makers – in short the music trade – which flourished and then faded in Dublin in the first half of the nineteenth century. Is it fair to suggest that this abundance was diminished by the increased polarisation of art and ethnic music as the century wore on?

Four essays in *Music and the Church* (1993), the second volume of Irish Musical Studies (also edited by Gillen and White), considerably advance the scrutiny of music in nineteenth-century Ireland, and two of them prefigure monographs which are substantially concerned with the same period. Joseph

Ryan – whose work is considered more extensively below – opens new ground with 'Assertions of distinction: the modal debate in Irish music'; Gerard Gillen contributes to the organology of nineteenth-century Ireland with an essay on 'William Telford and the Victorian organ in Ireland'; Nóirin Ní Riain identifies several important sources of sacred song in the ethnic tradition in 'The nature and classification of traditional religious songs in Irish' and the present writer assesses the writings of Heinrich Bewerunge (with a catalogue of Bewerunge's works by Nicholas Lawrence) in 'Towards a history of the Cecilian movement in Ireland'.

Ryan's essay is a vital one in several respects: it advances for the first time a history of Irish musical ideas which belongs to the nineteenth century and which was to endure well into the twentieth. Drawing especially on the writings of James Hardiman (1831), Eugene O'Curry (1862), Michael Conran (1846), James Culwick (1887), Richard Henebry (1903 and 1928), Heinrich Bewerunge (1903) and Carl Gilbert Hardebeck (1905), Ryan discusses the formation and development of modal perception in Irish music which he interprets principally as an attempt to integrate the provenance of Gaelic musical culture with the claims of nationalism and, *inter alia*, the intervallic structures of Gregorian chant. The result is a compelling and hitherto unresearched admixture of technical comment and outright ideology (particularly with regard to Conran and Henebry) in which the dim traces of antiquarianism are eclipsed by a vigorous admixture of musical theory and nationalist propaganda. The sheer identification of these musical sources represents a significant step in the recovery of Irish musical thought in the nineteenth century.

Gillen's essay on William Telford is of inherent interest to anyone concerned with the long and brilliant history of organ building, a subject which transcends nineteenth-century Ireland and which may at first glance appear to be of rather more relevance to the history of musical instruments. But in fact the presence of Telford, the international fame of his instruments and the long tenure of his (family) firm in Dublin (1834–1932) are indeed part of the rich if neglected fabric of musical life in Ireland. Gillen's technical (and admirably lucid) descriptions of Telford's instruments, together with the references that he makes to a strong tradition of organ building in Dublin in the nineteenth century, restore much detail to a long-neglected aspect of Irish musical life. This investigation of Telford's achievement – the sheer presence, design and technical capacity of the instruments attest to a vital culture of performance – implicitly argues the case for further research into the history of instrument manufacture in Ireland during this period.

In a detailed survey of religious music in the ethnic tradition in Ireland, Nóirin Ní Riain includes material from the Hoffmann (1877) and Stanford (1897) editions of Petrie's *Ancient Music of Ireland* (1855) which at once confirms the use of traditional melodies for religious texts and the general absence nevertheless of sources for this repertory. The apparent lack of a vernacular hymnology in Ireland (in the Roman Catholic tradition) until late in the century might seem a surprising one, given the intimate proximity of ethnic culture and religious belief. Ní Riain concludes that this absence is 'bound to the social history of the people' (p.206). Nevertheless, it may be that further research into the whole question of church music in Ireland could yield significant evidence of the kind of textual and musical cross-fertilisation which Ní Riain has discovered in early printed sources of the twentieth century.

Few figures in the history of music in Ireland during the nineteenth century possessed ideological zeal and technical expertise in equal measure, but Heinrich Bewerunge was one of them. Although Bewerunge's career was intimately connected to the Cecilian movement in Ireland (see below), it deserves to be reckoned on its own terms, given the extent of Bewerunge's scholarly prowess as a critic of plainchant and his trenchant position with regard to the aesthetics of (then) contemporary church music. 'Towards a History of the Cecilian Movement in Ireland' bears the more informative subtitle 'An Assessment of the Writings of Heinrich Bewerunge (1862–1923), With a Catalogue of his Publications and Manuscripts'. Although he cannot be properly understood in isolation from his Irish colleagues and predecessors in the reanimation of Catholic church music, Bewerunge's own writings, and the many controversies over musical style in which he involved himself, comprise a distinctive episode in the cultural history of music in Ireland. His forceful personality threw many issues in late nineteenth-century music into sharp relief: the provenance and potential of traditional music; the teaching of music in schools; the aesthetics of Renaissance and Counter-Reformation polyphony; the claims of Gaelic revivalism and its relevance to art music. As a musicologist, he combined a pragmatic (and astringent) expertise in the practice of plainchant with a sophisticated and uniquely informed range of techniques in textual scholarship. His settings and arrangements of Palestrina, included here in an excellent catalogue by Nicholas Lawrence, attest to his outstanding musicianship.

*Music and Irish Cultural History*, the third volume of the Irish Musical Studies series, appeared in 1995. Despite its title, only two essays in the volume, 'Nationalism and Irish music' by Joseph Ryan and Harry White's 'Music and the Irish literary imagination' are directly relevant to this report. (Because both subjects are more extensively treated by the same authors in monographs discussed later in this survey, they are not considered here.)

The publication of volumes 4 and 5 of Irish Musical Studies in 1996 marked a significant event in Irish musicology. *The Maynooth International Musicological Conference 1995: Selected Proceedings Parts One and Two*, edited by Patrick F. Devine and Harry White, runs to some 850 pages (in itself the largest single musicological publication to have appeared from an Irish press to date) and represents the first such gathering of musicologists to take place in the history of the state. Of the 57 papers published in these *Proceedings*, only five are directly concerned with music in nineteenth-century Ireland, but each of them is strongly suggestive of topics for future research.

Colette Moloney's 'Style and repertoire in the Gaelic harp tradition: evidence from the Bunting manuscripts and prints' offers a vital advance in the study of source transmission from the late eighteenth to the early nineteenth centuries. Moloney's scrutiny of Bunting's manuscripts in particular affords a detailed taxonomy of ornamentation and graces which Bunting's prints do not promptly disclose. Manuscript source study of this kind is comparatively commonplace in European musicology, but the kind of close reading that Moloney provides is rare in the domain of traditional music. As a mediator between two traditions, Edward Bunting was exercised by the problems of adapting western notation to Gaelic harp music, and Moloney sensitively records the processes by which he sought to notate and classify the music which he heard at the Belfast Harp Festival of 1792.

Barry Cooper's 'Beethoven's folksong settings as sources of Irish folk music' opens with the arresting sentence: 'It is remarkable that Beethoven composed more folksong settings than any other genre, and that more of them are Irish than any other nationality.' (p. 65) Although Cooper argues persuasively that the versions set by Beethoven 'deserve attention as a significant source for Irish folk music, providing information about some of the variants circulating in Ireland at the turn of the 19th century' (p. 77), his controversial suggestion that 'for Irish musicians [Beethoven's] fusion of styles resolves the dichotomy of resisting musical parochialism on the one hand and European cultural hegemony on the other' (p. 78), is one which is likely to invite sharp disagreement among musicologists, Irish or otherwise. Nevertheless, Cooper's expertise as a textual critic and the whole thrust of his paper are strongly suggestive of a more fundamental study of 'Ireland' as a musical idea in the European art tradition.[11] Whether or not we accept his assertion that 'only in Beethoven's settings . . . the rich musical potential of these Irish melodies is properly revealed . . . it takes a Beethoven to demonstrate what fine melodies they are' (p. 80), his reading of Beethoven's engagement with Irish music deserves to be more widely emulated.

Barra Boydell's 'The iconography of the Irish harp as a national symbol' is another paper which breaks new ground: musical iconography is itself a comparatively new discipline within the folds of musicology, and one which is of significant potential for music in Ireland. Boydell traces the strong associations between the harp and Ireland as an iconic emblem that was current at least by the end of the fifteenth century. In the early nineteenth century, its use by the United Irishmen not only as a symbol but also as a metaphor has been investigated by Helen Thuente among others (notably with regard to its visual and verbal presentation in ballad collections, and its prominence in Thomas Moore as the pre-eminent symbol of an Ireland free from colonial domination). Boydell, in this paper, is able to trace the revival, modification and dissemination of the harp as a political symbol throughout the nineteenth century in strictly visual terms (paintings, coinage, illustrations), a phenomenon which closely matches the symbolic status of Irish music itself during the same period. The ubiquitous presence of the harp in Irish visual materials fortifies the argument that music in Ireland was more successful as a suggestive or symbolic force than it was as an actual aesthetic presence.

In 'Dublin musical societies, 1850–1900', Ita Beausang, with characteristic concision and accuracy (her interventions in Irish musicology are all too rare), documents the plenitude of amateur musical societies in Dublin which, among other things, enabled the art music tradition to survive the cultural polarisation which tended so strikingly to hinder it throughout the nineteenth century.[12] Beausang points to the relationship between the Antient Concerts Society and the founding of the Irish Academy of Music in 1848, an initiative directly attributable to members of the society and in particular Joseph Robinson. The Philharmonic Society, likewise, maintained a vital presence for music in Dublin, notably in its performances of Beethoven (including the first performance in Ireland of the Choral Symphony, in 1856), notwithstanding the general perception, late in the century, of stagnation and limited opportunity. (This apathy was summarised, as Beausang demonstrates, by Bernard Shaw's scathing commentary on musical life in Dublin at the close of the century). The *ad hoc* nature of such musical associations silently attests to the impoverished condition of more durable infrastructures which might have overcome the tendency to duplicate already slender musical resources along denominational lines.[13]

Bennett Zon's paper on 'The revival of plainchant in the Roman Catholic Church in Ireland, 1777–1858: some sources and their commerce with England' is remarkable for its identification of Irish sources for the promotion of plainchant (and thereby Roman Catholicism) hitherto unknown to historians of music in Ireland. Noting the Jacobite tendencies of such publications, Zon investigates the role of the *Dublin Review*, which he describes as 'an organ for the promotion of plainchant' and church apologetics generally. The contribution of periodical literature (especially those long reviews so characteristic of Dublin magazines throughout the nineteenth century) to an understanding of the perception of music in Ireland richly repays the kind of scrutiny which Zon brings to it in this paper.

The seventh volume of Irish Musical Studies, *A Historical Anthology of Irish Church Music,* is edited by Gerard Gillen and Andrew Johnstone and was published in 2001. This book derives in part from a suggestion made in the afterword to the second volume of the series, namely that a modern edition which anthologised the style of Roman Catholic and Protestant church music in Ireland would considerably improve our grasp of this repertory as it is represented in extant sources. For the purposes of this survey, two features of *A Historical Anthology of Irish Church Music* are especially important. The first is that the extensive introduction to the anthology (pp. 13–39) identifies many hitherto neglected or little-noticed publications of Irish church music in the nineteenth century, together with important contemporary works of criticism and reference which deal with this topic, notably by W. H. Grindle, Kieran Daly, Barra Boydell, Patrick Brannon, Bennet Zon and other authors already considered in the present review. Gillen and Johnstone pay particular attention to the compositions of John Stevenson (1762–1833), John Smith, (1795–1861), Robert Prescott Stewart (1825–94) and George William Torrance (1835–1907) in the Protestant repertory, and acknowledge by contrast the almost complete dearth of a corresponding tradition of Roman Catholic music until very late in the century. For its bibliographical thoroughness alone, this introduction justifies the entire enterprise of the anthology and prefigures the exemplary editorial techniques applied to the repertory which is the book's mainstay.

The second feature is, of course, the generous representation of the music itself. This is impeccably edited and generously annotated. The inclusion of works by Stevenson, Robinson and Bewerunge next to each other, for example, gives a material notion of the scope and expressive reach of Irish church music in the nineteenth century. Just as importantly (because of the excellence of the commentaries attached to each item), the reader can see how certain parts of the repertory attained a quasi-liturgical permanence in the services especially at the two Dublin cathedrals.

Beyond *Irish Musical Studies*, music in nineteenth-century Ireland has been notably well served in four recent publications, each of which differently illustrates models of research which might be more widely applied in future projects.

*To Talent Alone: The Royal Irish Academy of Music 1848–1998*, edited by Richard Pine and Charles Acton, appeared in 1998. As a collaborative enterprise which enlists the expertise of several musicologists (including Richard Pine, Derek Collins, Jeremy Dibble and Axel Klein), *To Talent Alone* brilliantly realises its ambition to be a contextual study which places the Academy at the centre of Irish musical life during the past 150 years. In his introduction, Richard Pine writes of its coming into existence at a time when Ireland was struggling with the catastrophe of the Famine and undergoing a transformation of its political and social structures. Although he makes the case for a broad-based constituency of educational ideas on which the institution was founded, his attempts to relate the enterprise of systematic music education to that of Young Ireland do not strike one as absolutely persuasive, if only because of Young Ireland's explicit hostility to the European aesthetic in musical affairs. The Anglo-Irish complexion of the Academy (traces of which persisted well into the twentieth century) could be read alternatively as a 'benevolent' attempt to transcend the boundaries of a largely Protestant middle-class in the interests of disseminating music in Ireland. Nevertheless, Pine is scrupulously fair to both sides of this argument and the breadth of his research – as in his account of parliamentary lobbying in favour of the academy – is extremely impressive. The use of the Academy's own archives and contemporary newspapers throughout the book is a feature which results in much new information about the status and perception of music in the last century and a half.

*To Talent Alone* is organised in twelve chapters, of which four are directly relevant to this study. Derek Collins offers an astute survey of music in Dublin, 1800–48 which provides detailed evidence of an increase in Irish musical awareness and (mostly private) musical tuition, even if what Collins describes as 'public enthusiasm for private practice and participation in the ever-increasing number of musical societies and bands' (p. 23) does not compensate for the fragmented and reduced condition of professional public performance and the dearth of newly composed music during the same period. Pine himself charts the foundations of the Academy in two chapters (1848–70 and 1871–89) which are crowded with a densely filled narrative that brilliantly recovers the felt life (personalities, public and private exchanges, the overlap of political agitation with educational zeal) of the institution during its formative years. A chapter jointly authored by Dibble and Klein on 'The composer in the academy' begins with Dibble's remark that 'It would not be an exaggeration to say that the socio-political conditions of nineteenth-century Ireland were barely conducive to the nurturing of musical composition' (p. 400). The (entirely plausible) starkness of this declaration is nevertheless redeemed not only by Dibble's lucid assessment of those composers associated with the Academy (notably Stanford and Culwick) but also by the plenitude of detail which the book as a whole provides. Under Pine's excellent leadership, *To Talent Alone* stands as a vital advance in our understanding of music in nineteenth-century Ireland, precisely because it discloses and marshals in such unremitting detail the raw materials which are the book's sturdy foundation.

1998 seems to have been something of an *annus mirabilis* for Irish musicology. In addition to *To Talent Alone*, that year also marked the publication of Aloys Fleischmann's long-awaited *Sources of Irish Traditional Music c.1600–1855* (in two volumes). If *To Talent Alone* retrieves the life of a great Irish musical institution, Fleischmann's research represents a retrieval no less valuable, although significantly different in kind. *Sources of Irish Traditional Music* presents, for the first time, a *catalogue raisonée* of the traditional repertory insofar as such a thing is possible from printed and manuscript sources. But it is more than an annotated catalogue: the music itself is presented (some six thousand melodies in all to 1855), and this massive enterprise makes available not only an unparalleled (if not unprecedented) recension of Irish traditional music,[14] but also the material, the music itself, which is now restored to its pristine condition and shorn of the arrangements, adornments and verbal texts that are nevertheless themselves part of the history of music in Ireland.

Fleischmann and his collaborators (notably Mícheál Ó Súilleabháin and Paul McGettrick, among others) allow us access to music divested of all ideology: the book literally puts in order central rooms in the archive of Irish music. The lines out from that archive to the living tradition are undoubtedly difficult to trace (especially because of the sometimes confusing admixture of oral and printed sources in the tradition), but this catalogue at last affords the historian a reliable source for the transmission of music in Ireland in the first half of the nineteenth century. It also represents a fascinating and late example of German positivism brought productively to bear on a subject notoriously resistant to the ordinary canons of musicological discourse.

*Christ Church Cathedral Dublin: A History* edited by Kenneth Milne (2000) is another institutional record which embraces music in a compelling and central way: two chapters by Barra Boydell therein, 'Music in the nineteenth-century cathedral, 1800-70' and 'Optimism and decline: music, 1870-*c.*1970', are themselves emblematic of a recent and professional musicology in Ireland which decisively addresses questions of repertory, compositional and liturgical practice and aesthetic presence in a manner almost unknown in this country up to thirty years ago.[15] Boydell's contribution to the book as a whole is immense – five of the book's 18 chapters are his – and this, too, is emblematic of a long awaited recognition of the central role of music in Irish religious and cultural affairs. As far as the nineteenth century is concerned, Boydell's brief extends not only to the sung services but also to an incisive and (characteristically) authoritative discussion of the organs and bells in Christ Church Cathedral, in addition to much detailed discussion of individual vicars choral and other 'singing men'. This last feature bears especially on the vicissitudes of the choir and the eventual replacement of boys with women's voices. Although space does not permit an exhaustive consideration of Boydell's research, I can at least advert to the decisive historical record which Boydell, thanks to his painstaking recovery of documentary evidence, brings to bear on this seminal location for the professional practice of music in Ireland.

Finally, and briefly, it is instructive to record here the appearance of *Musical Constructions of Nationalism: Essays on the History and Ideology of European Musical Culture, 1800–1945* (2001), edited by Harry White and Michael Murphy. Murphy's enterprise in contextualising the phenomenon of nationalism as a central force in European musical thought is considerable. The focus and vision which stand behind the book are principally his, and he has enlisted an impressive roster of international specialists who examine this phenomenon in British, Scottish, French, Polish, Norwegian, Danish, German and Italian traditions of music. But the book also integrates the question of Irish nationalism and music into this broader fabric by means of two essays from Joseph Ryan and Harry White. Ryan's essay is a characteristically authoritative meditation on the cultural implications of interpreting Irish nationalism from a European musicological perspective, and this author pursues the argument that music in Ireland, mainly under the duress of nationalism, was subsumed by literature into a verbally dominated culture.

## MONOGRAPHS AND DISSERTATIONS

Monographs and dissertations on music in nineteenth-century Ireland divide easily into four areas of research: church music, opera, music education and cultural history.

Kieran Daly's *Catholic Church Music in Ireland 1878–1903* (1995) is principally a close reading of *Lyra Ecclesiastica*, the bulletin of the Irish Society of St Cecilia, which documented in sometimes quotidian detail the single most sustained and influential episode in the history of Irish church music in the second half of the nineteenth century. Daly reconstructs from the pages of *Lyra* a narrative which relates the question of Irish church music reform to two principal movements: the drive to romanise the Catholic Church in Ireland initiated by Paul Cardinal Cullen at the Synod of Thurles (1850) and the reform of church music begun in Germany, also in mid-century, which spread through the Society of St Cecilia to France and the United States and Ireland. Daly's monograph – which started life as an outstanding dissertation for Queen's University Belfast – charts the development of the Irish Society of St Cecilia and valuably corrects the hitherto generally accepted impression that its influence in church music reform was 'largely through the efforts of Henry Bewerunge'.[16] Although Bewerunge naturally plays a vital role in Daly's narrative, the author shows that the Irish Society was if anything *more* effective in the realisation of its objectives prior to Bewerunge's arrival in Ireland as professor of Church Chant and Organ at St Patrick's College, Maynooth in 1888. Moreover Daly foregrounds the impact on the Irish movement of William Walsh (Archbishop of Dublin) and Nicholas Donnelly (Bishop of Canea), whose expertise, technical knowledge and tact stand in contrast to Bewerunge's somewhat abrasive editorial style and trenchant, argumentative demeanour.

Personalities notwithstanding, Daly also shows that it was the 1903 *Motu proprio* (a papal encyclical which ratified the Solesmes-led Vatican edition of the chant) which dealt the death blow to the already waning presence of the society in Irish church music affairs. From within Ireland, the aesthetic crisis of the Cecilian ideal – its inability to countenance in any practical terms a contemporary church music other than that of spirited Renaissance pastiche – found a characteristic outlet not only in *Lyra Ecclesiastica* itself but in *The New Ireland Review* and other periodicals which voiced an antipathy to the conservative and sometimes reactionary stance of the Cecilian reform. Daly's book is also important because it nominates – again through its thoughtful perusal of *Lyra Ecclesiastica* – those personalities, publications, festivals and repertorial lists which gave the reform its distinctively European complexion.

Perhaps the most glaring lacuna in the history of nineteenth-century music in Ireland is the almost complete absence of research on opera during the greater part of the century. If Tom Walsh can make the startling claim in his book *Opera in Dublin 1798–1820* (1993) that 'the "Golden Age" of Italian opera in Dublin would be encompassed by the years between 1840 and 1878' (p. 4), it is a claim which is weakened not only by the paucity of opera research in this period but by the counter-impression left by the enduring popularity of ballad opera and the English operas of Balfe and Wallace in Dublin at the turn of the century.[17]

I mention Walsh's work with some diffidence in this review, because I am reluctant to criticise its author for failing to provide what he did not intend in the first place. *Opera in Dublin* is, as Walsh expressly states, a 'continuation' of *Opera in Dublin 1715–1797* (Dublin: Allen Figgis, 1973), a book subtitled 'The Social Scene'. As with its predecessor, this second volume is crowded with biography, newspaper reportage, the memoirs of singers, managers and composers, all of which collectively results in a book that is more akin to theatre history than to musicology, and a rather old-fashioned theatre history at that. But it is not sufficient or even fair to dismiss Walsh's work as outdated theatre history. The problem rather is that when we turn to European and Anglo-American musicology at the end of the twentieth century, we find that opera enjoys therein essentially two kinds of consideration. Either the genre is radically interpreted (or deconstructed) as an agent of cultural history, or individual works which transcend the international repertoire (the operas of Mozart or Wagner are obvious examples) receive sustained critical analysis. It *is* fair to say that Walsh's book points us in the direction of the first kind, but by virtue of its penetrating research it additionally confirms the irrelevance of the second kind to opera in Ireland. It is also fair to say that Tom Walsh, a connoisseur of European opera if ever there was one, made similarly important contributions to the history of French opera during the Second Empire and to opera in Monte Carlo. But his work would require the governing force of a prevailing idea (opera as an agent of political discourse, for example, or simply as a narrative discourse to cohere the entertaining multitude which crowds his pages) in order to weave it into the fabric of Irish musical history.

Although its principal energies are directed towards the nature of music education as a (sometimes conflicting) expression of cultural identity in the twentieth century, Marie McCarthy's *Passing It On: The Transmission of Music in Irish Culture* (1999) includes an informative survey of music education in Ireland in the nineteenth century. She identifies the central problem of Irish music education as a cultural act of dislocation in the following terms:

> The rich musical heritage which pupils such as [Patrick Weston] Joyce absorbed informally during their youth remained outside classroom hours . . . In contrast, school music was founded on a rationale that reproduced the values of high culture, ignoring the music familiar to students and meaningful in an Irish context. (p. 61)

This reading (in which Moore's *Melodies* are interpreted as a domesticated and thereby 'safe' conduit for the ethnic tradition) touches on the nerve-centre of the problem. The art music of Europe ('high culture'), mediated as it was by a colonial system which enforced it in socio-economic terms utterly irrelevant to its original milieu, became a shibboleth of repression at worst and at best an agent of cultural dislocation. The vast apparatus and expressive genius of European musical culture could scarcely survive the faintly ludicrous prospect of being forced through the medium of Victorian education policy and the dreary routines of the Hullah method. In some respects, the efforts of Her Majesty's government on behalf of music education in mid-nineteenth-century Ireland were about as enlightened as forcing a Bavarian peasant to learn and recite Wordsworth. Worse, in fact, because the Bavarian had only his own mad masters to contend with.

'Persistent discord is inimical to creative endeavour. Even Stanford's industry does not alter the sorry fact that the nineteenth century cannot supply a single Irish work of enduring quality.' Thus the conclusion (p. 463) of Joseph Ryan's dissertation, *Nationalism and Music in Ireland* (1991), which ranks without doubt as the most brilliant and penetrating contribution to the history of music in Ireland in any period, including the nineteenth century. Simply and by itself, Ryan's dissertation sets new standards for the perception of music in Irish culture and for Irish musicology to which many will aspire but few attain. The great strengths of Ryan's approach to music in Ireland are his acute understanding of nationalism and his integration of Irish culture in a European context. He thereby makes music in Ireland accessible to a much wider history of ideas than heretofore, with the result that the problems of music in Ireland become, as it were, part of the discourse of European cultural history. At the same time, he is the most deeply read and conversant scholar of Irish music of his generation, especially in the period 1800–1950. He understands with uncanny deliberation the imaginative conflicts which plagued Irish music throughout the century and he diagnoses the problem of reconciling European and Irish modes of musical thought with dispassionate clarity. Better than anyone else writing on this subject, Ryan understands the ways in which ideas of Irish music fostered nationalist discourse and how, in turn, that discourse was to curb and finally paralyse the emancipation of an Irish art music. Although *Nationalism and Music in Ireland* reaches beyond the nineteenth century to the 1950s, its chapters on Moore and Young Ireland, on indigenous musical culture, on 'the alternative tradition' and on 'the age of fusion' (the late nineteenth century) offer a reading of music in Ireland which is at once without useful precedent and now indispensable to further research. But the music for Ryan comes first and last. The abiding merit of this superb work is that it provides a history of ideas for music in Ireland which yet engages with the music itself in a reading that is masterly, secure and pro-vocative of fruitful disagreement. Whatever may be of value in my own work, for example, is permanently indebted to it. That it remains unpublished is a mystery and a scandal.

I leave it to others to asses the merits or otherwise of *The Keeper's Recital: Music and Cultural History in Ireland, 1770–1970* (1998). But it would be dis-ingenuous to pass silently over the fact that the book addresses the question of music in nineteenth-century Ireland from four different perspectives, nominated by the relevant chapter headings which are: 'History and roman-ticism: Bunting, Moore and the concept of Irish music in the nineteenth century'; 'Antiquarianism and politics: Davis, Petrie, Hyde and the growth of music in a sectarian culture'; 'Heinrich Bewerunge and the Cecilian move-ment in Ireland'; 'Music and the Literary Revival'. With the exception of the third of these chapters (which revisits my reading of Bewerunge's writings in the context of church music reform explicitly as an episode in Irish cultural history), *The Keeper's Recital* is concerned with the history of an idea which enjoyed formative influence in the nineteenth century. That idea may be summarised as the perception of music not merely as an agent of nationalist discourse but also as an emblem of colonial dispossession in terms which rivalled the so-called 'language problem' in Irish cultural history. The book argues that these rival perceptions of music not only produced a dislocation of music itself, but also led to a powerful secondary function for music, in which it dominated the political and literary imagination in Ireland as an image and symbol of regeneration.

CONCLUSION

Although the distinction between 'art' music and 'traditional' music obtains with reasonable clarity in Ireland after the Battle of Kinsale (1601) and the defeat of the Gaelic aristocracy, it reflects an ethnic divergence and a pre-eminence of English norms over an oral Gaelic culture that thereafter was preserved and developed in severely polarised circumstances. The fragmented polity of modern Ireland, no more clearly expressed than in the counter-claims of Gaelic and Anglo-Irish perceptions of high culture, has determined the understanding of orally transmitted music as a corpus of ethnic melodies, with its roots in the culture of Gaelic Ireland. The concept of 'art music' incorporates the norms of European (English, German, Italian) musical patronage assimilated as part of the colonial status quo, especially after the Battle of the Boyne.[18]

This reading of music, which opens the article on Ireland in *The New Grove Dictionary of Music, Revised Edition* (2001) is largely consonant with the work surveyed in this report. Even a glance at the bibliographies attached to the *New Grove* article confirms that whereas art music in Ireland has begun to stimulate a steady growth in scholarship, 'Irish traditional music research has been confined to a small group of interested individuals' (p. 567).[19] Nevertheless, the Irish World Music Centre established at the University of Limerick in 1995 has already begun to make a significant contribution to the history and criticism of the traditional repertory to judge by the large number of doctoral dissertations presently in progress there. One of its graduates, Colette Moloney, whose work I have surveyed here, has consolidated this work with the publication of *The Irish Music Manuscripts of Edward Bunting (1773–1843): An Introduction* (2000). David Cooper of Leeds University has likewise edited *The Petrie Collection of the Ancient Music of Ireland*, published by Cork University Press (2002).

But the divisions remain, in musicology as in music. The study of music in Ireland tends increasingly towards cultural history and criticism on one side and ethnomusicology and folklore on the other. If, as in my own work, these boundaries are occasionally transgressed, the result is not always to everyone's liking.[20]

The presence of Irish music (and of music in Ireland) in general or specialised works of reference has greatly increased: in addition to the articles on Irish subject matter in *The New Grove* (which appointed a national advisory editor for Ireland), *The Oxford Companion to Irish History*, ed. Sean Connolly (Oxford University Press, 1998; second edition, 2002) and the *Encyclopaedia of Ireland* (edited by Brian Lalor for Gill & Macmillan) give a much more prominent place to Ireland's musical history than was the case in such publications up to 1990. The *Companion to Irish Traditional Music* edited by Fintan Vallely (Cork University Press, 1999), is another important work of reference which could scarcely have been envisaged, let alone realised, a decade ago.

Taken together, these publications strongly support the view that an encyclopaedia of music in Ireland has an even more plausible case for publication than it had when I made this proposal in 1988 (and on several occasions thereafter). Ireland's scrutiny of music has never been more sustained or intense, and the state of research and of information technology are such as to enable the realisation of this project, to say nothing of the precedent which the *Encyclopedia of Music in Canada*, now in its second edition, provides. Nor have Irish publishers ever been more disposed to the encouragement of musicology as a discipline which enriches the gamut of Irish studies: as a matter of record, it was Irish Academic Press (under the leadership of Michael Adams) which first established a musicology list in this country, a commitment which Adams has sustained and increased with Four Courts Press. Cork University Press, likewise, has invested much in Irish musical scholarship, and it too promotes musicology as a self-standing discipline.

When we turn back to music in nineteenth-century Ireland and to the work surveyed here in the light of these developments, a number of conclusions can be tentatively offered.

Firstly, it is reasonable to suggest that although the discourse of Irish musicology is plural in its reach, its general tendency is towards cultural history and away from work-based criticism. Secondly, it is too soon to generalise about the promising but as yet uncertain development of generic, narrative and critical modes of musicology in Ireland, given that the discipline has so recently established itself and given, too, the lack of basic research which still abounds (notably in opera, in the recovery of printed and manuscript sources, and in that interface between art music and traditional music which – other than in terms of reception history – has scarcely been explored). Thirdly and finally, the writing of a narrative history of music in Ireland is, as with the proposed encyclopaedia, a much more realistic prospect now than it was before the appearance of such work as the Ryan thesis and the Fleischmann catalogue. It still seems to me that such a history must embrace the *actual* condition of music, not just as a dislocated presence in Irish affairs, but as a symbolic presence in the formation of Irish political and literary discourse. In these respects, musicology in Ireland enjoys a vigorous challenge by which it might define itself in relation to Anglo-American and European musicology on one side and to Ireland's cultural history on the other.

# CHAPTER II

# The Irish Diaspora in
# the Nineteenth Century

✳

*J. J. Lee.*

## INTRODUCTION

The challenge of addressing even a few of the issues that arise from the voluminous literature of the last decade on the Irish Diaspora would be yet more formidable but for the flood of bibliographical surveys, review articles and historiographical commentaries that alert readers to topics and titles far too numerous to mention here.[1] When Donald MacRaild can describe in 1998 the bibliography in *The Irish in Britain, 1815–1939*, edited by Roger Swift and Sheridan Gilley, and published only nine years earlier, as 'excellent, but now dated',[2] one gets some sense of the flood of subsequent publication in Britain alone. This surge, together with surges in other emigrant destinations, whose causes deserve an essay in their own right, is further reflected in the increased coverage of the diasporic dimension of the Irish experience in established journals, as well as in the emergence of new ones with a strong diasporic emphasis.[3]

These developments, supplemented by the appearance in 1999 of the (Notre Dame) *Encyclopedia of the Irish in America*,[4] edited by Michael Glazier, preclude any attempt at comprehensiveness in the present survey. So impossible has it become for a single scholar to keep fully abreast of all relevant publications in so extensive a field, relating to the history of several countries, that the focus here will concentrate instead on the vital issue of the use of evidence, taking a limited number of themes as case-studies. The references and the bibliography must therefore be severely selective, illustrative rather than comprehensive, though it would obviously be misleading to ignore completely highly influential studies relevant to the central theme published a little outside the strict chronological limits of the decade. The bibliography makes some space for important work on themes overlooked in the text by excluding some of the more specialised titles mentioned in the notes in favour of works not listed, but that still omits numerous fine studies. It would be unhistorical, however, to conclude even such rapid introductory remarks without saluting the contribution of Patrick O'Sullivan, through conceptualising, editing and introducing the six volumes of *The Irish World Wide*,[5] and through his inspirational web-site (http://www.jiscmail.ac.uk/). If it weren't to coin a phrase, one might say that never in the history of Irish diaspora studies have so many owed so much to so few!

### THE CONCEPT OF DIASPORA AND THE USE OF EVIDENCE

This entire essay could be devoted to the difficulties posed for scholarship on the nineteenth century by the virtually universal adoption of the once highly specific term, diaspora. However contested a concept in recent debate, the fact that it has become so universally popular so quickly reflects on the fashions of the present, and not only Irish ones.[6] Once applied to the past, however, the manner in which it is used has to be subject to the standard tests of historical scholarship to protect it from becoming merely the plaything of ideological fashion. Here we can only ponder some of the basic ambiguities inherent in the use of the term.

Donald Akenson, author of the first global survey, *The Irish Diaspora*, published in 1993, has recently distilled his mature thought into a definition:

> In *most* cultures the *sense of Irishness* (however defined) both changed and *diminished* over generations, but I would argue that for *at least two or three* generations it was a *significant* determinant of the behaviour of *most* people of Irish descent. Further I think that even after that, it remained (*and indeed remains*) as a(n) enduring stream, subterranean, but still *partially* determining personal behaviour, and this long after the individuals in question *ceased to think of themselves as Irish*. Any concept of Irish migration, then, must not be merely physical and must not deal only with the first generation, but must be cultural and institutional, and must deal with the *entire multi-generational ethnic group*. Operating with such a rich concept of migration is much more challenging than working with simple 'emigrant' history, but it has the potential to be infinitely more productive [italics mine].[7]

'Rich' though the concept may be, the question for the historian is how operationally valid is it? How subject is it to the standard rules of evidence, allowing the application of consistent scholarly standards?

To raise just a few queries, why was it that it was only in 'most' and not in all cultures that 'the sense of Irishness' developed in this manner? Are there criteria for determining why particular cultures must be excluded? What does 'at least two or three generations' mean? Why was it two generations in some cases, three generations in others, and an unspecified number of further generations in yet others? Why was it a 'significant determinant' of only 'most people' of Irish descent, and not of all? As there can be nothing inevitable about it if some escaped being so 'determined', once again what are the criteria for determining who the minority were – and how big could this minority be? For that matter, how does one know when 'significantly determined' has diminished to mere 'partially determined'? This issue becomes even more pressing with the next step in the definition. How does 'a sense of Irishness' remain until the present a 'partially determining' influence on even those who have long since ceased to think of themselves as Irish? Just how does this operate?

The concept of 'partially' becomes more problematic still after the third generation. If it apparently remains to the present day, by logical extension it must remain into the future, the diaspora comprising the 'entire multi-generational ethnic group' – presumably until the end of time, as the definition contains no mechanism for closure. But are there gradations within 'partial'? If not, do not certain difficulties ensue? It might after all seem logical to presume some decline in the intensity of the sense of identity in later generations in view of the fact that the definition posits a diminishing sense of Irishness in earlier generations – but presumably if the 'partially' were to continue to 'diminish' over time it would one day vanish? If not, we might finish up with the rather curious image of Irishness diminishing as a 'significant' determinant, but ceasing to 'diminish' once it had diminished far enough to become only 'partial'! Does the model, therefore, require the diasporic dimension to become frozen at some unspecified point along the line? What are the criteria for determining if the big freeze has set in – when, why, how? Can a thaw ever set in, a variation on Marcus Hansen's celebrated 'generations' model, according to which the third generation strives to remember what the second generation chooses to forget.[8]

If diaspora never ends, or even if it does, do we have an authorised (by whom?) checklist of 'Irish' traits against which we measure 'Irish' influence on behaviour unto the final generation? Can we pick and choose which traits we'll define as 'Irish' in any given circumstances, allowing us create the diaspora we want? If our definitions differ, can there be any productive dialogue? Does 'however defined' deserve a more prominent location than within brackets? How much interpretation revolves precisely around the validity of definitions? How much ethnic determinism is embedded in the definition? Are blood lines (real or imagined – and if imagined, why and in what way?) a constituent of 'a sense of Irishness' – or a prerequisite for such a 'sense'?

These are not abstract questions, even for the nineteenth century. If the question of when diaspora ends poses a central problem, did it, for purposes of this survey, end for anybody in the nineteenth century? How can we know? By what criteria? For we cannot just innocently think that all we have to do is establish the number of emigrants during the century and then follow their fortunes and that of their descendants (for how many generations?) during the period. For there were already substantial numbers of Irish-born emigrants, not to mention later generations, living abroad at the beginning of the century. By the end of the century there will have been substantial numbers of fifth and sixth-generation descendants in parts of Britain, and particularly the American South. How far they constituted a 'multi-generational ethnic group', however, much less a national one – for ethnic and national are not synonymous concepts – is itself a big unanswered question that can only be established by research, not by definition.

The whole concept of the 'multi-generational ethnic group' requires clarification for every diaspora in every destination. Otherwise there is a danger scholars, to say nothing of non-scholars, will find the diaspora they want. How many of the fabled seventy million Irish of the diaspora today are, well, fabled? It would be an odd methodology to study a country without any idea of the real size of the population. But we appear happy to work with the most casual idea of the size of the diaspora. The alleged American numbers alone concertina in and out in a manner which makes it essential to explore what they really mean – and to exercise elementary scholarly restraint in surmising the real orders of magnitude, past and present – until we can actually find a way of knowing what we are talking about. Such vagueness could allow all sorts of unscholarly misconceptions to take root under the cover of permissive definitions in the absence of serious source-criticism. Politicians and tourist boards may understandably frolic in these figures, but scholarship cannot have the same liberty. It would be a valuable pedagogic exercise if Michael Hout and Joshua Goldstein were to follow up their ingenious, if debatable, 1994 article, 'How 4.5 million Irish immigrants became 40 million Irish Americans: demographic and subjective aspects of the ethnic composition of white Americans',[9] based on the 1980 census, with a study of the implications for their interpretation of the results recorded in the 1990 and 2000 censuses.

An obvious question concerns the influence of inter-ethnic marriage on diasporic identities. What happens to the transmission of sense of origins, or behaviour patterns, when children of different diasporas marry, or when they marry into the indigenous population, as in Britain? 'Mixed marriage' of this type complicates the simplicity of the straight diasporic lines. Akenson himself, it is true, has a simple solution to one aspect of this, expressed in his denunciation of the American Census Bureau for having 'bungled' its question on ethnic origins by actually allowing respondents 'to list multiple ancestries, rather than a single dominant one, so that 55 per cent listed two or more in the 1980 census'.[10] Fancy that! One can certainly concede that all this was jolly

inconsiderate of the respondents. Did they not have the decency to be sufficiently ashamed of their mongrel status to conceal the miscegenating ancestral
impulses that laid such confusing trails? But might not forcing people to opt
for a solitary ancestral identity, to deny all but one of their ethnic origins when
they themselves are conscious of more, risk falsifying the record by compelling
the complexity of both past and present to be shrivelled to methodological
convenience, perhaps even prostituted to ideological imperatives if falling into
unscrupulous hands? But then perhaps people's sense of who they are, rather
than who they should be, may not be entirely irrelevant to the historian. It
goes without saying that exploring the functioning of 'memory' in those
circumstances requires the most sensitive of scalpels. But that is very different
from census commissioners imposing identity on the plain peoples of the
diaspora by assuming to themselves the functions of a new thought police.

'Diaspora', then, is a slippery concept. It can be useful, but only if rigorously
conceptualised. Even if the 'who' of diaspora could be agreed, 'what' a diasporic identity actually entails (or entailed historically at specific times and in
specific places) would still pose problems. An agreed definition will remain
highly elusive, for looseness of definition serves too useful a propagandistic
purpose for scholarly standards automatically to prevail in today's culture
wars in general, to say nothing of self-indulgent Irish self-images as reflected
in the feel-good rhetoric of the 'global Irish family', or the diasporic rhetoric
of the Good Friday Agreement, convenient body stockings to disguise the
emperor's sartorial deficiencies. It remains to be seen how far historical
scholarship can transcend this particular parochialism of the present.

It is worth lingering over Akenson's definition, however much clarification
it may require, to alert ourselves to how much more thinking is needed to
construct an historically valid and operationally feasible alternative, and to
warn of the potential for internal contradiction lurking in our own thinking,
unless we regularly review the consistency of our use of concepts, without
which there can be no serious scholarship. The best that can be hoped for is
that when we use the term for the nineteenth century we will define what we
mean by it as rigorously as we can, so that meaningful debate can be conducted,
and that we do not find ourselves hurtling past one another on different
trajectories because the looseness of the term conceals the fact that we are
talking about different things. In this chapter it refers purely descriptively, and
non-prescriptively, to the impact of their birth and/or socialisation in Ireland
on the lives of emigrants, or of their Irish ancestry on their descendants, during
the nineteenth century. That impact can range from very substantial, on the
one hand, to non-existent, on the other. In all cases it must be established
rather than assumed. We have no right to force immigrants or their descendants
into any particular category. Diaspora scholars have no mandate to ride as
gunhands to corral the children of the diaspora into the approved identity

pens. That should be left to the motley crew of propagandists scavenging the historical record in search of ammunition for current conflicts. Only open-minded research, based on respect for the evidence, can determine in any specific case the place of the diasporic dimension in the total life experience of emigrants themselves and of their descendants.

### 'A PECULIAR TRAMPING PEOPLE' AND THE USE OF EVIDENCE

It is not only the concept of diaspora that lacks rigour. The use of evidence on too many aspects of life in the Irish diaspora too often fails to satisfy the standard rules of historical inquiry. Even the basic issue of the size of the emigrant flow to various destinations has yet to be firmly established for the nineteenth century. Despite the plethora of publications in the past decade, it is disconcerting to observe that the implications of Cormac Ó Gráda's observations in his modestly titled but seminal 1975 'Note' concerning the inadequacy of the official statistics,[11] where he demonstrates that the post-Famine totals in general, and numbers going to Britain after about 1870 in particular, are under-recorded, have only fitfully been incorporated into wider analysis. And the post-Famine figures are probably generally more reliable than the pre-Famine ones, where the safest approach is to calculate orders of magnitude rather than precise numbers.[12] Unless and until the facts can be established with more confidence, many a generalisation about motives, timing, destinations and consequences must remain at least moderately, and in some cases distinctly, provisional.

It is not only the numerical evidence that requires revision. The obvious inadequacies in the handling of quantitative evidence may even have diverted attention from the problems posed by the traditional use of literary and oral evidence, which can often amount to little more than culling convenient quotations from a mass of material and stringing them together to 'prove' one's interpretation, with little discussion of the principles on which the 'evidence' was accumulated in the first place.

Some of the recent re-evaluation of oral and literary evidence comes from simple application of the standard rules of evidence. In his critique of the influence of commentators like Kay, Engels and Mayhew on the perceptions of scholars, MacRaild highlights an issue of wide-ranging import that has troubled others too.[13] The basic issue is the quality of the use of evidence by contemporaries who now count as authorities. MacRaild rightly notes the dominance of 'thousands of faceless local office-holders' among those who provide evidence on the Irish in England, observing sardonically that 'in an age when facts were revered among this legion of Gradgrinds, the extent to which hearsay and stereotype dominated attempts to understand the Irish is paradoxically noteworthy'.[14]

This issue, fundamental to all historical understanding, resonates with particular force for scholars seeking to reconstruct the reality of immigrant lives, and finding themselves employing distinctly dubious evidence.

Much of the evidence concerning the Irish born abroad comes from observers among the hosts looking in, and often looking down; observers usually distanced at least fourfold from the bulk of immigrants, by nationality, ethnicity, religion, and class and, from half of them, by gender, given that the vast majority of evidence comes from males. In Britain above all, they were programmed to judge the strangers by culturally different values, which they were largely conditioned, in turn, to assume to be 'normal', so that any deviation from them became 'peculiar'. This naturally spills over into their use of language, which requires the closest scrutiny.

These issues arise in the very title chosen by David Fitzpatrick for one of his scintillating chapters in the *New History of Ireland*: '"A peculiar tramping people": the Irish in Britain, 1801–70', a direct quotation from a Leeds poor law official pronouncing on Irish supplicants for poor-relief in 1847, whom Fitzpatrick cites in support of his depiction of the immigrants as 'living in an Irish condition of perpetual transience'.[15] In this image, Irish emigrants to Britain habitually thought of it as a second best, intending it as merely a staging post to America. 'Transients' in mind no less than body on arriving, incapable of settling down because of thinking of themselves as merely temporary sojourners, they kept constantly on the move in the attempt to acquire the resources they needed for the biggest 'transient' step of all, across the Atlantic. Not merely 'a peculiar tramping people', but ones inhabiting 'a curious middle place' in Britain,[16] even as late as 1911 they 'to some extent . . . were the residue of those drawn towards more enticing countries, united only in their disappointment at having missed the transatlantic boat'.[17]

Akenson, on the contrary, believes that the Irish 'found Scotland, Wales and especially England to their liking'.[18] But he not only accepts the image of perpetual Irish mobility within Britain. He even proposes a specific rate of mobility, giving as a model the Irish 'who lived in Manchester in 1851', and who 'would have moved away and been replaced by, say, 1871 with brand new migrants'.[19] Akenson's methodological rigour in quantifying the Irish propensity for taking to the open road challenges all others working in the field to turn their cards face up. That penchant for precision will bring into much sharper focus images of the Irish in Britain – just as soon as 'say' is supported by actual evidence for the country as a whole, or even in the first instance just for Manchester – where 'large numbers' of Irish were protected from removal under the Five years Residence Act of 1846 because they 'have been long term residents'[20] – and where for that matter, pedants might observe that even if the 46,000 Irish-born of the 1851 census had indeed 'moved away', they do not seem to have been quite 'replaced' by the 34,000 of the 1871 census.[21]

Although Fitzpatrick's review of Akenson[22] did not demur from this interpretation, their two models are virtually mutually exclusive. Whereas his own is based on the premise that the Irish were reluctant immigrants in Britain, who sought to get to America as fast as possible, Akenson's model, on the other hand, is based on the premise that the Irish liked Britain so much that they were keen on remaining. It was not that they disliked Britain at all, it was just that they couldn't stand any particular part of it for very long.

Fitzpatrick's model is beguiling. What is missing, however, is any sense of the order of magnitude – precise figures are obviously impossible – on just how many of the nearly 416,000 Irish born recorded in 1841, or the 781,000 recorded in 1871, actually did depart for North America. There is plenty of evidence of individual movement across the Atlantic – including some return migration, which raises other issues. But are we talking about 20 per cent of those resident at any particular time, or 40 per cent or 60 per cent, or 80 per cent, or what? The most explicit estimate proffered is that 'many migrants remained in Britain despite the impermanence of their intentions'.[23] However valid this may be, it is nearly of the same order of indeterminacy as Arthur Redford's contention of 1926, that 'many of the Irish regarded their stay in England simply as a means of earning sufficient money to take them to America'.[24]

The model distinguishes three main types of immigrant: permanent, vagrant pauper, and seasonal labourer.[25] But their relative size at any given time remains uncertain, and this uncertainty subverts the certainty of generalisations. Thus the image of the Irish as reluctant immigrants 'caught in the British web',[26] destined to tramp incessantly, is clinched by a quote, not a statistic: 'As a Stafford magistrate remarked of "a certain class of Irish" to a parliamentary inquiry in 1833, "they travel in a circle, and . . . the nearer they get to their own homes, the greater is their tendency to fly off".' Apart from the looseness of this formulation, the text here carries, very correctly, its own internal warning. The magistrate was referring only to 'a certain class of Irish', because the inquiry was not into the Irish, but into Irish vagrants. The boundaries of that class were certainly fluid. The Staffordshire magistrate himself, Edward Grove, defined those involved as 'labourers of a low cast, a migratory people; I'll call many of them vagrants'.[27] They included the sick, 'and women especially in a state very little short of nudity, and frequently in the last stage of pregnancy'.[28] 'Vagrant' was clearly an elastic concept. But that still gives little clue as to what percentage of immigrants they constituted at any particular date, and how the percentage changed over time.

Until we have the answer to these questions it is difficult to know how representative 'vagrants' were, and how far evidence about them, however liberally defined, can be generalised for immigrants as a whole. This problem of representativeness, essentially a quantitative one, dogged contemporaries.

The quantitative assertions of every editor, journalist, parliamentary witness, social commentator, etc. must therefore be subjected to the standard tests of source-criticism. One has to be conscious of how much opinion is based on quantitative conclusions by people unaccustomed to quantitative thinking. How did they convert qualitative observation, or even impressionistic quantitative observation, into quantitative conclusion sufficiently rigorous to serve as evidence?

In a notable later paper, 'The Irish in Britain: settlers or transients?', Fitzpatrick reinforced the argument about the 'transient' propensities of the Irish by invoking the authority of Rev. John Garwood's portrayal of Irish immigrants as 'temporary visitors, reluctantly caught in Britain en route for a promised land elsewhere', citing Garwood's observation that 'They generally simply desire to come, in order to obtain money to get over to America. The greater number succeed in this object'. 'The implications of Garwood's vision', Fitzpatrick observes, have yet to be explored', for 'if the Irish in Britain characteristically intended '"their resort here to be only a step" towards onward migration to the New World, their strategies concerning residence, occupation, marriage and institutional affiliation should have differed radically from those of intending settlers.'[29] This is an important observation. But it implies that 'the greater number' did actually make it to America. If they didn't, presumably at some stage a radical reappraisal of strategy occurred. Did they then cease their restless migratory life within Britain? Or maybe they met the woman of their dreams – or the man? (but we need to know much more about marriage patterns and customs among the migrants in Britain, as everywhere else). In real life, the 'failure' is likely to have been a concomitant of marrying in Britain. Did they then associate their marriage, and their spouse, with the stigma of failure in their lives? How many women tramped? How many women were determined to get to America? How many succeeded? Was there a gender difference in the degree of success? How do the proportions compare with those who left Ireland? If 'the greater number' of women left, was this because they felt 'oppressed' in Britain? If so, why did not indigenous British women also migrate in droves to 'liberation' across the Atlantic? Did those Irish who remained in Britain do so because they could not leave – or because they would not? Did their decision, or fate, depend on location? Shannon, noting in 1935 the 'peculiar' fall of the number of Irish-born in London from 109,000 to 66,000 between 1851 and 1891, surmised that 'the increased attraction of America would not only reduce the immigration to London, but would also swell the re-emigration of Irish-born out of it'.[30] No doubt it would. But did it? Shannon's observation, alas, has no supporting footnote. In fact it is a footnote itself.

The first question to be explored, then, concerns not 'the implications of Garwood's vision', but the more mundane one of its accuracy. Was Garwood right in claiming either that the Irish 'generally' came to Britain to get to America, or that 'the greater number succeed in this object'? How did Garwood know in either case? How compelling was his evidence? The problem is that he produced none.

The question of emigrants' expectations is not only a legitimate but a fundamental one. But delineating the trajectory of those expectations requires the closest sifting of evidence. Confidence in Garwood's unsubstantiated assertion is not enhanced by his conclusion, following 'a careful inquiry' in 1851 'by the missionaries of the London City Mission' that the number of 'Irish and Roman Catholic' in London, was 'nearly 200,000'.[31] This seems far stronger evidence than that cited by Redford in support of the same assumption that immigrants actually achieved their putative objective, on the basis of a quote from 1838, that the Irishman 'may in a few months realise a sufficient sum to enable him to seek his fortune in America'.[32] Apart from the fact that Garwood did not describe the methodology of his inquiry, the problem with his evidence is that another inquiry conducted the same year, the census itself, recorded only 109,000 Irish-born.[33] Even allowing for some census vagaries (but what about City Mission vagaries?) and for the Mission territory being nearly 10 per cent larger than the census area, Garwood's figure seems wildly inaccurate. It is true that Garwood's magazine did note that those who ought to be counted as Irish included the children, so that the real number of Irish far exceeded the census number,[34] but unfortunately Garwood had described his 'nearly 200,000' as 'all immigrants who have traversed the ocean to reach us'.[35] A decade later Pollard-Urquhart, having diligently canvassed the views of the local cognoscenti, could present a profile of Irish labourers in the East End without even alluding to the issue.[36] Garwood's account provides fascinating insights – but arguably less into the Irish in London than into the mindset of this passionate fundamentalist Evangelical, Clerical Secretary to the bitterly anti-Catholic London City Mission, whose credentials as a witness need to be subjected to standard source criticism before his conclusions can be accepted.

Innocence of rigorous quantitative thinking applied to all jurisdictions, of course, not just to Britain. In the United States, the records of the Emigrant Savings Bank in New York in the 1850s, and the archaeological excavations of one of the most notorious of all slums, the Five Points, significantly modify the conventional wisdom about the dehumanised nature of the denizens, most graphically described in celebrated comments by Charles Dickens.[37] If Dickens was not an indigenous observer, indigenous comment could be as uncomprehending, even that of commentators of real calibre, as Ellen Skerrett has shown with meticulous scholarship in the case of as celebrated a philanthropist as Jane Addams, even on conditions under her nose in Chicago.[38] How far can one test the 'top down' view of immigrants with evidence from the 'bottom up'? Would this not allow the voice from inside to be finally heard? Fitzpatrick has identified some fascinating inside sources, full of intrinsic human interest, in this regard. The problem is that it remains unclear how far they can be used as a basis for generalisation. Take 'the case of Isabella Charles, a lunatic pauper removed from Edinburgh to Ireland in 1849',[39] which it is claimed 'illustrates the "peculiar tramping" habits of the Irish migrant:

> Born in Kildare in about 1810, Isabella accompanied her Scottish mother to Castlehill, Edinburgh parish, in 1832. After three and a half years they moved to St Cuthbert's parish, and thence after a similar period to Old Assembly Close, city parish. After brief spells in the Close, in Dublin, and in Glasgow, Isabella returned for another two years to the Close, only to depart for further terms in Dublin and Glasgow. Just before her entry to the Morningside Asylum and consequent deportation, she spent a few weeks each in Edinburgh's Potter's Row and Crosscauseway.[40]

Fitzpatrick concludes from this that 'the concept of "settlement" had little relevance to the experience of much of Britain's Irish population, forever on the move in search of better jobs or cheaper lodgings.'[41]

This raises some questions. Isabella Charles was born in Kildare – but of a Scottish mother. Nothing is said about the father. The Scottish mother, with no father in sight, would explain why they went to Edinburgh, and kept to a Dublin–Glasgow–Edinburgh circuit, suggesting she, and not Isabella, was the initial decision maker. No doubt images of Irish women differ, but it may strike some as a shade odd to take the unfortunate lunatic daughter of a Scottish mother, fatherhood unspecified, to be representative of Irish migrant women. It may be suggested that the percentage of the poor woman's behaviour that can be attributed to her representative status as an Irish transient must remain, pending further evidence, not proven. The only really plausible conclusion on the case is that the mother was a Scottish transient, but whether that would suffice to call the Scots 'a peculiar tramping people' seems doubtful.

Isabella Charles fails to fully fit the 'transient' model not only because of these uncertainties, but because she did not go to America either. However, another case-study cited by Fitzpatrick in the previous chapter, that of Wilson Benson, conforms better to the model in this regard, even if it was to Canada rather than the United States that he migrated. In his celebrated 1975 study of Hamilton, Michael Katz drew extensively on the Memoir by Benson, whom Fitzpatrick describes as 'a not untypical Irishman'.[42] 'Not untypical' because he was a perpetual transient, who not only tramped in Ireland and Britain before emigrating to Canada, where in turn 'between 1841 and 1874 he had at least eight places of residence and twelve occupations'.[43] This is certainly evocative. Even here, however, it is possible to observe a different emphasis. Benson was indeed highly mobile in Canada for several years until at the age of 30 he settled down as a farmer for more than 20 years, and would presumably have continued for life only that an accident obliged him to forsake farming for storekeeping.[44]

For our immediate purposes, two points are relevant. Firstly, Benson was as mobile for about 10 years during his twenties in Canada, before settling down, as he had been in Scotland and Ireland before departure. The 'peculiar tramping people' were not confined to Britain. Or rather, the 'tramping people' were not. But no longer is there anything 'peculiar' about them. The historiographical perspective is generally different in North America, where Irish mobility is not seen through British lenses. Despite his fascination with Benson, Katz regards 'the amazing population mobility within nineteenth-century society' as a pervasive phenomenon, no more 'peculiar' to, or of, the Irish than anyone else.[45] Indeed Katz went so far as to describe Benson as 'a representative Canadian first and foremost because he was a transient'.[46] By British criteria, then, Benson still belonged to a 'peculiar' species stepping on the boat, only to be purged of his peculiarity by the alchemy of the Atlantic, able to step ashore the far side a 'representative' human being by Canadian criteria. The issues raised by the conflicting perspectives require systematic scrutiny.

In the USA, the Irish born were mobile too. But the tone of the historiography is again very different from that on Britain. Far from making them 'peculiar', or being 'peculiar' to them, this served only to make them, for Hasia Diner, 'like nineteenth-century Americans in general'.[47] Joseph Ferrie, in his 1999 *Yankeys Now*, confirms the impression of a highly mobile male population in the United States, with the Irish indeed at the higher end of mobility in mid-century, but with the other main immigrants of the period, the Germans, also more mobile than natives, who were themselves already highly mobile.[48] But Ferrie's perspective is the polar opposite of the preoccupation with the 'peculiar' Irish, when he reports that 'even the Irish experienced extensive mobility characteristic of antebellum immigrants in the years immediately after their arrival in the United States'.[49]

Ferrie has greatly advanced understanding of the modalities of migration within the United States, illustrating how perspectives can change in the light of new evidence. Thernstrom's pioneering 1964 and 1973 demographic studies of Newburyport and Boston, comparing the populations recorded in successive censuses, had fostered an image of immigrant groups as largely clustered and static.[50] Despite growing scepticism about this model, the big problem before Ferrie was that one could compare from census to census only the 40 per cent of 'persisters' who remained from one census to the next in Thernstrom's work. One had to guess how the remainder had fared. Ferrie's breakthrough occurred with his initiative in linking a systematic random sample of immigrants from passenger lists of ships landing in New York in the 1840s, to their census returns, wherever they were, for 1850 and 1860. Where Thernstrom surmised, but without the vital evidence, that the missing had fared worse than the 'persisters', Ferrie was able to conclude from actual evidence that they enjoyed higher social mobility than those who remained. However questionable some of Ferrie's skill categories appear to be, as when defining policemen, firemen, coachmen and drivers as unskilled, thus possibly underrating the competence required for these occupations,[51] and consequently skewing some of his conclusions concerning the relationship between skill and mobility, his work marks an important contribution to understanding the scale and pattern of internal male mobility.

Even in the USA, it is very difficult to estimate what the 'expected' rate of mobility of the Irish might have been – and therefore to calculate whether they were more, or less, mobile than their circumstances warranted. The most relevant reference group, the Germans, brought more capital with them, so that it is impossible to compare like with precise like around mid-century. As the Irish owned less property initially, they were less inhibited from moving than either natives or Germans by already having a stake in their immediate place of settlement. But all the mid-century variables involved require the most sensitive sifting, and it would be instructive to compare the mobility of the Irish-born in the later nineteenth century with that of the 'new' immigrants, or even the poorer Germans who came from east of the Elbe in the surge of the 1880s.

Part of the problem of understanding either the Irish immigrant response to Britain, or the indigenous response to the Irish, in contrast to the situation in Canada and the USA, is that there was no other major immigrant group present at the same time to alert observers to the necessity for disciplined as distinct from impressionistic comparison, and that observer analysis of mobile indigenes was unsystematic. As Ruth-Ann Harris has astutely observed, 'what attracted the attention of contemporaries then and historians now is not the typical but the unusual'. And the Irish fitted the bill, even if one must ask, with Harris, to what extent 'did their distinctive manner of dress and speech only make it appear that way'.[52]

One should not be too severe on the indigenes. After all, what was high mobility from the perspective of the Leeds poor-law official? He had no scholarly criteria for establishing the 'normal' geographical mobility of those in 'Irish' circumstances, holding all the other relevant variables constant, so that he could isolate the impact on 'tramping' of ethnicity alone. The question is not after all, for the student of diaspora, how mobile were immigrants in their new locations. It is how much of their mobility was due to their diasporic identity.

It may well be that in Britain, mobile though natives were, 'immigrants were more mobile than natives, and Irish immigrants were more mobile than most'.[53] But for the historian of diaspora, there are two problems with this.

First, plausible though the proposition appears (apart from the elusive category of 'most'), the evidence on the natives themselves is still disproportionately impressionistic. Hobsbawm's celebrated 1950 article on the tramping artisan did not have a detailed follow-up until Southall's 1991 article on the same subject, which certainly made its case that 'the economic history of internal migration in Britain is underdeveloped'.[54] Comparison between 'Irish' and 'British' averages is meaningless in the present state of knowledge, given the differences in circumstances. It may be that systematic scholarly comparison will substantiate contemporary impressions in this regard, but until then it is premature to hazard too sweeping generalisations.

The challenge is to find the appropriate control group against which to measure immigrant mobility. Ideally, it would have to be, at the very least, other immigrants of comparable initial occupation, skill, religion, and age, as well as family and sex structures. This poses a real interpretive problem in the case of Britain, given how few other immigrants there were until the coming of substantial numbers of Jews in the later nineteenth century. The problem is further exacerbated by the dearth of comparative work on the poorest layers of English and Scottish society. Although his research concentrates on artisans, Southall's conclusion that 'skilled manual workers did not differ markedly from unskilled workers'[55] begins to establish criteria potentially interesting for the study of most Irish immigrants. The behaviour of the immigrants must be related, in the first instance, to their specific occupations, as Gearóid Ó Tuathaigh observed in his classic 1981 paper.[56] Replete then though the literature be with references to Irish mobility, no conclusion can be regarded as more than an opinion unless the criteria of comparison are explicitly and precisely stated.

Why was there such contemporary British concern with the perceived mobility of the Irish? Large-scale internal migration was normal in all industrialising societies with rapid population growth. Britain may even have had lower rates than the United States or Canada. The differences in perception shift the focus sharply from the observed to the observers. On what evidence, then, can the Irish in Britain be designated 'a peculiar tramping people' throughout the century? Highly plausible for Famine immigrants in a period of economic slump – even for Southall's skilled workers, 'tramping activity was overwhelmingly concentrated into depression years'[57] – one can certainly imagine this applying to a high proportion of immigrants in 1847.[58] The inquiry at which Beckwith, the Leeds poor law official, coined the phrase was not, however, concerned with the 'Irish' in England, but with 'the operation of the Laws of Settlement and of the Poor Removal Act', or in effect with paupers. The phrase carries no more longer-term authority than Beckwith's range of observation, intelligence, and world-view. However relevant to the history of opinion about Irish immigrants in England, or even accurate about the situation within his purview in 1847 itself, its objective validity about the actual migration experience itself over a longer period has to be tested against other evidence. Only 13 years later, in this same Leeds, another Poor-Law official told another official inquiry that he could not say that many more Irish would have been removed but for the operation of the Irremovable Act, because 'many of them are very old residents'.[59] Although he is referring particularly to plaid workers who remained in Leeds after being brought across to work, he seems to regard them as representative.

Here it is necessary to sift evidence from impression. If we remain with Leeds, and note that Dillon, the historian of the Famine Irish in Leeds, duly observed that 'the Irish were noted for their extraordinary mobility' – he too invoking Beckwith's 'peculiar tramping people' as his clincher – we can also note that he proceeded to produce several economically rational reasons for their mobility without reference to a determination to get to America. So powerful is his image of mobility, however, that he then proceeds to structure his sentences in such a way as to play down evidence subversive of the model of perpetual movement:

> Although evidence from the place of birth of the first-born British child suggests that over 80 per cent (82 per cent in 1851 and 81 per cent in 1861) of the immigrant families came more or less directly to Leeds, making it their first place of settlement, and that of the remainder, 73 per cent in 1851, and 74 per cent in 1861, had children born in only one other place, it is clear that there remained a good deal of movement within the Irish community of the town.[60]

Frequent movement within local areas was commonplace in the period, for quite logical reasons. The above citation could have as easily been framed the other way around – that in spite of a high degree of movement within Leeds (though by no means necessarily exceptional for people in their circumstances), Irish families had a high degree of stability of location (though the historian might add here too 'by no means necessarily exceptional for people in their circumstances'). Without wishing to detract from Dillon's valuable study, his underlying assumptions clearly structured the presentation of the evidence.[61]

How far the 'peculiar, tramping people' are likely to have been the majority of Irish, except in special and transient circumstances, and just how many of the Irish throughout the country, and throughout the century, can best be understood from the perspective of ceaseless transience, must remain uncertain until sustained comparative work can be conducted. The importance of the issue transcends the specific British case. It is highly relevant for our understanding of the Irish in America. If, for instance, a substantial proportion of the Irish-born in the USA arrived not directly from rural Ireland but from urban England, are they not likely to have brought somewhat different perspectives on urban living with them than if they had come straight off the farm? For that matter, did they go to relatives? If they went on their own savings, rather than on pre-paid passages, like so many from Ireland, does this mean they had no relatives or friends in America to ease the way for them? Or had family relations broken down? How did they find jobs without a supportive network – or did they succeed in creating one very quickly? What was the gender distribution? Did they, male and/or female, travel in groups of single or mixed sex? Did they cling together after arrival? Did many head for textile towns if they had some experience of factory work in Britain? How many Protestants used Britain as a staging post – or were they less 'transient'? How many, of whatever denomination, headed for Canada rather than the United States? How did rates change over time? In short, these questions, and many more, posed by emigration directly to North America from Ireland must be asked of Irish migration from Britain, in addition to questions that arise from their specific British experience. The issue has important implications for our understanding of the entire emigrant experience not only in Britain but also in North America. But the first task must be to establish the likely order of magnitude of the numbers involved.

The issue is of course highly relevant to our understanding of English, Welsh and Scottish emigration as well as Irish. The study of Irish emigration from Britain has the potential to serve as a control on many of our generalisations about emigration from Ireland, and about the Irish experience in the United States and Canada – but that study must be subject to the standard laws of historical evidence. If 'the majority' of the Irish in England in 1851 succeeded, in Rev. John Garwood's estimate, in emigrating from Britain to America, did this mean that at least 364,000 of the 727,000 Irish recorded in that year's census rapidly became emigrants from Britain? If so, what implications has this for our understanding of the numbers of actual British emigrants during the 1850s? Does the history of British emigration require drastic revision to take account of this? – if it happened!

It is striking how much of our general image of the Irish in Britain during the century derives from a narrow class of observers during the Famine period. Even in Ireland itself, a disproportionate number of the sources on the motivation and behaviour of emigrants comes from external observers during the Famine. Consider the claims in 1849 by Col. Clarke, Poor Law Inspector for South Kerry, that husbands were particularly inclined to 'proceed to America immediately . . . and a great many when they get out there marry again'.[62] Husbands could certainly behave selfishly with regard to their families, even in a culture which took family obligations seriously. The scale of Clarke's 'a great many', however, remained unspecified. In any case, how did Clarke know? What were his sources of information?

The able-bodied men, he reveals, were 'going out by assistance from their friends on the other side: they get a remittance probably of 4 or 5 pounds, and leave their wives and families at home'.[63] As he was giving evidence in April 1849, his information (from whom?), given the communication system, must have referred to 1847–8. He must therefore have had his 'great many' married again soon after landing. How plausible is this? It meant that the husbands adapted with such impressive speed to American conditions that they were able to find jobs in no time at all, earn enough to pay off their 'friends', and then dangle irresistible attractions before their prospective brides. Presumably they remained in the circle of their 'friends', for by definition the information must have come to Clarke from someone who knew the newly wed husbands were already married at home – but curiously didn't apparently warn the unsuspecting brides. Or were the brides (Irish? Kerry?) so swept off their feet by enchanting Kerrymen that they just didn't care? Were they seduced mayhap by the soft sibylline sounds (of the ancestral tongue?) flowing from the liquid lips of the Cahirciveen charmers?

The whole scenario raises elementary questions about the depth of Clarke's understanding of native culture, emigrant culture, and the culture of poverty in relation to family decision making about survival in famine circumstances, where 'desertion' by the husband could be used as a method for procuring public relief for the 'deserted' wife and children.

Clarke was an 'official' witness. Lord Mounteagle, often cited as a genuine authority on Irish affairs, also felt that desertion and remarriage were frequent. But in his scenario, it was to England, rather than to America, the dastardly husbands took themselves off. In this case the source is Nassau Senior, who elicited these views in 1852 in connection with Mounteagle's locality of Foynes in Limerick.[64] Despite the fact that Senior's *Journals on Ireland* are a farrago of fundamentalist dogmatism and intellectual confusion, undisciplined by the tyranny of evidence, Mounteagle's testimony to the practice of 'desertion' could still carry weight if he produced any evidence whatever for his claim that England was the favourite destination of the deserters or for his belief that the remarried would stay there. (How could he know?)

Why linger over the likes of Clarke and Mounteagle? It is not because they, any more than the Staffordshire or Leeds officials, were necessarily hostile witnesses. Indeed commentators of this type could often appear as humane, if harassed, trying to do the decent thing to the best of their ability in difficult circumstances. It is rather because so much of the evidence cited by scholars on all aspects of nineteenth-century diaspora experience is of this type, with uncorroborated opinion equated with evidence. These opinions can soon assume canonical status, as reflected in the fact that as conscientious a scholar as Deirdre Mageean can now cite Clarke's interpretation as historically estab-lished.[65] Who can reproach less learned scholars from citing it in turn as definitive evidence? This then becomes one way in which unsubstantiated opinion, even historical myths, can seep into the standard literature and come to acquire the status of scholarly truth.

Can more weight be laid on media than on official or ascendancy opinion? Were journalists not fearless seekers after the 'facts', and socially closer to the ground? What weight should we lay, for instance, on the *Liverpool Times*, distinguishing the emigrants of hope, the small farmers, who emigrated to Canada and the US, to improve their condition, from the emigrants of despair, the poorest of the poor, 'who beg or borrow the trifle that is necessary to bring them over to this country'.[66] It is an appealing distinction, suggesting a certain symmetry in the modalities of migration. And it has a ring of plausibility about it – it was even cited in *The Nation*. But the verdict on 'the emigrants of hope' must remain at 'may' for the moment.

Why? A glance at the date, November 1846, counsels caution. The *Liverpool Times* is suggesting that the first winter migration in Irish history –the braving of the North Atlantic in sailing ships at a time of year that had deterred earlier emigrants – was based on 'hope'. Of course there would have been hope – in the sense of hoping for the best. But it is far more likely that the driving force was fear, the fear of something worse than even the North Atlantic gales if they did not take ship now. Yet for all one knows, the writer for the *Liverpool Times* may have known Ireland better than most English – or Irish – journalists. Many English journalists, and Irish ones too, were ignorant of data and precise circumstances, with a superficial view of Ireland, saturated in stereotype substituting for evidence, reporting second or third hand, even of local events, whether in Ireland or England. Important sources for opinion, they can be dubious ones for fact. Precisely because the press is often the main source we have, we need ever more refined techniques of analysis to test its reliability.[67]

Thackeray might lament in 1842 that in Ireland 'there are two truths, the Catholic truth and the Protestant truth'. If the real England was in fact as awash with alternative truths as Ireland, that is only a small part of the problem of establishing the historical truth. That most nineteenth-century commentators were innumerate did not deter them from confidently invoking the language of numeracy, if often at the 'many', or 'great many', level of rigour. 'Inside' commentators in Ireland are no different from outside ones in this respect. If their perspective may have been different, their innocence of quantitative reasoning, and their capacity for self-deception, was not. Grace Neville has drawn on the records of the Irish Folklore Commission to illuminate the mélange of confusion and internal contradictions among innumerate popular impressions and images, generalising wildly on the basis of anecdotal reasoning – often grossly inaccurate, though no less historically significant for that.[68] If there can indeed be few peoples in western Europe for whose circumstances we are so dependent on outside observers, this by no means implies that the evidence of insiders can be taken at face value, however different the motives for, and modalities of, misunderstanding may have been. All these claims are likely to tell us more about the observers than the observed.

It might seem that the discovery of letters, usually from the emigrant to the home family, would finally bring us evidence directly from the emigrants themselves. Study of letters has indeed made a major contribution to our understanding since Arnold Schrier's important 1958 volume, *Ireland and the American Emigration*.[69] If Kerby Miller's 1985 epic, *Emigrants and Exiles*,[70] remains the prime example of a general interpretation drawing heavily on letters which, however much contested, stands as a seminal achievement, Miller's latest study of letters, composed in conjunction with David Doyle, Bruce Boling and Arnold Schrier himself, *Irish Immigrants in the Land of Canaan*, is surely destined to stand as a monumental contribution not only to Irish but to Atlantic diaspora studies.[71] If only a minority of the letters relate chronologically to the nineteenth century, readers can marvel at the depth of the scholarship throughout.

Even with *Canaan*, however, as with Fitzpatrick's wonderful *Oceans of Consolation*, based on letters between Ireland and Australia,[72] which itself sets highly impressive standards of editing, and several other collections of letters, or contributions drawing heavily on letters,[73] which fillet their sources with skill and style, the original question remains: how representative is the material, how far can we go beyond it to say that it adds up to more than the sum of its parts? The assessment of how representative any particular letter, or collection of letters, may be, raises fundamental methodological issues in the use of evidence. However fascinating in their own right, the extent to which individual letters can in themselves answer the question of how representative of wider experience they may be has to be addressed case by case, and therefore requires the most painstaking and perceptive scholarly editing. It is fortunate that these issues have been discussed illuminatingly by most of the editors themselves.

Whatever the difficulties about using letters as a basis for generalisation, they can provide crucial control on generalisations based on other sources or none. They can give a voice to some of the otherwise voiceless, not least because many of them are by women, far more concerned in the nineteenth century with the domestic sphere than scholars habituated to exploring the public sphere. Margaret MacCurtain's lament that 'we need to hear the voices of women who are nuns, especially the self who is no longer annalist but the subject of the testimony',[74] could be extended to many others too,[75] reminding us how precious for deepening our understanding every expression by, and not only about, the individual human being can be – again evidence from the inside rather than the outside, however carefully that in turn must be handled.[76]

## CATHOLIC/PROTESTANT AND THE USE OF EVIDENCE

If letters are likely to be class skewed, so that we may already have learned more about middle-class women from their own pens than we will ever hear from the pens of working-class women, or indeed working-class men, they are an indispensable source for the study of otherwise elusive private Irish Protestant perspectives on diaspora issues.

Despite much welcome emphasis on Protestant emigration from Ireland in the literature of the past decade, it remains unclear how far even those most insistent on including the Protestant experience actually incorporate it in their wider thinking. This may be partly because the dominant elements in the host societies only sporadically did so, tending to equate Irish with Catholic in their own depictions of Irish identity. Only where direct violence erupted between Irish Catholic and Irish Protestant were host societies generally prone to think of Irish possibly including Protestant too. If W. J. Lowe could claim in 1989 that 'very little is known about Irish Protestants in Lancashire, or elsewhere in Britain, because they simply do not emerge from the available sources as distinctive, individually or as a group',[77] they now emerge more clearly from the sources further north, where MacRaild's study of Cumbria, stressing the intensity of conflict between Protestants and Catholics from Ireland, as well as the division between English Protestants and Irish Catholics, raises a further raft of questions about Protestants no less than Catholics in the diaspora, extending beyond such major centres of sectarian conflict as Liverpool, Glasgow and Toronto.[78] The instructive study by GrahamWalker of mainly Ulster Protestant immigrants in Scotland in the 1991 volume edited by Tom Devine on Irish immigrants in Scotland indicates how understanding of the totality of the diasporic experience there can be deepened.[79] New ways of exploring Catholic–Protestant identities, like the use of Christian names among immigrants to identify religious affiliation on Clydeside, as suggested by Foster, Houston and Madigan, may deepen insight into an important and challenging subject.[80]

The preoccupation with tracing Catholic–Protestant relations abroad has tended to obscure the question of relations among different Protestant denominations. Was it, for instance, the case abroad, as Lyons alleged at home, that 'between Ulster Presbyterians and Anglicans from the South, there was little contact and less affection'?[81] (Where this would leave the significant number of Anglicans from the North, who have suffered at least as much neglect in diaspora studies as Catholics from Ulster, is unclear.) The issue is the more salient in the light of Akenson's perceptive observation that the role of Anglican emigration from Ireland has been much neglected.[82]

Among the most arresting of Akenson's own numerous contentions, the claim, based on US census returns of 1980 and 1990 on ancestry and ethnicity, and on Andrew Greeley's NORC (National Opinion Research Center) inquiries, that the majority of Irish in America are, and always have been, Protestant, raises basic questions about the conceptualisation of ethnic, national and diasporic identities, and the use of evidence, which deserve thorough exploration.[83]

Catholics and Protestants nurtured intriguing images of one another in all the centres of settlement, but the degrees of continuity and change over the century would reward systematic comparison. This is a subject ripe for the effusions of propagandists, especially those concerned with fashioning their conclusions, of whatever hue, as weapons in the Northern Ireland conflict. Nevertheless the study of denominational images in the diaspora, of both self and other, raises issues that should not be neglected because of the potential abuse of them. The answers cannot be decreed by definition, but can only be determined by meticulous research of the type that Kerby Miller has so patiently pursued, either on his own or in conjunction with others, in a notable series of skilfully sculpted studies that seek to trace shifting sensibilities, Protestant and Catholic, mainly on the basis of letters, picking a carefully documented path through the propaganda-strewn minefields of this issue.[84]

There is an intriguing model that claims that weaker immigrant identities adapt to the images the stronger other has of them, so that they behave in accordance with the expectations of the dominant stereotype. A widespread British image of the Irish (Catholic) as thuggish, raucous, drunken layabouts, grievously deficient in the Protestant virtues, 'left its imprint on immigrant imagination', Fitzpatrick reports, 'causing many settlers to revel in misconduct that might otherwise have been a matter of shame'.[85] Patrick O' Farrell likewise records drunken Irish Catholic diggers deliberately behaving like 'Fenians' in 1868 in Australia.[86] The tendency reputedly persisted longer. O'Farrell reports Irish Catholic working-class Australians, relishing their lack of social mobility, revelling in defying an image Protestant Anglo-Saxon Australia held of them by vociferously embracing the image in the mid-twentieth century, although nowadays it is allegedly ex-Catholic Irish who indulge this style of behaviour, whereas 'most' Catholic Irish earn the encomium of being just like Protestant Irish, 'quiet, decent and respectable',[87] apparently having thus ascended, in O'Farrell's value system, to the purpose of life on earth.

It is not entirely clear how far one can pursue this line of reasoning. A logical implication would seem to be that if only Anglo-Saxon Protestant types around the world had cherished a more aromatic view of their Catholic Hibernian neighbours, these Hibernians would have striven to acquire appropriate habits of physical, moral and social hygiene. If the hosts, then, had not insisted on seeing the Irish as incorrigible Catholics, or so the logic of the argument would appear to suggest, the Irish would have been much less Catholic. And if only the hosts had nurtured an equally repulsive image of

Protestants from Ireland, the logic would seem to be that they would have chosen to behave accordingly. Then there is a Gilley argument, which deserves close analysis, that the (Catholic) Irish were themselves complicit in the construction of the 'Paddy' and 'Biddy' image, an interpretation that raises a range of fascinating – and for some students of human nature, maybe frightening – issues.[88]

How far does it make sense to proceed along any of these lines? For how does change occur at all, if Irish Catholics are so anxious to behave in the style attributed to them? Do they have to wait patiently – but then patience does not belong in the stereotype either – until the WASP image of them changes, and then they adjust their behaviour to conform to the image? If not, how does one explain within this model the rise of so many Catholic Irish immigrants in various locations – or for that matter the apparent relative decline of Irish Protestants in the United States, who apparently began to fall behind Catholics in the social mobility stakes within a generation or so of allegedly deciding they must distance themselves from the hordes of Catholic Irish by insisting they themselves weren't really Irish at all, coming to lag behind their sundered Catholic brethren who, again mainly on the basis of Greeley's NORC surveys, emerge in the twentieth century as far more 'successful' than the Protestant Irish?[89]

Images are important. Some do build their lives around them. Some can even kill and die for them. How people come to construct their images of the superiority or inferiority of themselves and others, who they define as 'them' and 'us', is a matter of supreme importance. But how these images work their way into the psyches of all those affected, one way or another, requires more relentless and refined probing. It is certainly the case that people – and not least those who are conscious that they are deemed inferior in the stereotypes of the dominant 'other' – can have their behaviour influenced by their perception of those images. Their response can vary widely, however, and all have to be placed in context. Questions of racism, stereotypes, hatred, discrimination, and intimately related issues of if, or how, the Irish became white, or whiter, are likely to remain live topics in diaspora studies for long to come.[90]

Perry Curtis, whose 1968 *Anglo-Saxons and Celts*, and 1973 *Apes and Angels* provided the first detailed analysis of English and American images of the Irish as ape-men and women, was sharply criticised by Sheridan Gilley, and more recently by Roy Foster, both attacking, if in different tactical formation, the attribution of anti-Irish racism to the English and to WASP America. Far from cowering Curtis, the assaults provoked him into a vigorous counter attack, in the revised 1997 edition of *Apes and Angels*. This controversy, which will run and run, merits the close attention of diaspora scholars, not only because of its intrinsic interest, but because it revolves, as far as scholarship goes, around inescapable issues about the use of evidence in an emotionally charged area.[91] The issues can cut to the core of the image scholars cherish of themselves, providing an acid test of the ability of those of us who claim to be, or aspire to be, scholars, to live up to our profession.

## THE SCOTTISH QUESTION AND THE USE OF EVIDENCE

MacRaild's study of Cumbria is notable not only for establishing the salience of the relationship between Irish Catholics and Irish Protestants, but for establishing equally graphically just how different Cumbria was from places further south, on which generalisations about England have normally been based. Together with the work of Neal and others on the Irish on Tyneside,[92] it reminds us how porous generalisations can be, based on small and perhaps skewed regional or local samples even for relatively small countries, much less for the USA, Canada or Australia.

The issue surfaces yet more emphatically when the 'region' happens to be historically an old country in its own right, with a sense of identity extending beyond the regional. In this regard, it is once again Fitzpatrick who most challengingly throws down the gauntlet by translating so many references to England in his sources into references to 'Britain' in his text. He confronts the issue uncompromisingly, setting the tone for the entire approach, in the opening lines of 'A peculiar tramping people'. The first sentence resoundingly proclaims that 'During the first seventy years of the union, the Irish and British peoples came more and more into contact with one another'.[93] Disconcertingly, however, this is immediately preceded by the introductory quote from Carlyle, which begins equally resoundingly with a reference not to Britain, but to England.[94] Then follow in the text several sequential mentions of British or Britain, where the footnotes refer to England.

The first textual statement assures us that 'as Gilley points out there was no universal British stereotype of the Irish immigrant'.[95] But Gilley's article is called 'English attitudes to the Irish in England, 1780–1900'. Gilley's title is immediately followed by a reference to Engels, *The Condition of the Working Class in England*, followed in turn by David Steele's 'The Irish presence in the North of England, 1850–1914'. Thereafter the allusions to 'Britain' in the text are based on references that jumble Britain and England together as interchangeable terms, interspersed with a few fleeting references to Scotland. Nor is this tendency of course confined to Fitzpatrick. To take an example from a valuable collection, the wide-ranging 2000 volume edited by Andy Bielenberg, *The Irish Diaspora*, begins with Graham Davis on Britain, followed by Richard McCready on Scotland, with nothing specifically on England.[96] This is not, however, as inconsistent as it sounds, for the Britain of Davis turns out to be overwhelmingly England.

The use of England to mean Britain, and vice-versa, is standard in English historiography. Irish usage is more mixed. F. S. L. Lyons asserted in 1978 that 'to speak of an "English" as opposed to a "British" culture may sound strange to some ears, but in Ireland, for most people outside north-east Ulster, the term British has always seemed a little anaemic. They have traditionally seen their relation with their neighbour as one with England rather than with the broader and more artificial concept, Britain.'[97]

The issue for historians of the diaspora in the nineteenth century, however, is not whether Britain is somehow a more 'artificial' concept than England. It is to reconstruct the assumptions of both the emigrants and the host populations. Did they think in these terms? And the answer, or answers to that – for answers may have varied among different people and at different times – must depend on research rather than assumptions. Did emigrants from Ireland think of themselves as going to Britain, or to England, Scotland, or indeed Wales, for whose distinctiveness Paul O'Leary strongly argues?[98] For that matter, how far did they think in terms of national units at all? The issue here is not in the first instance about ideologies of naming, but how to reconstruct emigrant perspectives.

Fitzpatrick's usage has the merit of reflecting a carefully considered decision to treat references to any part of the island of Britain as representative of the whole island, a decision that allows him, in contrast to the multitude of commentators who float mindlessly between 'England' and Britain', to achieve almost total consistency. Generalising for 'Britain', on the basis of evidence referring to specific areas, emerges as a guiding methodology, not only in the *New History* but in general. Rev. John Garwood, for instance, so emphatic in his profile of the Irish in London, was nevertheless quite explicit that he referred to London, and only to London, as indeed his title itself proclaimed in 1853: *The Million-Peopled City: One-half of the People of London Made Known to the Other Half.* Yet Garwood finds himself conscripted to speak for Britain.

Nor is this methodology necessarily always wrong. Britain is a historically valid term for several diasporic purposes. But its analytical appropriateness depends on the precise issue under discussion, and the criteria for correct use have to be specified according to the issue. Given, for instance, that England and Wales, on the one hand, and Scotland on the other, were deemed sufficiently separate ecclesiastical jurisdictions for Rome to be careful to 'restore' only England and Wales in 1850, Scotland having to wait until 1878, the idea of 'British' Catholicism requires clarification. Yet Fitzpatrick identifies as representative of something called 'British' Catholicism a statement by an archbishop of Westminster, who was careful to describe himself as a prelate 'in England and in London'.[99] Maybe this is justifiable in scholarly terms. But the choice of terms has to be explained, not pronounced ex-cathedra. Gilley has been scrupulous in distinguishing between England and Scotland in the series of scalpel-like studies that have made so valuable a contribution to scholarship, being careful to use the plural in referring to 'the British Catholic Churches', and not only because of his sensitivity to correct Catholic protocol, but because of the implications of the distinctiveness of Scottish Protestantism also.[100] All of us need to make the assumptions underlying our generalisation processes of this type as explicit as does Fielding, in giving as his reason for excluding Scotland from his absorbing study of class and ethnicity among Irish Catholics, that the experience of Irish immigrants in Scotland 'was too unique to collapse into a broader history'.[101] This may in turn be rejected – but if so it can only be through debate, not through decree.

The argument is sometimes made that we should devote more attention to the Irish in Scotland on the grounds that they form a higher proportion of the population than in England. In itself, however, this is not decisive, for it would make percentages, independent of absolute numbers, the chief criterion for dwelling on particular places, which can often be quite misleading. But the numbers involved in the Scottish case were substantial, hovering during the century between 25 per cent and 30 per cent of the recorded Irish-born population of the entire island.[102] It receives nothing like comparable attention in even the very best surveys of the Irish in Britain. This neglect may in turn be a reason for the neglect of Protestant emigration to Britain from Ireland, which probably went disproportionately to Scotland.

Devine, treating Scotland as a case in its own right, stresses the 'need to set the Scottish immigrant experience in context by comparing the Irish in Scottish cities and towns with their counterparts in English, American and Canadian urban centres. Only through imaginative use of comparative study will the distinctiveness of the Irish in Scotland be fully revealed'.[103] What then can comparison reveal?

### COMPARISON ACROSS PLACE AND THE USE OF EVIDENCE

While all historical writing is at least implicitly comparative, the literature is littered with both implicit and explicit pseudo-comparison and false comparison. However legion the demands for explicit comparison, exhortation tends to far outrun demonstration, for comparison depends heavily not only on information, but on perspective. All the more power then to Akenson, Belchem, Campbell, Doyle, Gallman, Jacobson, Jenkins, Kenny, MacRaild, Ó Gráda and others who attempt actual comparative work.[104]

Akenson is surely right to claim that 'to know very much about the Irish in America, one must first learn a good deal about the Irish elsewhere'.[105] If left in isolation, however, the sentence is misleading. It would be more historical to say that to know very much about the Irish (or anyone else) anywhere, one must first learn a good deal about them elsewhere. It would also be valid to say that to know much about the Irish (or anyone else) anywhere, one must know as much as one can about other diasporic experiences in similar circumstances. But 'elsewhere', however beloved of scholars as a comparative category, is too vacuous a designation to be operationally relevant for most comparative purposes. The reason that the experience of 'the Irish in America' has been, is, and always will be absolutely central to understanding the Irish diasporic experience in the nineteenth century is not only that the numbers involved were much bigger than those in even the next biggest destination, Britain, but that the sheer diversity of American life meant that the variety of Irish experience there illuminates so many aspects of diaspora existence in a wider range of circumstances than can be found anywhere else. Without rejecting Akenson's proposition in principle, one should also invert it to read 'to know very much about the Irish elsewhere, one must first learn a good deal about the Irish in America'.

It is instructive to observe how demands for 'comparison' emanate from critics of Irish America, or just of America, in Australia and Canada, for not employing comparison with – Australia and Canada! In a revealing episode, Akenson assured an Australian audience in 1993 of his complete confidence in 'both the inevitability and the magnitude of this historiographic tidal wave' through which Australia, 'by virtue of its resources and scholars, will be the place where the baneful hegemony of U.S. work on the history of the Irish diaspora will be overcome', adding that 'the Australian model, much more than the accepted American model of the Irish diaspora experience, is typical of the situation world-wide'.[106]

Far from being embarrassed by the fulsomeness of this tribute, the hosts succumbed to the apparently hallucinogenic impact of so mesmerising a vision by going yet a step further (perhaps summarising the exuberance of a verbal contribution?), attributing to Akenson the prophesy 'that the future of Irish Studies, not just within Australia, but worldwide, lies with Australian historical writing'.[107] So now it is not just the churls toiling in Irish Diaspora Studies, but in Irish Studies in general, who must wait with bated breath for the latest announcements and pronouncements of the new Antipodean ascendancy. It is precisely because Australian scholarship, as reflected in the admirable series of volumes emanating from the Irish-Australian conferences themselves,[108] and in the manner in which several Australian scholars, from Geoffrey Bolton through Patrick O'Farrell to Philip Bull, Mark Finnane, David Fitzpatrick and Elizabeth Malcolm, have enriched scholarship on Ireland, that one is tempted to wonder at the impulses behind the careless rapture of such hegemonic aspirations.

There is in fact no international 'model' of Irish diaspora historiography. American researchers do not dominate work on the Irish diasporic experience in Britain, or Canada, or Australia. Ironically the country outside the USA on which most American research has been conducted has been Ireland, with none other than Akenson himself as a prolific contributor. It would indeed be instructive to explore the impact of American historiography on Ireland, but pending comprehensive historiographical inquiry, based on the scholarly use of evidence, the invocation of 'baneful hegemony' seems as premature as it is immature. Not only is there no international model. There should be none. Researchers in every country are likely to learn something from those in every other, provided of course they are capable of approaching the subject in a scholarly spirit.

Malcolm Campbell, at the same conference, sought to justify Akenson's faith in the rise of Australian and the fall of American scholarship, with an assault on everyone tainted by the American virus, from Lawrence McCaffrey to Kerby Miller to David Doyle, for failing to see America through Australian eyes. That a scholar of Campbell's research record, who has himself done serious work on aspects of Irish emigrant experience in America and Australia, should commit himself to a perspective which, despite its pleas for comparison, remains profoundly insular, raises serious issues. It transpires that the rhetoric of the recognition of 'international' scholarship actually means recognition of Australasian and Canadian scholarship. But Campbell's example of Canadian historiography relies heavily on the American émigré, Akenson, leaving it unclear how comprehensively Canadian scholarship reaches the required 'international' standard.[109]

It appears too that for Campbell Ireland itself counts as no more 'international' than the United States, as he berates David Doyle for venturing to express reservations about the vaulting claims of self-styled 'international scholarship', as if Doyle himself were not 'international' in his range of research and reflection. Should one now have a new naming ritual where 'international scholarship' on the Irish diaspora means the scholarship of Australians anywhere, and of one American-in-Canada, and excludes as equally tainted both Americans outside Canada, and Irish (and the rest of the world?) anywhere? Rarely can the term 'international' have been so nationalised.

The issues of who is qualified to understand whom, the intensity of the anti-Irish-American, or just anti-American, resentments, themselves raise intriguing issues of motivation and psychology, which we must restrain the temptation to pursue here, however absorbing it might be to probe the impulses lurking beneath the surface. There are, in any case, likely to be impulses lurking beneath all our surfaces. The relevant issue is not the impulse, but how far the evidence supports the conclusions. At their most potentially fruitful, genuine 'international' approaches can be related to the increasing emphasis on the transnational perspective on American history. But this transnational perspective is still a matter of intense debate, much preached but little practised.[110] Something may still be achieved, however, beyond the merely descriptive, if it can be mobilised along the lines proposed by Kevin Kenny, who is properly sceptical of Robin Cohen's valiant but doomed effort to salvage analytical purpose for the concept of diaspora by proposing to distinguish five different types. Intelligent though Cohen's formulation be, it still leaves untouched the basic problem of operationalising the concept itself. Kenny instead proposes an alternative way of approaching the issues by suggesting how what he terms the trans-nationalism of a diasporic approach and the cross-nationalism of a comparative approach can be operationalised in practice.[111]

Kenny's approach transcends diaspora history in the conventional sense. An ambitious attempt, drawing on his researches on Irish-American labour history, and on his general synthesis of Irish-American history, to locate the Irish–American experience in the wider debate on the 'internationalising' of American history, and offering as a case study an interpretation of the Irish diasporic experience in Britain and the USA, it requires a daunting command of massive literatures, a familiarity with the evidence undergirding interpretations of the relevant general national histories, and a rare capacity for both conceptualisation and balanced judgement. This is no argument for resisting it, merely a warning that the bow will take some bending – and that it will require the manner in which history is generally taught to be radically reconceptualised.

Lawrence McCaffrey, on the other hand, expresses distinct scepticism about much of the comparative approach to the history of Irish America, rejecting what he sees as facile comparisons between the USA and anywhere else, arguing that American experience was unique, while also stressing striking differences within the USA. Much of this is still at the stage of an agenda for research rather than the definitive result of research: what is the evidence, for instance, that the Irish enjoyed more rapid upward social mobility in Baltimore than in other eastern cities, and that this explains why Cardinal Gibbon's concept of Catholicism was more 'liberal' than that of Archbishop Corrigan of New York?[112] Yet McCaffrey is right to stress the importance of seeing the USA whole, rather than impose generalisations based on the specific experience of any one centre. Oscar Handlin's 1941 study of Boston, in particular, was so singular an achievement that an entire generation grew up under its influence.[113] It has taken the work of a further succession of fine scholars – not least McCaffrey himself and his colleagues and students researching Chicago, as well as Doyle, Dennis Clark, David Emmons, David Gleeson, Tim Meagher, Jim Walsh, and many others – to explore and document the exhilarating variety of internal experience.[114]

It is precisely this celebration of variety in American historiography that allows Tim Meagher to deny that the experience of the Worcester Irish, which he has so brilliantly illuminated in *Inventing Irish America*, was typical, if only because 'there was no typical Irish-American experience' – an observation carrying all the greater weight coming from the joint editor of so major a collaborative venture in diaspora historiography as *The New York Irish*.[115] The very fact that there is no typical Irish centre in the USA makes a comparative approach to the internal experience all the more necessary for the general historian, for comparison can be translocal no less than transnational, posing equally demanding, if somewhat conceptually different, challenges. Numbers do count, however. Some experiences are more significant – if not more 'representative' – than others simply because they involve far more people. The Irish experience in New York City is certainly not typical of Irish experience in America. But then neither is New York itself 'typical' of America. But that does not detract from its significance, simply because of the scale and role of New York City in American history. That of course is no reason for neglecting anywhere else, and the sheer variety of experiences affecting substantial numbers of people within the United States ensures that there are still enough questions to keep generations of students at work.

But where should they work? McCaffrey comes to the sardonic conclusion that the best way to understand Irish America is to work on Irish America in America, rather than in Dublin or Belfast,[116] much less presumably in London, Liverpool or Edinburgh, Melbourne or Sydney, Toronto, Montreal or Quebec, not to mention Auckland, Cape Town, or Buenos Aires – and a host of more local archives.

Even those, however, like myself, who have some sympathy with McCaffrey's scepticism about current fashion, might wonder why the issue has to be framed as either–or, rather than both–and, depending on the precise topic. Whatever aspect of Irish America be studied, the quality of interpretation can only benefit from alertness to the external as well as the internal comparative dimension, properly conceived. This will vary widely, depending on the precise topic, and always runs the danger of confusing comparison with pseudo-comparison. But it has to be done because it is only by establishing how precisely the Irish diasporic experience is distinctive that the analytical accuracy of any statement purporting to identify the distinctiveness of that experience can be assessed. Indeed, if plausible evidence were to be adduced in support of Akenson's assertion that the superior Canadian source material allows us to infer American experience from Canadian data, then presumably American research students should be heading across the border in droves.[117]

It goes without saying that conceptualising comparison demands the highest degree of intellectual rigour and imagination. To revert for a moment to the issue of 'transience' in Britain, ponder how one would compare the implications of the model of the negative consequences of the mobility of the Irish in Britain with O'Farrell's attribution of what he regards as the rapid assimilation of the Irish in Australia partly to 'the mobility of a pioneering society'.[118] It is possible to list immediately reasons for both along the 'compare and contrast' axis – but proper comparison would have to go beyond instant responses, and might deepen understanding of both cases. That so much of what poses and passes as comparative is inadequately conceived is not itself a reason for abandoning the attempt to compare, least of all in diaspora history, for who says diaspora says comparison.


### COMPARISON ACROSS TIME AND THE USE OF EVIDENCE

Comparison embraces time as well as place. Comparison over place and time can fuse in many ways, as in Ó Gráda's studies of other famines over several countries and centuries, from which one may derive possible insights into the Irish experience, or Bob Scally's wide-ranging reflections on the same subject, or when Harris invokes Micheal Piore's study of recent Hispanic migrants in New York to illuminate possible attitudes towards housing of nineteenth-century Irish migrants to urban England.[119] Comparisons over time, when properly conceived, can be immensely rewarding, but here I will confine myself to the more limited issue of comparison within the nineteenth century itself, for there is a danger of treating the century as a whole, and making inadequate allowance for changes over the period. Aspinwall's three-phase periodisation for Scotland – 1815–46, 1848–67 (a pedant might wonder if 1847 has gone AWOL), and 1868 onward – may or may not be appropriate for other locations, or indeed for Scotland itself.[120] But by departing from the almost mechanical pre-Famine and post-Famine scenarios it obliges us to think about the fundamental issue of periodisation, which should certainly be explored more systematically.

Nevertheless, it may be hazarded that the spectre of the Famine will continue to loom large over nineteenth-century emigration, with pre-Famine and post-Famine remaining the two most frequent chronological categories. Here we can only look at the impact of the Famine, while stressing the importance of searching for both continuities and changes throughout the entire century. As with so much else concerning the Famine, the ghost at the feast (to turn a ghastly phrase) is the Famine itself. There are still too few studies that build on the splendid work of Ó Gráda, Donnelly, Neal, and Scally not only to bridge the Famine experience, but to explore that experience itself. Most either stop before the Famine, or begin after it. But how do the pre-Famine emigrants relate to the Famine ones, and both to the post-Famine ones? And how do the children and later descendants of the Famine migrants relate to the Famine experience?

If the Famine is central to nineteenth-century periodisation, the impact of the Famine itself depended partly on timing. Timing influenced not only the location but the gender and occupational structure of settlement patterns.

Timing normally reflects a combination of perceived demand for labour abroad and perceived prospects at home. The Famine significantly shifted the weight of these in popular perceptions. Thirty years earlier, for instance, an outflow of comparable proportions would have found far fewer female employment opportunities in the United States. The timing of the rise of an American urban middle class was to prove decisive for the location of Irish female Famine and post-Famine immigrants in the USA, where middle-class households were spawning a massive market for domestic servants. In general the timing of developments in foreign labour markets greatly affected the direction and timing of emigration.

The image of the Famine influenced many diasporic identities. Our understanding of how precisely, in what circumstances, through what mechanisms, remembering, transmuting, transmitting and forgetting, operated, has been greatly advanced by the work of the 1990s, much of it spurred by the impulse given by the sesquicentenary to establishing the full historical record of so epoch-making an event. Nevertheless much still remains to be understood. For if many Famine emigrants passed on bitter memories to their children, the issue is not only one of remembering the Famine – but of which Famine they remembered.[121]

Consider the disputed issue of the number of Famine dead. Whatever the role of Irish nationalist or humanitarian propaganda, the objective scale of the Famine, the recollection of the death and desolation they themselves witnessed, presumably affected memories and perceptions. Was it the Famine of a million or more dead, the figure most frequently cited in the literature until much lower figures, of a half million or less, were intimated or expressed, though without any supporting evidence, by some Revisionist historians in the 1970s and 1980s?[122] These have now been revised in turn, as scholarly research by Mokyr and Ó Gráda suggests a figure of a million or more once again.[123] Nothing on this subject can ever be deemed final, and the balance of probability may change again, whether upwards or downwards. But it can only change if Mokyr and Ó Gráda are refuted. That can only happen through engagement with evidence.

Or consider the relation between eviction and emigration. We do not know what proportion of emigrants had been evicted, or had seen relations or friends evicted. Nor do we know how that proportion may have varied between the main emigrant destinations. It seems reasonable to assume in general that those with personal experience of eviction, or of observation of eviction, may have carried bitter memories, nurtured them and transmitted them to their children, more passionately than those less directly affected. It therefore matters significantly for students of the impact of the Famine on diasporic memories whether the number evicted was the 250,000 of Vaughan[124] or more like the 600,000 of O'Neill,[125] which now holds the ground until and unless it can be refuted. Two hundred and fifty thousand would in itself have been enough to have made a vivid impression on those sensitive to such matters, but 600,000 would presumably have left more festering memories still. However 'local' personal memories of death and eviction will inevitably have been in the first instance, the number of 'locals' is crucial in determining the composition of the wider picture.

The issue is a central one for students of nineteenth-century emigration. For the impact of the Famine on diasporic identities was not only a matter of numbers, but of memories and mentalities. How far memories reflect the specific experiences of different categories, or how far individual memories came to be blended into a general collective memory, and for how long, may be impossible to establish precisely, but is nonetheless the type of question that must be asked. The variety of experiences chronicled in Margaret Crawford's *Hungry Stream* reminds us of how diverse might have been the recollections of those who came through Michael Quigley's Grosse Île, or from Trevor Parkhill's Ulster workhouses, or Patrick Duffy's Shirley Estate, or whether they flocked into Frank Neal's Liverpool or Edward O'Donnell's New York, both very different from Brenda Collins's Dundee.[126]

'Mentalities' have to be defined in the most inclusive possible manner because the long-term psychological and mental consequences of the Famine are likely to loom much larger than heretofore as the subject of systematic scholarly research, requiring collaboration between specialists in mental health, medical history and psychology, as well as more traditional types in history and literature. Knowledge of the medical history of the Famine itself has grown steadily thanks to the work of Laurence Geary and Margaret Crawford, building on William MacArthur's chapter in Edwards and Williams over 40 years ago, and the next step should involve a fusing of the research into physical and mental health among the survivors, at home and abroad.[127] The challenge of tracing 'memory' through successor generations, or for that matter the invention of memory in later generations, brings us back to the problem of unpacking and unscrambling the constituents of Akenson's 'multi-generational ethnic community' and how to probe the history of memory, including the creation of memory, across generations – what people cling to, what they let go, when, where, why, how, do some forget, and others remember. Why do others again identify with particular memories, internalise them, even if they have not come down to them directly through their own families? Famine memory may be one of the most extreme cases of all this, but in principle the issue affects all memory, and disaporic memory in a particular way.

Attempts to compute the likely number of emigrants in the absence of Famine, on the basis of projections from pre-Famine figures, however reasonable in themselves, are in danger of diverting attention from the impact of the Famine. It is possible that up to 800,000 of the 2 million or so who may have left between 1845 and 1855 would have emigrated anyway over that period. A cogent case can be made too that 'every distinctive aspect of Irish-America was discernible before the great famine'.[128] Nevertheless, those who left from 1846 would not have gone as Famine emigrants, and therefore not with the same memories. In political terms, 'No Famine, no Fenians' may be too lapidary a formulation – but the sequence is inherent in the contribution of the Famine to political culture. And although politics is one of the several topics omitted for reasons of space from the present survey, the place of politics in the diaspora, not least for the manner in which it illuminates issues of identity, deserves deep reflection.

Just as understanding Irish circumstances is a prerequisite for understanding the emigrant experience, so can evidence from the diaspora have implications for understanding Ireland. Who could have guessed that so many of those habitually stereotyped as lazy, feckless and improvident on the eve of the Famine could have embarked on one of the great savings surges of history so soon after disembarking in North America, had Marion Casey's discovery of the New York Emigrant Savings Bank records, whose riches both she herself and Ó Gráda have already begun to mine, not salvaged information about savings behaviour inconceivable from Irish sources, one of the many 'hidden Irelands' of the Diaspora that is rewarding excavation.[129]

Teaching the Famine in all its dimensions, and not least its diasporic consequences, is one of the great challenges to both the intellectual rigour and the intellectual integrity of students of the Irish experience. This is not the place to assess how far that test has been met, although if one were inclined to be suspicious of conclusions that conveniently happen to coincide with the ideological convictions of the writer, one might wonder how much of Famine scholarship would be left standing. The scale of the challenge makes the success of Maureen Murphy, Director of the Great Irish Famine project on behalf of the New York State Human Rights Curriculum, all the more impressive, in crafting one of the great pedagogical achievements of our era, in the Famine Curriculum for New York schools.[130]

If teaching the Famine involves the most obvious challenge to scholarly standards, given the ideological impulses influencing so much of the controversy on the topic, the teaching of diaspora history in general poses challenges of both content and presentation that deserve more systematic reflection. American scholarship is particularly productive in this respect, as evident for instance in the discussion of Kevin Kenny's *American Irish* in the *Journal of American Ethnic History*.[131]

## RESEARCH AGENDA AND THE USE OF EVIDENCE

Tim Meagher's summary of the results of recent research on the Irish-American experience probably holds for everywhere:

> the key environmental influences on ethnic development are the vitality of local economies and the breadth of opportunities that they afforded; the rules of politics; the ethnic origins, power, and endurance of local elites; and the time of arrival, cultural predilections, and numbers of other immigrant or racial groups.[132]

But this very summary also constitutes a challenge, for how many studies are able to encompass all these variables?

Here one can identify only a handful of topics, in addition to those already mentioned, deserving immediate attention. Methodological issues concerning the most fruitful approach to diasporic topics should loom large, not least in the light of Mary Hickman's critique of approaches 'bequeathed by either American sociology or Irish historiography', to the study of the Irish in England, which she believes lead to a neglect of 'the role of the state in shaping Irish experience'.[133] Her particular criticisms of what she sees as Fitzpatrick's misuse of the concept of 'community' have been criticised in turn by Fitzpatrick.[134] It must be hoped that the respective viewpoints will be further expounded, for the issues could be fruitfully pondered for all locations. It must always be kept in mind, of course, that studies of diaspora must strive to understand the host societies as intimately as the immigrants and their descendants, for it is out of the interaction between them that diasporic identities emerge.

It is instructive that it should be Davis McCaughey in Australia who chose to stress what he saw as an Irish genius for institution building, whether in political parties, churches, trade unions, or education systems, emphasising the role of the Irish as an important subgroup in preventing the dominance of either extreme individualist or extreme dirigiste ideologies.[135] McCaughey's approach, like Hickman's, if from a different perspective, allows the role of education in society to be located in the context of the nature of the state. Given the potential importance of education in the formation of world-views, it is extraordinary how little the study of the subject has yet been incorporated in systematic detail into diaspora studies – by education meaning the content of education, and the identity and formation of teachers, as well as the politics and administration of education. The Irish model of the churches, and particularly the Catholic Church, keeping the state at a distance, while at the same time using the state for their own purposes, was destined to travel around the diasporic world, influencing the nature of the host societies in a way that went well beyond the Irish component of those societies. Yet the Irish component itself still requires extensive research, even in the USA, where Janet Nolan has opened up the whole issue of teaching and Philip Gleason can bluntly state as recently as 1999 that the 'historical role of the Irish in American higher education has never been studied in a systematic way'. Studies of the impact of education at all levels and in all places are urgently needed.[136]

Gender relations are as central to the history of the Irish diaspora as to the general history of the human race. No history of the nineteenth-century diaspora that concentrates exclusively on males or females can provide a full understanding of the experience for the vast majority. It is only through reconstructing their interaction that the totality of the diasporic experience can be recaptured. The main weakness in Ferrie's work, for instance, is that however far it pushes back the frontiers of understanding of American internal migration, it relates only to males, whereas much of real diasporic life in the nineteenth century revolved around the relations of men and women in the context of the family. Capturing that complexity may be a counsel of perfection, but even within the confines of single-sex history Anne O' Connell is surely right to call for greater nuance in delineating the contours of late nineteenth-century female emigration, pointing to the potential variety of women's experience, venturing beyond the catechism-like recitation of self-evident truths which so often substitutes for exploration of the cross-grained texture of lives actually lived, whether of women or men.[137]

If the lunatic pauper, Isabella Charles, can hardly stand as a representative woman, her mother, who watched over her unfortunate daughter, may have been closer to being a representative mother. But how often do mothers feature in diaspora studies – even though O'Leary's reference to 'the matrifocal orientation of Irish migrant culture' in Wales[138] could probably be extended generally to diaspora culture in the nineteenth century? The study of parenthood in general, and of motherhood in particular, the most consuming role in the life of the big majority of women in the diaspora during the century, remains astoundingly neglected.

The biggest single gap in our knowledge concerns the demographic history of the diaspora, both in terms of the marriage history of the emigrants them-selves, and of their children. Making all due allowance for the problems with the statistical evidence, the finding of Marc Foley and Tim Guinnane that the age at marriage of Irish female emigrants in America was much more 'normal' than has been assumed, casts serious doubt on many of the claims made about the unique problems imposed on women by the Irish (Catholic) inheri-tance, and alerts us to the potential scale of the revisions probably now required.[139] Comparative fertility studies too can penetrate value systems and behaviour patterns in an especially illuminating manner, which in turn can call into question much of the oral and anecdotal evidence on which research has tended to rely in this field as in so many others.[140]

Central though parenthood was to nineteenth-century diasporic experience, no history that concentrates exclusively on an adult population in the
prime of life can convey the fullness of that experience. We tend to jump from
active adult generation to active adult generation in their adult prime, without
tracing through the lifecycle experience of any single generation. Children
and the elderly are people too, however rarely they attract the attention of
scholars who are, for the most part, neither children nor elderly.

Marriage, or at least the coming of children, was likely to be the great
divide between lifestyles of relative mobility and of relative stability. Relatively
few are likely to have tramped incessantly as families after the birth of their
children, or to have courted, except in the terror of the Famine, the conditions
that could leave the three-month-old Anthony O'Sullivan lying lifeless on the
roadside at his mother's milkless breast in April 1847 outside Manchester.[141]

Decision making about marriage was not only central to the lives of
individual women and men, but to the entire diasporic experience. Scholars
of Neal's stature who have laboured in the census material can justifiably
claim that 'there is a need to move beyond census data',[142] but for many there
is still an urgent need to get as far as it first before they can move beyond it.
They must of course resist the temptation to succumb to what Tony Wrigley
described three decades ago as the 'delusive clarity and apparent authority' of
official statistics, above all the census. Quantitative evidence can be as potentially misleading as oral or literary evidence, and perhaps even more dangerous
precisely because of its 'apparent authority'.[143] But census schedules are essential for testing, for instance, Akenson's claim that the Irish settled for no more
than 20 years anywhere in Britain against Patrick Joyce's view that 'the integrity
and longevity of Irish neighbourhood communities [are] very striking'.[144]

Census linkage is so obviously essential, if not sufficient, for the adequate
study of family formation that when a report comes to be made on research
during the current decade one hopes it will be able to harvest the fruits of
sustained inquiry in the census schedules of the relevant countries, despite all
the familiar problems of source-criticism that attach to their use in various
jurisdictions.

O'Sullivan, in a graphic phrase, observed that interdisciplinary study of
Irish migration 'puts the song next to the census'.[145] But that still remains
much more the ideal than the reality. One might wish that there was far more
study of both, although the recent explosion in the study of the music of the
diaspora, with all its potential for illuminating so much of the wider experience,
offers encouraging portents of more to come. It may indeed be that the best
hope of overcoming the subordination of scholarship to personal and ideological agendas, to whatever modest extent human nature allows, lies with the
musical fraternity, whose love of their art can transcend even fraught personal
relations, spanning the oceans and the traditions in common devotion to the

music itself. However that may be, Busteed has shown how ballads can be effectively mobilised as source material transcending more prosaic texts even in the relatively unfamiliar English context.[146]

O'Sullivan and Fanning rightly stress the variety of techniques employed by historians, sociologists, sociolinguists, literary critics, artists, architects and folklorists, to mention no more, in the study of diasporic experience.[147] But the caveat must be entered, on behalf of earlier generations, that they all require the unifying framework of historical thought. Otherwise specialist perspectives may distort more than they illuminate, because there is only one ultimate unifying feature among them all – they are all dealing with the historical past. The danger of approaching that past unhistorically is that decontextualised content not only plays into the hands of propagandists of all stripes, but simply falsifies the experience of the dead generations. This is not a plea to confine the history of diaspora to historians as academically defined. It is a plea to think historically about the past instead of simply plunging in as if the past were merely a backward extension of the present – which we are all prone to do, so difficult is it to think historically. As one modest but essential preliminary step in that direction, one elementary but fundamental technique of the historians' craft with respect to the use of evidence, that should be obligatory in the scholarly study of the diaspora, irrespective of the subject or topic involved, concerns reference systems. The proliferation of meaningless lists of titles, without specific page references, masquerading as critical footnotes, but failing to relate to the precise argument or alleged evidence in the text, that appears to be the standard practice in some disciplines (and even among historians in some countries), should be simply unacceptable as source-criticism among serious scholars. It is instrumental in allowing slovenly assertions pass unchallenged as scholarly truth.

The diaspora history of the nineteenth century is a genre that draws from, but transcends, all other disciplines, and all specialist sub-disciplines, in its aspiration of seeing the diaspora whole. Far more can be done to incorporate several disciplines, not least the visual, in the writing and teaching of diaspora studies. Here I will mention only two points. The first concerns the relationship between historical and literary studies. Both need to become more sensitive to the perspectives of the other. No study of the impact of the Famine on mentalities, for instance, could afford to ignore the critical work of Margaret Kelleher, Christopher Morash or Charles Fanning, on the one hand, or of Peter Quinn's historical fiction, on the other, or indeed of Thomas Keneally's blending of different genres. When done well, these can provide perspectives, insights, and a depth of understanding, that transcend the observations of the official, mind. On the other hand, literary critics must become more aware of how often historians are baffled by the manner in which they can invoke a fictional representation as if were a valid record of the actual history of an event or period.

Much of what it may suit a later generation to consider an imaginative insight may be no more than self-indulgent distortion, however seductive the style, or ideologically appealing, the perspective. The historical mind can of course succumb to such temptation itself, but at least it is then likely to be exposed in due course as transgressing the professional standards of the discipline. As the relation between history and literature is central to understanding of the human condition, the manner in which the historical mind relates to literature, and the literary mind relates to history, needs to be pondered more systematically, as of course do the very meanings of 'history' and 'literature'.[148]

The second point concerns the case for economic history, not simply in its own right – the case can be made for many a subject in its own right – but because the idea of 'success' haunts the Irish case. Issues of identity in Ireland revolved inescapably around the relationships between conquerors and conquered. So many of the images fostered by those relationships revolved in turn around the relative capacity of the 'natives' and 'settlers' to achieve economic 'success' that the economic performance of the diaspora became a propaganda weapon to be wielded by the protagonists in the racial and religious conflicts, at home and abroad, to a degree probably unrivalled in the history of any other western European people. It is one of the ironies of diaspora discourse that whichever religion found favour in the eyes of God was often held to be measured by the material success of its members, when the doctrines in conflict spent much of their time denouncing materialism. Protestant, or at least Calvinist, theology was more flexible in accommodating itself to the needs of money-makers, allowing them to make their money with the clear conscience that it was really God's Will they were fulfilling, whereas Catholics (or at least the theologically sensitive souls among them) had to make money while persuading themselves they did so in a fit of absence of mind, in so far as, for instance, 'American Catholic culture perceived wealth as a symbol of betrayal'.[149]

It is therefore disconcerting that so little relative attention is devoted to economic history. One need not go as far as Chris McConville in claiming that 'the multifarious variations of migration can only be revealed by an historian who's more interested in counting than in quoting',[150] for both approaches should complement one another. But one must certainly be able to count as well as quote – it is after all elementary innumeracy that leaves so much of the 'evidence' paraded in so much diaspora historiography as inadequate, if not grossly misleading. Numeracy is a prerequisite for understanding the economic aspects of emigration, including attempts to assess the significance of immigrant labour supplies for the economic fortunes of the recipient countries. Verdicts on this issue that do not engage with the work of Timothy Hatton, Jeffrey Williamson, Kevin O'Rourke, Ó Gráda and Guinnane simply cannot carry conviction.[151] This does not mean that one must accept uncritically the conclusions of even the most eminent practitioners in the field, whose reliance on macroeconomic perspectives can raise doubts among those working at the microeconomic level, who may see little correlation between the models purporting to reflect the big picture and their perceptions at grassroots level.[152] But it does mean one must engage explicitly with the conclusions, rather than ignore them.

It means too that one must admit the artificiality of defining diaspora by century, however inescapable as a chronological category, for economic processes are notoriously indifferent to calendar chronology. In the present case of nineteenth-century studies, special effort should therefore be devoted to determining the linkages at the beginning and end of the period, to identifying what was carried forward into the century, and out of the century. The later connections are already relatively well established, mainly because many of the same scholars often work on the nineteenth and twentieth centuries. As fewer of the specialists on the pre-nineteenth century do not, however, work equally on the nineteenth century, and vice-versa, there is a danger that the findings of scholars like Bric, Canny, Cullen and Griffin may not be adequately incorporated into thinking about later periods. All the more valuable then are the types of study by Doyle and Miller that transcend the chronological divide. Whatever the misunderstandings about the dynamics of emigration that lead to so many studies ending or beginning at the irrelevant political dates of 1921 or 1922, establishing the links going forward into the nineteenth century – or ceasing to go forward – whether with reference to North America, Britain, or the European continent, to which much valuable work has been recently devoted, is the more immediate task.

The axiomatic assumption that predominantly Irish speakers would be necessarily helpless abroad may require revision, at least in some circumstances, in the light of the exasperated description by Leeds poor law officials of their importunities, and of the implications of their family customs, in which the women played a far from passive role, raising wider issues about the place of women in Irish language culture, and the consequences of Anglicisation in the diaspora for the status of Irish-speaking women.[153] Attitudes towards language issues have been saturated on all sides with assumptions that owe little to scholarship. That makes it all the more instructive that the cool comparative eye Ferrie casts on the relative economic performance of Irish and German immigrants in mid-century America does not find superior Irish knowledge of English to have translated into obvious material advantage.[154] Complex though the issues be, conventional assumptions about the relationship between language and economic success in diaspora experience now require systematic scrutiny.

One could proceed with an almost endless list of neglected topics, not least sport.[155] More important even than topic, however, is perspective. There is a dire need for all of us to become more explicitly self-interrogatory about our own motives and assumptions. If few of us are likely to be as combatively forthright as Patrick O'Farrell, nevertheless his explanation of the inspiration behind his celebrated 1986 study, *The Irish in Australia*, illuminates his perspective:

> I see our culture – our Catholic and our Irish culture – Catholic in particular – the broad Irish culture, as being very much in danger in this country. I see it as perishing, as dying for remembrance of things past. I think that would be a disaster . . . the overlay of recent immigrants are entitled to themselves and their culture, and good luck to them. But we are entitled to ours – very much so – because we've done things in this country that nobody else has done . . . the book is a celebration in many ways. But it's like any decent celebration, a critical celebration . . . but I do feel that we are no mean people and I'd like that to be the message that people would get out of that book.[156]

Of course self-portraiture has to be as subject to critical evaluation as any other – indeed O'Farrell himself sketched a variety of not always compatible self-images.[157] But self-reflection as a genre can move the subject significantly forward by revealing silent assumptions and their possible origins, and can help us understand how we come to select the evidence, consciously or unconsciously, on which our conclusions are based. McCaffrey, for instance, attributes much of the difference of emphasis between himself and Kerby Miller to their different personal trajectories, partly reflecting their different generational backgrounds and the changing circumstances of their country.[158] Though this in turn deserves debate, McCaffrey raises issues about how we acquire our perspectives which should help us all grow in awareness about why we look at our subject the way we do.

Graham Davis refers illuminatingly to British attitudes towards Irish immigrants as 'a cultural filter that mirrors the values of the host nation without fully reflecting the variety of Irish migrant experience'.[159] It is important for us all to interrogate ourselves as to how far we are influenced by nationality, ethnicity, gender, religion, class and/or the pressure of current events – the Northern Ireland conflict has obviously left its imprint here as elsewhere, for better and for worse – not only to think in particular ways, but to subordinate the scholarly use of evidence to other purposes. How far can any of us stand outside our own ideology and look in on ourselves?

In cross-examining ourselves we must also try to locate ourselves in the longer historiography of the subject, a much neglected aspect of diaspora scholarship, but one essential to historical perspective, both on earlier generations and on ourselves. The work of scholars during the 1990s must be placed in the context of their own earlier research. The contributions of not only McCaffrey and Miller, but of several others, whose corpus stretches back far beyond the nineties, like Akenson, Clark, Dolan, Doyle, Edwards, Fanning, Fitzpatrick, Gilley, Greeley, Meagher, O'Farrell and Ó Gráda, needs to be located in the totality of their œuvre. The historiography of Irish Studies in general still sadly lacks more than a handful of examples of sustained critical engagement with the full body of work of individual scholars, despite the potential of this approach.

This approach requires too the systematic analysis of individual books, articles, hypotheses, and of the evidence adduced to sustain interpretations, seeking to evaluate strengths and weaknesses, in the manner of Bielenberg's judicious assessment of Akenson's contentions concerning the Irish role in the British Empire.[160]

MacRaild's warning that scholars have swallowed uncritically too much of the evidence of contemporary witnesses should alert us to our own suscep-tibility in this regard. How many of us are condemned by our own value-systems to gaze as uncomprehendingly at the real history of the diaspora in the nineteenth century as the contemporaries through whose eyes scholars for so long viewed the diasporic experience? How far are late twentieth-century scholars 'distanced' by one or more of the values of nationality, ethnicity, religion, class, gender and language from their subjects?[161] All of this makes the close scrutiny of the use of evidence in even the most standard works essential. How much of the deluge of words of recent years will survive as added value, when purged of all repetition, recycling, and unsubstantiated claims, remains to be seen. A subject ultimately advances not in relation to the number of words published on it, but in relation to the extent to which the supporting evidence survives scholarly scrutiny. The indispensable task for the future remains exactly the same as for the past – the testing of the concepts with which we work, and the testing of the evidence on which interpretation is based. The first step towards achieving scholarly standards is to be aware of all the impulses to lapse from them. That awareness is possibly even more important in the case of diasporic than of domestic studies in that no reader can be expected to be fully familiar with the assumptions underlying the work of so many contributors from so many diverse backgrounds. Deconstructing the observer begins with ourselves. Human nature being what it is, none of us is ever likely to fully achieve this objective. But that does not absolve us from the effort of constantly striving for it. There is no more important continuing task for diaspora scholarship.[162]

# Notes

❋

*Abbreviations used in the Notes and Select Bibliography*

IHS    *Irish Historical Studies*
IPA    Institute of Public Administration
NGI    National Gallery of Ireland
NLI    National Library of Ireland
NUI    National University of Ireland
QUB    The Queen's University of Belfast
TCD    Trinity College, Dublin
UCD    University College Dublin

## CHAPTER I: POLITICAL HISTORY

1    *Irish Historical Studies*; *Irish Economic and Social History*; *Saothar: Journal of the Irish Labour History Society*.

2    R. F. Foster, 'Anglo-Irish relations and Northern Ireland: historical perspectives', in Dermot Keogh and Michael Haltzel (eds), *Northern Ireland and the Politics of Reconciliation* (Cambridge and Washington: Cambridge University Press and Woodrow Wilson Centre Press, 1993), p. 32.

3    Ibid., p. 29.

4    For an interesting comment see Alvin Jackson, 'Review articles: twentieth-century foxes? Historians and late modern Ireland', *IHS* 32, 126 (Nov. 2000), pp. 272–7.

5    Titles include: Chris Morash and Richard Hayes (eds), *'Fearful Realities': New Perspectives on the Famine* (Dublin: Irish Academic Press, 1996); Margaret Kelleher and James H. Murphy (eds), *Gender Perspectives in Nineteenth-Century Ireland* (Dublin: Irish Academic Press, 1997); Tadhg Foley and Sean Ryder (eds), *Ideology and Ireland in the Nineteenth Century* (Dublin: Four Courts, 1998); Glenn Hooper and Leon Litvack (eds), *Regionalism and Nineteenth-Century Ireland* (Dublin: Four Courts, 2000); and Laurence M. Geary (ed.), *Rebellion and Remembrance in Modern Ireland* (Dublin: Four Courts, 2001).

6    Foley and Ryder (eds), *Ideology and Ireland*, p. 7.

7    Ibid.; see also Sean Hutton and Paul Stewart (eds), *Ireland's Histories: Aspects of State, Society and Ideology* (London: Routledge, 1991).

8    For a Marxist critic's cultural analysis see Terry Eagleton, *Heathcliff and the Great Hunger: Studies in Irish Culture* (London: Verso, 1995), and *Scholars and Rebels in Nineteenth-Century Ireland* (Oxford: Blackwell, 1999).

9    The cultural critics most closely associated with the Field Day publications: Seamus Deane, Luke Gibbons, Kevin Whelan, David Lloyd; also Declan Kiberd, and the Galway group of Tadhg Foley, Lionel Pilkington, Sean Ryder and Thomas Boylan.

10 A good example is Seamus Deane, *Strange Country: Modernity and Nationhood in Irish Writing since 1790* (Oxford: Clarendon, 1997). The major project is Seamus Deane (general editor), *The Field Day Anthology of Irish Writing*, 3 vols (Derry: Field Day, 1991).

11 Reviews of the *Field Day Anthology* made this point: for a sharp comment see Edna Longley's review in *London Review of Books*, 9 Jan. 1992. For a critical commentary, see Stephen Howe, *Ireland and Empire: Colonial Legacies in Irish History and Culture* (Oxford: Oxford University Press, 2000).

12 The approach is well demonstrated in Ranajit Guha, *Dominance Without Hegemony: History and Power in Colonial India* (Cambridge, Mass: Harvard University Press, 1997).

13 This is the case, for example, with 'assessments' of Ireland's economic performance in the twentieth century: See K. Kennedy, T. Giblin and D. McHugh, *The Economic Development of Ireland in the Twentieth Century* (London: Routledge, 1988); J. J. Lee, *Ireland 1912–85: Politics and Society* (Cambridge: Cambridge University Press, 1989).

14 Margaret MacCurtain and Mary O'Dowd (eds), *Women in Early Modern Ireland, 1500–1800* (Edinburgh: Edinburgh University Press, 1991); Margaret Ward, *The Missing Sex: Putting Women into Irish History* (Dublin: Attic Press, 1991); Maria Luddy, *Women in Ireland, 1800–1918: A Documentary History* (Cork: Cork University Press, 1995); Janice Holmes and Diane Urquhart (eds), *Coming into the Light: The Work, Politics, and Religion of Women in Ulster 1840–1940* (Belfast: Institute of Irish Studies, QUB, 1994); Maria Luddy, 'An agenda for women's history in Ireland: Part II, 1800–1900', *IHS* 28, 109 (1992), pp. 19–37; Maryann G. Valiulis and Mary O'Dowd (eds), *Women and Irish History* (Dublin: Wolfhound, 1997); For more private but sharply political opinions, see Jean Agnew (ed.), *The Drennan–McTier Letters, 1776–1819*, 3 vols (Dublin: Women's History Project, 1998, 1999).

15 See Maria Luddy, 'The women's history project', *Women's Studies Review* 7 (2000), pp. 6–80.

16 See, for example, Joanna Bourke, *Husbandry to Housewifery: Women, Economic Change and Housework in Ireland, 1890–1914* (Oxford: Clarendon, 1993).

17 Review by Valiulis of Roger Sawyer's '*We Are But Women': Women in Ireland's History* (London: Routledge, 1993), in *Irish Economic and Social History* 21 (1994), p. 137.

18 Laura E. Lyons, 'The state of gender in Irish Studies: a review essay', *Éire-Ireland* 32, 4; 33, 1; 33, 2 (1997/8), pp. 236–60.

19 Anthony Bradley and Maryann G. Valiulis (eds), *Gender and Sexuality in Modern Ireland* (Amherst: University of Massachusetts Press, 1997); Kelleher and Murphy (eds), *Gender Perspectives in Nineteenth-Century Ireland*; Carol Coulter, *The Hidden Tradition: Feminism, Women and Nationalism in Ireland* (Cork: Cork University Press, 1993); T. P. Foley et al. (eds), *Colonialism and Gender* (Galway: University of Galway Press, 1995); David Fitzpatrick, 'Women, gender and the writing of Irish history', *IHS* 27, 108 (1991), pp. 267–73; Cliona Murphy, 'Women's history, feminist history, gender history?', *Irish Review* 12 (1992), pp. 21–36; see also T. A. Boylan and Timothy P. Foley, 'From hedge schools to hegemony: intellectuals, ideology and Ireland in the nineteenth century', in Liam O'Dowd (ed.), *On Intellectuals and Intellectual Life in Ireland* (Belfast: Institute of Irish Studies, QUB, 1996), pp. 98–115.

20 Lyons, 'The state of gender in Irish Studies', pp. 236–60.

21 Margaret Kelleher, *The Feminization of the Famine: Expressions of the Inexpressible?* (Cork: Cork University Press and Durham NC: Duke University Press, 1997).

22  A good example is R. F. Foster (ed.), *Oxford Illustrated History of Ireland* (Oxford: Clarendon, 1989).

23  The early exchanges on mobilisation between David Miller and L. M. Cullen may be followed in issues of *Irish Economic and Social History*.

24  Kevin Whelan, *The Tree of Liberty: Radicalism, Catholicism and the Construction of Irish Identity, 1760–1830* (Cork: Cork University Press and South Bend: University of Notre Dame Press, 1996). Both Bartlett and Whelan had rehearsed their theses on politicisation and socialisation in *Culture et Pratiques Politiques en France et en Irlande, XVIᵉ–XVIIIᵉ Siècle, Actes du Colloque de Marseille* (Paris: Centre de Recherches Historiques, 1988).

25  Whelan, *The Tree of Liberty*, pp. 54–5.

26  Thomas Bartlett, *The Fall and Rise of the Irish Nation: The Catholic Question 1690–1830* (Dublin: Gill & Macmillan, 1992); see also C. D. A. Leighton, 'Gallicanism and the Veto controversy: church, state and the Catholic community in early nineteenth-century Ireland', in R. V. Comerford et al. (eds), *Religion, Conflict and Coexistence in Ireland* (Dublin: Gill & Macmillan, 1990), pp. 135–58.

27  C. D. A. Leighton, *Catholicism in a Protestant Kingdom: A Study of the Irish Ancien Régime* (Dublin: Gill & Macmillan, 1994).

28  Vincent McNally, *Reform, Revolution and Reaction: Archbishop John Thomas Troy and the Roman Catholic Church in Ireland, 1787–1817* (Lanham and London: University of America Press, 1996). See also Brian McDermot, *The Irish Catholic Petition of 1805: The Diary of Denys Scully* (Dublin: Irish Academic Press, 1992).

29  For a local study, see Fergus O'Ferrall, 'The emergence of the political community in Longford, 1824–29', in Raymond Gillespie and Gerard Moran (eds), *Longford: Essays in County History* (Dublin: Lilliput, 1991), pp. 123–51.

30  Patrick J. Corish, 'James Caulfield, Bishop of Ferns (1786–1814)', *Journal of the Wexford Historical Society* 16 (1996/7), pp. 114–25.

31  The concept of the 'challenging collectivity' was first applied to Irish popular politics by Samuel Clark, *Social Origins of the Irish Land War* (Princeton, NJ: Princeton University Press, 1989).

32  Geraldine Grogan, *The Noblest Agitator: Daniel O'Connell and the German Catholic Movement 1830–1850* (Dublin: Veritas, 1991); also articles by Peter Alter (on O'Connell and German politics) and by Pierre Joannon (on O'Connell, Montalembert and Christian Democracy in France) in Maurice R. O'Connell (ed.), *Daniel O'Connell: Political Pioneer* (Dublin: IPA, 1991).

33  Maurice R. O'Connell (ed.), *Daniel O'Connell: Political Pioneer*, and O'Connell (ed.), *O'Connell, Education, Church and State* (Dublin: IPA, 1992).

34  The 1990s volumes included Kilkenny, Waterford, Cork, Wicklow, Donegal, Galway, Down, Offaly, Laois, Derry/Londonderry, Tyrone.

35  For example, Gillespie and Moran (eds), *Longford*; Raymond Gillespie (ed.), *Cavan: Essays on the History of an Irish County* (Dublin: Irish Academic Press, 1995).

36  For example, Jim Lenehan, *Politics and Society in Athlone, 1830–1885: A Rotten Borough* (Dublin: Irish Academic Press, 1999).

37  For another local town study, see Sean O'Donnell, *Clonmel 1840–1900: Anatomy of an Irish Town* (Dublin: Geography Publications, 1999).

38  For a good example, see Anne Coleman, *Riotous Roscommon: Social Unrest in the 1840s* (Dublin: Irish Academic Press, 1999).

39  Peter Jupp and Stephen A Royle, 'The social geography of Cork city elections, 1801–30', *IHS* 29, 113 (May 1994), pp. 13–43. See also John B. O'Brien, 'Population, politics and society in Cork, 1780–1900', in Patrick O'Flanagan and Cornelius Buttimer (eds), *Cork: History and Society* (Dublin: Geography Publications, 1993), pp. 699–717; and Ian d'Alton, 'A perspective upon historical process: the case of Southern Irish Protestantism', in F. B. Smith (ed.), *Ireland, England and Australia* (Canberra and Cork: Australian National University and Cork University Press, 1990), pp. 70–91.

40  Jacqueline Hill, *From Patriots to Unionists: Dublin Civic Politics and Irish Protestant Patriotism, 1660–1840* (Oxford: Clarendon, 1997).

41  For a later episode, see Martin Maguire, 'The organization and activism of Dublin's Protestant working class 1883–1935', *IHS* 29, 113 (1994), pp. 65–87.

42  B. M. Walker, *Ulster Politics: The Formative Years 1868–86* (Belfast: Institute of Irish Studies, QUB, 1989).

43  Patrick Maume makes the comparison between these Irish Tories and Walter Scott, sharing an antipathy to 'homogenising' Whig reformers. See his *The Long Gestation: Irish Nationalist Life, 1891–1918* (Dublin: Gill & Macmillan, 1999), p. 5.

44  Joseph Spence, 'Isaac Butt, nationality and Irish Toryism, 1833–1852', *Bullán* 2, 1 (1995), pp. 45–60; D. G. Boyce, 'Trembling solicitude: Irish conservatism, nationality and public opinion, 1833–86', in D. G. Boyce et al. (eds), *Political Thought in Ireland Since the Seventeenth Century* (London: Routledge, 1993); Damien Murray, *Romanticism, Nationalism and Irish Antiquarian Societies, 1840–80* (Maynooth: Dept of Old and Middle Irish, NUI Maynooth, 2000).

45  Gréagóir Ó Dúill, *Samuel Ferguson: Beatha agus Saothar* (BÁC: An Clóchomhar, 1993).

46  Robert Sloan, 'O'Connell's liberal rivals in 1843', *IHS* 30, 117 (1996), pp. 47–65; also D. G. Boyce, 'Federalism and the Irish question', in Andrea Bosco (ed.), *The Federal Idea. Vol. 1: The History of Federalism from the Enlightenment to 1945* (London: Lothian Foundation, 1991).

47  For example, Sean Ryder, 'Male autobiography and Irish cultural nationalism: John Mitchel and James Clarence Mangan', *Irish Review* 13 (1992–3), pp. 70–7.

48  See, also, Takashi Koseki, *Dublin Confederate Clubs and the Repeal Movement* (Tokyo: Hosei University, 1992).

49  Breandán Ó Cathaoir, *John Blake Dillon: Young Irelander* (Dublin: Irish Academic Press, 1990); David N. Buckley, *James Fintan Lalor: Radical* (Cork: Cork University Press, 1990); John N. Molony, *A Soul Came into Ireland: Thomas Davis 1814–1845: A Biography* (Dublin: Geography Publications, 1995); Richard Davis, *Revolutionary Imperialist: William Smith O'Brien 1803–1864* (Dublin: Lilliput, 1998); Gerard O'Brien, 'Charles Gavan Duffy 1816–1903', in Gerard O'Brien and Peter Roebuck (eds), *Nine Ulster Lives* (Belfast: Ulster Historical Foundation, 1992), pp. 87–98.

50  Gary Owens, 'Constructing the Repeal spectacle: monster meetings and people power in pre-Famine Ireland', in Maurice O'Connell (ed.), *People Power: Proceedings of the Third O'Connell Workshop* (Dublin: IPA, 1993), pp. 80–93; Gary Owens, 'Constructing the image of Daniel O'Connell', *History Ireland* 7, 1 (1999), pp. 32–6; Gary Owens, 'Nationalism

without words: symbolism and ritual behaviour in the Repeal "monster meetings" of 1843–1845', in James S. Donnelly, Jr and Kerby Miller (eds), *Irish Popular Culture 1650–1850* (Dublin: Irish Academic Press, 1998); Gary Owens, 'Visualizing the Liberator: self-fashioning dramaturgy and the construction of Daniel O'Connell', *Éire-Ireland* 33, 3; 33, 4; 34, 1 (1998–9), pp. 103–30. See also Lawrence McBride (ed.), *Images, Icons and the Irish Nationalist Imagination* (Dublin: Four Courts, 1999).

51  See, for example, Brian M. Walker, *Dancing to History's Tune: History, Myth and Politics in Ireland* (Belfast: Institute of Irish Studies, QUB, 1996).

52  Raymond Gillespie and Brian P. Kennedy (eds), *Ireland: Art Into History* (Dublin: Town House, 1994).

53  This is the subtitle of D. George Boyce's general history *Nineteenth-Century Ireland: The Search for Stability* (Dublin: Gill & Macmillan, 1990).

54  See, for the Westminster context, Peter Mandler, *Aristocratic Government in the Age of Reform: Whigs and Liberals 1830–1852* (Oxford: Clarendon, 1990).

55  For an exemplary publication of local source material see the *Clogher Record* special issues on the Famine, published in 2000 and 2001.

56  James S. Donnelly, Jr, 'Mass eviction and the Great Famine', in Cathal Póirtéir (ed.), *The Great Irish Famine* (Cork: Mercier, in association with RTÉ, 1995), pp. 155–73; Christine Kinealy, *This Great Calamity: The Irish Famine 1845–52* (Dublin: Gill & Macmillan, 1994); Tim P. O'Neill, 'Famine evictions', in Carla King (ed.), *Famine, Land and Culture in Ireland* (Dublin: UCD Press, 2000), pp. 29–70.

57  Donal A. Kerr, *'A Nation of Beggars'? Priests, People and Politics in Famine Ireland 1846–52* (Oxford: Clarendon, 1994), and Peter Gray, *Famine, Land and Politics: British Government and Irish Society 1843–50* (Dublin: Irish Academic Press, 1999).

58  See, for example, Ambrose Macauley, *William Crolly: Archbishop of Armagh, 1835–1849* (Dublin: Four Courts, 1994); Thomas McGrath, *Politics, Interdenominational Relations and Education in the Public Ministry of Bishop James Doyle of Kildare and Leighlin, 1786–1843* (Dublin: Four Courts, 1999) and Thomas McGrath, *Religious Renewal and Reform in the Pastoral Ministry of James Doyle of Kildare and Leighlin, 1786–1843* (Dublin: Four Courts, 1999).

59  See Thomas Boylan and Tadhg Foley, *Political Economy and Colonial Ireland: The Propagation and Ideological Function of Economic Discourse in the Nineteenth Century* (London: Routledge, 1992).

60  Gray, *Famine, Land and Politics*.

61  Ibid., p. 338.

62  See Mandler, *Aristocratic Government*; also E. A. Smith, *Lord Grey 1764–1845* (Oxford: Clarendon, 1990), and Boyd Hilton, 'The ripening of Robert Peel', in Michael Bentley (ed.), *Public and Private Doctrine* (Cambridge: Cambridge University Press, 1993), pp. 63–83.

63  Virginia Crossman, *Local Government in Nineteenth-Century Ireland* (Belfast: Institute of Irish Studies, QUB, 1994); Virginia Crossman, *Politics, Law and Order in Nineteenth-Century Ireland* (Dublin: Gill & Macmillan, 1996).

64  Crossman, *Politics, Law and Order*, p. 3. See also Elizabeth A. Muenger, *The British Military Dilemma in Ireland: Occupation Politics 1870–1914* (Lawrence, Ka: University of Kansas Press, 1991).

65   Thomas Bartlett and Keith Jeffery (eds), *A Military History of Ireland* (Cambridge: Cambridge University Press, 1996); Brian Griffin, 'Religious opportunity in the Irish police forces 1836–1914', in Comerford et al. (eds), *Religion, Conflict and Coexistence in Ireland*, pp. 219–34.

66   W. E. Vaughan, *Landlords and Tenants in Mid-Victorian Ireland* (Oxford: Clarendon, 1994).

67   K. T. Hoppen, 'Grammars of electoral violence in nineteenth-century England and Ireland', *English Historical Review* 59 (1994), pp. 519–620; K. T. Hoppen, 'Nationalist mobilization and governmental attitudes: geography, politics and nineteenth-century Ireland', in Laurence Brockliss and David Eastwood (eds), *A Union of Multiple Identities: The British Isles, c. 1750–c. 1850* (Manchester: Manchester University Press, 1997); K. T. Hoppen, 'Roads to democracy: electioneering and corruption in nineteenth-century England and Ireland', *History* 81 (1996), pp. 553–71; S. R. Knowlton, *Popular Politics and the Irish Catholic Church: The Rise and Fall of the Independent Irish Party, 1850–59* (New York and London: Garland, 1991).

68   Oliver Rafferty, *Catholicism in Ulster, 1603–1983* (London: Hurst, 1994).

69   David Hempton and Myrtle Hill, *Evangelical Protestantism in Ulster, 1740–1890* (London: Routledge, 1992); Alan Ford, James McGuire and Kenneth Milne (eds), *As by Law Established: The Church of Ireland Since the Reformation* (Dublin: Lilliput, 1995); Finlay Holmes, *Irish Presbyterians 1642–1992* (Belfast: Presbyterian Historical Society of Ireland, 1992); David Hempton, *Religion and Political Culture in Britain and Ireland from the Glorious Revolution to the Decline of the Empire* (Cambridge: Cambridge University Press, 1996).

70   R. V. Comerford, 'Comprehending the Fenians', *Saothar* 17 (1992), pp. 52–7; R. V. Comerford, 'Fenianism revisited: past-time or revolutionary movement? *Saothar* 17 (1992), pp. 46–52; Gerard Moran, *A Radical Priest in Mayo: Father Patrick Lavelle, the Rise and Fall of an Irish Nationalist, 1825–86* (Dublin: Four Courts, 1994); Eva Ó Cathaoir, 'Patrick Lennon, 1841–1901: Dublin Fenian leader', *Dublin Historical Record* 44, 2 (1991), pp. 38–50; Pádraig G. Ó Laighin, *Éadbhard Ó Dufaigh 1840–1868* (BÁC: Coiscéim, 1994); Takagami Shin-ichi, 'The Fenian rising in Dublin, March 1867', *IHS* 29, 115 (May 1995), pp. 340–62; Oliver P. Rafferty, *The Church, the State and the Fenian Threat, 1861–75* (Basingstoke: Macmillan, 1999).

71   Gerard Moran, 'The Fenians in Tipperary politics 1868–1880', *Tipperary Historical Journal* (1994), pp. 73–9.

72   See below note 97.

73   E.g. D. George Boyce and Alan O'Day (eds), *The Making of Modern Irish History: Revisionism and the Revisionist Controversy* (London: Routledge, 1996); Peter Collins (ed.), *Nationalism and Unionism: Conflict in Ireland 1885–1921* (Belfast: Institute of Irish Studies, QUB, 1994); Frank Callanan, *The Parnell Split 1890–91* (Cork: Cork University Press, 1992).

74   D. George Boyce and Alan O'Day (eds), *Parnell in Perspective* (London: Routledge, 1991); Paul Bew, *C. S. Parnell* (Dublin: Gill & Macmillan, 1980); Donal McCartney (ed.), *Parnell: The Politics of Power* (Dublin: Wolfhound, 1991).

75   Patrick Maume, 'Parnell and the IRB oath', *IHS* 29, 115 (May 1995), pp. 363–70.

76   R. F. Foster, 'Parnell, Wicklow, nationalism', in McCartney (ed.), *Parnell*, pp. 19–35.

77   See works cited in note 74 above, and also Callanan, *The Parnell Split*.

78   For a long-term perspective, see Pauric Travers, 'The financial relations question 1800–1914', in Smith (ed.), *Ireland, England and Australia*, pp. 41–69.

79   Sally Warwick-Haller, *William O'Brien and the Irish Land War* (Dublin: Irish Academic Press, 1990); Philip Bull, *Land, Politics and Nationalism: A Study of the Irish Land Question* (Dublin: Gill & Macmillan, 1996); for an excellent collection of essays, see King (ed.), *Famine, Land and Culture in Ireland*; see, also, the early sections of Eamon Phoenix, *Northern Nationalism: Nationalist Parties, Partition and the Catholic Minority in Northern Ireland 1890–1940* (Belfast: Ulster Historical Foundation, 1994). See also, Alan O'Day, 'Review article: politics after Parnell', *IHS* 30, 120 (1997), pp. 602–10.

80   Donald E. Jordan, Jr, *Land and Popular Politics in Ireland: County Mayo from the Plantation to the Land War* (Cambridge: Cambridge University Press, 1994).

81   See, most recently, Gerard Moran, 'James Daly and the rise and fall of the Land League in the west of Ireland, 1879–82', *IHS* 29, 114 (1994), pp. 189–208.

82   Paul Bew, *Conflict and Conciliation in Ireland 1890–1910: Parnellites and Radical Agrarians* (Oxford: Clarendon, 1987), p. 221.

83   Bull, *Land, Politics and Nationalism*, p. 176.

84   Padraig G. Lane, 'The Land and Labour Association 1894–1914', *Journal of the Cork Historical and Archaeological Society* 98 (1993), pp. 90–106; Padraig G. Lane, 'The organisation of rural labourers 1870–1890', *Journal of the Cork Historical and Archaeological Society* 100 (1995), pp. 149–60; Padraig G. Lane, 'Agricultural labourers and rural violence', *Studia Hibernica* 27 (1999), pp. 77–87; Padraig G. Lane, 'Agricultural labourers and the land question', in King (ed.), *Famine, Land and Culture*, pp. 101–15. David Seth Jones, *Graziers, Land Reform and Political Conflict in Ireland* (Washington: Catholic University of America Press, 1995); for a good local study, see Jim Gilligan, *Graziers and Grasslands: Portrait of a Rural Meath Community 1854–1914* (Dublin: Irish Academic Press, 1999).

85   Frank Callanan, *T. M. Healy* (Cork: Cork University Press, 1996).

86   Eugene J. Doyle, *Justin McCarthy* (Dundalk: Historical Association and Dundalgan Press, 1996); Áine Ní Chonghaile, *F. H. O'Donnell 1848–1916: A Shaol agus a Shaothar* (BÁC: Coiscéim, 1992).

87   Paul Bew, *John Redmond* (Dundalk: Historical Association and Dundalgan Press, 1996).

88   Terence A. Dooley, 'Why Monaghan Protestants opposed Home Rule', *Clogher Record* 14, 3 (1993), pp. 42–6; and Terence A. Dooley, 'The organisation of unionist opposition to Home Rule in counties Monaghan, Cavan and Donegal, 1885–1914', *Clogher Record* 16, 1 (1997), pp. 46–70. See also Br Conal Thomas, *The Land for the People: The United Irish League and Land Reform in North Galway 1898–1912* (Corrandulla, Co. Galway, Annaghdown Heritage Society, 1999).

89   Íde Ní Liatháin, *The Life and Career of P. A. McHugh, a North Connacht Politician 1859–1909: A Footsoldier of the Party* (Dublin: Irish Academic Press, 1999).

90   Marie-Louise Legg, *Newspapers and Nationalism: The Irish Provincial Press 1850–1892* (Dublin: Four Courts, 1998).

91   Emmet Larkin, *The Roman Catholic Church and the Emergence of the Modern Irish Political System, 1874–78* (Dublin: Four Courts, 1996); Senia Pašeta, *Before the Revolution: Nationalism, Social Change and Ireland's Catholic Elite, 1879–1922* (Cork: Cork University Press, 1999); see, also, Lawrence W. McBride, *The Greening of Dublin Castle: The Transformation of Bureaucratic and Judicial Personnel in Ireland, 1892–1922* (Washington: Catholic University of America Press, 1991).

92   Larkin, *The Roman Catholic Church*. See, for a portrait of a bishop in politics, Liam
Bane, *The Bishop in Politics: Life and Career of John McEvilly* (Westport: Westport Historical
Association, 1993). For radical priests, see Gerard Moran (ed.), *Radical Irish Priests
1660–1970* (Dublin: Four Courts, 1998); Denis Carroll, *Unusual Suspects: Twelve Radical
Clergy* (Dublin: Columba, 1998).
93   Margaret O'Callaghan, *British High Politics and Nationalist Ireland: Criminality, Land
and the Law under Foster and Balfour* (Cork: Cork University Press, 1994).
94   Publisher's note on dust jacket of Alan O'Day, *Irish Home Rule 1867–1921* (Manchester:
Manchester University Press, 1998).
95   Ibid.; see especially O'Day's first chapter, for definitions and interpretations.
96   See note 43 above.
97   For a recent portrait of the Parnell women, see Jane McL. Côté, *Fanny and Anna
Parnell: Ireland's Patriot Sisters* (Basingstoke: Macmillan, 1991). See also Margaret Ward,
*Hanna Sheehy Skeffington: A Life* (Cork: Attic Press and Cork University Press, 1997);
Louise Ryan, 'Traditions and double moral standards: the Irish suffragists' critique of
nationalism', *Women's History Review* 4 (1995), pp. 487–503; Mary Cullen and Maria Luddy
(eds), *Women, Power and Consciousness in Nineteenth-Century Ireland: Eight Biographical
Studies* (Dublin: Attic Press, 1995). Marie O'Neill, *From Parnell to de Valera: A Biography of
Jennie Wyse Power 1858–1941* (Dublin: Blackwater, 1991).
98   Fergus D'Arcy, 'The Irish trade union movement in the nineteenth century', in Donal
Nevin (ed.), *Trade Union Century* (Cork and Dublin: Mercier, in association with ICTU
and RTÉ, 1994); Dermot Keogh, 'Founding and early years of the Irish TUC 1894–1912',
in ibid., pp. 19–32; John Foster, 'Completing the first task: Irish labour in the nineteenth
century', *Saothar* 15 (1990), pp. 65–9; Fintan Lane, *The Origins of Modern Irish Socialism,
1881–1896* (Cork: Cork University Press, 1997). For a neglected urban perspective see,
B. J. Graham and Susan Hood, 'Town tenant protest in late nineteenth and early twentieth-
century Ireland', *Irish Economic and Social History* 21 (1994), pp. 39–57.
99   Maura Cronin, *Country, Class or Craft? The Politicization of the Skilled Artisan in
Nineteenth-Century Cork* (Cork: Cork University Press, 1994); also, John Cunningham,
*Labour in the West of Ireland* (Belfast: Athol, 1995).
100   For a local town study, see Sean O'Donnell, *Clonmel*; see note 37 above.
101   See, for example, general histories by Jackson and Boyce, cited herein. Also Richard
English and Graham Walker (eds), *Unionism in Modern Ireland* (Basingstoke: Palgrave
Macmillan, 1996); James Loughlin, *Ulster Unionism and British National Identity Since 1885*
(London: Pinter, 1995). For a long-term view, see Frank Wright, *Two Lands on One Soil:
Ulster Politics before Home Rule* (Dublin: Gill & Macmillan, 1996).
102   For a discussion of these issues, see Ciaran Brady (ed.), *Interpreting Irish History*
(Dublin: Irish Academic Press, 1994).
103   See e.g. R. F. Foster, *The Story of Ireland*, Inaugural Lecture, University of Oxford
(Oxford: Clarendon, 1995); For a concise historiographical review, see Alvin Jackson,
'Twentieth-century foxes? Historians and late modern Ireland', *IHS* 32, 126 (2000), pp. 272–7.
104   Alvin Jackson, *Ireland 1798–1998: Politics and War* (Oxford: Blackwell, 1999); quoted
comment from publisher's dust jacket.
105   D. George Boyce, *Nineteenth-Century Ireland: The Search for Stability* (Dublin: Gill &
Macmillan, 1990); D. George Boyce, *Ireland 1828–1923: From Ascendancy to Democracy*

(Oxford: Blackwell, 1992); Jonathan Bardon, *A History of Ulster* (Belfast: Blackstaff, 1992; updated edn, 2001); also Alan J. Ward, *The Irish Constitutional Tradition: Responsible Government and Modern Ireland 1872–1922* (Washington: Catholic University of America Press, 1994); W. E. Vaughan (ed.), *A New History of Ireland*, VI, *Ireland Under the Union 1870–1920* (Oxford: Clarendon, 1996).

106 These perspectives are handled in a balanced way by Jackson, see note 104 above.

107 For an elegant profile of a Liberal Unionist see Donal McCartney, *W. E. H. Lecky: Historian and Politician 1838–1903* (Dublin: Lilliput, 1994); also, R. B. McDowell, *Crisis and Decline: The Fate of Southern Unionism* (Dublin: Lilliput, 1997); Aiken McClelland, *William Johnston of Ballykilbeg* (Lurgan, Co. Armagh: Ulster Society, 1990); James Loughlin, 'T. W. Russell, the tenant farmers' interest, and progressive unionism in Ulster, 1886–1900', *Éire-Ireland* 25, 1 (1990), pp. 44–63.

108 Alvin Jackson, *Colonel Edward Saunderson: Land and Loyalty in Victorian Ireland* (Oxford: Clarendon, 1995). See also Jackson's short but stimulating *Sir Edward Carson* (Dundalk: Historical Association of Ireland and Dundalgan Press, 1995), and the same author's 'Unionist myths', *Past and Present* 136 (1992), pp. 164–85.

109 Jackson, *Ireland 1798–1998*, p. 215.

110 Ian S. Lustick, *Unsettled States, Disputed Lands: Britain and Ireland, France and Algeria, Israel and the West Bank Gaza* (Ithaca and London: Cornell University Press, 1993).

111 T. G. Fraser, 'Ireland and India', in Keith Jeffery (ed.), *An Irish Empire? Aspects of Ireland and the British Empire* (Manchester: Manchester University Press, 1996), pp. 77–122.

112 Jeffery (ed.), *An Irish Empire?*

113 S. B. Cook, *Imperial Affinities: Nineteenth-Century Analogies and Exchanges Between India and Ireland* (New Delhi, Newbury Park and London: Sage, 1992); also, David M. Anderson and David Killingray (eds), *Policing the Empire: Government, Authority and Control 1830–1940* (Manchester: Manchester University Press, 1991). Michael Holmes and Denis Holmes (eds), *Ireland and India: Connections, Comparisons, Contrasts* (Dublin: Blackwater, 1997).

114 S. J. Connolly, R. A. Houston and R. J. Morris (eds), *Conflict, Identity and Economic Development: Ireland and Scotland 1600–1939* (Preston: Carnegie, 1995); Also, T. M. Devine and J. F. McMillan (eds), *Celebrating Columba: Irish–Scottish Connections 597–1997* (Edinburgh: John Donald, 1999); Ron Weir, 'The Scottish and Irish unions: the Victorian view in perspective', in S. J. Connolly (ed.), *Kingdoms United: Integration and Diversity* (Dublin: Four Courts, 1999), pp. 56–66.

115 I. S. Wood, *Scotland and Ulster* (Edinburgh: Mercat, 1994); Graham Walker, *Intimate Strangers: Political and Cultural Interaction between Scotland and Ulster in Modern Times* (Edinburgh: John Donald, 1995).

116 The pioneer of this approach was Hugh Kearney. For recent contributions see S. J. Connolly (ed.), *Kingdoms United?*; Brockliss and Eastwood (eds), *A Union of Multiple Identities*; Bernard Crick (ed.), *National Identities: The Constitution of the United Kingdom* (Oxford: Blackwell, 1991).

117 Paul O'Leary, 'Accommodation and resistance: a comparison of cultural identities in Ireland and Wales, *c.* 1880–1914', in Connolly (ed.), *Kingdoms United?* pp. 123–34; and 'Religion, nationality and politics: disestablishment in Ireland and Wales', in J. R. Guy and W. S. Neely (eds), *Contrasts and Comparisons: Studies in Irish and Welsh Church History*

(Llandysul and Keady: Welsh Religious History Society and Church of Ireland Historical Society, 1999), pp. 89–113.
118 A good example is T. M. Devine (ed.), *Irish Immigrants and Scottish Society in the Nineteenth and Twentieth Centuries* (Edinburgh: John Donald, 1991). Also Graham Davis, *The Irish in Britain 1815–1914* (Dublin: Gill & Macmillan, 1991). There is an extensive and growing literature on all aspects of the Irish diaspora: see chapter 11 of this volume.

CHAPTER 2: SOCIAL HISTORY

1   For example, the bibliography expanded from 15 pages in 1989 to 39 pages in 1999.
2   These included *Bullán, History Ireland, Irish Studies Review, and New Hibernia Review/Iris Éireannach Nua*. An abundance of useful information on Irish social history also became available on that ever-burgeoning offspring of the 1990s, the World Wide Web.
3   See, for example, James Livesey and Stuart Murray, 'Post-colonial theory and modern Irish culture', *IHS* 30, 119 (1997), pp. 452–61; Terence Brown, 'New literary histories', *IHS* 30, 119 (May 1997), pp. 462–70; Niall Ó Ciosáin, 'Round towers and square holes: exoticism in Irish culture', *IHS* 31, 122 (1998), pp. 259–73; and Richard Dunphy, 'Gender and sexuality in Ireland', *IHS* 31, 124 (1999), pp. 549–57.
4   Patrick Joyce, 'The return of history: postmodernism and the politics of academic history in Britain', *Past and Present* 158 (Feb. 1998), p. 229.
5   See, for example, Lynn Hunt (ed.), *The New Cultural History* (Berkeley: University of California Press, 1989); Peter Burke, 'Overture: the new history, its past and its future', in Peter Burke (ed.), *New Perspectives on Historical Writing* (Cambridge: Polity, 1994), pp. 1–23 and *passim*; Adrian Wilson (ed.), *Rethinking Social History* (Manchester: Manchester University Press, 1994); and Gary Owens, 'Pre-Famine Ireland and the "New History"', *Irish Literary Supplement* 15, 2 (1996), pp. 26–7.
6   Joe Lee was the only contributor to discuss the Famine. His essay cited roughly a dozen publications dealing with the subject, almost all of them being short articles concerned with specific localities. J. J. Lee, 'Irish economic history since 1500', in J. J. Lee (ed.) *Irish Historiography, 1970–9* (Cork: Cork University Press, 1981), p. 182.
7   Joel Mokyr, *Why Ireland Starved: A Quantitative and Analytical History of the Irish Economy, 1800–1850* (London: Allen & Unwin, 1983); Mary E. Daly, *The Famine in Ireland* (Dundalk: Dundalgan Press and Dublin Historical Association, 1986); Cormac Ó Gráda, *The Great Irish Famine* (London: Macmillan, 1989); W. E. Vaughan (ed.), *A New History of Ireland*, v, *Ireland Under the Union, I: 1801–70* (Oxford: Clarendon, 1989).
8   Christine Kinealy, *A Death-Dealing Famine: The Great Hunger in Ireland* (London: Pluto, 1997), p. 1.
9   Besides the countless publications devoted to the Famine, it became the subject of academic courses in second- and third-level institutions in Ireland, Britain and North America; entire websites were devoted to it; Irish bookshops permanently set aside special sections for Famine literature; and, by the time of the sesquicentenary, one observer had even detected the appearance of 'faminists – people who make their professional careers (or at least major portions of those careers) – by studying and curating and writing about the Great Famine'. Donald Harman Akenson, 'A midrash on "galut", "exile" and "diaspora"

rhetoric', in E. Margaret Crawford (ed.), *The Hungry Stream: Essays on Famine and Emigration* (Belfast: Institute of Irish Studies, QUB, 1997), p. 5.

10  For an overview of recent Famine historiography and a flavour of the debates, see S. J. Connolly, 'Revisions revised: new work on the Irish Famine', *Victorian Studies* 39 (1996), pp. 205–16; Mary E. Daly, 'Revisionism and Irish history: the Great Famine', in D. G. Boyce and Alan O'Day (eds), *The Making of Modern Irish History: Revisionism and the Revisionist Controversy* (London: Routledge, 1996), pp. 71–89; Mary E. Daly, 'Historians and the Famine: a beleaguered species?', *IHS* 30, 120 (1997), pp. 591–601; Cormac Ó Gráda, 'Making Irish famine history in 1995', *History Workshop Journal* 42 (1996), pp. 87–104 and Cormac Ó Gráda, 'New perspectives on the Irish Famine', *Bullán* 3, 2 (1997–8), pp. 103–15.

11  David Fitzpatrick, 'The failure: representations of the Irish Famine in letters to Australia', in Crawford (ed.), *Hungry Stream*, p. 161.

12  See especially David Fitzpatrick, *Oceans of Consolation: Personal Accounts of Irish Migration to Australia* (Cork: Cork University Press, 1994) and Kerby A. Miller, *Emigrants and Exiles: Ireland and the Irish Exodus to North America* (Oxford: Clarendon, 1985).

13  Fitzpatrick, 'The failure', p. 161.

14  Ibid., p. 163. Another source relating directly to individual experiences of the Famine is that of folklore. Cathal Póirtéir published a generous sample of this material in his *Famine Echoes* (Cork: Mercier, 1995). Niall Ó Ciosáin provides a more critical perspective in his 'Famine memory and the popular culture of scarcity', in Ian McBride (ed.), *History and Memory in Modern Ireland* (Cambridge: Cambridge University Press, 2001), pp. 95–117. See also Cormac Ó Gráda, *Black '47 and Beyond: The Great Irish Famine in History, Economy, and Memory* (Princeton NJ: Princeton University Press, 1999).

15  Líam Kennedy, et. al., *Mapping the Great Irish Famine: A Survey of the Famine Decades* (Dublin: Four Courts, 1999).

16  Other volumes arising from the database include: L. A. Clarkson, E. M. Crawford and M. A. Litvack (eds), *The Occupations of Ireland, 1841*, 4 vols (Belfast: Department of Economic and Social History, QUB, 1995) and Líam Kennedy, *An Historical Database of Irish County Statistics* (Belfast: Department of Economic and Social History, QUB, 1996). The database, which includes material drawn from the population censuses and a range of other sources, covers the period 1821–1971 and is intended as a launching pad for more explorations in Irish social and economic history.

17  Kennedy, et. al., *Mapping the Great Irish Famine*, p. 211.

18  Robert J. Scally, *The End of Hidden Ireland: Rebellion, Famine and Emigration* (Oxford: Clarendon, 1995).

19  See especially the work of Emmanuel Leroy Ladurie, Natalie Davis, and Carlo Ginzburg.

20  Another good example is Angela Bourke, *The Burning of Bridget Cleary* (London: Pimlico, 1999).

21  See Mary E. Daly, 'Recent writings on modern Irish history: the interaction between past and present', *Journal of Modern History* 69 (1997), pp. 522–4; and Niall Ó Ciosáin's review of Scally's book in *IHS* 30, 120 (1997), pp. 622–4. Since 1994, Professor Charles Orser of Illinois State University and his assistants have conducted a series of excavations in the County Roscommon townlands of Gortoose and Ballykilcline. Summaries of the early stages of this work and discussions of the application of archaeology to the study of nineteenth-century history are found in: Charles E. Orser, Jr, 'Can there be an archaeology

of the Great Famine?' in Chris Morash and Richard Hayes (eds), *'Fearful Realities': New Perspectives on the Famine*, (Dublin: Irish Academic Press, 1996), pp. 77–89; Charles E. Orser, Jr, 'Archaeology and modern Irish history', *Irish Studies Review* 18 (1997), pp. 2–7.

22 Among them is the absence of abundant evidence concerning the community of Ballykilcline which forces Scally to rely on material relating to other places, much of it found in secondary sources. Another issue is the familiar one of typicality: how representative of other communities across Ireland was Ballykilcline?

23 James S. Donnelly Jr, *The Great Irish Potato Famine* (Stroud: Sutton, 2001). See also Christine Kinealy, *The Great Irish Famine: Impact, Ideology and Rebellion* (Basingstoke and New York: Palgrave, 2002); Colm Tóibín and Diarmaid Ferriter, *The Irish Famine* (London: Profile, 2002). Despite its political focus, there is much for the social historian in Peter Gray's outstanding *Famine, Land and Politics: British Government and Irish Society 1843–50* (Dublin: Irish Academic Press, 1999).

24 Vaughan, (ed.), *A New History of Ireland*, v, *Ireland Under the Union, i: 1801–70*.

25 J. G. Kohl, *Travels in Ireland* (London, 1844), pp. 186–7.

26 The term is Nina Witoszek's who has written perhaps more than anyone on the subject, though she is concerned with funerary culture from the middle ages to the present. See her book, co-written with Pat Sheeran, *Talking to the Dead: A Study of Irish Funerary Traditions* (Amsterdam: Rodopi, 1998); Nina Witoszek, *The Theatre of Recollection: A Cultural Study of the Modern Dramatic Traditions of Ireland and Poland* (Stockholm, 1988); Nina Witoszek, 'Ireland: a funerary culture?', *Studies* 76 (1987), pp. 206–17; Lawrence J. Taylor, 'Bás in Éirinn: cultural constructions of death in Ireland', *Anthropological Quarterly* 62 (1989), pp. 175–87; and his *Occasions of Faith: An Anthropology of Irish Catholics*, (Dublin: Lilliput, 1995).

27 The literature on the subject is vast and growing, but see especially Ralph Houlbrooke (ed.), *Death, Ritual, and Bereavement* (London: Routledge, 1989); Pat Jalland, *Death in the Victorian Family* (Oxford: Clarendon, 1996); J. J. Farrell, *Inventing the American Way of Death, 1830–1920*, (Philadelphia: Temple University Press, 1980); Philippe Ariès, *The Hour of Our Death* (New York: Alfred A. Knopf, 1981); John McManners, *Death and Enlightenment: Changing Attitudes to Death Among Christians and Unbelievers in Eighteenth-Century France* (Oxford: Clarendon, 1981).

28 Michel Vovelle, 'On death', in his *Ideologies and Mentalities* (Chicago University Press, 1990), p. 65.

29 These are some of the matters discussed in Thomas A. Kselman's *Death and the Afterlife in Modern France* (Princeton NJ: Princeton University Press, 1993), a book concerned mainly with the nineteenth century that deserves an Irish equivalent.

30 Gearóid Ó Crualaoich, 'The "merry wake"', in James S. Donnelly, Jr, and Kerby Miller (eds), *Irish Popular Culture, 1650–1850* (Dublin: Irish Academic Press, 1998), pp. 173–200.

31 Ibid., p. 173. The anthropologist Lawrence Taylor makes a similar observation that is particularly applicable to nineteenth-century Ireland: 'Where moral authority is unclear, and the dominant religion either disestablished, in a state of crisis, or by doctrine unsympathetic to the generation of symbolic forms, the way is left open to a more general competition in the definition of death, as part of a wider context over meaning and moral authority. In such cases, the competition is through the generation of rituals and other

symbolic cultural forms which compete for hegemony among various segments of the population.' Lawrence J. Taylor, 'The uses of death in Europe', *Anthropological Quarterly* 62 (1989), p. 150.

32  Ruth Richardson, *Death, Dissection and the Destitute* (Harmondsworth: Penguin, 1988).

33  Jacinta Prunty, *Dublin Slums, 1800–1925: A Study in Urban Geography* (Dublin: Four Courts, 1997), p. 337.

34  Maura Cronin notes, for example, how newspaper coverage of Dublin petty sessions and even the heckling of public speakers might tell us something about the self-perceptions and value-systems of the urban poor. See *IHS* 31, 123 (1999), pp. 441–2. Marie-Louise Legg's splendid *Newspapers and Nationalism: The Irish Provincial Press, 1850–1892* (Dublin: Four Courts, 1999) is the first major study of Irish newspapers and deserves an equivalent that covers the national press over the whole of the nineteenth century.

35  Greta Jones and Elizabeth Malcolm (eds), *Medicine, Disease and the State in Ireland, 1650–1940* (Cork: Cork University Press, 1999), p. 9.

36  Ibid., p. 1.

37  Laurence M. Geary, 'Prince Hohenlohe, Signor Pastorini and miraculous healing in early nineteenth-century Ireland'; Peter Froggatt, 'Competing philosophies: the "preparatory" medical schools of the Royal Belfast Medical Institution and the Catholic University of Ireland, 1835–1909'; Maria Luddy, '"Angels of mercy": nuns as workhouse nurses, 1861–1898', in Jones and Malcolm (eds), *Medicine, Disease and the State*, pp. 40–58, 59–84, 102–20.

38  Markus Reuber, 'Moral management and the "unseen eye": public lunatic asylums in Ireland, 1800–1845', in Jones and Malcolm (eds), *Medicine, Disease and the State*, pp. 208–33. Mention should also be made of Ronald D. Cassell's study of the Irish medical dispensary system before and after the Great Famine, *Medical Charities, Medical Politics: The Irish Dispensary System and the Poor Law, 1836–1872* (London: Royal Historical Society, 1997). Though it is more conventional in its methodology, it is notable for its meticulous research and for being the first work of modern scholarship on the topic. It lucidly demonstrates how Ireland's impressive but ramshackle health system came to be reformed after mid-century until, by the 1870s, it could boast 'the most comprehensive free medical care system in the British Isles'. What is now needed are studies that show what these changes meant at 'ground level' to the professionals who worked in the system and, above all, to the ordinary people they were meant to benefit.

39  Joseph Robins, *The Miasma: Epidemic and Panic in Nineteenth-Century Ireland* (Dublin: IPA, 1995).

40  Modern interest in the subject might be said to have begun only a quarter-century ago with the appearance of T. D. Williams (ed.), *Secret Societies in Ireland* (Dublin and New York: Gill & Macmillan, 1973). Donnelly was perhaps the most prolific of those who wrote on agrarian secret societies over the next two decades, though much of his work focused upon the eighteenth century. A collection of his work on this subject is forthcoming from Irish Academic Press.

41  Samuel J. Clark and James S. Donnelly, Jr, 'The unreaped harvest', in Clark and Donnelly (eds), *Irish Peasants: Violence and Political Unrest, 1780–1914* (Manchester: Manchester University Press, 1983), pp. 420–1.

42   For example, M. R. Beames, *Peasants and Power: The Whiteboy Movements and Their Control in Pre-Famine Ireland* (New York: Harvester, 1983); Tom Garvin, 'Defenders, Ribbonmen and others: underground political networks in pre-Famine Ireland', *Past and Present* 96 (1982), pp. 133–55; James S. Donnelly, Jr, 'The social composition of agrarian rebellions in early nineteenth-century Ireland: the case of the Carders and Caravats, 1813–1816', in P. J. Corish (ed.), *Radicals, Rebels and Establishments: Historical Studies* XV (Belfast: Appletree, 1985), pp. 151–69.

43   Kevin Kenny, *Making Sense of the Molly Maguires* (Oxford: Clarendon, 1998).

44   The Rockite movement is the subject of a work in progress by Donnelly who also published a brief sketch of the Terry Alts: 'The Terry Alt movement, 1829–31', *History Ireland* 2, 4 (1994), pp. 30–5.

45   Peter Sahlins, *Forest Rites: The War of the Demoiselles in Nineteenth-Century France* (Cambridge, Mass: Harvard University Press, 1994).

46   Luke Gibbons, 'Identity without a centre: allegory, history and Irish nationalism', in his *Transformations in Irish Culture* (Cork: Cork University Press, 1996), pp. 134–47; David Lloyd, 'Violence and the constitution of the novel', in his *Anomalous States: Irish Writing and the Post-colonial Moment* (Dublin: Lilliput, 1993), pp. 125–55.

47   David Lloyd, 'Nationalisms against the state', in Lloyd, *Ireland After History* (Cork: Cork University Press, 1999), p. 26.

48   See, for example, Ranajit Guha and Gayatri Chakravorty Spivak, *Selected Subaltern Studies* (Oxford: Clarendon, 1988) and David Lloyd, 'Outside history: Irish new histories and the "subalternity effect"', in *Ireland After History*, pp. 77–88.

49   Clark and Donnelly, 'Unreaped harvest', p. 421.

50   Apart from a smattering of articles that appeared over the past decade, recent research on the subject has been negligible. But see Gary Owens, '"A moral insurrection": faction-fighters, public demonstrations and the O'Connellite campaign, 1828', *IHS* 30, 120 (1997), pp. 513–41; M. B. Kiely and W. Nolan, 'Politics, land and rural conflict in County Waterford, *c.* 1830–1845', in William Nolan and Thomas Power (eds), *Waterford: History and Society* (Dublin, 1992), pp. 459–94. Outstanding studies of factional warfare in other countries, albeit in the early modern period, include Edward Muir, *Mad Blood Stirring: Vendetta and Factions in Friuli During the Renaissance* (Baltimore and London: Johns Hopkins University Press, 1993) and Robert C. Davis, *The War of the Fists: Popular Culture and Public Violence in Late Renaissance Venice* (Oxford: Clarendon, 1994).

51   See Carolyn A. Conley, *Melancholy Accidents: The Meaning of Violence in Post-Famine Ireland* (Lanham MD: Lexington Books, 1999), esp. ch. 2, 'Recreational violence'.

52   This is the subject of a forthcoming book by Professor Sean Farrell of Newberry College.

53   Brian Henry's *Dublin Hanged: Crime, Law Enforcement and Punishment in Late Eighteenth-Century Dublin* (Dublin: Irish Academic Press, 1994) is the only book-length Irish study. Particularly outstanding examples of work in other countries and models for work in an Irish context are: V. A. C. Gatrell, *The Hanging Tree: Execution and the English People, 1770–1868* (Oxford: Clarendon, 1994); Richard J. Evans, *Rituals of Retribution: Capital Punishment in Germany, 1600–1987* (Oxford: Clarendon, 1996); and Louis P. Masur, *Rites of Execution: Capital Punishment and the Transformation of American Culture* (Oxford: Clarendon, 1989).

54  Gatrell, *Hanging Tree*, p. 8 and fn.

55  Ibid., p. 56.

56  Burke, 'Overture: the new history', p. 3. For a superb analysis of this and related themes, together with an invaluable survey of historiography in the 'new history' vein, see Raphael Samuel, 'Reading the signs', *History Workshop Journal* 32 (1991), pp. 88–109 and 'Reading the signs: II. Fact-grubbers and mind-readers', *History Workshop Journal* 33 (1992), pp. 220–51.

57  Cormac Ó Gráda, *Ireland: A New Economic History, 1780–1939* (Oxford: Clarendon, 1994); Alvin Jackson, *Ireland, 1798–1998: Politics and War* (Oxford: Blackwell, 1999).

### CHAPTER 3: WOMEN'S HISTORY

1  See for instance, Joan Wallach Scott, *Feminism and History* (Oxford: Clarendon, 1998); Judith Bennett, 'Feminism and history', *Gender and History* 1, 3 (1989), pp. 251–72; Kathleen Canning, 'Dialogue: the turn to gender and the challenge of poststructuralism', *Journal of Women's History* 5, 1 (1993), pp. 104–13; Joan Hoff, 'Gender as a postmodern category of paralysis', *Women's History Review* 3, 2 (1994), pp. 149–68.

2  Margaret MacCurtain and Donncha Ó Corráin (eds), *Women in Irish Society: The Historical Dimension* (Dublin: Arlen House/Women's Press, 1978).

3  Caitriona Clear, *Nuns in Nineteenth-Century Ireland* (Dublin: Gill & Macmillan, 1987).

4  Caitriona Clear, 'Walls within walls: nuns in nineteenth-century Ireland', in Chris Curtin, Pauline Jackson and Barbara O'Connor (eds), *Gender in Irish Society* (Galway: Galway University Press, 1987), pp. 134–51 and her, 'The limits of female autonomy: nuns in nineteenth-century Ireland', in Maria Luddy and Cliona Murphy (eds), *Women Surviving: Studies in Irish Women's History in the 19th and 20th Centuries* (Dublin: Poolbeg, 1990), pp. 15–50. Marie O'Connell, 'The genesis of convent foundations and their institutions in Ulster, 1840–1920', in Janice Holmes and Diane Urquhart (eds), *Coming into the Light: The Work, Politics and Religion of Women in Ulster, 1840–1940* (Belfast: Institute of Irish Studies, QUB, 1994), pp. 179–206. For an account of nuns as nurses see Maria Luddy, '"Angels of mercy": nuns as workhouse nurses, 1861–1898', in Greta Jones and Elizabeth Malcolm (eds), *Medicine, Disease and the State in Ireland, 1650–1940* (Cork: Cork University Press, 1999), pp. 102–17.

5  Mary Peckham Magray, *The Transforming Power of the Nuns: Women, Religion and Cultural Change in Ireland, 1750–1900* (New York: Oxford University Press, 1998).

6  A significant addition to the literature on nuns is Mary C. Sullivan's *Catherine McAuley and the Tradition of Mercy* (Dublin: Four Courts, 1995), which includes original letters, memoirs and extracts from convent annals by many of the first generation of Mercy Sisters.

7  Jacinta Prunty, *Lady of Charity, Sister of Faith: Margaret Aylward 1810–1889* (Dublin: Four Courts, 1999).

8  Jacinta Prunty, *Dublin Slums, 1800–1925: A Study in Urban Geography* (Dublin: Irish Academic Press, 1998).

9  See P. J. Corish, 'Women and religious practice', in Mary O'Dowd and Margaret MacCurtain (eds), *Women in Early Modern Ireland* (Dublin: Wolfhound, 1991), pp. 212–20.

10   Erin I. Bishop, *The World of Mary O'Connell, 1778–1836* (Dublin: Lilliput, 1999), ch. 7.

11   S. J. Connolly, *Priests and People in Pre-Famine Ireland* (Dublin: Gill & Macmillan, 1982).

12   David Hempton and Myrtle Hill, *Evangelical Protestantism in Ulster Society, 1740–1890* (London: Routledge, 1992).

13   Janice Holmes, '"The world turned upside down": women in the Ulster revival of 1859', in Holmes and Urquhart, *Coming Into The Light*, pp. 126–53; see the same author's *Religious Revival in Britain and Ireland 1859–1905* (Dublin: Irish Academic Press, 2000). See also, Myrtle Hill, 'Ulster awakened: the '59 revival reconsidered', *Journal of Ecclesiastical History* 41, 3 (1990), pp. 443–62. Hill does not focus particularly on women though much of the evidence she provides relates directly to them.

14   Andrea Ebel Brożyna, *Labour, Love and Prayer: Female Piety in Ulster Religious Literature 1850–1914* (Belfast and Montreal: Institute of Irish Studies/McGill–Queen's University Press, 1999). See also her articles, '"The cursed cup hath cast her down": constructions of female piety in Ulster evangelical temperance literature, 1863–1914', in Holmes and Urquhart, *Coming into the Light*, pp. 154–78; '"The right to labour, love and pray": the creation of the ideal Christian woman in Ulster Roman Catholic and Protestant religious literature, 1850–1914', *Women's History Review* 6, 4 (1997), pp. 505–25.

15   Magray, *Transforming Power*, pp. 90–4; S. J. Connolly, *Religion and Society in Nineteenth-Century Ireland* (Dundalk: Dundalgan Press, 1985).

16   See James S. Donnelly, Jr, 'The Marian shrine of Knock: the first decade', *Éire-Ireland* 28, 2 (1993), pp. 218–36.

17   Connolly, *Religion and Society*.

18   Maria Luddy, *Women and Philanthropy in Nineteenth-Century Ireland* (Cambridge: Cambridge University Press, 1995). See also her 'Religion, philanthropy and the state in late eighteenth and early nineteenth-century Ireland', in Hugh Cunningham and Joanna Innes (eds), *Charity, Philanthropy and Reform from the 1690s to 1850* (London: Macmillan, 1998), pp. 148–67.

19   Luddy, *Women and Philanthropy*, ch. 6.

20   Margaret Preston, 'Discourse and hegemony: race and class in the language of charity in nineteenth-century Dublin', in Tadhg Foley and Sean Ryder (eds), *Ideology and Ireland in the Nineteenth Century* (Dublin: Four Courts, 1998), pp. 100–12.

21   See Luddy, *Women and Philanthropy*, pp. 183–7 and her 'Religion, philanthropy and the state'.

22   Mary E. Daly, *Women and Work in Ireland* (Dundalk: Dundalgan Press, 1997). For a general discussion of women and work in the nineteenth century see Maria Luddy, 'Women and work in nineteenth and early twentieth-century Ireland', in Bernadette Whelan (ed.), *Women and Paid Work in Ireland 1500–1930* (Dublin: Four Courts, 2000), pp. 44–56.

23   Mary Cullen, 'Breadwinners and providers: women in the household economy of labouring families, 1835–36', in Luddy and Murphy, *Women Surviving*, pp. 98–111.

24   Anne McKernan, 'War, gender and industrial innovation: recruiting women weavers in early nineteenth-century Ireland', *Journal of Social History* 28, 1 (1995), pp. 109–24.

25   Marilyn Cohen, *Linen, Family, and Community in Tullylish, County Down, 1690–1914* (Dublin: Four Courts, 1997).

26   Brenda Collins, 'Sewing and social structure: the flowerers of Scotland and Ireland', in Rosalind Mitchison and Peter Roebuck (eds), *Economy and Society in Scotland and Ireland,*

*1500–1939* (Edinburgh: John Donald, 1988), pp. 242–52. See also the same author's 'The organisation of sewing outwork in late nineteenth-century Ulster', in Maxine Berg (ed.), *Markets and Manufacture in Early Industrial Europe* (London: Routledge, 1991), pp. 139–56.

27 Margaret Neill, 'Homeworking in Ulster', in Holmes and Urquhart (eds), *Coming Into The Light*, pp. 2–32; David M. Smith, '"I thought I was landed!": the Congested Districts Board and the women of western Ireland', *Éire-Ireland* 31, 3 & 31, 4 (1996), pp. 209–27.

28 Joanna Bourke, *Husbandry to Housewifery: Women, Economic Change and Housewifery in Ireland 1890–1914* (Oxford: Clarendon, 1993). See also the following articles by the same author, 'Women and poultry in Ireland', *IHS* 25, 99 (1987), pp. 293–310; 'The health caravan: female labour and domestic education in rural Ireland 1890–1914', *Éire-Ireland* 24, 4 (1989), pp. 21–38; 'Dairywomen and affectionate wives: women in the Irish dairy industry, 1890–1914', *Agricultural History Review* 38, 11 (1991), pp. 149–64; 'Working women: the domestic labour market in rural Ireland, 1890–1914', *Journal of Interdisciplinary History* 21, 3 (1991), pp. 479–99; '"The best of all homerulers: the economic power of women in Ireland, 1800–1914', *Irish Economic and Social History* 18 (1991), pp. 34–47.

29 Daly, *Women and Work*, pp. 19–24.

30 Bourke, *Husbandry to Housewifery*, passim.

31 Mona Hearn, *Below Stairs: Domestic Service Remembered in Dublin and Beyond, 1880–1922* (Dublin: Lilliput, 1993).

32 Ibid., p. 111.

33 Theresa Moriarty, *Work in Progress: Episodes from the History of Irish Women's Trade Unionism* (Brighton: Irish Labour History Society/Unison, 1994).

34 Dympna McLoughlin, 'Workhouses and Irish female paupers, 1840–70', in Luddy and Murphy, *Women Surviving*, pp. 117–47, see also her 'Superfluous and unwanted dead-weight: the emigration of nineteenth-century Irish pauper women', in Patrick O'Sullivan (ed.), *The Irish World Wide*, IV, *Irish Women and Irish Migration* (London: Leicester University Press, 1995), pp. 66–88.

35 Rena Lohan, 'The treatment of women sentenced to transportation and penal servitude, 1790–1898'. (Unpublished MLitt thesis, TCD, 1989). This is an excellent account of the treatment of convict women.

36 See the following: Joy Damousi, *Depraved and Disorderly: Female Convicts, Sexuality and Gender in Colonial Australia* (Cambridge: Cambridge University Press, 1997); Deborah Oxley, *Convict Maids: The Forced Migration of Women to Australia* (Cambridge: Cambridge University Press, 1996). See also the earlier work by Portia Robinson, *The Women of Botany Bay* (Melbourne: Macquarie Library, 1993), and Trevor McClaughlin (ed.), *Irish Women in Colonial Australia* (St Leonards, NSW: Allen & Unwin, 1998).

37 For instance, Kerby Miller, *Emigrants and Exiles: Ireland and the Irish Exodus to North America* (Oxford: Clarendon, 1985), has been hailed as a valuable and comprehensive treatment of its subject. Miller has, however, little to say on Irish women emigrants.

38 O'Sullivan (ed.), *Irish Women and Irish Migration*.

39 Hasia R. Diner, *Erin's Daughters in America: Irish Immigrant Women in the Nineteenth Century* (Baltimore: Johns Hopkins University Press, 1983).

40 On the links between emigration and modernisation see David Fitzpatrick, 'The modernisation of the Irish female', in P. O'Flanagan, P. Ferguson and K. Whelan (eds), *Rural Ireland, 1600–1900: Modernisation and Change* (Cork: Cork University Press, 1987),

pp. 167–80; David Fitzpatrick, '"A share of the honeycomb": education, emigration and Irishwomen', in Mary E. Daly and David Dickson (eds), *The Origins of Popular Literacy in Ireland: Language Change and Educational Development, 1700–1920* (Dublin: TCD, 1990), pp. 167–87.

41  See, K. Miller, D. N. Doyle and P. Kelleher, '"For love and liberty": Irish women, migration and domesticity in Ireland and America, 1815–1920', in O'Sullivan (ed.), *Irish Women and Irish Migration*, pp. 41–61.

42  David Fitzpatrick, *Oceans of Consolation: Personal Accounts of Irish Migration to Australia* (Cork: Cork University Press, 1995). See in particular the section on the Doorleys, pp. 334–58.

43  Martha Kanya-Forstner, 'Defining womanhood: Irish women and the Catholic Church in Victorian Liverpool', in D. M. McRaild (ed.), *The Great Famine and Beyond: Irish Migrants in Britain in the Nineteenth and Twentieth Centuries* (Dublin: Irish Academic Press, 1999), pp. 168–88.

44  Miller et al., 'Love and liberty'. See also, Deirdre Mageean, 'To be matched or to move: Irish women's prospects in Munster'; Deirdre Mageean, 'Making sense and providing structure: Irish-American women in the parish neighborhood', in Christiane Harzig (ed.), *Peasant Maids, City Women: From the European Countryside to Urban America* (Ithaca and London: Cornell University Press, 1997), pp. 57–97, 223–60. See also, Grace Neville, '"She never then after that forgot him": Irish women and emigration to North America in Irish folklore', *Mid-America: A Historical Review* 74 (1992), pp. 271–89.

45  John Logan, 'The dimensions of gender in nineteenth-century schooling', in Margaret Kelleher and James Murphy (eds), *Gender Perspectives in Nineteenth-Century Ireland: Public and Private Spheres* (Dublin: Irish Academic Press, 1997), pp. 36–49.

46  Anne V. O'Connor, 'Influences affecting girls' secondary education in Ireland, 1860–1910', *Archivium Hibernicum* 141 (1986), pp. 83–98; Anne V. O'Connor, 'The revolution in girls' secondary education in Ireland, 1860–1910', in Mary Cullen (ed.), *Girls Don't Do Honours: Irishwomen in Education in the Nineteenth and Twentieth Centuries* (Dublin: Women's Education Bureau, 1987), pp. 31–54. For an overview of the educational opportunities available to Irish women see Anne V. O'Connor, 'Education in the nineteenth century', in A. Bourke et al. (eds), *The Field Day Anthology of Irish Writing: Irish Women's Writing and Traditions* v (Cork and New York: Cork University Press and New York University Press, 2002), pp. 647–67. See also, Anne V. O'Connor and Susan Parkes, *Gladly Learn and Gladly Teach: A History of Alexandra College and School, Dublin, 1866–1916* (Dublin: Blackwater, 1983).

47  Alison Jordan, *Margaret Byers, Pioneer of Women's Education and Founder of Victoria College, Belfast* (Belfast: Institute of Irish Studies, QUB, 1991); Maria Luddy, 'Isabella M. S. Tod', and Anne V. O'Connor, 'Anne Jellicoe', in Mary Cullen and Maria Luddy (eds), *Women, Power and Consciousness in Nineteenth-Century Ireland* (Dublin: Attic Press, 1995), pp. 197–230 and pp. 125–60. For third-level education see Eibhlin Breathnach, 'Charting new waters: women's experience in higher education, 1879–1908', in Cullen, *Girls Don't Do Honours*, pp. 55–78.

48  See Senia Pašeta, *Before the Revolution: Nationalism, Social Change and Ireland's Catholic Elite, 1879–1922* (Cork: Cork University Press, 1999) which briefly explores some of the issues pertinent to the education of Catholic women at this time.

49  See Maria Luddy, *Women in Ireland 1800–1914: A Documentary History* (Cork: Cork University Press, 1995), pp. 239–330, for examples of women's political activity.

50  Carmel Quinlan, *Genteel Revolutionaries: Anna and Thomas Haslam and the Irish Women's Movement* (Cork: Cork University Press, 2002). A brief survey of the early suffrage campaign is provided in Rosemary Cullen Owens, *Smashing Times: The History of the Irish Suffrage Movement, 1890–1922* (Dublin: Attic Press, 1998).

51  For an account of the suffrage campaign directed from Ulster see Luddy, 'Isabella Tod'. This campaign is covered briefly in Diane Urquhart, *Women in Ulster Politics, 1890–1940* (Dublin: Irish Academic Press, 2000), ch. 1.

52  Virginia Crossman, *Local Government in Nineteenth-Century Ireland* (Belfast: Institute of Irish Studies, QUB, 1994), pp. 83–5.

53  Maria Luddy, 'Women and politics in nineteenth-century Ireland', in Mary O'Dowd and Maryann Valiulis (eds), *Women and Irish History* (Dublin: Wolfhound, 1997), p. 105.

54  Ibid., pp. 89–108.

55  See Brigitte Anton, 'Northern voices: Ulsterwomen in the Young Ireland movement' in Holmes and Urquhart, *Coming into the Light*, pp. 60–92; Jan Cannavan, 'Romantic Revolutionary Irishwomen: Women, Young Ireland and 1848', in Kelleher and Murphy, *Gender Perspectives*, pp. 212–20.

56  Anna Parnell, *Tale of a Great Sham*, ed. Dana Hearne (Dublin: Arlen House, 1986). For recent writings on the Ladies' Land League see Margaret Ward, 'The Ladies' Land League and the Irish Land War 1881/1882: defining the relationship between women and nation', in Ida Blom, Karen Hagemann and Catherine Hall (eds), *Gendered Nations: Nationalism and Gender Order in the Long Nineteenth Century* (Oxford: Berg, 2000), pp. 229–47;

57  See Jane McL. Côté, *Fanny and Anna Parnell: Ireland's Patriot Sisters* (Dublin: Gill & Macmillan, 1991); Jane McL. Côté and Dana Hearne, 'Anna Parnell, 1852–1911', in Cullen and Luddy, *Women, Power and Consciousness*, pp. 263–93.

58  Janet T. TeBrake, 'Irish peasant women in revolt: the Land League years', *IHS* 28, 109 (1992), pp. 63–80.

59  Joel A. Hollander, '"Beauty and the beast": depiction of Irish female types during the era of Parnell, *c*.1881–1891', in Lawrence W. McBride (ed.), *Images, Icons and the Irish Nationalist Imagination* (Dublin: Four Courts, 1999), pp. 53–72; Niamh O'Sullivan, 'The iron cage of femininity: visual representation of women in the 1880s land agitation', in Foley and Ryder, *Ideology and Ireland*, pp. 181–96.

60  Virginia Crossman, 'The *Shan Van Vocht*: women, republicanism, and the commemoration of the 1798 rebellion', *Eighteenth-Century Life* 22, 3 (1998), pp. 128–39.

61  Patricia Lysaght, 'Perspectives on women during the Great Irish Famine from the oral tradition', *Béaloideas* 64–5 (1996–7), pp. 63–130. See the same author's 'Women and the Great Famine: vignettes from the Irish oral tradition' in Arthur Gribben (ed.), *The Great Famine and the Irish Diaspora in America* (Amherst: University of Massachusetts Press, 1999), pp. 21–47.

62  Asenath Nicholson, *Annals of the Great Famine in Ireland*, ed. Maureen Murphy (Dublin: Lilliput, 1998). See also Margaret Kelleher, 'The female gaze: Asenath Nicholson's Famine narrative', in Chris Morash and Richard Hayes (eds), *'Fearful Realities': New Perspectives on the Great Famine* (Dublin: Irish Academic Press, 1996), pp. 119–30.

63  Mary E. Daly, *The Great Famine in Ireland* (Dundalk: Dundalgan Press and Dublin Historical Association, 1986); Cormac Ó Gráda, *The Great Irish Famine* (London: Macmillan,

1989) and Cormac Ó Gráda, *Black '47 and Beyond: The Great Irish Famine* (Princeton NJ: Princeton University Press, 1999).

64  David Fitzpatrick, 'Women and the Great Famine', in Kelleher and Murphy, *Gender Perspectives*, pp. 50–69.

65  Ibid., p. 68.

66  McLoughlin, 'Workhouses and Irish female paupers' and 'Superfluous and unwanted deadweight'.

67  Helen Burke, *The People and the Poor Law in Nineteenth-Century Ireland* (Dublin: Women's Education Bureau, 1987).

68  Grainne Blair, '"Equal sinners": Irish women utilising the Salvation Army rescue network', in Kelleher and Murphy, *Gender Perspectives*, pp. 179–92.

69  Frances Finnegan, *Do Penance or Perish: A Study of Magdalen Asylums in Ireland* (Piltown, Co. Kilkenny: Congrave Press, 2000).

70  Luddy, *Women and Philanthropy*, ch. 4.

71  Elizabeth Malcolm, 'Women and madness in Ireland, 1600–1850', in Margaret MacCurtain and Mary O'Dowd (eds), *Women in Early Modern Ireland* (Dublin: Wolfhound, 1991), pp. 318–34; '"The house of strident shadows": the asylum, the family and emigration in post-Famine rural Ireland', in Malcolm and Jones (eds), *Medicine, Disease and the State in Ireland*, pp. 177–91.

72  Oonagh Walsh, '"A lightness of mind": gender and insanity in nineteenth-century Ireland', in Kelleher and Murphy, *Gender Perspectives*, pp. 159–67. See also her article, '"The designs of providence": race, religion and Irish insanity', in Joseph Melling and Bill Forsythe (eds), *Insanity, Institutions and Society, 1800–1914* (London: Routledge, 1999), pp. 223–42.

73  See the following by Maria Luddy, 'An outcast community: the "Wrens" of the Curragh', *Women's History Review* 1, 3 (1992), pp. 341–55; Maria Luddy, 'Abandoned women and bad characters: prostitution in nineteenth-century Ireland', *Women's History Review* 6, 4 (1997), pp. 485–503; Maria Luddy, 'Irish women and the Contagious Diseases Acts', *History Ireland* 1, 1 (1993), pp. 32–4; 'The army and prostitution in nineteenth-century Ireland: the case of the Wrens of the Curragh', *Bullán* 6, 1 (2001), pp. 67–83.

74  Carolyn A. Conley, 'Irish criminal records, 1865–1892', *Éire-Ireland* 28, 1 (1993), pp. 97–106, and her 'No pedestals: women and violence in nineteenth-century Ireland', *Journal of Social History* 17, 3 (1995), pp. 800–18. See also, Elizabeth Steiner-Scott, '"To bounce a boot off her now & then . . .": domestic violence in post-Famine Ireland', in O'Dowd and Valiulis, *Women and Irish History*, pp. 125–43.

75  M. Luddy, C. Cox, L. Lane, D. Urquhart et al., *Sources for Women's History in Ireland* (Dublin: Women's History Project, 1999). Web address: www.nationalarchives. ie/wh. For other sources on women's history in this period see Maria Luddy, *Women in Ireland, 1800–1918: A Documentary History* (Cork: Cork University Press, 1995, 2nd edn, 1999).

76  See in particular Jean Agnew (ed.), *The Drennan–McTier Letters, 1776–1819*, 3 vols (Dublin: Irish Manuscripts Commission/Women's History Project, 1998–9). See also *Irish Women's Writing 1830–1890*, 6 vols (London: Thoemmes/Routledge, 1998). This collection includes the following works: Catherine Alexander, *Friendly Advice to Irish Mothers*; Mary Leadbeater, *The Leadbeater Papers*; A. Carroll, *Leaves from the Annals of the Sisters of Mercy*;

M. F. Cusack, *My Autobiography*; Lady Morgan, *Woman and Her Master*; and Annie Keary, *Castle Daly: The Story of an Irish Home Thirty Years Ago*.

77  See for instance, Alvin Jackson, *Ireland 1798–1998: Politics and War* (Oxford: Blackwell, 1999) and K. T. Hoppen, *Ireland Since 1800: Stability and Change* (London: Longmans, 1990, rev. edn, 1999).

### CHAPTER 4: RELIGIOUS HISTORY

1  The framework of this introduction is developed further in my 'Irish Christianity and revolution' in Jim Smyth (ed.), *Revolution, Counter-Revolution and Union, Ireland in the 1790s* (Cambridge: Cambridge University Press, 2000), pp. 195–210, and in my 'Radicalism and ritual in East Ulster', in Thomas Bartlett, David Dickson, Dáire Keogh and Kevin Whelan (eds), *1798: A Bicentenary Perspective* (Dublin: Four Courts, 2003), pp. 195–211.

2  For a perceptive argument that Protestantism formed the basis for a British sense of nationhood in the eighteenth century see Linda Colley, *Britons: Forging the Nation, 1707–1837* (New Haven: Yale University Press, 1992), pp. 11–54.

3  Jim Smyth, 'The making and undoing of a confessional state: Ireland, 1660–1829', *Journal of Ecclesiastical History* 44 (1993), pp. 506–13. See also his 'Manning the ramparts: Ireland and the agenda of the Roman Catholic Church', *History of European Ideas* 20 (1996), pp. 681–7. See Donal A. Kerr, 'Government and Roman Catholics in Ireland, 1850–1940', in Donal A. Kerr, Mordechai Breuer, Sheridan Gilley and Ernst Christoph Suttner (eds), *Religion, State and Ethnic Groups: Comparative Studies on Governments and Non-dominant Ethnic Groups in Europe: 1850–1940*, II (Aldershot: Dartmouth Publishing Co., 1992), pp. 277–312.

4  J. J. Lee, 'On the birth of the modern Irish state: the Larkin thesis', in Stewart J. Brown and David W. Miller (eds), *Piety and Power: Essays in Honour of Emmet Larkin* (Belfast: Institute of Irish Studies, QUB, 2000), pp. 130–57.

5  C. D. A. Leighton, 'Gallicanism and the Veto controversy: church, state and Catholic community in early nineteenth-century Ireland', in R. V. Comerford, Mary Cullen, Jacqueline R. Hill and Colm Lennon (eds), *Religion, Conflict and Coexistence in Ireland: Essays presented to Monsignor Patrick J. Corish* (Dublin: Gill & Macmillan, 1990), pp. 135–58. Fergus O'Ferrall, 'Liberty and Catholic politics 1790–1990', and Pierre Joannon, 'O'Connell, Montalembert and the birth of Christian Democracy in France', in Maurice R. O'Connell (ed.), *Daniel O'Connell: Political Pioneer* (Dublin: IPA, 1991), pp. 35–56, 98–109, as well as Geraldine Grogan, 'Daniel O'Connell and European Catholic thought', *Studies* 80 (1991), pp. 56–64, shed light on links between continental Catholic thought and Irish Catholicism in O'Connell's time.

6  Important articles on the careers of particular prelates include Aisling Walsh, 'Michael Cardinal Logue, 1840–1924, Part 1', *Seanchas Ard Mhacha* 17 (1997), pp. 108–62; Liam Bane, 'John MacEvilly and the Catholic Church in Galway, 1857–1902', in Gerard Moran (ed.), *Galway, History and Society: Interdisciplinary Essays on the History of an Irish County* (Dublin: Geography Publications, 1996), pp. 421–44; Donal Kerr, 'Dublin's forgotten Archbishop: Daniel Murray, 1768–1852', in James Kelly and Dáire Keogh (eds), *History of the Catholic Diocese of Dublin* (Dublin: Four Courts), pp. 247–67; Ciaran O'Carroll, 'The

pastoral politics of Paul Cullen', in Kelly and Keogh (eds), *History of the Catholic Diocese,* pp. 294–312; and Stephen McLaughlin, 'The development of the Catholic Church in Derry under the leadership of Bishop Francis Kelly (1849–88)', in Henry A. Jefferies and Ciarán Devlin (eds), *History of the Diocese of Derry from Earliest Times* (Dublin: Four Courts, 2000), pp. 224–39. C. J. Woods's article, 'Parnell and the Catholic Church', in D. George Boyce and Alan O'Day (eds), *Parnell in Perspective* (London: Routledge, 1991), pp. 9–37, provides a critical synthesis of work on that topic by a generation of scholars, including himself.

7   John F. Quinn, 'The "vagabond friar": Father Mathew's difficulties with Irish bishops 1840–56', *Catholic Historical Review* 78 (1992), pp. 542–56.

8   Anna Kinsella, '1798 claimed for Catholics: Father Kavanagh, Fenians and the centenary celebrations', in Dáire Keogh and Nicholas Furlong (eds), *The Mighty Wave: The 1798 Rebellion in Wexford* (Dublin: Four Courts, 1996), pp. 139–55.

9   John F. Ryan, 'Gerald O'Donovan: priest, novelist and Irish revivalist', *Journal of the Galway Archaeological and Historical Society* 48 (1996), pp. 1–47; Frank A. Biletz, 'The *Irish Peasant* and the conflict between Irish-Ireland and the Catholic bishops, 1903–1910', and Donal A. Kerr, 'Priest, pikes and patriots: the Irish Catholic Church and political violence from the Whiteboys to the Fenians', in Brown and Miller, *Piety and Power*, pp. 16–42, 108–29; Thomas Morrissey, 'The paradox of James Connolly, Irish Marxist socialist, 1868–1916, and the papal encyclicals, 1891–1991', *Milltown Studies* (1991), pp. 24–40.

10  R. H. McIlrath, 'Classon Porter: A short account of the life and work of a nineteenth-century non-subscribing minister in Larne', *Ulster Local Studies* 15 (1993), pp. 13–37; Duncan Scarlett, 'Conflict during the incumbency of the Reverend August B. R. Young, Rector of Ballybay, Co. Monaghan, 1872–1920, Prebendary of Devenish 1906–1911, and Precentor of Clogher, 1911–1920', *Clogher Record* 16 (1998), pp. 182–200.

11  Peter Nockles, 'Church or Protestant sect? The Church of Ireland, high churchmanship and the Oxford Movement, 1822–69', *Historical Journal* 41 (1998), pp. 457–93. David Degiustino, 'Finding an archbishop: the Whigs and Richard Whately in 1831', *Church History* 64 (1995), pp. 218–36. Kenneth Milne, 'The stripping of the assets, 1830–1960', in Milne, *Christ Church Cathedral, Dublin: A History* (Dublin: Four Courts, 2000), pp. 315–38.

12  Kenneth Milne, 'Principle or pragmatism: Archbishop Brodrick and church education policy', in Alan Ford, James McGuire and Kenneth Milne (eds), *As by Law Established: The Church of Ireland Since the Reformation* (Dublin: Lilliput, 1995), pp. 187–94. Sean Griffin, 'Catholic Book Society and its role in the emerging system of national education 1824–1834', *Irish Educational Studies* 11 (1992), pp. 82–98, and his 'Archbishop Murray of Dublin and the episcopal clash on the interdenominational school scripture lessons controversy, 1835–41', *Recusant History* 22 (1995), pp. 370–408. Geraldine Grogan, 'The Colleges Bill, 1845–49', in Maurice R. O'Connell (ed.), *O'Connell, Education, Church and State: Proceedings of the Second Annual Daniel O'Connell Workshop* (Dublin: IPA, 1992), pp. 19–34. Paul Connell, *Parson, Priest and Master: National Education in Co. Meath, 1824–1841* (Dublin: Irish Academic Press, 1995). Francis Duffy, 'Education in Cavan, 1825–32', *Breifne* 8 (1995), pp. 587–606. George Beale, 'Shore Street National School, Donaghadee, 1861–1917: a case study in local Presbyterian education', *Ulster Local Studies* 19 (1997),    pp. 52–60.

13  Micheál Ó Cearúil (ed.) *Gniomhartha na mBráithre* (Baile Átha Cliath: Coiscéim, 1996).

14  Mary Kenny, *Goodbye to Catholic Ireland: A Social, Personal and Cultural History from the Fall of Parnell to the Realm of Mary Robinson* (London: Sinclair Stevenson, 1997).

15  Emmet Larkin, 'The devotional revolution in Ireland, 1850–75', *American Historical Review* 77 (1972), pp. 625–52.

16  Ibid., p. 650.

17  Raymond Gillespie, 'Popular and unpopular religion: a view from early modern Ireland', in James S. Donnelly, Jr and Kerby A. Miller (eds), *Irish Popular Culture, 1650–1850* (Dublin: Irish Academic Press, 1998), pp. 30–2.

18  Emmet Larkin, 'The rise and fall of stations in Ireland, 1750–1850', in Michel Lagrée, *Chocs et Ruptures en Histoire Religieuse: Fin XVIIIe–XIXe Siècles* (Rennes: Presses Universitaires de Rennes, 1998), pp. 19–32.

19  David W. Miller, 'Irish Catholicism and the Great Famine', *Journal of Social History* 9 (1975), pp. 81–98.

20  David W. Miller, 'Mass attendance in Ireland in 1834', in Brown and Miller, *Piety and Power*, pp. 172–3.

21  Patrick Corish, *The Irish Catholic Experience: A Historical Survey* (Dublin: Gill & Macmillan, 1985), p. 233.

22  Ignatius Murphy, *The Diocese of Killaloe, 1800–50* (Dublin: Four Courts, 1992), p. 347.

23  Ibid., pp. 344–7; Ambrose Macaulay, *William Crolly, Archbishop of Armagh, 1835–49* (Dublin: Four Courts, 1994), pp. 114–20.

24  Desmond J. Keenan, *The Catholic Church in Nineteenth-Century Ireland: A Sociological Study* (Dublin: Gill & Macmillan, 1983), pp. 244–5. Dáire Keogh, '"The pattern of the flock": John Thomas Troy, 1786–1823', in Kelly and Keogh, *Catholic Diocese of Dublin*, pp. 225–8.

25  Hugh Fenning, 'Prayer-books and pamphlets: 1700–1829', *Seanchas Ard Mhacha* 16 (1994), pp. 93–9, contains valuable information and guidance for the historian of spirituality seeking devotional material printed before emancipation. Vincent Ryan describes his *The Shaping of Sunday: Sunday and Eucharist in the Irish Tradition* (Dublin: Veritas, 1997) as 'a pastoral rather than a scholarly work' (p. 9). The same description might be applied to Peter O'Dwyer, *Towards a History of Irish Spirituality* (Dublin: Columba, 1995). Both books are very valuable for their evocation of styles of devotion in the past, but less so for their assessment of the impact of those styles.

26  Murphy, *Killaloe, 1800–50*, p. 371.

27  Ignatius Murphy, *The Diocese of Killaloe, 1850–1904* (Dublin: Four Courts, 1995), pp. 52–3, 472–3.

28  Desmond Mooney, 'Popular religion and clerical influence in pre-Famine Meath', in Comerford, et al., *Religion, Conflict and Coexistence*, pp. 188–218.

29  Daniel Gallogly, 'Priests and people of Kilmore, 1800–1950', *Breifne* 8 (1995), pp. 515–52. James Kelly is also attentive to these issues in 'The formation of the modern Catholic Church in the Diocese of Kilmore, 1580–1880', in Raymond Gillespie (ed.), *Cavan: Essays on the History of an Irish County* (Dublin: Irish Academic Press, 1999), pp. 115–38; and in 'The Catholic Church in the Diocese of Ardagh, 1650–1870', in Raymond Gillespie and Gerard Moran (eds), *Longford: Essays in County History* (Dublin: Lilliput, 1991), pp. 63–91. See also Séamas Ó Maitiú, 'Donnybrook fair: carnival versus Lent', *History Ireland* 4 (1996), pp. 21–6; and Diarmuid Ó Giolláin, 'The Pattern', in Donnelly and Miller, *Irish Popular Culture*, pp. 201–21.

30  Peter Harbison, *Pilgrimage in Ireland* (London: Barrie & Jenkins, 1991). Michael Dames, *Mythic Ireland* (London: Thames & Hudson, 1992). Walter L. Brennemann, and Mary G. Brennemann, *Crossing the Circle at the Holy Wells of Ireland* (Charlottesville: University Press of Virginia, 1995).

31  Gearóid Ó Crualaoich, 'The "merry wake"', in Donnelly, and Miller, *Irish Popular Culture*, pp. 173–200.

32  Laurence M. Geary, 'Prince Hohenlohe, Signor Pastorini and miraculous healing in early nineteenth-century Ireland', in Greta Jones and Elizabeth Malcolm (eds), *Medicine, Disease and the State in Ireland, 1650–1940* (Cork: Cork University Press, 1999), pp. 40–58.

33  James S. Donnelly, Jr, 'Lough Derg: The making of the modern pilgrimage', in William Nolan, Liam Ronayne and Mairead Dunlevy (eds), *Donegal, History and Society: Interdisciplinary Essays on the History of an Irish County* (Dublin: Geography Publications, 1995), pp. 491–508.

34  John White, 'The Cusack papers: new evidence on the Knock apparition', *History Ireland* 4 (1996), pp. 39–43; Paul Bew, 'A vision to the dispossessed? Popular poety and revolutionary politics in the Irish land war, 1879–82', in Judith Devlin and Ronan Fanning (eds), *Religion and Rebellion: Historical Studies* xx (Dublin: UCD Press, 1997); Walter L. and Mary G. Brennemann, *Crossing the Circle*, pp. 110–23. For a very informative study by a folklorist of the Brigantine devotions see Séamas Ó Catháin, *The Festival of Brigit: Celtic Goddess and Holy Woman* (Blackrock: DBA Publications, 1995).

35  William A. Christian, *Local Religion in Sixteenth-Century Spain* (Princeton NJ: Princeton University Press, 1981).

36  David Hempton and Myrtle Hill, *Evangelical Protestantism in Ulster Society, 1740–1890* (London: Routledge, 1992), pp. 12–14.

37  Miller, 'Irish Christianity and revolution'. See also Joseph Liechty, 'The popular reformation comes to Ireland: the case of John Walker and the foundation of the Church of God, 1804', in Comerford et al, *Religion, Conflict and Coexistence*, pp. 159–87, which is as valuable for its careful placement of Irish popular Protestantism within a longer temporal context as it is for its treatment of the particular case of the Church of God.

38  Stewart J. Brown, 'Presbyterian communities, transatlantic visions and the Ulster Revival of 1859', in J. P. Mackey (ed.), *The Cultures of Europe: The Irish Contribution* (Belfast: Institute of Irish Studies, QUB, 1994), pp. 103–4.

39  I. R. McBride, *Scripture Politics: Ulster Presbyterians and Irish Radicalism in the Late Eighteenth Century* (Oxford: Clarendon, 1998).

40  Alfred Russell Scott, *The Ulster Revival of 1859: Enthusiasm Emanating from Mid-Antrim* (Ballymena: Mid-Antrim Historical Group, 1994). Myrtle Hill, 'Ulster awakened: the '59 revival reconsidered', *Journal of Ecclesiastical History* 41 (1990), pp. 443–62. Janice Holmes, 'Ignorant, ill-mannered and excitable: clerical attitudes towards the laity in the Ulster Revival of 1859', *Ulster Local Studies*, 13 (1991), pp. 27–37, and her 'The "world turned upside down": women in the Ulster revival of 1859', in Janice Holmes and Diane Urquhart (eds), *Coming into the Light: The Work, Politics, and Religion of Women in Ulster, 1840–1940* (Belfast: Institute of Irish Studies, QUB, 1994), pp. 126–53. Brown, 'Presbyterian communities', pp. 87–108.

41  Recently, for example, in Brian Girvin, 'Making nations: O'Connell, religion and the creation of political identity', in O'Connell, *Daniel O'Connell: Political Pioneer*, pp. 13–34;

and Hugh Kearney, '1875: faith or fatherland? the contested symbolism of Irish nationalism', in Brown and Miller, *Piety and Power*, pp. 65–80.

42   Maria Luddy, *Women and Philanthropy in Nineteenth-Century Ireland* (Cambridge: Cambridge University Press, 1995), p. 216. See also Margaret Preston, 'Women and philanthropy in nineteenth-century Dublin', *Historian* 58 (1996), pp. 763–76; Oonagh Walsh, 'Protestant female philanthropy in Dublin in the early twentieth century', *History Ireland* 5 (1997), pp. 27–31; Maureen Murphy, 'Asenath Nicholson and the Famine in Ireland', in Maryann Gialanella Valiulis and Mary O'Dowd (eds), *Women and Irish History: Essays in Honour of Margaret MacCurtain* (Dublin: Wolfhound, 1997), pp. 109–24; Gráinne M. Blair, '"Equal sinners": Irish women utilising the Salvation Army rescue network for Britain and Ireland in the nineteenth century', in Margaret Kelleher and James H. Murphy (eds), *Gender Perspectives in Nineteenth-Century Ireland: Public and Private Spheres* (Dublin: Irish Academic Press, 1997), pp. 179–92.

43   Contributions on interdenominational relations include Irene Whelan, 'The stigma of souperism', in Cathal Póirtéir (ed.), *The Great Irish Famine* (Cork: Mercier, 1995), pp. 135–54; Stewart J. Brown, 'The new reformation movement in the Church of Ireland, 1801–29', in Brown and Miller, *Piety and Power*, pp. 180–208; and Andrew Finlay, 'Sectarianism in the workplace: the case of the Derry shirt industry, 1868–1968', *Irish Journal of Sociology* 3 (1993), pp. 79–94. John D. Brewer and Gareth I. Higgins's *Anti-Catholicism in Northern Ireland, 1600–1998: The Mote and the Beam* (New York: St Martin's, 1998), while dependent on secondary literature for its historical component, offers a very promising typology for understanding anti-Catholicism in the nineteenth century. Another important work by a social scientist on late twentieth-century sectarian issues which contains a critical review of historical literature is John Fulton, *The Tragedy of Belief: Division, Politics and Religion in Ireland* (Oxford: Clarendon, 1991). Joseph Liechty, 'The problem of sectarianism and the Church of Ireland', in Ford et al., *As by Law Established*, pp. 204–22 offers a splendidly nuanced analysis of interdenominational relations.

44   Luddy, *Women and Philanthropy*, p. 21. See also Séamus Enright, 'Women and Catholic life in Dublin, 1766–1852', in Kelly and Keogh, *Catholic Diocese of Dublin*, pp. 268–93.

45   Alison Jordan, *Who Cared? Charity in Victorian and Edwardian Belfast* (Belfast: Institute of Irish Studies, QUB, 1993), pp. 197–8.

46   For another analysis of the relationship between Catholicism and economics see T. Fahey, 'Catholicism and industrial society in Ireland', in J. H. Goldthorpe and C. T. Whelan (eds), *The Development of Industrial Society in Ireland: 3rd Joint Meeting of the Royal Academy and the British Academy, Oxford, 1990* (Oxford and London: Clarendon and British Academy, 1992), pp. 241–63.

47   Patrick Hogan, 'Fr. Robert O'Keefe, Parish Priest and the Callan controversy 1869–1881', in William Nolan and Kevin Whelan (eds), *Kilkenny, History and Society: Interdisciplinary Essays on the History of an Irish County* (Dublin: Geography Publications, 1990), pp. 507–40.

48   Líam Kennedy, K. A. Miller, and M. Graham, 'The long retreat: Protestants, economy and society, 1660–1926', in Gillespie and Moran, *Longford*, pp. 31–62. Miriam Moffitt, *The Church of Ireland Community of Killala and Achonry, 1870–1940* (Dublin: Irish Academic Press, 1999). Lindsay T. Brown, 'The Presbyterians of Co. Monaghan', and 'The

Presbyterian dilemma (part 2 of a series on the Monaghan Presbyterians)', *Clogher Record* 13 (1990), pp. 7–54, and 14 (1995), pp. 30–68. John Tunney, 'The marquis, the reverend, the grandmaster and the major: Protestant politics in Donegal, 1868–1933', in Nolan, et al., *Donegal, History and Society*, pp. 674–96. Ian D'Alton, 'Keeping faith: an evocation of the Cork Protestant character, 1820–1920', in Patrick O'Flanagan and Cornelius G. Buttimer (eds), *Cork: History and Society: Interdisciplinary Essays on the History of an Irish County* (Dublin: Geography Publications, 1993), pp. 759–92. Myrtle Hill, 'Religion and society: Protestantism in nineteenth-century County Down', and Oliver Rafferty, 'The Catholic Chapel and the Catholic community: observance and tradition in nineteenth-century County Down', in Lindsay J. Proudfoot (ed.), *Down, History and Society: Interdisciplinary Essays on the History of an Irish County* (Dublin: Geography Publications, 1997), pp. 489–522, 523–46.

49 This discussion focuses on middle-class history, but of course important work continues to be done on working class history. Recent publications relevant to religion include Martin Maguire, 'The Church of Ireland and the problem of the Protestant working class of Dublin, 1870s–1930s', in Ford et al., *As by Law Established*, pp. 195–203, and Peter A. Murray, 'A militant among the Magdalens? Mary Ellen Murphy's incarceration in High Park Convent during the 1913 Lockout', *Saothar* 20 (1995), pp. 41–55.

50 Eugene Hynes, 'The great hunger and Irish Catholicism', *Societas* 8 (1978), pp. 137–56.

51 Another area in which much remains to be done is the recruitment and career patterns of clergy, though Kenneth D. Brown's 'Life after death: a preliminary survey of the Irish Presbyterian ministry in the nineteenth century', *Irish Economic and Social History* 22 (1995), pp. 49–63, is a useful beginning.

52 Eugene Hynes, 'Nineteenth-century Irish Catholicism, farmers' ideology and national religion: explorations in cultural explanation', in Roger O'Toole (ed.), *Sociological Studies in Roman Catholicism: Historical and Contemporary Perspectives* (Lewiston: Edwin Mellen Press, 1990), pp. 45–69.

53 Oliver P. Rafferty, *The Church, the State and the Fenian Threat, 1861–75* (Basingstoke: Macmillan, 1999), p. x.

54 Ibid., pp. 148, 116–19.


CHAPTER 5: HISTORICAL GEOGRAPHY


1 See A. R. H. Baker as quoted in Catherine Nash and Brian Graham, 'The making of modern historical geographies', in Brian Graham and Catherine Nash (eds), *Modern Historical Geographies* (Edinburgh: Pearson Education, 2000), pp. 1–9, see p. 4. The relationship between geography and local history is successfully explored in P. J. Duffy, 'Locality and changing landscape: geography and local history', in Raymond Gillespie and Myrtle Hill (eds), *Doing Irish Local History: Pursuit and Practice* (Belfast: Institute of Irish Studies, QUB, 1998), pp. 24–46.

2 Dismissed as a 'population geographer' by Anngret Simms, T. W. Freeman (1908–1988) was Professor of Geography at TCD from 1936 to 1949 and at Manchester University from 1950 to 1977. See Anngret Simms, 'Perspectives on Irish settlement studies', in Terry Barry (ed.), *A History of Settlement in Ireland* (London: Routledge, 2000),

pp. 228–47, see p. 228. Recently retired, Anngret Simms was Professor of Geography at UCD. She continues to be active in geographical research after her retirement, most notably as editor of the *Historic Town Atlas* series published by the Royal Irish Academy.

3    T. W. Freeman, 'Land and people, *c.*1841', in W. E. Vaughan (ed.), *A New History of Ireland*, V, *Ireland under the Union, 1: 1801–70* (Oxford: Clarendon, 1989), pp. 242–71.

4    See, for example, E. E. Evans, 'Some survivals of the Irish openfield system', *Geography* 24 (1939), pp. 24–36. For a survey of Evans's career see M. Stout, 'Emyr Estyn Evans and Northern Ireland: the archaeology and geography of a new state', in J. Atkinson, I. Banks and J. O'Sullivan (eds), *Nationalism and Archaeology* (Glasgow: Cruithne Press, 1996), pp. 112–27. Emyr Estyn Evans (1905–1989) was Professor of Geography at QUB from 1928 to 1968 and first director of the Institute of Irish Studies until his retirement in 1970

5    T. W. Freeman, *Pre-Famine Ireland: A Study in Historical Geography* (Manchester: Manchester University Press, 1957).

6    Ibid., p. 243. The words are those of the compilers of the 1841 census.

7    Ibid., pp. 244.

8    Ibid., p. 249.

9    Ibid., pp. 262–3.

10   Ibid., p. 253.

11   Ibid. See also W. J. Smyth, 'Landholding changes, kinship networks and class transformation in rural Ireland: a case study from County Tipperary', *Irish Geography* 16 (1983), pp. 16–35, table 1.

12   Freeman, 'Land and people', p. 264.

13   Ibid., pp. 245–6. With due credit to the pioneering work of Paul Ferguson, the system of poor law unions still await their historical geographer if not their historian; see Christine Kinealy, 'The response of the Poor Law to the Great Famine in County Galway', in Gerard Moran and Raymond Gillespie (eds), *Galway: History and Society* (Dublin: Geography Publications, 1996), pp. 375–94; Christine Kinealy, 'The workhouse system in County Waterford, 1838–1923', in William Nolan and T. P. Power (eds), *Waterford: History and Society* (Dublin: Geography Publications, 1992), pp. 479–596.

14   Freeman, 'Land and people', p. 259.

15   Cormac Ó Gráda, *Ireland Before and After the Famine: Explorations in Economic History, 1800–1925* (Manchester: Manchester University Press, 1988).

16   Joel Mokyr, *Why Ireland Starved: A Quantitative and Analytical History of the Irish Economy 1800–1850* (London: Allen & Unwin, 1983) remains the classic quantitative study of this period. Mokyr and Ó Gráda are among the 'new economic historians', a school of history written by people taught as economists rather than historians. Cliometrics is the study of economic history using statistics and computer analysis.

17   Ó Gráda, *Ireland Before and After the Famine*, pp. 7–8.

18   Quoted in ibid., p. 10.

19   Ibid., pp. 35.

20   Ibid., pp. 109–10.

21   Ibid., p. 86.

22   Ibid., p. 87.

23   Ibid., p. 33.

24  Ibid., pp. 28–30.

25  Ibid., pp. 57, 59, table 17.

26  Ibid., p. 46.

27  A choropleth map is one which displays a quantitative attribute as a uniform symbol or shading applied to a territorial unit such as a county or poor law union.

28  Freeman, 'Land and people', p. 248.

29  Ibid.

30  Kevin Whelan, 'The modern landscape: from plantation to present', in F. H. A. Aalen, Kevin Whelan and Matthew Stout (eds), *Atlas of the Irish Rural Landscape* (Cork: Cork University Press, 1997), pp. 67–103.

31  Tom Jones Hughes was Professor of Geography at UCD between 1950 and 1987. His major contribution to historical geographical studies was his use of *Griffith's Valuation* to identify a more complex geography than the 'two Irelands model'; most importantly, the indentification of the Nore, Suir and Barrow valleys as a cockpit of Catholic institutional development. Within the regions, he further identified a far more complex class structure and land tenure than had been acknowledged in previous research. His students dominate the field of historical geography in Ireland today. For a review of his contribution see J. H. Andrews, 'Jones Hughes's Ireland: a literary quest', in W. J. Smyth and Kevin Whelan (eds), *Common Ground: Essays on the Historical Geography of Ireland* (Cork: Cork University Press, 1988), pp. 1–22.

32  Whelan, 'The modern landscape', pp. 70–88.

33  W. J. Smyth, 'Social, economic and landscape transformations in County Cork from the mid-eighteenth to the mid-nineteenth century', in Patrick O'Flanagan and C. G. Buttimer (eds), *Cork: History and Society* (Dublin: Geography Publications, 1993), pp. 655–98, see p. 655.

34  Whelan, 'The modern landscape', pp. 79–88; For additional detail about the west of Ireland before the famine see Kevin Whelan, 'Pre and post-Famine landscape change', in Cathal Póirtéir (ed.), *The Great Irish Famine* (Cork and Dublin: Mercier and RTÉ, 1995), pp. 19–33.

35  Whelan, 'The modern landscape', fig. 33, p. 80.

36  Smyth, 'Transformations in County Cork', p. 680.

37  William Nolan, 'Society and settlement in the valley of Glenasmole *c.*1750–*c.*1900', in F. H. A. Aalen and Kevin Whelan (eds), *Dublin City and County: From Prehistory to Present* (Dublin: Geography Publications, 1992), pp. 181–228, see p. 208.

38  M. B. Kiely and William Nolan, 'Politics, land and rural conflict in County Waterford', in Nolan and Power (eds), *Waterford: History and Society*, pp. 459–94, see p. 470. Like so much research in Irish historical geography, this essay draws on the groundbreaking work of John Andrews; see J. H. Andrews, 'Limits of agricultural settlement in pre-Famine Ireland', in L. M. Cullen and F. Furet (eds), *Irlande et France XVIIe–XXe Siècles, pour une Histoire Rurale Comparée* (Paris: Editions de l'école des hautes études en sciences sociales, 1980), pp. 47–58.

39  Kiely and Nolan, 'Politics, land and rural conflict in County Waterford', p. 471.

40  House clusters or clachans are unplanned groups of houses lacking the central place functions of a true village. The term 'clachan' is a Scottish one, never applied to these clusters by their inhabitants. E. Estyn Evans and subsequent QUB geographers have suggested that this settlement phenomenon had its roots deep in Irish history. Geographers from the

tradition of Tom Jones Hughes at UCD sought to establish how the clachan form of settlement was a response to rapid population growth. The change of nomenclature was an attempt to clearly establish a break with past research.

41  Jack Burtchaell, 'A typology of settlement and society in County Waterford *c.* 1850', in Nolan and Power (eds), *Waterford: History and Society*, pp. 541–78, see p. 565.

42  Smyth, 'Transformations in County Cork', p. 685.

43  Ibid., p. 692.

44  Tom Yager, 'What was rundale and where did it come from?', *Béaloideas* 70 (2002), pp. 153–86.

45  Rundale was condemned as early as 1845: 'The system was necessarily attended with every evil, and improvement precluded'. Quoted in Whelan, 'Pre and post-Famine landscape change', pp. 30–1.

46  Yager, 'What was rundale?', pp. 170–1.

47  Ibid., p. 182.

48  P. J. Duffy, 'Trends in nineteenth- and twentieth-century settlement', in Terry Barry (ed.), *A History of Settlement in Ireland* (London: Routledge, 2000), p. 214.

49  Jack Burtchaell, 'The South Kilkenny farm villages', in Smyth and Whelan (eds), *Common Ground*, pp. 110–23.

50  Kevin Whelan, 'Landscape and society on Clare Island 1700–1900', in Críostóir Mac Cárthaigh and Kevin Whelan (eds), *New Survey of Clare Island 1: History and Cultural Landscape* (Dublin: Royal Irish Academy, 1999), pp. 73–98.

51  Ibid., p. 75.

52  Ibid., p. 81.

53  In addition to Whelan's work there is a extensive literature on the historical geography of the west of Ireland; see, for example, Stephen Royle, *A Geography of Islands: Small Island Insularity* (London: Routledge, 2001); Tim Robinson, *Stones of Aran: Pilgrimage* (Mullingar and Dublin: Lilliput and Wolfhound, 1986).

54  Smyth, 'Transformations in County Cork', p. 661.

55  Ibid., p. 673–4.

56  Kevin Whelan, 'The regional impact of Irish Catholicism 1700–1850', in Smyth and Whelan (eds), *Common Ground*, pp. 253–77.

57  Ibid., p. 274.

58  Ibid., p. 255, fig. 13. 2. See also Kevin Whelan, 'The Catholic Church in County Tipperary, 1700–1900', in W. Nolan (ed.), *Tipperary: History and Society* (Dublin: Geography Publications, 1985), pp. 215–55.

59  Ibid., p. 261, fig. 13. 4.

60  Ibid., pp. 256–7, fig. 13. 3.

61  Ibid., pp. 264–6, fig. 13. 5.

62  Kevin Whelan, 'The geography of hurling', *History Ireland* 1 (1993), pp. 27–31.

63  Smyth, 'Transformations in County Cork', pp. 675–8.

64  Ibid., pp. 678–9.

65  Ibid., p. 679.

66  Ibid., p. 689.

67  Ibid., pp. 684–5; James S. Donnelly, Jr, *The Land and the People of Nineteenth-Century Cork: The Rural Economy and the Land Question* (London: Routledge & Kegan Paul, 1975).

68   L. J. Proudfoot, 'Regionalism and localism: religious change and social protest, *c.* 1700 to *c.* 1900', in B. J. Graham and L. J. Proudfoot (eds), *An Historical Geography of Ireland* (London: Academic Press, 1993), pp. 185–218, see p. 185.

69   Lindsay Proudfoot, 'The estate system in mid nineteenth-century County Waterford', in Nolan and Power (eds), *Waterford: History and Society*, pp. 519–40, see p. 528.

70   L. M. Cullen, 'Catholics under the penal laws', *Eighteenth-Century Ireland* 1 (1986), pp. 23–37, see p. 27.

71   D. W. Miller, 'Mass attendance in Ireland in 1834', in S. J. Brown and D. W. Miller (eds), *Piety and Power in Ireland 1760–1960: Essays in Honour of Emmet Larkin* (Belfast: Institute of Irish Studies, QUB, 2000), pp. 158–79. See also Kiely and Nolan, 'Politics, land and rural conflict in County Waterford', pp. 487–9. Miller's study builds on his earlier essay that examined the growth of radical conservatism in Ireland; see D. W. Miller, 'Irish Catholicism and the Great Famine', *Journal of Social History* 9 (1975), pp. 81–98. This period has been described as the 'devotional revolution' in the seminal study by Emmet Larkin; see Emmet Larkin, 'The devotional revolution in Ireland, 1850–75', *American Historical Review* 77 (1972), pp. 625–52.

72   Miller, 'Mass attendance', p. 173, fig. 7. 5.

73   Kevin Whelan, 'Daniel O'Connell: the Kerry proteus', in Kevin Whelan (ed.), *Daniel O'Connell* (Dublin: Keough Notre Dame Centre, 2002), pp. 22–9.

74   Whelan, 'Regional impact', pp. 268–9, table 13.3.

75   James Grant, 'The Great Famine in County Tyrone', in Charles Dillon and H. A. Jefferies (eds), *Tyrone: History and Society* (Dublin: Geography Publications, 2000), pp. 587–615; Kinealy, 'The response of the Poor Law in County Galway', pp. 375–94.

76   Liam Kennedy, P. S. Ell, E. M. Crawford and L. A. Clarkson, *Mapping the Great Irish Famine: A Survey of the Famine Decades* (Dublin: Four Courts, 1999). Compare this work with the intimate knowledge of the historic landscape evident in P. J. Duffy, *Landscapes of South Ulster: A Parish Atlas of the Diocese of Clogher* (Belfast: Institute of Irish Studies, QUB, 1993).

77   Kennedy, et al., *Mapping the Great Irish Famine*; see for example, 'Gender ratios', p. 46; 'Methodists', pp. 91–2; 'Males in domestic service', p. 154.

78   An isopleth map is one which features lines drawn through points of equal value. For example, elevation contours on a topographical map are isopleths.

79   Brian MacDonald, *'A Time of Desolation': Clones Poor Law Union 1845–50* (Enniskillen: Clogher Historical Society, 2001). See also *Clogher Record* 17 (2000, 2001), two volumes of Famine archives compiled by Brian MacDonald and his team as part of the New Millennium Project of the Clogher Record Society.

80   MacDonald, *'A Time of Desolation'*, p. 110.

81   Ibid., pp. 17, 24.

82   Ibid., pp. 17, 40.

83   Ibid., p. 56.

84   Ibid., p. 59.

85   Ibid., pp. 65–6.

86   C. E. Orser Jr., 'Can there be an archaeology of the Great Famine?', in Chris Morash and Richard Hayes (eds), *'Fearful Realities': New Perspectives on the Famine* (Dublin: Irish Academic Press, 1996), pp. 77–89.

87  R. J. Scally, *The End of Hidden Ireland: Rebellion, Famine, and Emigration* (Oxford: Clarendon, 1995).

88  S. J. Campbell, *The Great Irish Famine: Words and Images from the Famine Museum, Strokestown Park, County Roscommon* (Strokestown Famine Museum, 1994).

89  C. E. Orser Jr., 'Archaeology and nineteenth-century rural life in County Roscommon', *Archaeology Ireland* 11 (1997), pp. 14–17, see p. 17.

90  Orser Jr., 'Can there be an archaeology of the Great Famine?', p. 89.

91  Jack Burtchaell, 'The demographic impact of the Famine', in Des Cowman (ed.), *The Famine in Waterford 1845–1850: Teacht na bPrátaí Dubha* (Dublin: Geography Publications, 1995), pp. 263–88.

92  Ibid., p. 277.

93  Smyth, 'Landholding changes', pp. 16–35. See also W. J. Smyth, 'Land values, land-ownership and population patterns in Co. Tipperary for 1641–1660 and 1841–1850: some comparisons', in L. M. Cullen and F. Furet (eds), *Irlande et France XVIIᵉ–XXᵉ Siècles*, pp. 59–84. Historical geographers working on the post-Famine period owe a debt of gratitude to Raymond Crotty's 1966 foundation study: R. D. Crotty, *Irish Agricultural Production: Its Volume and Structure* (Cork: Cork University Press, 1966). See also Michael Turner, *After the Famine: Irish Agriculture, 1850–1914* (Cambridge: Cambridge University Press, 1996).

94  Smyth, 'Landholding changes', p. 22, table 1.

95  Ibid., p. 28.

96  Kennedy, et al., *Mapping the Great Irish Famine*, p. 57, table 3.

97  Matthew Stout, 'The geography and implications of post-Famine population decline in Baltyboys, County Wicklow', in Morash and Hayes (eds), *'Fearful Realities'*, pp. 15–37.

98  Despite three publications based on these diaries, we still lack a complete edition of Smith's Irish writings; the best is Patricia Pelly and Andrew Tod (eds), *The Highland Lady in Ireland, Journals 1840–50 by Elizabeth Grant* (Edinburgh: Canongate, 1991). See also David Thomson and Moyra McGusty (eds), *The Irish Journals of Elizabeth Smith, 1840–1850: A Selection* (Oxford: Clarendon, 1980); Dermot James and Séamas Ó Maitiú (eds), *The Wicklow World of Elizabeth Smith, 1840–1850* (Dublin: Woodfield Press, 1996).

99  Matthew Stout, 'Post-Famine population decline in Baltyboys', p. 32.

100  See, for example, J. J. Mannion, *Point Lance in Transition: The Transformation of a Newfoundland Outport* (Toronto: McClelland & Steward, 1976).

101  Kevin Kenny, 'Diaspora and comparison: the global Irish as a case study', *Journal of American History* 90 (2003), pp. 134–62.

102  P. J. Duffy, 'The nuts and bolts of making landscape in the mid-nineteenth century', *Group for the Study of Irish Historic Settlement Newsletter* 8 (1997), pp. 13–16; P. J. Duffy, 'Management problems on a large estate in mid nineteenth-century Ireland: William Steuart Trench's report of the Shirley estate in 1843', *Clogher Record* 16 (1997), pp. 101–23.

103  Duffy, 'Nuts and bolts of making landscape', p. 13.

104  Ibid., p. 15.

105  Ibid., pp. 14–15.

106  Ibid., pp. 15–16.

107  Proudfoot, 'The estate system in mid nineteenth-century County Waterford', p. 533.

108  Ibid., p. 537.

109 P. G. Lane, 'The Encumbered Estates Court and Galway land ownership, 1849–58', in Moran and Gillespie (eds), *Galway: History and Society*, pp. 395–417, see pp. 415–17.

110 Proudfoot, 'The estate system in mid nineteenth-century County Waterford', pp. 532–3.

111 Ibid., p. 526.

112 Ibid., pp. 525–6.

113 Burtchaell, 'A typology of settlement and society in County Waterford' pp. 541–78; Geraldine Stout, *Newgrange and the Bend of the Boyne* (Cork: Cork University Press, 2002).

114 Still the best guide to these sources is William Nolan, *Tracing the Past: Sources for Local Studies in the Republic of Ireland* (Dublin: Geography Publications, 1982), now sadly out of print.

115 Burtchaell, 'Typology of settlement and society in County Waterford', pp. 555–65.

116 Geraldine Stout, *Newgrange and the Bend of the Boyne,* p. 149. Stout established that there was a strong statistical correlation ($r= 0.841$) between a house's value and the value of the lands associated with that house.

117 Ibid., p. 154.

118 Ibid., p. 160. See also Whelan, 'The modern landscape', p. 75, fig. 18 for a model of settlement relating to large tillage farming.

119 Donald Jordan, 'The Famine and its aftermath in County Mayo', in Morash and Hayes (eds), *'Fearful Realities'*, pp. 35–48.

120 Ibid., pp. 37–9.

121 Ibid., pp. 42–4.

122 Ibid., p. 48.

123 Whelan, 'Landscape and society on Clare Island', pp. 83–4.

124 Whelan, 'The modern landscape', pp. 87, 89.

125 F. H. A. Aalen, 'Constructive unionism and the shaping of modern Ireland', *Rural History* 4 (1993), pp. 137–64. See also William Nolan, 'New farms and fields: migration policies of state land agencies 1891–1980', in Smyth and Whelan (eds), *Common Ground*, pp. 296–319.

126 Whelan, 'The modern landscape', p. 93.

127 Whelan, 'Landscape and society on Clare Island', p. 84.

128 Whelan, 'The modern landscape', p. 94.

129 Whelan, 'Landscape and Society on Clare Island', maps 1 and 2.

130 Nash and Graham, 'Modern historical geographies', p. 2.

131 Kevin Whelan, 'Towns and villages', in Aalen, Whelan and Stout (eds), *Atlas of the Irish Rural Landscape*, pp. 180–96, see p. 190. For an early but highly influential study of the development of the road network see J. H. Andrews, 'Road planning in Ireland before the railway age', *Irish Geography* 5 (1964), pp. 17–41.

132 Whelan, 'Towns and villages'; See also Kevin Whelan, 'The Catholic parish, the Catholic chapel and village development in Ireland', *Irish Geography* 16 (1983), pp. 1–15.

133 Whelan, 'Towns and villages', p. 193.

134 Anngret Simms and Patricia Fagan, 'Villages in County Dublin: their origins and inheritance', in Aalen and Whelan (eds), *Dublin City and County*, pp. 79–120, see pp. 106–8.

135 L. M. Cullen, 'The growth of Dublin 1600–1900: character and heritage', in Aalen and Whelan (eds), *Dublin City and County*, pp. 251–78, see p. 265.

136 Ibid., pp. 265–7.

137 Ibid., pp. 271–2.

138 Jacinta Prunty, *Dublin Slums, 1800–1925: A Study in Urban Geography* (Dublin: Irish Academic Press, 1998). Prunty's work and methodology have their origins in two studies published in 1988: J. H. Martin, 'Social geography of mid nineteenth-century Dublin City', in Smyth and Whelan (eds), *Common Ground*, pp. 173–88; Brian Murnane, 'The recreation of the urban historical landscape: Mountjoy ward Dublin *circa* 1901', in Smyth and Whelan (eds), *Common Ground*, pp. 189–207.

139 Prunty, *Dublin Slums*, pp. 276–8.

140 Quoted in ibid., p. 286.

141 See also F. H. A. Aalen, 'Health and housing in Dublin *c.*1850– 1921', in Aalen and Whelan (eds), *Dublin City and County*, pp. 279–304.

142 Prunty, *Dublin Slums*, p. 61.

143 Ibid., pp. 151–2; See aslo Aalen, 'Health and housing'.

144 Prunty, *Dublin Slums*, ch. 7, pp. 234–73.

145 The Iveagh Trust's pioneering efforts to re-house the poor have been analysed by Fred Aalen, see F. H. A. Aalen, *The Iveagh Trust: The First Hundred Years, 1890–1990* (Dublin: Iveagh Trust, 1990). Aalen's work on the nineteenth century combines historical geography with an intimate knowledge of architectural history.

146 Des Cowman, 'Trade and society in Waterford City 1800–1840', in Nolan and Power (eds), *Waterford: History and Society*, pp. 427–59.

147 Ibid., p. 443.

148 Ibid., p. 449.

149 Anngret Simms and J. H. Andrews (eds), *Irish Country Towns* (Dublin and Cork: Mercier Press and RTÉ, 1994). Anngret Simms and J. H. Andrews (eds), *More Irish Country Towns* (Cork and Dublin: Mercier Press and RTÉ, 1995). H. B. Clarke (ed.), *Irish Cities* (Cork and Dublin: Mercier Press and RTÉ, 1995). Despite the obvious visual appeal of the landscape, a serious treatment of historical geography has yet to find a place on Irish television. However, the 'Thomas Davis series' of radio lectures featured the Irish town and cities series as well as the survey of historical geography ultimately published as William Nolan (ed.), *The Shaping of Ireland: The Geographical Perspective* (Cork and Dublin: Mercier and RTÉ, 1986).

150 William Nolan and Anngret Simms (eds), Ríonach Ní Néill and Yvonne Whelan (comp.), *Irish Towns: A Guide to Sources* (Dublin: Geography Publications, 1998).

151 Duffy, 'Trends in nineteenth- and twentieth-century settlement', p. 206.

152 Geraldine Stout, *Newgrange and the Bend of the Boyne*, p. 155.

153 See Department of the Environment and Local Government, *An Introduction to the Architectural Heritage of Fingal* (Dublin: Dúchas, The Heritage Service, 2002).

154 For a full list of maps see J. H. Andrews, *A Paper Landscape: The Ordnance Survey in Nineteenth-Century Ireland* (1st edn, Oxford: Clarendon, 1975; 2nd edn, Dublin: Four Courts, 2002), pp. 333–7, appendix G. An indispensable guide to OS maps has recently been reprinted, see J. H. Andrews, *History in the Ordnance Map: An Introduction for Irish Readers* (1st edn, Dublin: Ordnance Survey of Ireland, 1974; reprinted Newton, Montgomeryshire: David Archer, 1993).

155 For an account of Andrews's remarkable career see Kevin Whelan, 'Beyond a paper landscape – John Andrews and Irish historical geography', in Aalen and Whelan (eds), *Dublin City and County*, pp. 379–424.

156 Andrews, *A Paper Landscape*.

157 J. H. Andrews, *Shapes of Ireland: Maps and their Makers 1664–1839* (Dublin: Geography Publications, 1997); see also J. H. Andrews, *Plantation Acres: An Historical Study of the Irish Land Surveyor and His Maps* (Belfast: Ulster Historical Foundation, 1985).

158 Patrick McWilliams (ed.), *Ordnance Survey Memoirs of Ireland: Index of Peoples and Places* (Belfast: Institute of Irish Studies, QUB, 2003).

159 To date, Four Masters Press, Dublin, have published the OS letters for Donegal, Down, Kildare, Kilkenny and Meath.

160 Brian Friel, *Translations* (London: Faber, 1981). The historian and playwright held public discussions about what Andrews regarded as the play's distortion of the historical record. The literature inspired by the Andrews/Friel controversy is detailed in the 2001 paperback edition of Andrews, *A Paper Landscape*, pp. vi (i–j).

161 Andrews, *A Paper Landscape*, p. iii.

162 W. H. Crawford, 'Introduction', in W. H. Crawford and R. H. Foy (eds), *Townlands in Ulster: Local History Studies* (Belfast: Ulster Historical Foundation and Federation of Ulster Local Studies, 1998), pp. 1–5, see p. 5. See also the earlier study inspired by the same controversy, Tony Canavan (ed.), *'Every Stoney Acre has a Name': A Celebration of the Townland in Ulster* (Belfast: Federation for Ulster Local Studies, 1991).

163 Angela Bourke, *The Burning of Bridget Cleary: A True Story* (London: Pimlico, 1999).

164 Jack Johnston, 'Society in the Clogher valley, *c.*1750–1900', in Dillon and Jefferies (eds), *Tyrone: History and Society*, pp. 543–65, see p. 548.

165 Billy Colfer, *The Hook Peninsula* (Cork: Cork University Press, 2004), pp. 125–6.

166 Kevin Whelan, 'The memories of "The Dead"', *Yale Journal of Criticism* 15 (2002), pp. 59–97, see p. 59.

167 Ibid., p. 70.

168 Ibid., pp. 78–80.

169 Ibid., p. 87.

170 William Nolan, *Fassadinin: Land, Settlement and Society in South-East Ireland 1600–1850* (Dublin: Geography Publications, 1979).

171 I welcome the publication of John Feehan, *Farming in Ireland: History, Heritage and Environment* (Dublin: Faculty of Agriculture, UCD, 2003).

172 Jonathan Bell, 'Changing farming methods in Donegal', in William Nolan, Liam Ronayne and Mairead Dunlevy (eds), *Donegal: History and Society* (Dublin: Geography Publications, 1995), pp. 471–90. See also numerous contributions to the journal *Ulster Folklife*.

173 Eavan Boland, *In a Time of Violence* (Manchester: Carcanet, 1994). The poem is reproduced by kind permission of the author.

CHAPTER 6: ANTHROPOLOGICAL AND SOCIOLOGICAL STUDIES

1 Franz Boas, 'The study of geography' (1897); reprinted in G. W. Stocking, Jr (ed.), *Volksgeist as Method and Ethic: Essays on Boasian Ethnography and the German Anthropological Tradition* (Madison WI: University of Wisconsin Press, 1996). See also Greta Jones, 'Contested territories: Alfred Cort Haddon, progressive evolutionism and Ireland', *History of European Ideas* 24, 3 (1998), pp. 195–211.

2   Eric R. Wolf, *Anthropology* (1964; new edn, Englewood-Cliffs NJ: Prentice-Hall, 1974), pp. 88–9, 90, 96.

3   Lawrence J. Taylor, 'Stories of power, powerful stories: the drunken priest in Donegal', in Ellen Badone (ed.), *Religious Orthodoxy and Popular Faith in European Society* (Princeton NJ: Princeton University Press, 1990), p. 104; Joan Vincent, 'A political orchestration of the Irish Famine: County Fermanagh, May 1847', in Marilyn Silverman and Philip H. Gulliver (eds), *Approaching the Past: Historical Anthropology through Irish Case Studies* (New York: Columbia University Press, 1992), pp. 75–98.

4   Wolf, *Anthropology*, p. 88.

5   For the latter historiography, see Marilyn Cohen, 'Beyond boundaries: towards an interdisciplinary Irish studies', *Éire-Ireland* 31, 1 & 2 (1996), pp. 137–62.

6   Karl Polanyi, *The Great Transformation: The Political and Economic Origins of our Time* (London: Rinehart, 1944). A fact of interest to Irish studies is that Conrad Arensberg was Polanyi's collaborator at Columbia University in research that contributed to the establishment of the sub-field of economic anthropology.

7   David Lloyd and Paul Thomas, *Culture and the State* (London: Routledge, 1998).

8   Eamonn Slater and Terrence McDonough, 'Bulwark of landlordism and capitalism: the dynamics of feudalism in nineteenth century Ireland', *Research in Political Economy* 14 (1994), pp. 63–118.

9   Denis O'Hearn, 'Innovation and the world-system hierarchy: British subjugation of the Irish cotton industry', *American Journal of Sociology* 100 (1994), pp. 587–621.

10   Denis O'Hearn, 'Irish linen: a peripheral industry', in Marilyn Cohen (ed.), *The Warp of Ulster's Past: Interdisciplinary Perspectives on the Irish Linen Industry, 1700–1920* (New York: St Martin's, 1997), pp. 161–90.

11   Jane Gray, 'Rural industry and uneven development: the significance of gender in the Irish linen industry', *Journal of Peasant Studies* 20 (1993), pp. 590–611; Jane Gray, 'Gender and uneven working-class formation in the Irish linen industry', in L. L. Frader and Sonya O. Rose (eds), *Gender and Class in Modern Europe* (Ithaca NY: Cornell University Press, 1996), pp. 37–56.

12   Jane Gray, 'The Irish and Scottish linen industries in the eighteenth century: an incorporated comparison', in Cohen (ed.), *The Warp*, pp. 37–69.

13   Marilyn Cohen, 'Peasant differentiation and proto-industrialisation in the Ulster countryside: Tullylish 1690–1825', *Journal of Peasant Studies* 17 (1990), pp. 413–32; 'Peasant differentiation and proto-industrialisation in the Ulster countryside: petty commodity producers in Tullylish, 1690–1825', in Alice Littlefield and Hill Gates (eds), *Marxist Approaches in Economic Anthropology*. Monographs in Economic Anthropology, No. 9 (Lanham: University Press of America, 1991), pp. 37–64.

14   Marilyn Silverman and Philip H. Gulliver, 'Inside historical anthropology: scale reduction and context', *Focaal* 26/27 (1996), a special issue on 'Historical anthropology: the unwaged debate'.

15   Marilyn Silverman, 'The non-agricultural working-class in nineteenth-century Thomastown', in William Murphy (ed.), *In the Shadow of the Steeple*, II (Tullaherin Heritage Society, 1990), pp. 86–104; Marilyn Silverman, 'The voices of conflict: the inland salmon fishery of the River Nore, 1911', in William Murphy (ed.), *In the Shadow of the Steeple*, III (Tullaherin Heritage Society, 1992), pp. 66–80.

16   Marilyn Silverman, 'From fisher to poacher: public right and private property in the salmon fisheries of the River Nore in the nineteenth century', in Silverman and Gulliver (eds), *Approaching the Past*, p. 132.

17   P. H. Gulliver, 'Shopkeepers and farmers in South Kilkenny, 1840–1981', in Silverman and Gulliver, *Approaching the Past*, pp. 176–204.

18   Marilyn Silverman and P. H. Gulliver, *Merchants and Shopkeepers: A Historical Anthropology of an Irish Market Town, 1200–1991* (Toronto: University of Toronto Press, 1995).

19   Marilyn Silverman, *An Irish Working Class: Explorations in Political Economy and Hegemony, 1800–1950* (Toronto: University of Toronto Press, 2001). See also Silverman, 'The Inhabitants vs the Sovereign' in Pat Caplan (ed.), *Understanding Disputes: The Politics of Argument* (London: Berg, 1995), pp. 111–36; Silverman, 'From fisher to poacher'; and Silverman, 'The voices of conflict'.

20   Marilyn Cohen, 'Rural paths of capitalist development: class formation, paternalism and gender and County Down's linen industry', in Lindsay Proudfoot (ed.), *Down: History and Society* (Dublin: Geography Publications, 1997), pp. 567–97; Marilyn Cohen, *Linen, Family and Community in Tullylish, Co. Down, 1690–1914* (Dublin: Four Courts, 1997).

21   Marilyn Cohen, 'Urbanisation and the milieux of factory life: Gilford/Dunbarton, 1825–1914', in Chris Curtin, Hastings Donnan and Thomas M. Wilson (eds), *Irish Urban Cultures* (Belfast: Institute of Irish Studies, QUB, 1993), pp. 227–42.

22   Joan Vincent, 'A political orchestration of the Irish Famine', in Silverman and Gulliver, *Approaching the Past*, pp. 75–98; Joan Vincent, 'Conacre: the political economy of an Irish custom', in Jane Schneider and Rayna Rapp (eds), *Articulating Hidden Histories: Exploring the Influence of Eric R. Wolf* (Berkeley CA: University of California Press, 1994), pp. 82–93; Joan Vincent, *Seeds of Revolution: The Cultural Politics of the Great Irish Famine* (New York: Palgrave, 2004); Jonathan Bell, 'Miserable hovels and substantial habitations: the housing of rural labourers in Ireland since the eighteenth century', *Folk Life* 34 (1995), pp. 43–56.

23   Jonathan Bell, 'Donegal women as migrant workers in Scotland', *Review of Scottish Culture* 7 (1991), pp. 73–80.

24   Vincent, 'Conacre: the political economy', p. 85.

25   Marilyn Cohen, 'Religion and social inequality in Ireland', *Journal of Interdisciplinary History* 25 (1994), pp. 1–21.

26   Marilyn Cohen, 'Survival strategies in female-headed households: linen industry workers in Tullylish, County Down, 1901', *Journal of Family History* 17 (1992), pp. 303–18.

27   Mary J. Hickman, *Religion, Class and Identity* (Aldershot: Ashgate, 1995); Mary J. Hickman, 'Incorporating and denationalising the Irish in England: the role of the Catholic Church', in Patrick O'Sullivan (ed.), *The Irish World Wide*, v, *Religion and Identity* (London: Leicester University Press, 1996), pp. 196–216; Mary J. Hickman, 'Constructing the nation, segregating the Irish: the education of Irish Catholics in nineteenth-century Britain', *Aspects of Education* 53 (1997), pp. 33–54.

28   Mary J. Hickman, 'Integration and segregation? The education of the Irish in Britain in Roman Catholic voluntary-aided schools', *British Journal of Sociology of Education* 14 (1993), pp. 285–300.

29   Marilyn Cohen, 'The migration experience of female-headed households: Gilford, Co. Down to Greenwich, New York', in O'Sullivan (ed.), *The Irish World Wide*, IV, *Irish Women*

*and Irish Migration* (London: Leicester University Press, 1995), pp. 131–45; '"A girdle around the globe": spinning transnational bonds between Gilford, Ireland and Greenwich, New York, 1880–1920', in Marilyn Cohen and Nancy J. Curtin (eds), *Reclaiming Gender: Transgressive Identities in Modern Ireland* (New York: St Martin's, 1999), pp. 185–204.

30  Jane Gray, 'Folk poetry and working-class identity in Ulster: an analysis of James Orr's "The Penitent"', *Journal of Historical Sociology* 6 (1993), pp. 249–75.

31  Jane Gray, 'Gender and plebian culture in Ulster', *Journal of Interdisciplinary History* 24 (1993), pp. 251–70.

32  Marilyn Cohen, 'Toward a historical anthropology of work: structure and subjectivity among linen workers in Tullylish, County Down, 1900–1920', in Cohen, *The Warp*, pp. 253–75.

33  Silverman, *An Irish Working Class*, passim.

34  Lawrence J. Taylor, '"There are two things that people don't like to hear about themselves": the anthropology of Ireland and the Irish view of anthropology', *The Southwest Atlantic Quarterly* 95 (1996), p. 223.

35  Lawrence J. Taylor, 'Peter's pence: official Catholic discourse and Irish nationalism in the nineteenth century', *History of European Ideas* 16 (1993), pp. 103–7.

36  Lawrence J. Taylor, 'The languages of belief: nineteenth-century religious discourse in Southwest Donegal', in Silverman and Gulliver, *Approaching the Past*, pp. 142–75.

37  Taylor, 'Stories of power', pp. 163–84.

38  Eugene Hynes, 'Nineteenth-century Irish Catholicism, farmers' ideology, and national religion: explorations in cultural explanation', in Roger O'Toole (ed.), *Sociological Studies of Roman Catholicism. Studies in Religion and Societies*, xxiv (Lewiston: Edwin Mellen Press, 1989), pp. 45–69.

39  E. Doyle McCarthy, *Knowledge as Culture: The New Sociology of Knowledge* (London: Routledge, 1996); Donna Haraway, 'Situated knowledges: the science question in feminism and the privilege of partial perspective', *Feminist Studies* 14, 3 (1988), pp. 575–99. For use of the concept, see Marilyn Cohen, '"Drifting with denominationalism": a situated examination of Irish national schools in nineteenth-century Tullylish, County Down', *History of Education Quarterly* 40 (2000), pp. 49–70.

40  F. H. A. Aalen, Kevin Whelan and Matthew Stout (eds), *Atlas of the Irish Rural Landscape* (Cork: Cork University Press, 1997), p. 92; Taylor, 'There are two things . . .', p. 216.

41  Jones, 'Contested territories', pp. 195–211.

42  Eamonn Slater, 'Contested terrains: differing interpretations of Co. Wicklow Landscape', *Irish Journal of Sociology* 3 (1993), pp. 23–55.

43  A. Jamie Saris, 'Mad kings, proper houses, and an asylum in rural Ireland', *American Anthropologist* 98 (1996), pp. 690–710; Saris, 'The asylum in Ireland: a brief institutional history and some local effects', in Anne Cleary and Margaret P. Treacy (eds), *The Sociology of Health and Illness in Ireland* (Dublin: UCD Press, 1997), pp. 208–23; Saris, 'Producing persons and developing institutions in rural Ireland', *American Ethnologist* 26 (1999), pp. 690–710.

44  Saris, 'The asylum in Ireland', p. 210.

45  Saris, 'Producing persons', p. 692.

46  For example, Vincent, 'Political orchestration', pp. 75–98; Cohen, *Linen, Family and Community*, ch. 7; Marilyn Cohen, 'Paternalism and poverty: contradictions in the

schooling of working class children in Tullylish, County Down, 1825–1914', *History of Education* 21 (1992) pp. 291–306.

47 Tanya M. Cassidy, 'Irish drinking worlds: a socio-cultural reinterpretation of ambivalence', *International Journal of Sociology and Social Policy* 16 (1996), pp. 5–25; and her 'Alcoholism in Ireland', in Cleary and Treacy (eds), *The Sociology of Health and Illness*, pp. 176–92.

48 Nancy Scheper-Hughes, *Saints, Scholars and Schizophrenics: Mental Illness in Rural Ireland* (Berkeley and London: California University Press, 1979). Unfortunately this more recent ethnographic research on the institutionalisation of mental illness in Ireland has yet to receive the attention it deserves.

49 Seamus Heaney, *Preoccupations: Selected Prose 1968–1978* (London: Faber & Faber, 1980), p. 131.

50 Joan Vincent, 'The land war in the Irish northwest: "agitation" and its unintended consequences', in Cohen and Curtin, *Reclaiming Gender*, p. 241.

51 Saris, 'Mad kings', p. 551, n. 31.

52 Conrad Arensberg, *The Irish Countryman: An Anthropological Study* (New York: Macmillan, 1937), pp. 39–42; Henry Glassie, *Passing the Time in Ballymenone: Culture and History of an Ulster Community* (Dublin: O'Brien, 1982). Donna Birdwell-Pheasant's published work includes the following articles: 'The early twentieth-century Irish stem family: a case study from County Kerry', in Silverman and Gulliver (eds), *Approaching the Past*, pp. 205–35; 'The "home place": centre and periphery in Irish house and family systems', in Donna Birdwell-Pheasant and Denise Lawrence-Zuniga (eds), *House Life: Space, Place and Family in Europe* (Oxford and New York: Berg, 1999), pp. 105–29; 'Family systems and the foundations of class in Ireland and England', *History of the Family* 3, 1 (1998), pp. 17–34. See also Lawrence J. Taylor, 'Re-entering the west room: on the power of domestic spaces', in Birdwell-Pheasant and Lawrence-Zuniga (eds), *House Life*, pp. 223–7.

53 Birdwell-Pheasant, 'The "home place": centre and periphery', pp. 118–19.

54 Timothy Guinnane, *The Vanishing Irish: Households, Migration, and the Rural Economy in Ireland, 1850–1914* (Princeton NJ: Princeton University Press, 1997).

55 Charles E. Orser, Jr, 'Can there be an archaeology of the Great Famine?' in Chris Morash and Richard Hayes (eds), *'Fearful Realities': New Perspectives on the Irish Famine* (Dublin: Irish Academic Press, 1996), pp. 77–89; Charles E. Orser Jr, 'Of dishes and drains: an archaeological perspective on rural life in the Famine era', *New Hibernia Review* 1 (1997), pp. 120–35.

56 Ethnographic essays include Joan Vincent, 'Political orchestration' and Marilyn Cohen, 'Historicising capitalist development during the Great Famine, Tullylish, 1847–51', in Cohen, *Linen, Family and Community*, pp. 134–55. Three more conceptual essays are Marilyn Silverman and P. H. Gulliver, 'Historical verities and verifiable history: locality-based ethnography and the Great Famine in Southeastern Ireland', *Europaea* 3, 2 (1997); Joan Vincent, 'Interpreting silences: an anthropological perspective on the Great Irish Famine', *Éire-Ireland* 32, 2 & 3 (1997), pp. 21–39; and Vincent, 'Historicising the Great Irish Famine: uneven capitalist development in the parish of Tullylish, County Down, 1841–52', in David Nugent (ed.) *Locating Capitalism in Time and Place* (Berkeley CA: University of California Press, 2001).

57 Cohen's account of the Famine is part of a larger study of economic and political transformation in County Down; Vincent's is embedded in a political and cultural history

of Fermanagh within the Irish northwest; and Gulliver and Silverman's local ethnography of Thomastown spans the entire nineteenth century.

58 Anne Byrne and Ronit Lentin (eds), *(Re)Searching Women: Feminist Research Methodologies in the Social Sciences in Ireland* (Dublin: IPA, 2000); Hilary Tovey, 'Creating and recreating modernity: peasantisation and de-peasantisation in Ireland', in Leo Graberg, Irme Kovách and Hilary Tovey (eds), *Europe's Green Ring* (Aldershot: Ashgate, 2001) pp. 306–29.

59 Anne Byrne, Ricca Edmondson and Tony Varley, 'Arensberg and Kimball and anthropological research in Ireland', introduction to Conrad M. Arensberg and Solon T. Kimball, *Family and Community in Ireland*, 3rd edn (1940; Ennis: Clasp Press, 2001), pp. i–ci.

### CHAPTER 7: LITERATURE IN ENGLISH

1    Thomas Kinsella, *The New Oxford Book of Irish Verse* (Oxford: Clarendon, 1980), p. xxvii.
2    Thomas Kinsella, *Davis, Mangan, Ferguson? Tradition and the Irish Writer* (Dublin: Dolmen, 1970), p. 58.
3    W. J. Mc Cormack, *From Burke to Beckett: Ascendancy, Tradition and Betrayal in Literary History* (Cork: Cork University Press, 1994), p. 6.
4    Daniel Corkery, *Synge and Anglo-Irish Literature* (1931; Cork: Mercier, 1966), pp. 19–22.
5    Ibid., pp. 7–8.
6    Ibid., pp. 10, 18–19.
7    Gerry Smyth, *Decolonisation and Criticism: The Construction of Irish Literature* (London: Pluto, 1998), p. 155.
8    Joep Leerssen, *Remembrance and Imagination: Patterns in the Historical and Literary Representation of Ireland in the Nineteenth Century* (Cork: Cork University Press, 1996), p. 60.
9    Ibid., p. 143.
10   Ibid., p. 156.
11   Ibid., p. 5.
12   Seamus Deane, *Strange Country: Modernity and Nationhood in Irish Writing since 1790* (Oxford: Clarendon, 1997), pp. 17–18.
13   Ibid., p. 197.
14   Ibid., p. 145.
15   Declan Kiberd, *Inventing Ireland: The Literature of the Modern Nation* (London: Cape, 1995), p. 41.
16   Terry Eagleton, *Crazy Jane and the Bishop, and Other Essays on Irish Culture* (Cork: Cork University Press, 1998), p. ix.
17   Ibid.
18   Both in Terry Eagleton, *Heathcliff and the Great Hunger: Studies in Irish Culture* (London: Verso, 1995).
19   Ibid., p. 279.
20   Terry Eagleton, *Scholars and Rebels in Nineteenth-Century Ireland* (Oxford: Blackwell, 1999), p. vi.
21   David Lloyd, *Nationalism and Minor Literature: James Clarence Mangan and the Emergence of Irish Cultural Nationalism* (Berkeley, University of California Press, 1987).

22  David Lloyd, *Anomalous States: Irish Writing and the Post-Colonial Moment* (Dublin: Lilliput, 1993), p. 150.

23  Robert Welch, 'Language and tradition in the nineteenth century', in *Changing States: Transformations in Modern Irish Writing* (London and NY: Routledge, 1993), pp. 17–18.

24  Mc Cormack, *From Burke to Beckett*, p. 200.

25  Norman Vance, *Irish Literature: A Social History*, 2nd edn (Dublin: Four Courts, 1999), p. 153.

26  Siobhán Kilfeather, 'Sex and sensation in the nineteenth-century novel', in Margaret Kelleher and James H. Murphy (eds), *Gender Perspectives in Nineteenth-Century Ireland: Public and Private Spheres* (Dublin: Irish Academic Press, 1997), p. 85.

27  See *The Works of Maria Edgeworth*, a twelve-volume project by London publishers Pickering & Chatto, general editor is Marilyn Butler and volume editors include Claire Connolly, Susan Manly and Clíona Ó Gallchóir. See also Anne Fogarty (ed.), *Irish Women Novelists, 1800–1940*, special issue of *Colby Quarterly* 36, 2 (2000), with essays on Edgeworth, Owenson, Emily Lawless and Charlotte Riddell.

28  Sean Ryder, 'Gender and the discourse of Young Ireland cultural nationalism', in T. P. Foley et al. (eds), *Gender and Colonialism* (Galway: Galway University Press, 1995), pp. 210–24.

29  Jan Cannavan, 'Romantic revolutionary Irishwomen: women, Young Ireland and 1848', in Kelleher and Murphy (eds), *Gender Perspectives*, pp. 212–20; Brigitte Anton, 'Women of *The Nation*', *History Ireland* 3, 3 (1995), pp. 34–7; Joy Melville, *Mother of Oscar: The Life of Jane Francesca Wilde* (London: John Murray, 1994).

30  Marjorie Howes, 'Tears and blood: Lady Wilde and the emergence of Irish cultural nationalism', in Tadhg Foley and Sean Ryder (eds), *Ideology and Ireland in the Nineteenth Century* (Dublin: Four Courts, 1998), pp. 151–72.

31  Margaret Kelleher, *The Feminization of Famine: Expressions of the Inexpressible?* (Cork: Cork University Press, 1997; Durham NC: Duke University Press), p. 100.

32  Tony Bareham (ed.), *Charles Lever: New Evaluations* (Gerrards Cross: Colin Smythe, 1991).

33  James H. Murphy, *Catholic Fiction and Social Reality in Ireland, 1873–1922* (Westport, CT: Greenwood, 1997).

34  Adrian Frazier, *George Moore 1852–1933* (New Haven: Yale University Press, 2000).

35  James W. Flannery, *Dear Harp of My Country: The Irish Melodies of Thomas Moore* (Nashville: Sanders: 1997). Flannery's harp accompaniment is, of course, a departure from Moore's piano-based performances.

36  Augustine Martin, et al. (eds), *The Collected Poems of James Clarence Mangan*, 4 vols (Dublin: Irish Academic Press, 1996–1999); Sean Ryder (ed.), *James Clarence Mangan: Selected Writings* (Dublin: UCD Press, 2004); Ellen Shannon-Mangan, *James Clarence Mangan: A Biography* (Dublin: Irish Academic Press, 1996); Jacques Chuto, *James Clarence Mangan: A Bibliography of his Works* (Dublin: Irish Academic Press, 1999).

37  Peter Denman, *Samuel Ferguson: The Literary Achievement* (Gerrards Cross: Colin Smythe, 1990); Colin Graham, *Ideologies of Epic: Nation, Empire and Victorian Epic Poetry* (Manchester: Manchester University Press, 1998).

38  R. F. Foster, *W. B. Yeats: A Life*, 1 (Oxford and NY: Oxford University Press, 1997); Terence Brown, *The Life of W. B. Yeats: A Critical Biography* (Dublin: Gill & Macmillan, 1999).

39  Cited in Owen Dudley Edwards, 'Oscar Wilde: the soul of man under Hibernicism', in Sarah Briggs, Paul Hyland and Neil Sammells (eds), *Reviewing Ireland: Essays and Interviews from Irish Studies Review* (Bath: Sulis Press, 1998), pp. 105–14.

40  Website addresses: www. ucc. ie/celt/ and www. pgil-eirdata. org/html/index. htm.

41  Website address: www. bodley. ox. ac. uk/ballads/.

42  Gary Owens, 'Nationalism without words: symbolism and ritual behaviour in the Repeal "Monster Meetings" of 1843–5', in James S. Donnelly, Jr and Kerby A. Miller (eds), *Irish Popular Culture 1650–1850* (Dublin: Irish Academic Press, 1998), pp. 242–69.

43  Wayne E. Hall, *Dialogues in the Margin: A Study of the Dublin University Magazine* (Washington: Catholic University Press of America, 2000); Elizabeth Tilley, 'Charting culture in the *Dublin University Magazine*', in Leon Litvack and Glenn Hooper (eds), *Ireland in the Nineteenth Century: Regional Identity* (Dublin: Four Courts, 2000), pp. 58–66; Leslie Williams, 'Irish identity and the *Illustrated London News*, 1846–1851', in Susan Shaw Sailer (ed.), *Representing Ireland: Gender, Class, Nationality* (Gainesville: University Press of Florida, 1997), pp. 59–93, and most recently, Tom Clyde, *Irish Literary Magazines: An Outline History and Descriptive Bibliography* (Dublin: Irish Academic Press, 2002).

CHAPTER 8: GAELIC CULTURE AND LANGUAGE SHIFT

1  Seán de Fréine, *Saoirse gan Só* (Dublin: Foilseacháin Naisiúnta, 1960) [trans. as *The Great Silence*, Cork: Mercier, 1965].

2  Mairéad Nic Craith, *Malartú Teanga: An Ghaeilge i gCorcaigh sa Naoú hAois Déag* (Bremen: Verlag für E. S. I. S.-Publikationen, 1994), ch. 6.

3  Geraint Jenkins (ed.), *Language and Community in the Nineteenth Century* (Cardiff: University of Wales Press, 1998); Geraint Jenkins (ed.), *The Welsh Language and its Domains 1801–1911* (Cardiff: University of Wales Press, 2000); Dot Jones, *Statistical Evidence relating to the Welsh Language, 1801–1911* (Cardiff: University of Wales Press, 1998); Mari Williams and Gwenfair Parry, *The Welsh Language and the 1891 Census* (Cardiff: University of Wales Press, 1999).

4  D. George Boyce, *Nineteenth-Century Ireland: The Search for Stability* (Dublin: Gill & Macmillan, 1990); Alvin Jackson, *Ireland 1798–1998: Politics and War* (Oxford: Blackwell, 1999).

5  Ralph Grillo, *Dominant Languages: Language and Hierarchy in Britain and France* (Cambridge: Cambridge University Press, 1989), p. 4.

6  David Lloyd, *Anomalous States: Irish Writing and the Post-colonial Moment* (Dublin: Lilliput, 1993), quotation on p. 7; Lloyd, 'Outside history: Irish new histories and the "subalternity effect"', *Subaltern Studies* 9 (1996), pp. 261–80, reprinted in Lloyd, *Ireland after History* (Cork: Cork University Press, 1999), pp. 77–88; Robert James Scally, *The End of Hidden Ireland: Rebellion, Famine and Emigration* (Oxford: Clarendon, 1995).

7  Seamus Deane (ed.), *The Field Day Anthology of Irish Writing*, 3 vols (Derry: Field Day, 1991).

8  J. J. Lee, *Ireland 1912–85: Politics and Society* (Cambridge: Cambridge University Press 1989), pp. 662–70.

9  Seamus Deane, *A Short History of Irish Literature* (London: Hutchinson, 1986), p. 28; Joep Leerssen, *Remembrance and Imagination: Patterns in the Historical and Literary Representation of Ireland in the Nineteenth Century* (Cork: Cork University Press, 1996), p. 1.

10   Gearóid Denvir, 'Decolonising the mind: language and literature in Ireland', *New Hibernia Review* 1 (1997), pp. 44–68.

11   Brian Ó Cuív, 'Irish language and literature 1691–1845', in T. W. Moody and W. E. Vaughan (eds), *A New History of Ireland*, IV, *Eighteenth-Century Ireland* (Clarendon: Oxford: Clarendon, 1986), pp. 374–473; Ó Cuív, 'Irish language and literature 1845–1921', in W. E. Vaughan (ed.), *A New History of Ireland*, VI, *Ireland under the Union, II* (Oxford: Clarendon, 1996), pp. 385–435.

12   Cathal Ó hÁinle, 'Ó Chaint na nDaoine go dtí an Caighdeán Oifigiúil', in Kim McCone et al. (eds), *Stair na Gaeilge* (Maynooth: Department of Old Irish, 1994), pp. 745–93.

13   Máire Ní Mhurchú and Diarmuid Breathnach, *1782–1881: Beathaisnéis* (Dublin: An Clóchomhar, 1999).

14   Tony Crowley, *The Politics of Language in Ireland 1366–1922: A Sourcebook* (London: Routledge, 2000).

15   Maureen Wall, 'The decline of the Irish language', in Brian Ó Cuív (ed.), *A View of the Irish Language* (Dublin: Stationery Office, 1969), pp. 81–90; Máirtín Ó Murchú, *Urlabhra agus Pobal / Language and Community* (Dublin: Stationery Office, 1970); Oliver MacDonagh, *States of Mind: A Study of Anglo-Irish Conflict 1780–1980* (London: Allen & Unwin, 1983), ch. 7, 'The politics of Gaelic'; Lee, *Ireland 1912–85*, pp. 662–70.

16   Karen P. Corrigan, '"For God's sake, teach the children English": emigration and the Irish language in the nineteenth century', in Patrick O'Sullivan (ed.), *The Irish World Wide: The Irish in the New Communities* (London: Leicester University Press, 1992), p. 144; Brighid Ní Mhóráin, *Thiar sa Mhainistir atá an Ghaoluinn Bhreá: Meath na Gaeilge in Uíbh Ráthach* (Dingle: An Sagart, 1997), p. 33; Liam De Paor, *Landscape with Figures* (Dublin: Four Courts, 1998), ch. 17, 'The ebb of Irish'.

17   Donald H. Akenson, *Small Differences: Irish Catholics and Irish Protestants 1815–1922* (Kingston, Canada : McGill-Queen's University Press, 1988), pp. 135–6; Reg Hindley, *The Death of the Irish Language: A Qualified Obituary* (London: Routledge, 1990), p. 13; Liam Kennedy, 'Out of history: Ireland, that "most distressful country"', in *Colonialism, Religion and Nationalism in Ireland* (Belfast: Institute of Irish Studies, QUB, 1996) pp. 182–223, particularly pp. 204–8 'Language and language change'.

18   Hindley, *The Death of the Irish Language* p. 13; Lee, *Ireland 1912–85*, p. 664; Brinley Thomas, 'A cauldron of rebirth: population and the Welsh language in the nineteenth century', *Welsh Historical Review* 13 (1987), pp. 418–37. Thomas's influential argument was originally made as far back as 1959, but is almost never cited in the Irish literature: see Thomas, 'Wales and the Atlantic economy', *Scottish Journal of Political Economy* 6 (1959), pp. 169–92.

19   Joel Mokyr and Cormac Ó Gráda, '"Poor and getting poorer?": Living standards in Ireland before the Famine', *Economic History Review* 41 (1988), pp. 209–35, quotation on p. 211; Lee, *Ireland 1912–85*, pp. 662–3.

20   Garret FitzGerald, 'Estimates for baronies of minimum level of Irish speaking amongst successive decennial cohorts', *Proceedings of the Royal Irish Academy* 84 (1984), pp. 117–55; Fitzgerald, 'The decline of the Irish language 1771–1871', in M. Daly and D. Dickson (eds), *The Origins of Popular Literacy in Ireland: Language Change and Educational Development 1700–1920* (Dublin: UCD and TCD, 1990), pp. 59–72.

21   Nic Craith, *Malartú Teanga*; Ní Mhóráin, *Thiar sa Mhainistir*.

22 Hindley, *The Death of the Irish Language*, ch. 2, 'Irish in the nineteenth century: from collapse to revival'.

23 Máirtín Ó Murchú, 'Language and society in nineteenth-century Ireland', in Jenkins (ed.), *Language and Community*, pp. 341–68; S. J. Connolly, 'Popular culture: patterns of change and adaptation', in Connolly, R. A. Houston and R. J. Morris (eds), *Conflict, Identity and Economic Development: Ireland and Scotland 1600–1939* (Preston: Carnegie, 1995), pp. 103–13; Seán De Fréine, 'An Gorta agus an Ghaeilge', in Cathal Póirtéir (ed.), *Gnéithe den Ghorta* (Dublin, Coiscéim, 1995), pp. 55–68.

24 Michel Flot, 'Gerald Griffin et la conversion linguistique de l'Irlande', and Grace Neville, '"He spoke to me in English: I answered him in Irish": language shift in the Folklore Archives', both in J. Brihault (ed.), *L'Irlande et ses Langues* (Rennes: Presses Universitaires de Rennes n. d. [1992]), pp. 147–56, 19–32.

25 Corrigan, 'For God's sake'; Máirín Nic Eoin, 'Irish language and literature in County Kilkenny in the nineteenth century' , in William Nolan and Kevin Whelan (eds), *Kilkenny: History and Society* (Dublin: Geography Publications, 1990), pp. 465–79.

26 Mary E. Daly, 'Literacy and language change in the late nineteenth and early twentieth centuries', in Daly and Dickson (eds), *The Origins of Popular Literacy*, pp. 153–66.

27 Aodh Ó Canainn, 'An Cúlra', in Ó Canainn and S. Watson (eds), *Scian a Caitheadh le Toinn: Scéalta agus Amhráin as Inis Eoghain agus Cuimhne ar Ghaeltacht Iorrais* (Dublin: Coiscéim, 1990), pp. 1–27.

28 Anon, 'The Irish language in Inishowen', *Donegal Annual* 45 (1993), pp. 29–42; M. Ó hEarcáin, 'Meath na Gaeilge i gCluain Maine agus in Iorras', *Donegal Annual* 47 (1995), pp. 106–12; Bernadette Friel, 'Language change in Urris', *Donegal Annual* 50 (1998), pp. 66–75.

29 Ciaran Devine, 'The Irish language in County Down', in Lindsay J. Proudfoot (ed.), *Down: History and Society* (Dublin: Geography Publications, 1997): pp. 431–87.

30 Máirín Ní Dhonnchadha, 'Neamhlitearthacht agus Gaeilge: eagna na staraithe?', *Comhar* 50 (1991), pp. 22–5; Daly and Dickson (eds), *The Origins of Popular Literacy*.

31 Dermot McGuinne, *Irish Type Design: A History of Printing Types in the Irish Character* (Dublin: Irish Academic Press, 1992).

32 Niall Ó Ciosáin, 'Printed popular literature in Irish: presence and absence', in Daly and Dickson (eds), *The Origins of Popular Literacy*, pp. 45–57; Ó Ciosáin, 'Printing in Irish and O'Sullivan's *Miscellany*', in Gerard Long (ed.), *Books Beyond the Pale: Aspects of the Provincial Book Trade in Ireland before 1850* (Dublin: Dublin: Rare Books Group of the Library Association of Ireland, 1996), pp. 87–99; Ó Ciosáin, *Print and Popular Culture in Ireland 1750–1850* (London: Macmillan, 1997).

33 Malachy McKenna, 'A textual history of *The Spiritual Rose*', *Clogher Record* 14 (1991), pp. 52–73; see also McKenna, 'Historically long-stressed vowels in a south-east Ulster text', *Celtica* 21 (1990), pp. 265–72.

34 Fionnuala Uí Fhlannagáin, *Micheál Ó Lócháin agus An Gaodhal* (Dublin: An Clóchomhar, 1990); Caoilfhionn Nic Pháidín, *Fáinne an Lae agus an Athbheochan 1898–1900* (Dublin: Cois Life, 1998); *An Gaodhal* has been put in the context of the Irish emigrant press as a whole by Dorothy Ní Uigínn, 'An Iriseoireacht Ghaeilge i Meiriceá agus in Éirinn: An Cúlra Meiriceánach', in Ruairí Ó hUigínn (ed.), *Iriseoireacht na Gaeilge* (Maynooth: An Sagart, 1998), pp. 25–47.

35  Breandán Ó Conchúir, *Clár Lámhscríbhinní Gaeilge in Ollscoil Chorcaí: Cnuasach Uí Mhurchú* (Dublin: Institute for Advanced Studies, 1991); Pádraig Ó Macháin, *Catalogue of Irish Manuscripts in Mount Melleray Abbey, County Waterford* (Dublin: Institute for Advanced Studies, 1994); Ó Macháin, 'Additions to the collection of Irish Manuscripts at Mount Melleray Abbey', *Éigse* 30 (1997) pp. 92–108; Ronald Black, 'Four O'Daly manuscripts', *Éigse* 26 (1992), pp. 43–7.

36  Kenneth Nilsen, 'Mícheál Ó Broin agus Lámhscríbhinní Gaeilge Ollscoil Wisconsin', *Celtica* 22 (1991), pp. 112–18; Edgar Slotkin, 'Two Irish literary manuscripts in the midwest', *Éigse* 25 (1991), pp. 56–80.

37  L. M. Cullen, 'Patrons, teachers and literacy in Irish, 1700–1850', in Daly and Dickson (eds), *The Origins of Popular Literacy*, pp. 15–44; Éamon Ó hÓgáin, 'Scríobhaithe Lámhscríbhinní Gaeilge i gCill Chainnigh 1700–1870', in Nolan and Whelan (eds), *Kilkenny: History and Society*, pp. 405–36; Eoghan Ó Súilleabheain, 'Scríobhaithe Phort Láirge 1700–1900', in William Nolan, T. P. Power and Des Cowman (eds), *Waterford: History and Society: Interdisciplinary Essays on the History of an Irish County* (Dublin: Geography Publications, 1992), pp. 265–308; one Waterford scribe and writer is discussed in Kathleen Laffan, 'James Scurry (1790–1828): A South Kilkenny Scholar', *Decies* 50 (1994), pp. 60–6.

38  William Mahon, 'Scríobhaithe Lámhscríbhinní Gaeilge i nGaillimh 1700–1900', in Gerard Moran and Raymond Gillespie (eds), *Galway: History and Society: Interdisciplinary Essays on the History of an Irish County* (Dublin: Geography Publications, 1996), pp. 623–50; L. M. Cullen, 'Filíocht, cultúr agus polaitíocht', in M. Ní Dhonnchadha (ed.), *Nua-Léamha: Gnéithe de Chultúr, Stair agus Polaitíocht na hÉireann c.1600–1900* (Dublin: An Clóchomhar, 1996), pp. 170–93 (in Irish) and L. M. Cullen, 'Poetry, culture and politics', *Studia Celtica Japonica* 8 (1996), pp. 1–26 (in English); Cathal Ó hÁinle, 'Ceo Meala: an Craoibhín agus na hAmhráin Ghrá', *Irish Review* 14 (1993), pp. 33–47.

39  Meidhbhín Ní Úrdail, *The Scribe in Eighteenth and Nineteenth-Century Ireland: Motivations and Milieu* (Münster: Nodus, 2000); Rónán Ó Donnchadha, *Mícheál Óg Ó Longáin, File* (Dublin: Coiscéim, 1994); Tom Dunne, 'Subaltern voices? Poetry in Irish, popular insurgency and the 1798 Rebellion', *Eighteenth-Century Life* 22 (1998), pp. 31–44.

40  Ciarán Dawson, *Peadar Ó Gealacáin, Scríobhaí* (Dublin: An Clóchomhar, 1992); Séamus Mac Gabhann, 'Salvaging cultural identity: Peter Gallegan, 1792–1860', *Ríocht na Midhe* 9, 1 (1995), pp. 70–86; Séamus Mac Gabhann, 'Forging identity: Michael Clarke and the hidden Ireland', *Ríocht na Midhe* 9, 2 (1996), pp. 73–96.

41  Eilís Ní Dheá, 'Mícheál Ó Raghallaigh – scríobhaí ó Inis Díomáin', *The Other Clare*, (Apr. 1992), pp. 18–20; Ní Dheá, 'Mícheál Ó hAnnracháin agus a chomhscríobhaithe i gCill Ruis', *The Other Clare* (Apr. 1993), pp. 45–7; Ní Dheá, 'Ár n-Oidhreacht Lámhscríbhinní ó Dhún Átha Thiar agus ón gCeantar Máguaird', in Pádraig Ó Fiannachta (ed.), *Ómós do Eoghan Ó Comhraí* (Dingle: An Sagart, 1995), pp. 31–42; Nessa Ní Shéaghdha, 'Gairmeacha beatha roinnt scríobhaithe ón 18ú agus an 19ú céad', *Celtica* 21 (1990), pp. 567–75.

42  Neil Buttimer, 'Gaelic literature and contemporary life in Cork, 1700–1840', in Buttimer and P. O'Flanagan (eds), *Cork: History and Society* (Dublin: Geography Publications, 1993), pp. 585–653.

43  Neil Buttimer, 'Degré de perception de la France dans l'Irlande Gaélique de la pré-famine, 1700–1840', in *Irlande et Bretagne: Vingt Siècles d'Histoire* (Rennes: Presses

Universitaires de Rennes, 1994), pp. 178–89; Buttimer, 'A Gaelic reaction to Robert Emmet's rebellion', *Journal of the Cork Historical and Archaeological Society* 97 (1992), pp. 36–53; Buttimer, 'A Cork Gaelic text on a Napoleonic campaign', *Journal of the Cork Historical and Archaeological Society* 95 (1990), pp. 107–23; Buttimer, 'Pláig fhollasach, pláig choimhtheach: obvious plague, strange plague', *Journal of the Cork Historical and Archaeological Society* 102 (1997), pp. 41–68.

44  Diarmaid Ó Muirithe, 'Prayers for O'Connell and emancipation', *Éigse* 25 (1991), pp. 102–4; Pádraig A. Breatnach, 'Meascra ar an saol in Éirinn, 1841–44', *Éigse* 25 (1991), pp. 105–12.

45  Tom Dunne, '"Tá Gaedhil bhocht cráidhte": memory, tradition and the politics of the poor in Gaelic poetry and song', in Laurence M. Geary (ed.), *Rebellion and Remembrance in Modern Ireland* (Dublin: Four Courts, 2001), pp. 93–111; Ríonach Uí Ógáin, *Immortal Dan* (Dublin: Geography Publications, n.d. [1995]), a translation of Uí Ógáin, *An Rí gan Choróin: Dónall Ó Conaill sa Bhéaloideas* (Dublin: An Clóchomhar, 1984); Maura Cronin, 'Memory, story and balladry: 1798 and its place in popular memory in pre-Famine Ireland', in Geary, *Rebellion and Remembrance*, pp. 112–34; Gearóid Denvir, 'Filíocht Antaine Raiftearaí', in Denvir, *Litríocht agus Pobal* (Indreabhán: Cló Iar-Chonnachta, 1997), pp. 295–307; Proinsias Ó Drisceoil, *Ar Scaradh Gabháil: an Fhéiniúlacht in 'Cín Lae Amhlaoibh Uí Shúilleabháin'* (Dublin: An Clóchomhar, 2000); L. M. Cullen, 'Humphrey O'Sullivan's Callan: before and after', in Noreen McDonnell (ed.), *Callan Co-operative Agricultural and Dairy Society Ltd., 1899–1999* (Callan Co-operative, 1999), pp. 11–28.

46  Antain Mac Lochlainn, 'The Famine in Gaelic tradition', *Irish Review* 17/18 (1995), pp. 90–108; Neil Buttimer, '"A stone on the cairn": the Great Famine in later Gaelic manuscripts', in Chris Morash and Richard Hayes (eds), *'Fearful Realities': New Perspectives on the Famine* (Dublin: Irish Academic Press, 1996), pp. 93–109.

47  Victor Durkacz, *The Decline of the Celtic Languages* (Edinburgh: John Donald, 1983); Michel Lagrée, *Religion et Cultures en Bretagne: 1850–1950* (Paris: Fayard, 1992); Lagrée, 'Foi et langue en Bretagne et en Irlande au XIXᵉ siècle', in *Chrétientés de Basse-Bretagne et d'Ailleurs: Les Archives au Risque de l'Histoire* (Quimper: Société Archéologique du Finistère, 1998), pp. 275–81.

48  Wall, 'The decline of the Irish language'; Gearóid Ó Tuathaigh, 'An Chléir Chaitliceach, an Léann Dúchais agus an Cultúr in Éirinn, 1750–1850', in P. Ó Fiannachta (ed.), *Léachtaí Cholmcille* XVI (1986), pp. 110–39.

49  Roger Blaney, *Presbyterians and the Irish Language* (Belfast: Institute of Irish Studies, QUB, 1996); Séamus Ó Saothraí, *An Ministir Gaelach: Uilliam Mac Néill 1774–1821* (Dublin: Coiscéim, 1992); Anthony D. Buckley, 'The case of the Cushendall schoolmaster', *The Glynns* 20 (1992), pp. 30–5.

50  Risteárd Giltrap, *An Ghaeilge in Eaglais na hÉireann* (Dublin: Cumann Gaelach na hEaglaise, 1990); Pádraig de Brún, 'The Irish Society's Bible teachers, 1818–27', *Éigse* 24 (1990), pp. 71–120, *Éigse* 25 (1991), pp. 113–49, *Éigse* 26 (1992), pp. 131–72.

51  Ó Tuathaigh, 'An Chléir Chaitliceach'; Gearóid Ó Tuathaigh, 'Maigh Nuad agus Stair na Gaeilge', in Etaín Ó Síocháin (ed.), *Maigh Nuad: Saothrú na Gaeilge 1795–1995* (Maynooth: An Sagart, 1995), pp. 13–25; Séamus Mac Gabhann, 'Father Paul O'Brien of Cormeen (1763–1820): Folk-poet and Maynooth professor', *Ríocht na Midhe* 10 (1999), pp. 125–51; Diarmuid Ó Muirithe, 'An t-Athair Pól Ó Briain', in Pádraig Ó Fiannachta

(ed.), *Maigh Nuad agus an Ghaeilge* (Maynoooth: An Sagart, 1993), pp. 8–43; Liam P. Ó Caithnia, 'Tábhacht na teangan – Éamon Rís agus an Ghaeilge' and A. P. Caomhánach, 'Na Bráithre Críostaí agus an Ghaeilge', in M. Ó Cearúil (ed.), *Gníomhartha na mBráithre* (Dublin: Coiscéim, 1996), pp. 21–50 and 123–56.

52 Tadhg Ó Dúshláine, 'Gealán Dúluachra: Seanmóireacht na Gaeilge *c.*1600–1850', in Ruairí Ó hUiginn (ed.), *Léann na Gaeilge: Súil siar, súil chun cinn* (Maynooth: An Sagart, 1996), pp. 83–122.

53 William Mahon (ed.), *Doctor Kirwan's Irish Catechism by Thomas Hughes* (Cambridge, Mass: Pangur Publications, 1991); Pádraigín Riggs et al. (eds), *Saoi na hÉigse: Aistí in Onóir do Sheán Ó Tuama* (Dublin: An Clóchomhar, 2000): Breandán Ó Buachalla, 'Marbhchaoine an athar Seán Ó Maonaigh', pp. 197–208; Seán Ua Súilleabháin, 'Tioreamh an athar Diarmada Uí Uallacháin', pp. 209–18.

54 Pádraig Ó Fiannachta (ed.), *Ómós do Eoghan Ó Comhraí* (Dingle: An Sagart, 1995): Ó Madagáin, 'Eoghan Ó Comhraí agus Amhráin Ghailge an Chláir', pp. 43–57; de Barra, 'Saol agus Saothar Eoghain', pp. 5–22; Ó Riain, 'Saothar Suaithinseach de Chuid Eoghain Uí Chomhraí', pp. 23–30; Ó Dúshláine, 'Eoghan Ó Comhraí: Dr. Johnson na Gaeilge', pp. 116–31; Ó Maolfabhail, 'Eoghan Ó Comhraí agus an tSuirbhéireacht Ordanáis', pp. 145–84; Ó Murchú, 'Dán ar Réimeas Shéarlais II le hEoghan Ó Comhraí 1828–34', pp. 79–95.

55 Nollaig Ó Muraíle, Introduction to Eugene O'Curry, *On the Manners and Customs of the Ancient Irish*, facsimile edn (Dublin: Edmund Burke, 1996).

56 Nollaig Ó Muraíle, 'Seán Ó Donnabháin', in Ruairí Ó hUigínn (ed.), *Scoláirí Gaeilge* (Maynooth: An Sagart, 1997), pp. 11–82.

57 Joep Leerssen, 'Language revivalism before the twilight', in J. Leerssen et al. (eds), *Forging in the Smithy: National Identity and Representation in Anglo-Irish Literary History* (Amsterdam: Rodopi, 1995) pp. 133–44; Breandán Ó Conchúir, 'Thomas Swanton, réamhchonraitheoir in Iar Chairbre', *Journal of the Cork Historical and Archaeological Society* 98 (1993), pp. 50–60; Pádraig Ó Macháin, 'Patrick Carmody, Irish Scholar', *Decies* 53 (1997), pp. 133–43.

58 Kerby Miller, Bruce Boling and David Doyle, 'Emigrants and exiles: Irish cultures and Irish emigration to North America 1790–1922', *IHS* 22 (1980), pp. 97–125.

59 Angela Bourke, 'The baby and the bathwater: cultural loss in nineteenth-century Ireland', in Tadhg Foley and Seán Ryder (eds), *Ideology and Ireland in the Nineteenth Century* (Dublin: Four Courts, 1998), pp. 79–92.

60 Declan Kiberd, *Irish Classics* (London: Granta, 2000), ch. 18: '*Love Songs of Connaught*'.

61 Niall Ó Ciosáin, 'Boccoughs and God's poor: deserving and undeserving poor in Irish popular culture', in Foley and Ryder (eds), *Ideology and Ireland*, pp. 93–9.

62 *Galway Patriot*, 5 Apr. 1837, quoted in Richard McMahon, 'The courts of petty sessions and the law in pre-Famine Galway' (MA thesis, NUI Galway, 1999), p. 104.

63 Jarlath Waldron, *Maamtrasna: the Murders and the Mystery* (Dublin: Edmund Burke, 1992).

64 James S. Donnelly, Jr, 'The Marian shrine of Knock: the first decade', *Éire-Ireland* 28, 2 (1993), pp. 55–99.

65 Michel Lagrée, 'Langue céleste et langue régionale au XIX$^e$ siècle', *Annales de Bretagne et des Pays de l'Ouest* 98 (1991), pp. 121–9; René Merle, 'L'Apparition de La Salette et les "patois"', *Lengas* 31 (1992), pp. 69–105.

66  Gérard Cholvy, 'Régionalisme et clergé catholique au XIX$^e$ siècle', in *Région et Régionalisme en France du XVII$^e$ siècle à nos jours* (Paris: Presses Universitaires de France, 1977), pp. 187–201; Lagrée, 'Foi et langue'.

## CHAPTER 9: ART HISTORY

1  Recent surveys on aspects of twentieth-century art include James Christen Steward (ed.), *When Time Began to Rant and Rage: Figurative Painting from Twentieth-Century Ireland* (London: Merrell Holberton, 1998); Dorothy Walker, *Modern Art in Ireland* (Dublin: Lilliput, 1997); Liam Kelly, *Thinking Long: Contemporary Art in the North of Ireland* (Kinsale: Gandon, 1996); S. B. Kennedy, *Irish Art and Modernism 1880–1950* (Belfast: Institute of Irish Studies, QUB, 1991). There have also been many studies on individual artists, for example Bruce Arnold's two books, *Jack Yeats* (New Haven and London: Yale University Press, 1998) and *Mainie Jellett and the Modern Movement in Ireland* (New Haven and London: Yale University Press, 1991).

2  See Edward McParland, 'A bibliography of Irish architectural history', *IHS* 26, 102 (1988), pp. 161–212.

3  For studies on art institutions see Catherine de Courcy, *The Foundation of the National Gallery of Ireland* (Dublin: NGI, 1985) and Homan Potterton's 'Introduction', *National Gallery of Ireland: Illustrated Summary Catalogue of Paintings* (Dublin: Gill & Macmillan, 1981), xi–xxxxii; Peter Murray, *Illustrated Summary Catalogue of the Crawford Municipal Art Gallery* (Cork: City of Cork Vocational Education Committee, 1992); Eileen Black, 'The development of Belfast as a centre of art 1760–1888' (unpublished PhD thesis, QUB, 1998), and her article, 'Practical patriots and true Irishmen. The Royal Irish Art Union 1839–59', *Irish Arts Review Yearbook* 14 (1998), pp. 140–6.

4  John Turpin, *A School of Art in Dublin since the Eighteenth Century: A History of the National College of Art and Design* (Dublin: Gill & Macmillan, 1995).

5  Cyril Barrett, *Irish Art in the Nineteenth Century*, an exhibition of Irish Victorian art at the Crawford Municipal School of Art (Cork, 1971), p. 6.

6  Art Gallery of the Corporation of London, *Catalogue of the Exhibition of Works by Irish Painters* (London, 1904).

7  Anne Crookshank and the Knight of Glin, The *Painters of Ireland c.1660–1920* (London: Barrie and Jenkins, 1978) and *Ireland's Painters 1600–1940* (New Haven and London: Yale University Press, 2002).

8  Cyril Barrett, 'Irish nationalism and art 1800–1921', *Studies* 64 (1975), pp. 393–409.

9  *Irish Portraits 1660–1860*, catalogue by Anne Crookshank and the Knight of Glin (London: Paul Mellon Foundation for British Art, 1969). See for example the entry on the portrait painter Stephen Catterson Smith, no. 106: 'The Earl of Bessborough' (NGI), and no. 107: 'Miss Emily Murphy' from the O'Conor Don's estate, p. 72.

10  Barrett, 'Irish nationalism and art', p. 408.

11  David Lloyd, *Anomalous States: Irish Writing and the Post-Colonial Moment* (Dublin: Lilliput, 1993), pp. 136–44.

12  Jeanne Sheehy, *The Rediscovery of Ireland's Past: The Celtic Revival, 1830–1920* (London: Thames & Hudson, 1980).

13   Walter Strickland, *A Dictionary of Irish Artists*, 2 vols (Dublin and London: Maunsel, 1913).

14   Eric Adams, *Francis Danby* (New Haven and London: Yale University Press, 1973); Katryn Moore Heleniak, *William Mulready* (New Haven and London: Yale University Press, 1980); but see also Marica Pointon, *Mulready* (London: Victoria and Albert Museum, 1986), which takes a more thematic and less biographical approach to the artist's career; Arts Council of Great Britain, *Daniel Maclise* (London: National Portrait Gallery, 1972) and Nancy Weston, *Daniel Maclise: An Irish Artist in Victorian London* (Dublin: Four Courts, 2000); John Hutchinson, *James Arthur O'Connor* (Dublin: NGI, 1985); Julian Campbell, *Nathaniel Hone* (Dublin: NGI, 1991); Julian Campbell, *Frank O'Meara 1853–1888* (Dublin: Hugh Lane Municipal Gallery of Modern Art, 1989); Roy Johnston, *Roderic O'Connor* (London and Belfast: Barbican Art Gallery and Ulster Museum, 1985); Jonathan Benington, *Roderic O'Connor: A Biography* (Dublin: Irish Academic Press, 1992); Fintan Cullen, *The Drawings of John Butler Yeats, 1839–1922* (Albany Institute of History & Art, 1987); Jeanne Sheehy, *Walter Osborne* (Ballycotton, Co. Cork: Gifford and Craven, 1974).

15   See A. L. Rees and F. Borzello (eds), *The New Art History* (London: Camden Press, 1986).

16   Julian Campbell has produced the following catalogues: *The Irish Impressionists: Irish Artists in France and Belgium* (Dublin: NGI, 1984), *Hone*, and *O'Meara*, see note 14 and most recently, *Peintres Irlandais en Bretagne* (Musée de Pont-Aven, 1999); Jeanne Sheehy, *Walter Osborne* (Dublin: NGI, 1983).

17   See James Holloway and Lindsay Errington, *The Discovery of Scotland* (Edinburgh: National Gallery of Scotland, 1978); Fiona Pearson (ed.), *Virtue and Vision: Sculpture and Scotland 1540–1990* (Edinburgh: National Galleries of Scotland, 1991); Lindsay Errington, *Tribute to Wilkie* (Edinburgh: National Gallery of Scotland, 1985); Helen Smailes and Duncan Thomson, *The Queen's Image: A Celebration of Mary Queen of Scots* (Edinburgh: Scottish National Portrait Gallery, 1987) or most recently *O Caledonia! Sir Walter Scott and the Creation of Scotland* (Edinburgh, National Galleries of Scotland CD-Rom, 1999).

18   Niamh O'Sullivan, *Aloysius O'Kelly: Re-Orientations: Painting, Politics and Popular Culture* (Dublin: Hugh Lane Municipal Gallery of Modern Art, 1999).

19   Commemorations of 1798 fared better, even if the visual material could have been examined more fully; see Kevin Whelan, *Fellowship of Freedom: The United Irishmen and 1798. Companion volume to the Bicentenary Exhibition by the National Library and the National Museum of Ireland at Collins Barracks, Dublin, 1998* (Cork: Cork University Press, 1998) and W. A. Maguire (ed.), *Up in Arms: The 1798 Rebellion in Ireland. A Bicentenary Exhibition* (Belfast: Ulster Museum, 1998). See also Fintan Cullen, 'Radicals and reactionaries: portraits of the 1790s in Ireland', in Jim Smyth (ed.), *Revolution, Counter Revolution and Union* (Cambridge: Cambridge University Press, 2000), pp. 161–94 and S. J. Campbell, *The Great Irish Famine: Words and Images from the Famine Museum Strokestown Park, County Roscommon* (Strokestown: Famine Museum, 1994).

20   Belinda Loftus, *Mirrors: William III and Mother Ireland* (Dundrum: Picture Press, 1990); Adele Dalsimer (ed.), *Visualizing Ireland: National Identity and the Pictorial Tradition* (Boston and London: Faber, 1993); Raymond Gillespie and Brian P. Kennedy (eds), *Ireland: Art into History* (Dublin: Town House, 1994).

21   See also, Belinda Loftus, *Mirrors: Orange and Green* (Dundrum: Picture Press, 1994).

22  Loftus, *Mirrors: William III and Mother Ireland*, p. 16.

23  Marina Warner, *Monuments and Maidens: The Allegory of the Female Form* (London: Weidenfeld & Nicolson, 1985).

24  For further discussion of this image, as both a painting and an engraved illustration to Tom Moore's poem, see Fintan Cullen, *Visual Politics:The Representation of Ireland, 1750–1930* (Cork: Cork University Press, 1997), pp. 47–8 and L. Perry Curtis, Jr, 'The four Erins: feminine images of Ireland, 1780–1900', *Éire-Ireland* 33, 3 & 4; 34, 1 (1998–9), pp. 70–102; see also Fintan Cullen and Roy Foster, *'Conquering England': Ireland in Victorian London* (London: National Portrait Gallery, 2005), pp. 56–9.

25  Rosalind M. Elmes, *Catalogue of Engraved Irish Portraits Mainly in the Joly Collection* (Dublin: NLI, 1932); for discussion of portraits of O'Connell see Fintan Cullen, *Visual Politics*, pp. 90–101 and Leon Litvack, 'Exhibiting Ireland, 1851–3: Colonial Mimicry in London, Cork and Dublin', in Glenn Hooper and Leon Litvack (eds), *Ireland in the Nineteenth Century: Regional Identity* (Dublin: Four Courts, 2000), pp. 52–6.

26  R. F. Foster (ed.), *The Oxford Illustrated History of Ireland* (Oxford: Clarendon, 1989); W. E. Vaughan (ed.), *A New History of Ireland*, v, *Ireland Under the Union, I: 1801–70* (Oxford: Clarendon, 1989); W. E. Vaughan (ed.), *A New History of Ireland*, vi, *Ireland Under the Union, II: 1870–1921* (Oxford: Clarendon, 1996).

27  Peter Gray, *The Irish Famine* (London: Thames & Hudson, 1995); Tommy Graham (ed), *History Ireland* (since 1993). The latter is lavishly illustrated and frequently uses nineteenth-century paintings and other artworks to accompany articles. Unfortunately the authors rarely use them in a meaningful way. A number of art historians have begun to publish articles in this award winning journal: for example, Niamh O'Sullivan, 'Through Irish eyes: the works of Aloysius O'Kelly in the *Illustrated London News*', *History Ireland* 3, 3 (1995), pp. 10–16; Catherine Marshall, 'Painting Irish history: the Famine', *History Ireland* 4, 3 (1996), pp. 46–50; John Turpin, '1798, 1898 and the political implications of Sheppard's monuments', *History Ireland* 6, 2 (1998), pp. 44–8; Fintan Cullen, 'Lord Edward FitzGerald: the creation of an icon', *History Ireland* 6, 4 (1998), pp. 17–20.

28  Foster (ed.), *Illustrated History*, pp. 187 and 195. The NLI's extensive collection of photographs is slowly being made more accessible; see Sarah Rouse, *Into the Light: An Illustrated Guide to the Photographic Collections in the NLI* (Dublin: NLI, 1998).

29  Cyril Barrett and Jeanne Sheehy, 'Visual arts and society', in Vaughan (ed.), *A New History of Ireland*, vi, pp. 436–99. For further comment on these two chapters see Fintan Cullen, *Irish Arts Review Yearbook* 15 (1999), pp. 188–9.

30  Vaughan (ed.), *A New History of Ireland*, v, figs. 10 a & b, see also p. xxxiii.

31  Vaughan (ed.), *A New History of Ireland*, v, pp. 108–133.

32  This was one of my main concerns in writing *Visual Politics*. I wished to place Irish visual material, be it by Irish artists or not, firmly within the framework of Irish historical and postcolonial debate. Chapter 4 of that book (pp. 116–46) discusses 'The peasant, genre painting and national character', where imagery, both high art paintings and more ephemeral cartoons, are examined in the context of a visual tradition. See also Sighle Bhreathnach-Lynch, 'Framing the Irish: Victorian paintings of the Irish peasant', *Journal of Victorian Culture* 2, 2 (1997), pp. 245–63.

33  For recent art historical examples outside Irish Studies, see Julie Codell and Dianne Sachko Macleod (eds), *Orientalism Transposed: The Impact of the Colonies on British Culture*

(London, Ashgate, 1998). Recent developments in the study of American art in the nineteenth century offer instructive models for improving the state of Irish art historiography; see Wanda M. Corn, 'Coming of age: historical scholarship in American art', in Mary Ann Calo (ed.), *Critical Issues in American Art: A Book of Readings* (Boulder, CO: Westview, 1998), pp. 1–34.

34   L. Perry Curtis, Jr, *Anglo-Saxons and Celts: A Study of Anti-Irish Prejudice in Victorian England* (Bridgeport, CT: Conference on British Studies, 1968) and *Apes and Angels: The Irishman in Victorian Caricature* (Newton Abbot: David & Charles, 1971; rev. ed., Washington and London: Smithsonian Institution Press, 1997); R. F. Foster, *Paddy and Mr Punch: Connections in Irish and English History* (London: Allen Lane, 1993), pp. 171–94; Sheridan Gilley, 'English attitudes to the Irish in England 1780–1900', in Colin Holmes (ed.), *Immigrants and Minorities in British Society* (London: George Allen & Unwin, 1978), pp. 81–110.

35   Richard Ned Lebow, *White Britain and Black Ireland: The Influence of Stereotypes on Colonial Policy* (Philadelphia: Institute for the Study of Human Issues, 1976); Frankie Morris, *John Tenniel, Cartoonist: A Critical and Sociocultural Study in the Art of the Victorian Political Cartoon* (Ann Arbor: University Microfilms International, 1985) and the highly polemical Liz Curtis, *Nothing But the Same Old Story: The Roots of Anti-Irish Racism* (London: Information on Ireland, 1984). See also, H. L. Malchow, 'Frankenstein's monster and images of race in nineteenth-century Britain', *Past and Present* 139 (1993), pp. 124–5 and William Vaughan, 'The Englishness of British art', *Oxford Art Journal* 13, 2 (1990), pp. 11–23.

36   I discuss this issue in ch. 3 of *Visual Politics*.

37   Foster, *Paddy and Mr Punch*, p. 174.

38   Luke Gibbons in Seamus Deane (ed.), *The Field Day Anthology of Irish Writing*, 3 vols (Derry: Field Day Publications, 1991), III, p. 585, n. 8.

39   Curtis, *Apes and Angels* (1997 edn), pp. 109–20 and 189–93.

40   Ibid., pp. 84–6.

41   Recent publications on popular illustrations include Margarita Cappock, 'Aloysius O'Kelly and the *Illustrated London News*', *Irish Arts Review Yearbook* 12 (1996); see also her unpublished doctoral thesis, 'Irish subjects in the *Illustrated London News* and elsewhere, 1842–1900', National College of Art and Design, Dublin, 1998; Niamh O'Sullivan, 'Painters and illustrators: Aloysius O'Kelly and Vincent Van Gogh', *Irish Arts Review Yearbook* 14 (1998), pp. 134–39 and her 'The iron cage of femininity: visual representation of women in the 1880s land agitation', in Tadhg Foley and Sean Ryder (eds), *Ideology and Ireland in the Nineteenth Century* (Dublin: Four Courts, 1998), pp. 181–96; Leslie Williams, 'Irish identity and the *Illustrated London News*, 1846–1851: famine to depopulation', in Susan Shaw Sailer (ed.), *Representing Ireland: Gender, Class, Nationality* (Gainesville: University Press of Florida, 1997), pp. 59–93; Lawrence W. McBride, 'Visualising '98: Irish nationalist cartoons commemorate the revolution', *Eighteenth-Century Life* 22 (1998), pp. 103–17 and various relevant essays in Lawrence W. McBride (ed.), *Images, Icons and the Irish Nationalist Imagination* (Dublin: Four Courts, 1999).

42   In *Visual Politics*, I examine oil portraits of O'Connell and juxtapose them with the *Punch* view of him as 'The Irish Frankenstein'. Later, I explore Ford Madox Brown's *Work* (1852–63) and examine the Irish emigrants who appear in the painting; see *Visual Politics*, pp. 90–2; 135–46. For other studies of O'Connell in popular cartoons see, Miles

L. Chappell and James N. McCord, Jr, 'John Doyle, Daniel O'Connell "The Great Liberator", and Rubens: The appropriate and appropriation in political culture', *South Eastern College Art Conference Review* 11 (1987), pp. 127–34; James N. McCord, 'The image in England: the cartoons of HB', in Maurice O'Connell (ed.), *Daniel O'Connell: Political Pioneer* (Dublin: IPA, 1991), pp. 57–71; Gary Owens, 'Visualizing the Liberator: self-fashioning, dramaturgy, and the construction of Daniel O'Connell', *Éire-Ireland* 33, 3 & 4; 34, 1 (1998–9), pp. 103–30. For a comparable study of Brown's painting to my own, see Joel A. Hollander, 'Ford Madox Brown's *Work* (1865): the Irish question, Carlyle, and the Great Famine', *New Hibernia Review* 1, 1 (1997), pp. 100–19.

43 For an illuminating discussion on recent trends in art historiography, see Richard Shiff, 'Art history and the nineteenth century: realism and resistance', *The Art Bulletin* 70 (1988), pp. 25–48.

44 Luke Gibbons, 'Romanticism, realism and Irish cinema', in Kevin Rockett, Luke Gibbons and John Hill (eds), *Cinema and Ireland*, (London: Routledge, 1987), pp. 194–257; Luke Gibbons, 'Between Captain Rock and a hard place: art and agrarian insurgency', in Foley and Ryder (eds), *Ideology and Ireland in the Nineteenth Century*, pp. 23–44. See also his '"A shadowy narrator": history, art and romantic nationalism in Ireland 1750–1850', in Ciaran Brady (ed.), *Ideology and the Historians*, (Dublin: Lilliput, 1991), pp. 99–127.

45 This area is now greatly aided by the publication of exhibition lists by Ann Stewart, see details in the Select Bibliography in this volume. See also John Turpin, 'Dublin Exhibitions of Art and Industry, 1865–1885', *Dublin Historical Record* 35, 2 (1982); Brendan Rooney, 'The Irish Exhibition at Olympia, 1888', *Irish Architectural and Decorative Studies: Journal of the Irish Georgian Society* 1 (1998), pp. 101–19; Eileen Black, doctoral thesis, 1998, see note 3; Fintan Cullen, 'Union and display in nineteenth-century Ireland', in Dana Arnold (ed.), *Cultural Identities and the Aesthetics of Britishness* (Manchester: Manchester University Press, 2003), pp. 111–33.

46 Adele Dalsimer and Vera Kreilkamp, 'Introduction', in Dalsimer (ed.), *Visualizing Ireland*, p. 7. Andrew Hemingway, *Landscape Imagery and Urban Culture in Early Nineteenth-Century Britain* (Cambridge: Cambridge University Press, 1992).

47 Fintan Cullen, *Sources in Irish Art: A Reader* (Cork: Cork University Press, 2000), pp. 59–61, 65–74 and 243–8. Another figure worthy of reassessment is the Irish-born Anna Jameson (1794–1860), see Adele M. Holcomb, 'Anna Jameson: the first professional English art historian', *Art History* 6, 2 (1983), pp. 171–87; Sheridan Gilley, 'Victorian feminism and Catholic art: the case of Mrs Jameson', in Diana Wood (ed.), *The Church and the Arts* (Oxford: 1992), pp. 381–91; Judith Johnston, *Anna Jameson: Victorian, Feminist, Woman of Letters* (Aldershot, Scolar Press, 1997)

48 Irish Architectural Archive (Merrion Square, Dublin 2) publications include *The Architecture of Richard and William Vitruvius Morrison* (Dublin, 1989) and David Griffin and Simon Lincoln, *Drawings from the Irish Architectural Archive* (Dublin, 1993). Another recent architectural publication is Frederick O'Dwyer, *The Architecture of Deane and Woodward* (Cork: Cork University Press, 1997).

49 National Photographic Archive, Meeting House Square, Temple Bar, Dublin 2. Rouse, *Into the Light*, is a useful guide to the collection. See also Sean Sexton, *Ireland: Photographs, 1840–1930*, introduction by J. J. Lee (London: Lawrence King, 1994); Peadar Slattery, 'The uses of photography in Ireland, 1839–1900', unpublished doctoral dissertation,

3 vols, TCD, 1992; and Fintan Cullen, 'Marketing national sentiment: lantern slides of evictions in late nineteenth-century Ireland', *History Workshop Journal* 54 (2002), pp. 162–79. See also, Edward Chandler, *Photography in Ireland: The Nineteenth Century* (Dublin: Edmund Burke, 2001).

50  Nicola Gordon Bowe and Elizabeth Cumming, *The Arts and Crafts Movements in Dublin and Edinburgh* (Dublin: Irish Academic Press, 1998). See also T. J. Edelstein (ed.), *The Celtic Revival, 1840–1940* (Chicago: David and Alfred Smart Museum of Art, University of Chicago, 1992); Paul Larmour, *The Arts and Crafts Movement in Ireland* (Belfast: Friar's Bush Press, 1992) and Sheehy, *The Rediscovery of Ireland's Past*.

51  See John Turpin, *John Hogan: Irish Neo-Classical Sculptor in Rome 1800–1858* (Dublin: Irish Academic Press, 1982) and Judith Hill, *Irish Public Sculpture: A History* (Dublin: Four Courts, 1998).

52  Paula Murphy, 'The politics of the street monument', *Irish Arts Review Yearbook* 10 (1994), pp. 202–8 and her 'The O'Connell monument in Dublin: the political and artistic context of a public sculpture', *Apollo* (Mar. 1996), pp. 22–6.

53  Julian Campbell's *The Irish Impressionists* is subtitled *Irish Artists in France and Belgium*. The first chapter of Cullen, *Visual Politics*, is entitled, 'Artists on the make: Irish artists in London', pp. 14–49.

54  See Doreen Bolger et al. (eds), *William M. Harnett* (New York: Harry N. Abrams, Inc., 1992), pp. 298–9 (illustrated p. 202). Anne Crookshank and the Knight of Glin have a chapter on 'The Irish in America and the colonies' in *The Watercolours of Ireland: Works on Paper in Pencil, Pastel and Paint c.1660–1914* (London: Barrie & Jenkins, 1994), pp. 237–58.


CHAPTER 10: MUSICOLOGY


1    For a useful overview of European and Anglo-American musicology which explains in greater detail the relationship of musical research to philology, art history and criticism, see Joseph Kerman, *Musicology* (London: Fontana, 1985).

2    The term 'imaginary museum of musical works' originates with Franz Liszt, and was first employed in the musicological literature by Carl Dahlhaus. The phrase is used by Dahlhaus to describe that mode of music history which assumes the autonomy of the musical object as a donnée and repudiates any real consideration of the socio-cultural processes from which music arises. See Dahlhaus, *Foundations of Music History* (Cambridge: Cambridge University Press, 1983), pp. 60–71 and *passim*.

3    See Gary Tomlinson, *Monteverdi and the End of the Renaissance* (Oxford: Clarendon, 1987), p. 1.

4    The secondary literature growing around this question of re-engagement and the more general impact of postmodernist discourse on musicology is considerable. See Lawrence Kramer, *Classical Music and Postmodern Knowledge* (Berkeley: University of California Press, 1995), and Pieter Van den Toorn, *Music, Politics and the Academy* (Berkeley: University of California Press, 1995) for discussions of this question which respectively support and reject the postmodernist approach of contemporary American musicology.

5    I have discussed these alternatives in 'American musicology and "The archives of Eden"', *Journal of American Studies* 32, 1 (1998), pp. 1–18.

6    For a discussion of this approach, which countenances the acute problem of sources, see Kerman, *Musicology*, pp. 155–81.

7    Harry White, *The Keeper's Recital: Music and Cultural History in Ireland, 1770–1970* (Cork: Cork University Press, 1998), p. 9.

8    Harry White, 'Musicology in Ireland', *Acta Musicologica* 60 (1988), fasc. III, pp. 290–305.

9    For convenience, full citations for the published materials discussed in this essay are available in the bibliography appended to this chapter's notes on pp. 276–7 below. Publications are also listed in the general bibliography.

10   Shields's work on the sources of Irish ballads in general (in the twentieth as well as the nineteenth century) is consolidated in *Narrative Singing in Ireland: Lays, Ballads, Come-all-yes and Other Songs* (Dublin: Irish Academic Press, 1993).

11   The reception by European composers of Irish music came principally through the poetry and musical settings of Thomas Moore. One of these is considered in the Maynooth *Proceedings*, namely Berlioz's *Irlande*. See Julian Rushton, 'Berlioz and *Irlande*: From romance to melodie', in *The Maynooth International Musicological Conference 1995, Selected Proceedings, Part Two*, pp. 224–40.

12   See Ita Margaret Hogan [Beasuang], *Anglo-Irish Music 1780–1830* (Cork: Cork University Press, 1966).

13   It is tempting to conclude that religious denomination (sometimes modifiied as the integrity of tradition) – in education as in music – regularly dissipated Dublin's resources.

14   Fleischmann would not have wanted the pioneering work of Donal O'Sullivan and the London-based Irish Folk Song Society (most active in the first decades of the twentieth century) to be overlooked in assessing the scholarly importance of these volumes.

15   It is only fair to add that Harry Grindle's study of Irish cathedrals and their repertory, *Irish Cathedral Music* (Belfast: Institute of Irish Studies, QUB), which appeared in 1989, is an important precedent for Boydell's work, although its publication date (1989) falls just beyond the perimeters of the present study. Barra Boydell's *A History of Christ Church Cathedral Dublin* (Woodbridge: Boydell Press, 2004) appeared too late to be included in the present report.

16   See, Karl Gustav Fellerer, 'Caecilianismus', in F. Blume (ed.), *Die Musik in Geschichte und Gegenwart* (Basle: Bärenreiter, 1973), Bd. 2, p. 625, where the establishment of the Cecilian movement in Ireland is attributed to Bewerunge in 1876, i.e., 12 years before his arrival in Ireland.

17   Even in Walsh's own book, we find only 11 Italian operas recorded as having been given in Dublin between 1808 and 1820, as against some 50 English works – many of which appear to be 'afterpieces' – between 1798 and 1820.

18   Harry White and Nicholas Carolan, 'Ireland', in Stanley Sadie (ed.), *The New Grove Dictionary of Music and Musicians*, 2nd edn (London: Macmillan, 2001), XII, pp. 556–68.

19   This remark by Nicholas Carolan comes at the end of his survey of traditional music in Ireland.

20   See Harry White, 'The preservation of music and Irish cultural history', *International Review of the Aesthetics and Sociology of Music* 27, 2 (1996), pp. 123–38.

MUSICOLOGY: SELECT BIBLIOGRAPHY

Connolly, S. J. (ed.), *The Oxford Companion to Irish History* (Oxford: Oxford University Press, 1998; rev. edn, 2002), incl. Entries on 'music' and 'musical institutions and venues' by Harry White, pp. 373–76.

Cooper, David (ed.), *The Petrie Collection of the Ancient Music of Ireland* (Cork: Cork University Press, 2002).

Daly, Kieran, *Catholic Church Music in Ireland 1878–1903* (Dublin: Four Courts, 1995).

Devine, Patrick F. and Harry White (eds), *The Maynooth International Musicological Conference 1995: Selected Proceedings, Part One*, Irish Musical Studies IV (Dublin: Four Courts, 1996), incl. Colette Moloney, 'Style and repertoire in the Gaelic harp tradition: evidence from the Bunting manuscripts and prints', pp. 310–34.

Devine, Patrick F. and Harry White (eds), *The Maynooth International Musicological Conference 1995: Selected Proceedings, Part Two*, Irish Musical Studies V (Dublin: Four Courts Press, 1996), incl. Barry Cooper, 'Beethoven's folksong settings as sources of Irish folk music', pp. 65–81; Barra Boydell, 'The iconography of the Irish harp as a national symbol', pp. 131–45; Ita Beausang, 'Dublin musical societies, 1850–1900', pp. 169–78; Julian Rushton, 'Berlioz and *Irlande*: from romance to melodie', pp. 224–40; Bennett Zon, 'The revival of plainchant in the Roman Catholic Church in Ireland, 1777–1858: some sources and their commerce with England', pp. 251–61.

Fleischmann, Aloys (ed.), *Sources of Irish Traditional Music c.1600–1855*, 2 vols (London and New York: Garland, 1998).

Gillen, Gerard and Andrew Johnstone (eds). *A Historical Anthology of Irish Church Music* Irish Musical Studies VI (Dublin: Four Courts, 2001).

Gillen, Gerard and Harry White (eds), *Musicology in Ireland*, Irish Musical Studies I (Dublin: Irish Academic Press, 1990), incl. Hugh Shields, 'The history of *The Lass of Aughrim*', pp. 58–73; Barra Boydell: 'The flageolet in Ireland', pp. 150–68; Harry White, 'Musicology, positivism and the case for an encyclopedia of music in Ireland', pp. 295–300.

Gillen, Gerard and Harry White (eds), *Music and the Church*, Irish Musical Studies II (Dublin: Irish Academic Press, 1993), incl. Joseph J. Ryan, 'Assertions of distinction: the modal debate in Irish music', pp. 62–76; Harry White and Nicholas Lawrence, 'Towards a history of the Cecilian movement in Ireland', pp. 78–107; Gerard Gillen, 'William Telford and the Victorian organ in Ireland', pp. 108–28; Andrew Johnstone, 'Incongruous music in an Irish cathedral', pp. 149–63; Nóirin Ní Riain, 'The nature and classification of traditional religious songs in Irish', pp. 190–253.

Gillen, Gerard and Harry White (eds), *Music and Irish Cultural History*, Irish Musical Studies III (Dublin: Irish Academic Press, 1995), incl. Joseph J. Ryan, 'Nationalism and Irish music', pp. 101–15; Frank Heneghan, 'Music in Irish education', pp. 153–98; Harry White, 'Music and the Irish literary imagination', pp. 212–28.

Grindle, W.H., *Irish Cathedral Music* (Belfast: Institute of Irish Studies, QUB, 1989).

Lalor, Brian (ed.), *Encyclopaedia of Ireland* (Dublin: Gill & Macmillan, 2003).

McCarthy, Marie, *Passing It On: The Transmission of Music in Irish Culture* (Cork: Cork University Press, 1999).

Milne, Kenneth (ed.), *Christ Church Cathedral Dublin: A History* (Dublin: Four Courts, 2000), incl. Barra Boydell, 'Music in the nineteenth-century cathedral, 1800–1870', pp. 339–52; Barra Boydell, 'Optimism and decline: music, 1870–*c.*1970', pp. 374–85.

Moloney, Colette, *The Irish Music Manuscripts of Edward Bunting (1773–1843): An Introduction* (Dublin: Irish Traditional Music Archive, 2000).

Pine, Richard and Charles Acton (eds), *To Talent Alone: The Royal Irish Academy of Music 1848–1998* (Dublin: Gill & Macmillan, 1998), incl. Richard Pine, 'Introduction', pp. 1–11; Derek Collins, 'Music in Dublin, 1800–1848', pp. 12–27; Richard Pine, 'Foundations I, 1848–1870', pp. 33–95; Richard Pine, 'Foundations II, 1871–1870'; Jeremy Dibble, 'The composer in the academy (1) 1850–1940', pp. 400–18.

Ryan, Joseph J., 'Nationalism and music in Ireland', PhD dissertation, National University of Ireland, Maynooth (1991).

Shields, Hugh, *Narrative Singing in Ireland: Lays, Ballads, Come-all-yes and Other Songs* (Dublin: Irish Academic Press, 1993).

Vallely, Fintan (ed.), *Companion to Irish Traditional Music* (Cork: Cork University Press, 1999).

Walsh, T. J., *Opera in Dublin 1798–1820* (Oxford: Oxford University Press, 1993).

White, Harry, *The Keeper's Recital: Music and Cultural History in Ireland, 1770–1970* Field Day Critical Conditions Series (Cork: Cork University Press and Indiana: University of Notre Dame Press, 1998).

White, Harry and Nicholas Carolan, 'Ireland', in Stanley Sadie (ed.), *The New Grove Dictionary of Music and Musicians*, 2nd edn (London: Macmillan, 2001), XII, pp. 556–68.

White, Harry and Michael Murphy (eds), *Musical Constructions of Nationalism: Essays on the History and Ideology of European Musical Culture 1800–1945* (Cork: Cork University Press, 2001), incl. Joseph Ryan, 'The tone of defiance', pp. 197–211; Harry White, 'Nationalism, colonialism and the cultural stasis of music in Ireland', pp. 256–70.

CHAPTER 11: THE IRISH DIASPORA IN THE NINETEENTH CENTURY

This text has been greatly improved by the painstaking criticism of the editors and of an anonymous reader. The usual disclaimer applies with particular emphasis.

1    As a small sample see the bibliographies in Donald M. MacRaild, *Irish Migrants in Modern Britain 1750–1922* (Houndmills: Macmillan, 1999); Kevin Kenny, *The American Irish: A History* (Harlow: Longman, 2000); Roger Swift and Sheridan Gilley (eds), *The Irish in Victorian Britain: The Local Dimension* (Dublin: Four Courts, 1999); Robert J. Grace, *The Irish in Quebec: An Introduction to the Historiography* (Québec: Institut québécois de recherche sur la culture, 1993); Ann M. Shea and Marion R. Casey, *The Irish Experience in New York City: A Select Bibliography* (New York: New York Irish History Roundtable, 1995); Patrick J. Blessing, *The Irish in America: A Guide to the Literature and the Manuscript Collections* (Washington, DC: Catholic University of America Press, 1992); Patrick O'Farrell, *The Irish in Australia: 1788 to the Present* (Cork: Cork University Press, 2001). David N. Doyle, 'Cohesion and diversity in the Irish diaspora', *IHS* 21, 123 (1999), pp. 411–34, provides a remarkably wide-ranging and incisive survey of recent work.

2 Donald M. MacRaild, *Culture, Conflict and Migration: The Irish in Victorian Cumbria* (Liverpool: Liverpool University Press, 1998), p. 212. Roger Swift and Sheridan Gilley (eds), *The Irish in Britain: 1815–1939* (London: Pinter; Savage, Md.: Barnes & Noble, 1989).

3 New periodicals include the *Journal of Scotch–Irish Studies* (1, 2000–), *Radharc* (1, 2000–) and the *Australian Journal of Irish Studies* (1, 2001–). The contents up to 2002 of an older specialised journal, *New York Irish History* (1986–) can be accessed at http://www.irishnyhistory.com/NYIH.htm. Notable is the Special Issue of *Éire-Ireland* 36, 1 & 2 (2001), edited by Kevin Kenny, devoted to Irish-America (Part 1: to 1900).

4 Michael Glazier (ed.), *Encyclopedia of the Irish in America* (South Bend: Notre Dame University Press, 1999).

5 Patrick O'Sullivan (ed.), *The Irish World Wide*, 6 vols (London: Leicester University Press): *Patterns of Migration* (1992); *The Irish in the New Communities* (1992); *The Creative Migrant* (1994); *Irish Women and Irish Migration* (1995); *Religion and Identity* (1996); *The Meaning of the Famine* (1997).

6 Mary Hickman, '"Locating" the Irish diaspora', *Irish Journal of Sociology* 11, 2 (2002), pp. 8–26, offers invigorating insight from a sympathetic perspective into the potential and problems of the term in current discourse. Patrick O'Sullivan, 'Developing Irish diaspora studies: a personal view', *New Hibernia Review* 7, 1 (2003), pp. 130–48 provides a meditation on the whole issue which should promote intense reflection by students of the nineteenth-century diaspora.

7 Donald Harman Akenson, 'No petty people: Pakeha history and the historiography of the Irish diaspora', in Lyndon Fraser (ed.), *A Distant Shore: Irish Migration and New Zealand Settlement* (Dunedin: University of Otago Press, 2000), p. 18.

8 For a discussion of the Hansen thesis see Peter Kivisto and Dag Blanck (eds), *American Immigrants and their Generations* (Urbana: University of Illinois Press, 1990).

9 Michael Hout and Joshua R. Goldstein, 'How 4.5 million Irish immigrants became 40 million Irish Americans: demographic and subjective aspects of the ethnic composition of white Americans', *American Sociological Review* 59 (1994), pp. 64–82.

10 Donald Harman Akenson, *The Irish Diaspora: A Primer* (Belfast: Institute of Irish Studies, QUB, 1993), p. 225 and p. 302 nn. 8, 9.

11 Cormac Ó Gráda, 'A note on nineteenth-century Irish emigration statistics', *Population Studies* 29 (1975), pp. 143–9.

12 David Fitzpatrick, 'Emigration 1801–70', in W. E. Vaughan (ed.), *A New History of Ireland*, v, *Ireland under the Union, 1: 1801–70* (Oxford: Clarendon, 1989), pp. 564ff; David N. Doyle, 'The Irish in North America, 1776–1845', ibid., pp. 682–3, 692–3, 702–5.

13 Donald M. MacRaild, 'Irish immigration and the "condition of England" question: the roots of an historiographical tradition', *Immigrants and Minorities* 14, 1 (1995); Mervyn A. Busteed, Robert I. Hodgson and Thomas F. Kennedy, 'The myth and reality of Irish migrants in mid-nineteenth century Manchester: a preliminary study', in O'Sullivan (ed.), *The Irish in the New Communities*, pp. 26–51; Ruth-Ann M. Harris, *The Nearest Place that Wasn't Ireland: Early Nineteenth Century Labour Migration* (Ames: University of Iowa Press, 1994), p. 26ff.

14 MacRaild, 'Irish immigration', p. 69.

15 David Fitzpatrick, '"A peculiar tramping people": the Irish in Britain, 1801–70', in Vaughan (ed.), *A New History of Ireland*, v, p. 636.

16   David Fitzpatrick, '"A curious middle place": the Irish in Britain 1871–1921', in Swift and Gilley (eds), *The Irish in Britain: 1815–1939*, pp. 10–59.

17   David Fitzpatrick, 'The Irish in Britain, 1871–1921', in W. E. Vaughan (ed.), *A New History of Ireland*, VI, *Ireland under the Union II: 1870–1921* (Oxford: Clarendon 1996), p. 655.

18   Akenson, *The Irish Diaspora*, pp. 149–50.

19   Ibid., p. 200.

20   Frank Neal, *Black '47: Britain and the Famine Irish* (Houndmills: Macmillan, 1998), p. 220.

21   W. J. Lowe, *The Irish in Mid-Victorian Lancashire: The Shaping of a Working-Class Community* (New York: Lang, 1989), p. 47.

22   *IHS* 29, 115 (1995), pp. 423–5.

23   Fitzpatrick, 'Peculiar tramping people', p. 625.

24   Arthur Redford, *Labour Migration in England 1800–1850*, 2nd edn, ed. W. H. Chaloner (Manchester: Manchester University Press, 1964), p. 160.

25   Fitzpatrick, 'Peculiar tramping people', pp. 624–5.

26   Ibid. p. 625.

27   *Report from the Select Committee on Irish Vagrants, with the minutes of evidence taken before them*, HC 1833 (394), xvi, p. 362.

28   Ibid., p. 363.

29   David Fitzpatrick, 'The Irish in Britain: settlers or transients?', in P. Buckland and J. Belchem (eds), *The Irish in British Labour History* (Liverpool: Institute of Irish Studies, University of Liverpool, 1992), p. 1.

30   H. A. Shannon, 'Migration and the growth of London 1841–91', *Economic History Review* 5, 2 (1935), p. 83, n. 1.

31   Rev. John Garwood, *The Million-Peopled City: One-Half of the People of London Made Known to the Other Half* (London, 1853), pp. 245–6.

32   Redford, *Labour Migration*, p. 161.

33   Lynn Hollen Lees, *Exiles of Erin: Irish Migrants in Victorian London* (Ithaca: Cornell University Press, 1979), p. 47.

34   *City Mission Magazine*, 1854, p. 193.

35   Garwood, *The Million-Peopled City*, p. 246.

36   Willliam Pollard-Urquhart, 'Condition of the Irish labourers in the East of London', *Transactions of the National Association for the Promotion of Social Science* (London: Parker, Son & Bourne, 1863), pp. 744–50.

37   Tyler Anbinder, *Five Points* (New York: Free Press, 2001). Rebecca Yamin (ed.), *Tales of Five Points: Working Class Life in Nineteenth-Century New York*, 6 vols (Westchester, PA, 2000); Cormac Ó Gráda, *Black '47 and Beyond: The Great Irish Famine in History, Economy and Memory* (Princeton NJ: Princeton University Press, 1999), pp. 116–20; Charles Dickens, *American Notes* (London: Chapman & Hall, 1842), pp. 42–3.

38   Ellen Skerrett, 'The Irish of Chicago's Hull-House neighbourhood ', in Charles Fanning (ed.), *New Perspectives on the Irish Diaspora* (Carbondale: Southern Illinois University Press, 2000), pp. 189–222, esp. 191–2.

39   Fitzpatrick, 'Peculiar tramping people', p. 636.

40   Ibid., pp. 636–7.

41   Ibid., p. 637.

42  Michael B. Katz, *The People of Hamilton, Canada West* (Cambridge, Mass: Harvard University Press, 1975), p. 110; Fitzpatrick, 'Emigration, 1801–70', p. 564.

43  Fitzpatrick, 'Emigration, 1801–70', p. 564.

44  Katz, *Hamilton*, pp. 103, 106.

45  Ibid., pp. 115–16.

46  Fitzpatrick, 'Emigration, 1801–70', p. 564.

47  Hasia Diner, '"The most Irish city in the Union": the era of the Great Migration, 1844–1877', in Ronald J. Bayor and Timothy J. Meagher (eds), *The New York Irish* (Baltimore: Johns Hopkins University Press, 1996), p. 93.

48  Joseph P. Ferrie, *Yankeys Now: Immigrants in the Antebellum United States, 1840–1860* (New York: Oxford University Press, 1999), pp. 144–5.

49  Ibid., p. 185.

50  Stephen Thernstrom, *Poverty and Progress: Social Mobility in a Nineteenth-Century City* (Cambridge, Mass: Harvard University Press, 1964); *The Other Bostonian: Poverty and Progress in the American Metropolis, 1880–1970* (Cambridge, Mass: Harvard University Press, 1973).

51  Ferrie, *Yankeys Now*, p. 210.

52  Harris, *The Nearest Place*, pp. 168, 156.

53  Fitzpatrick, 'Peculiar tramping people', p. 624.

54  E. J. Hobsbawm, 'The tramping artisan', *Economic History Review* 2nd ser., III (1951), pp. 299–320; Humphrey R. Southall, 'The tramping artisan revisits; labour mobility and economic distress in early Victorian England', *Economic History Review* 44, 2 (1991), pp. 272–96, at p. 273.

55  Southall, 'The tramping artisan', p. 291.

56  M. A. G. Ó Tuathaigh, 'The Irish in nineteenth-century Britain: problems of integration', originally in *Transactions of the Royal Historical Society* 5th series, 31 (1981), pp. 149–73, reprinted in Roger Swift and Sheridan Gilley (eds), *The Irish in the Victorian City* (London: Croom Helm, 1985), pp. 13–36, and in Colin Holmes (ed.), *Migration in European History*, I (Cheltenham: Edward Elgar, 1996), pp. 51–75.

57  Southall, 'The tramping artisan', p. 294.

58  See Frank Neal, *Black '47*; and his 'Lancashire, the famine and the poor laws', *Irish Economic and Social History* 22 (1995), pp. 26–48.

59  *Minutes of Evidence taken before the Select Committee on Irremovable Poor*, 22 June 1860, HC 1860 (520), xvii, q. 2533, ev. A. Moore.

60  T. Dillon, 'The Irish in Leeds, 1851–61', *Publications of the Thoresby Society* 54, pt. I, no. 119, 1974, pp. 5–6.

61  See the probing, perceptive approach to this topic in Brenda Collins, 'The Irish in Britain, 1780–1921', in B. J. Graham and L. J. Proudfoot (eds), *Historical Geography of Ireland* (London: Academic Press, 1993), p. 378.

62  Quoted in Fitzpatrick, 'Emigration, 1801–70', p. 601.

63  *Fourth Report from the Select Committee of the HL appointed to inquire into the Operation of the Irish Poor Law*, HC 1849 (365), XVI, 779, ev. Col. W. A. Clarke, q. 7793.

64  Fitzpatrick, 'Emigration, 1801–70', pp. 601–2; Nassau Senior, *Journals, Conversations and Essays Relating to Ireland* (London: Longmans Green, 1868), p. 302.

65   Deirdre Mageean, 'To be matched or to move: Irish women's prospects in Munster', in Christiane Harzig (ed.), *Peasant Maids–City Women: From the European Countryside to Urban America* (Ithaca: Cornell University Press, 1997), p. 83.

66   *Liverpool Times*, quoted by Graham Davis, 'The Irish in Britain, 1815–1939', in Andy Bielenberg (ed.), *The Irish Diaspora* (Harlow and New York: Longman, 2000), p. 19.

67   Owen Dudley Edwards and Patricia J. Storey, 'The Irish press in Victorian Britain', in Swift and Gilley (eds), *The Irish in the Victorian City*, pp. 158–78, provide a tantalising taste of the potential riches awaiting the labourers in the bigger vineyard of the indigenous press.

68   Grace Neville, '"Land of the fair, land of the free: the myth of America in Irish folklore', in Anthony Coulson (ed.), *Exiles and Migrants: Crossing Thresholds in European Culture and Society* (Brighton: Sussex Academic Press, 1997), pp. 57–71.

69   Arnold Schrier, *Ireland and the American Emigration* (Minneapolis: University of Minnesota Press, 1958).

70   Kerby Miller, *Emigrants and Exiles* (Oxford: Clarendon, 1985).

71   Kerby Miller, David N. Doyle, Bruce Boling and Arnold Schrier (eds), *Irish Immigrants in the Land of Canaan: Letters and Memoirs from Colonial and Revolutionary America, 1675–1815* (New York: Oxford University Press, 2003).

72   David Fitzpatrick, *Oceans of Consolation: Personal Accounts of Irish Migration to Australia* (Cork: Cork University Press, 1994).

73   Cecil J. Houston and William J. Smyth, *Irish Emigration and Canadian Settlement: Patterns, Links and Letters* (Toronto: University of Toronto Press, 1990); Lawrence W. McBride (ed.), *The Reynolds Letters: An Irish Emigrant Family in Late Victorian Manchester* (Cork: Cork University Press, 1999); Angela McCarthy, '"In Prospect of a Happier Future": private Letters and Irish women's migration to New Zealand, 1840–1925', in Fraser (ed.), *A Distant Shore*, pp. 105–16; Ruth-Ann M. Harris, 'Come all you courageously; Irish women in America write home', *Éire-Ireland* 36, 1 & 2 (2001), pp. 166–84.

74   Suellen Hoy and Margaret MacCurtain, *From Dublin to New Orleans: Nora and Alice's Journey to America, 1889* (Dublin: Attic Press, 1994), p. 138.

75   Bernard Canavan, 'Story-tellers and writers: Irish identity in emigrant labourers' autobiographies 1870–1970', in O'Sullivan (ed.), *Creative Migrant*, pp. 154–69.

76   For an impressive analysis see Virginia Yans-McLaughlin, 'Metaphors of self in history: subjectivity, oral narrative, and immigration studies', in Virginia Yans-McLaughlin (ed.), *Immigration Reconsidered: History, Sociology, and Politics* (New York: Oxford University Press, 1990), pp. 254–90.

77   Lowe, *The Irish in Mid-Victorian Lancashire*, pp. 2–3.

78   MacRaild, *Culture, Conflict and Migration*; MacRaild, 'Wherever Orange is worn: Orangeism and Irish migration in the nineteenth and early twentieth centuries', *Canadian Journal of Irish Studies* 28, 2 (2002), pp. 98–117; Michael Cottrell, 'Green and Orange in mid-nineteenth century Toronto: the Guy Fawkes Day episode of 1864', *Canadian Journal of Irish Studies* 19, 1 (1993), pp. 12–21; Elaine McFarland, *Protestants First: Orangism in Nineteenth Century Scotland* (Edinburgh: Edinburgh University Press, 1990).

79   Graham Walker, 'The Protestant Irish in Scotland', in T. M. Devine (ed.), *Irish Immigration and Scottish Society in the Nineteenth and Twentieth Centuries* (Edinburgh: John Donald, 1991), pp. 44–66.

80  John Foster, Muir Houston and Chris Madigan, 'Distinguishing Catholics and Protestants among Irish immigrants to Clydeside: a new approach to immigration and ethnicity in Victorian Britain', *Irish Studies Review* 10, 2 (2002), pp. 171–220.

81  F. S. L. Lyons, *Culture and Anarchy in Ireland* (Oxford: Clarendon: 1980), p. 25.

82  Akenson, *The Irish Diaspora*, pp. 28ff.

83  Ibid., p. 219.

84  See relevant entries in bibliography for a sample.

85  Fitzpatrick, 'Peculiar tramping people', p. 651.

86  O'Farrell, *Irish in Australia*, p. 299.

87  O'Farrell, 'Writing the history of Irish-Australia', in Oliver MacDonagh and W. F. Mandle (eds), *Ireland and Irish-Australia: Studies in Cultural and Political History* (London; Croom Helm, 1986), p. 227.

88  Sheridan Gilley, 'English attitudes to the Irish in England, 1789–1900', in Colin Holmes (ed.), *Immigrants and Minorities in British Society* (London: Allen & Unwin, 1978), p. 84.

89  Andrew Greeley, 'Achievement of the Irish in America', in Glazier (ed.), *Encyclopedia*, pp. 1–4.

90  David R. Roediger, *The Wages of Whiteness: Race and the Making of the American Working Class* (London: Verso, 1991); Matthew Frye Jacobson, *Special Sorrows: The Diasporic Imagination of Irish, Polish and Jewish Immigrants in the United States*, rev. edn (Berkeley: University of California Press, 2002).

91  L. Perry Curtis, Jr, *Apes and Angels: The Irishman in Victorian Caricature*, rev. edn (Washington: Smithsonian Press, 1997), pp. 109ff; Gilley, 'English attitudes', in Holmes (ed.), *Immigrants and Minorities*, pp. 90–1; R. F. Foster, *Paddy and Mr Punch* (Harmondsworth: Penguin, 1993).

92  Frank Neal, 'The foundations of the Irish settlement in Newcastle upon Tyne: the evidence in the 1851 Census', in Donald M. MacRaild (ed.), *The Great Famine and Beyond: Irish Migrants in Britain in the Nineteenth and Twentieth Centuries* (Dublin: Irish Academic Press, 2000), pp. 71–93.

93  Fitzpatrick 'Peculiar tramping people', p. 623.

94  Ibid.

95  Ibid.

96  Davis, 'Irish in Britain', in Bielenberg (ed.), *Diaspora*, pp. 19–36; Richard B. McCready, 'Revising the Irish in Scotland; the Irish in nineteenth-and early twentieth-century Scotland', in Bielenberg, ibid., pp. 37–50.

97  Lyons, *Culture and Anarchy*, p. 7, n. 12.

98  Paul O'Leary, *Immigration and Integration: The Irish in Wales 1798–1922* (Cardiff: University of Wales Press, 2000).

99  David Fitzpatrick, 'The Irish in Britain, 1871–1921', in Vaughan (ed.), *New History of Ireland*, VI, pp. 675.

100 Sheridan Gilley, 'Roman Catholicism and the Irish in England', in MacRaild (ed), *The Great Famine*, p. 149, and Gilley, 'Irish Catholicism in Britain', in Donal Kerr (ed.), *Religion, State and Ethnic Groups* (Aldershot: European Science Foundation, 1992), p. 242. Despite the 'Britain' of the latter title, the text distinguishes regularly between England and Scotland. For an early indication in Gilley's work of the importance of the distinction between

Protestant perspectives in the two countries, see his 'Protestant London, No-popery and the Irish poor, 1830–60 (Part I)', *Recusant History* 10, 4 (1970), p. 212.

101 Steven Fielding, *Class and Ethnicity: Irish Catholics in England, 1880–1939* (Buckingham: Open University Press, 1993), p. xiii.

102 McCready, 'Revising the Irish', p. 39.

103 Devine (ed.), *Irish Immigrants*, p. vii.

104 See entries in bibliography under named authors.

105 Akenson, *The Irish Diaspora*, p. 5.

106 Akenson, 'Irish lives: confession of a biographical recidivist', in Rebecca Pelan (ed.), *Irish-Australian Studies: Papers Delivered at the Seventh Irish-Australian Conference July 1993* (Sydney: Crossing Press, 1994), pp. 139–40. See also Akenson, *The Irish Diaspora*, p. 91.

107 Editorial in Pelan, *Irish-Australian Studies*, pp. iv–v.

108 See the thoughtful critiques by Val Noone, 'Commentary and analysis. Publications from the Irish-Australian Conferences', in Philip Bull, Frances Devlin-Glass and Helen Doyle (eds), *Ireland and Australia, 1798–1998: Studies in Culture, Identity and Migration* (Sydney: Crossing Press: 2000), pp. 349–66, and Bob Reece, 'Writing about the Irish in Australia', in John O'Brien and Pauric Travers (eds), *The Irish Emigrant Experience in Australia* (Swords: Poolbeg, 1991), pp. 226–42.

109 Malcolm Campbell, 'Exploring comparative history: the Irish in Australia and the United States', in Pelan (ed.), *Irish-Australian Studies*, pp. 342–54; for an expanded version, see Campbell, 'The other immigrants: comparing the Irish in Australia and the United States', *Journal of American Ethnic History* 14, 3 (1995), pp. 3–22.

110 For an informative overview of the current situation, see Thomas Bender (ed.), *Rethinking American History in a Global Age* (Berkeley: University of California Press, 2002).

111 Kevin Kenny, 'Diaspora and comparison: the global Irish as a case-study', *Journal of American History* 90 (2003), pp. 134–62.

112 Lawrence J. McCaffrey, 'Diaspora comparisons and Irish-American uniqueness', in Charles Fanning (ed.), *New Perspectives on the Irish Diaspora* (Carbondale: Southern Illinois University Press, 2000), p. 24.

113 Oscar Handlin, *Boston's Immigrants 1790–1865; A Study in Acculturation* (Cambridge, Mass: Harvard University Press, 1941).

114 See entries in bibliography under named authors.

115 Timothy J. Meagher, *Inventing Irish America* (South Bend: University of Notre Dame Press, 2001); Bayor and Meagher (eds), *The New York Irish*.

116 McCaffrey, 'Diaspora comparisons', p. 25.

117 Akenson, *The Irish Diaspora*, pp. 228–9.

118 Patrick O'Farrell, 'The Irish in Australia and New Zealand, 1870–1990', in W. E. Vaughan (ed.), *A New History of Ireland*, VI, p. 704.

119 Cormac Ó Gráda and Tim Dyson (eds), *Famine Demography* (Oxford: Clarendon, 2002); Robert Scally, 'External forces in the Famine emigration from Ireland', in E. Margaret Crawford (ed.), *The Hungry Stream: Essays on Emigration and Famine* (Belfast: Institute of Irish Studies, QUB, 1997), pp. 17–24; Harris, *Nearest Place*, n. 163, p. 226.

120 Bernard Aspinwall, 'A long journey: the Irish in Scotland', in O'Sullivan (ed.), *Religion and Identity*, p. 147.

121 See James S. Donnelly, Jr, 'Constructing the memory of the Famine', in Donnelly, *The Great Irish Potato Famine* (Thrupp, Stroud: Sutton, 2001), pp. 209–45.

122 Edward Norman, *A History of Modern Ireland* (London: Penguin, 1971), pp. 116–17; Mary E. Daly, *A Social and Economic History of Ireland* (Dublin: Education Company, 1981), p. 24.

123 J. Mokyr, *Why Ireland Starved* (London: Allen & Unwin, 1983), pp. 264ff; C. Ó Gráda, *Ireland: A New Economic History, 1780–1939* (Oxford: Clarendon, 1994), pp. 178ff.

124 W. E. Vaughan, *Landlords and Tenants in mid-Victorian Ireland* (Oxford: Clarendon, 1994), pp. 28 and 230–1.

125 Tim P. O'Neill, 'Famine evictions', in Carla King (ed.), *Famine, Land and Culture in Ireland* (Dublin: UCD Press, 2000), p. 48.

126 Crawford (ed.), *The Hungry Stream*. Michael Quigley, 'Grosse Île: the most important and evocative Great Famine site outside of Ireland', in ibid., pp. 25–40; Trevor Parkhill, '"Permanent deadweight": emigration from Ulster workhouses during the Famine', ibid., pp. 87–100; Patrick J. Duffy, 'Emigrants and the estate office in the mid-nineteenth century: a compassionate relationship?', ibid., pp. 71–86; Neal, 'Black '47: Liverpool and the Famine Irish', ibid., pp. 123–36; Edward T. O'Donnell, '"The scattered debris of the Irish nation": the Famine Irish and New York City, 1845–55', ibid., pp. 49–60; Brenda Collins, 'The linen industry and emigration to Britain during the mid-nineteenth century', ibid., pp. 151–60.

127 E. Margaret Crawford, 'Migrant maladies: unseen lethal baggage', in Crawford (ed.), *Hungry Stream*, pp. 137–50; Laurence M. Geary, 'Famine, fever and the bloody flux'; in Cathal Poirteir (ed.), *The Great Irish Famine* (Cork: Mercier, 1995), pp. 74–85; Geary, 'What people died of during the famine', in Cormac Ó Gráda (ed.), *Famine 150: Commemorative Lecture Series* (Dublin: Teagasc/UCD, 1997), pp. 95–111; Geary, 'The late disastrous epidemic: medical relief and the Great Famine', in Chris Morash and Richard Hayes (eds), *'Fearful Realities': New Perspectives on the Famine* (Dublin: Irish Academic Press, 1996), pp. 49–59; Geary, 'A psychological and sociological analysis of the Great Famine in Ireland', in Robert Dare (ed.), *Food, Power and Community: Essays in the History of Food and Drink* (Kent Town, South Australia: Wakefield Press, 1999), pp. 181–92; Geary, '"The living were out of their feeling": a socio-cultural analysis of the great Irish famine', in Brendan Ó Conaire (ed.), *The Famine Lectures: Comhdháil an Chraoibhín* 1995–97 (Boyle: Roscommon County Council, 2001), pp. 308–28; Liam Greenslade, 'White skin, white masks; psychological distress among the Irish in Britain', in O'Sullivan (ed.), *The Irish in the New Communities*, pp. 201–25; Alan M. Kraut, 'Illness and medical care among Irish immigrants in antebellum New York', in Bayor and Meagher (eds), *The New York Irish*, pp. 153–68.

128 Doyle, 'Irish in North America, 1776–1845', p. 700.

129 Marion R. Casey, 'Friends in need: financing emigration from Ireland', *Seaport (New York's History Magazine)* (May, 1996), pp. 30–3; Casey, 'Refractive history: memory and the founders of the Emigrant Savings Bank', *Radharc* 3 (2002), pp. 74–107; Ó Gráda, *Immigrants, Savers and Runners: The Emigrant Industrial Savings Bank in the 1850s* (Dublin: Department of Economics, UCD, 1998).

130 Maureen Murphy (ed.), *The Great Irish Famine Curriculum* (New York: New York State Education Department, 2001). On the important subject of teaching see also Thomas J. Archdeacon, 'The Irish Famine in American school curricula', *Éire-Ireland* 37, 1 & 2 (2002), pp. 130–52; Lawrence Bickford, 'Famine, emigration and Boston', in Crawford,

*Hungry Stream*, pp. 205–12; Evelyn Cardwell, 'Interpreting Famine emigration with children at the Ulster-American Folk Park', ibid., pp. 199–204.

131 Kevin Kenny, 'Teaching Irish-American history', *Journal of American Ethnic History* 21, 4 (2002), pp. 30–9; Jay P. Dolan, 'Comment: teaching Irish-American history', ibid. pp. 40–3; Marion R. Casey, 'Comment: Irish-American studies and undergraduate pedagogy', ibid., pp. 44–50; Timothy J. Meagher, 'Comment: teaching Irish-American history', ibid., pp. 51–4.

132 Timothy J. Meagher, *Inventing Irish America* (South Bend: University of Notre Dame Press, 2001), pp. 14–15.

133 Mary J. Hickman, 'Alternative historiographies of the Irish in Britain; a critique of the segregation/assimilation model', in Swift and Gilley (eds), *The Irish in Victorian Britain*, pp. 236–53; Hickman, 'Incorporating and denationalizing the Irish in England; the role of the Catholic Church', in O'Sullivan (ed.), Hickman, *Religion and Identity*, pp. 196–216; Hickman, *Religion, Class and Identity: The State, the Catholic Church and the Education of the Irish in Britain* (Aldershot: Avebury, 1995).

134 David Fitzpatrick, review of Roger Swift and Sheridan Gilley (eds), *The Irish in Victorian Britain: The Local Dimension*, in *Irish Economic and Social History* 38 (2001), p. 158.

135 Davis McCaughey, 'Patrick O'Farrell on the Irish in Australia', in Bull, Devlin-Glass and Doyle (eds), *Ireland and Australia*, pp. 269–70. For a stimulating survey of the situation in the USA and Canada, see David N. Doyle, 'Irish elites in North America and liberal democracy 1820–1920', *Radharc* 3 (2002), pp. 51–73.

136 Philip Gleason, 'Higher education', in Glazier (ed.), *Encyclopedia*; Janet Nolan, 'Education; Irish-American teachers in public schools: 1880–1920', in ibid.

137 Anne O'Connell, '"Take care of the immigrant girls": The migration process of late nineteenth-century Irish women', *Éire-Ireland* 35, 3 & 4 (2000–1), pp. 102–33.

138 Paul O'Leary, 'From the cradle to the grave; popular Catholicism among the Irish in Wales', in O'Sullivan (ed.), *Religion and Identity*, p. 192.

139 Marc. C. Foley and Timothy W. Guinnane, 'Did Irish marriage patterns survive the emigrant voyage? Irish-American nuptiality, 1880–1920', *Irish Economic and Social History* 26 (1999), pp. 15–34.

140 The Yale-centred research in progress by Guinnane and Ó Gráda promises to greatly deepen understanding of the crucial demographic variables.

141 Neal, *Black '47*, p. 178.

142 Ibid., p. 11. See too the perceptive critique of census, and other, evidence, in Roger Swift, 'The historiography of the Irish in nineteenth-century Britain: some perspectives', in O'Sullivan (ed.), *The Irish World Wide*, 11, *The Irish in the New Communities*, pp. 52–81.

143 Quoted by P. L. Garside, 'London and the Home Counties', in F. M. L. Thompson (ed.), *The Cambridge Social History of Britain, 1750–1950*, 1 (Cambridge: Cambridge University Press, 1990), p. 498, in the course of his own warnings about possible pitfalls in the use of census material, pp. 498–500.

144 Patrick Joyce, 'Work', in Thompson (ed.), *Cambridge History*, 11 (1990), p. 143.

145 O'Sullivan (ed.), *The Irish World Wide*, 1, *Patterns of Migration*, p. xv; Mick Moloney, *Far from the Shamrock Shore* (New York; Crown Books, 2002); W. H. A. Williams, *Twas Only an Irishman's Dream: The Image of Ireland and the Irish in American Popular Song Lyrics, 1800–1920* (Urbana: University of Illinois Press, 1996); John P. Cullinane, 'Irish dance

world-wide; Irish emigrants and the shaping of traditional Irish dance', in O'Sullivan (ed.), *Creative Migrant*, pp. 192–210.

146 Mervyn Busteed, 'Little Islands of Erin: Irish settlement and identity in mid-nineteenth-century Manchester', in MacRaild (ed.), *Great Famine*, pp. 116–22; '"I shall never return to Hibernia's bowers": Irish migrant identities in early Victorian Manchester', *The North West Geographer* 2 (2000), pp. 15–30, and his further articles there cited.

147 O'Sullivan (ed.), *Patterns of Migration*, p. xv; Fanning (ed.), *New Perspectives*, editor's introduction, passim.

148 See, for instance, Keith Thomas, *History and Literature* (Swansea: University College of Swansea, 1988).

149 Colleen McDannell, 'Catholicism and the Irish-American male', *American Studies* 27, 2 (1986), p. 31.

150 Chris McConville, 'Patrick O'Farrell on the Irish in Australia', in Philip Bull, Chris McConville and Noel McLachlan (eds), *Irish-Australian Studies* (Melbourne: La Trobe University, 1991), p. 260.

151 See entries in bibliography under named authors.

152 See Frank Neal's reservations about some of Williamson's conclusions, 'The foundations of Irish settlement in Newcastle-upon-Tyne: the evidence in the 1851 census', in MacRaild (ed.), *The Great Famine*, p. 93, n. 16.

153 *Sixth report from the select committee on settlement, and poor removal; together with the minutes of evidence and appendix*, HC 1847(409), xi, qs. 4048, 4051, ev. J. Beckwith, q. 4053, ev. C. Heaps.

154 Ferrie, *Yankeys*, pp. 120–2.

155 See, for instance, Mike Cronin and David Mayall (eds), *Sporting Nationalisms: Identity, Ethnicity, Immigration and Assimilation* (London: Cass, 1998); Jerrold Casway, 'Baseball: the early years', in Glazier (ed.), *Encyclopedia*, pp. 42–7.

156 Patrick O'Farrell, 'Patrick O'Farrell on the Irish in Australia', in Bull et al. (eds), *Irish-Australian Studies*, p. 273.

157 Ibid.; Patrick O'Farrell, 'Writing the history of Irish-Australia', in Oliver MacDonagh and W. F. Mandle (eds), *Ireland and Irish-Australia: Studies in Cultural and Political History* (London: Croom Helm, 1986), pp. 218–19; O'Farrell, 'Varieties of New Zealand Irishness', in Fraser (ed.), *A Distant Shore*, pp. 25–35.

158 Lawrence J. McCaffrey, *Textures of Irish America* (Syracuse: Syracuse University Press, 1992), pp. xi–xiv.

159 Graham Davis, 'The Irish in Britain, 1815–1939', in Bielenberg (ed.), *The Irish Diaspora*, p. 19.

160 Andy Bielenberg, 'Irish emigration to the British Empire, 1700–1914', in Bielenberg (ed.), *The Irish Diaspora*, pp. 215–34.

161 Gilley, 'Roman Catholicism and the Irish', in MacRaild (ed.), *The Great Famine*, pp. 147–8, has pertinent observations on the difficulty for secularists in understanding the role of religion in general, and Catholicism in particular.

162 For an avowedly 'Revisionist' perspective on diaspora research, see Alan O'Day, 'Revising the diaspora', in D. G. Boyce and Alan O'Day (eds), *The Making of Modern Irish History: Revisionism and the Revisionist Controversy* (London: Routledge, 1996), pp. 188–215. Some of the themes in the present survey are also noted, with reference to the USA, in J. J. Lee, 'Millennial reflections on Irish-American history', *Radharc* 1 (2000), pp. 1–76.

# Select Bibliography

❋

*For abbreviations used in the Select Bibliography see p. 223.*

Aalen, F. H. A., *The Iveagh Trust: The First Hundred Years, 1890–1990* (Dublin: Iveagh Trust, 1990).

Aalen, F. H. A., 'Constructive unionism and the shaping of modern Ireland', *Rural History* 4 (1993), pp. 137–64.

Aalen, F. H. A., 'Health and housing in Dublin c.1850–1921', in Aalen and Whelan (eds), *Dublin City and County*, pp. 279–304.

Aalen, F. H. A. and Kevin Whelan (eds), *Dublin City and County: From Prehistory to Present* (Dublin: Geography Publications, 1992).

Aalen, F. H. A., Kevin Whelan and Matthew Stout (eds), *Atlas of the Irish Rural Landscape* (Cork: Cork University Press, 1997).

Acheson, Alan, *A History of the Church of Ireland* (Dublin: Columba, 1997).

Agnew, Jean (ed.), *The Drennan–McTier Letters, 1776–1819*, 3 vols (Dublin: Irish Manuscripts Commission/Women's History Project, 1998–9).

Akenson, Donald H., *Small Differences: Irish Catholics and Irish Protestants 1815–1922* (Kingston, Canada:McGill-Queen's University Press, 1988), pp. 135–6.

Akenson, Donald Harman, *The Irish Diaspora: A Primer* (Toronto: P. D. Meaney, 1993).

Akenson, Donald Harman, 'No petty people: Pakeha history and the historiography of the Irish diaspora', in Fraser (ed.), *A Distant Shore*, pp. 12–24.

Akenson, Donald Harman, 'Irish lives: confession of a biographical recidivist', in Pelan (ed.), *Irish-Australian Studies*, pp. 139–50.

Anbinder, Tyler, *Five Points* (New York: Free Press, 2001).

Andrews, J. H., 'Road planning in Ireland before the railway age', *Irish Geography* 5 (1964), pp. 17–41.

Andrews, J. H., *History in the Ordnance Map: An Introduction for Irish Readers* (Dublin: Ordnance Survey of Ireland, 1974; repr. Newton, Montgomeryshire: David Archer, 1993).

Andrews, J. H., *A Paper Landscape: The Ordnance Survey in Nineteenth-Century Ireland* (1st edn, Oxford: Clarendon, 1975; 2nd edn, Dublin: Four Courts, 2002).

Andrews, J. H., *Shapes of Ireland: Maps and Their Makers 1664–1839* (Dublin: Geography Publications, 1997).

Andrews, J. H., 'Jones Hughes's Ireland: a literary quest', in Smyth and Whelan (eds), *Common Ground*, pp. 1–22.

Andrews, J. H., 'Limits of agricultural settlement in pre-Famine Ireland', in Cullen and Furet (eds), *Irlande et France XVIIᵉ–XXᵉ Siècles*, pp. 47–58.

Anon, 'The Irish language in Inishowen', *Donegal Annual* 45 (1993), pp. 29–42.

Anton, Brigitte, 'Women of *The Nation*', *History Ireland* 1, 3 (1993), pp. 34–7.

Archdeacon, Thomas J., 'The Irish Famine in American school curricula', *Éire-Ireland* 37, 1 & 2 (2002), pp. 130–52.

Arensberg, Conrad M. and Solon T. Kimball, *Family and Community in Ireland*, 3rd edn ([1940]; Ennis: Clasp Press, 2001).

Arts Council of Great Britain, *Daniel Maclise* (London: National Portrait Gallery, 1972).

Aspinwall, Bernard, 'A long journey: the Irish in Scotland', in O'Sullivan (ed.), *The Irish World Wide*, V, *Religion and Identity*, pp. 146–82.

Aspinwall, Bernard, 'The Catholic Irish and wealth in Glasgow', in Devine (ed.), *Irish Immigration and Scottish Society*, pp. 91–115.

Bane, Liam, *The Bishop in Politics: Life and Career of Jon McEvilly* (Westport: Westport Historical Association, 1993).

Bardon, Jonathan, *A History of Ulster* (Belfast: Blackstaff; updated edn, 2001).

Bareham, Tony (ed.), *Charles Lever: New Evaluations* (Gerrards Cross: Colin Smythe, 1991).

Barrett, Cyril, *Irish Art in the Nineteenth Century*, an exhibition of Irish Victorian art at the Crawford Municipal School of Art (Cork, 1971).

Barrett, Cyril, 'Irish nationalism and art 1800–1921', *Studies* (Winter 1975), pp. 393–409.

Barrett, Cyril and Jeanne Sheehy, 'Visual arts and society 1850–1921', in Vaughan (ed.), *A New History of Ireland*, VI, pp. 436–99.

Barry, Terry (ed.), *A History of Settlement in Ireland* (London: Routledge, 2000).

Bartlett, Thomas, *The Fall and Rise of the Irish Nation: The Catholic Question 1690–1830* (Dublin: Gill & Macmillan, 1992).

Bartlett, Thomas and Keith Jeffery (eds), *A Military History of Ireland* (Cambridge: Cambridge University Press, 1996).

Bayor, Ronald H. and Timothy J. Meagher (eds), *The New York Irish* (Baltimore, MD: Johns Hopkins University Press, 1996).

Belchem, John (ed.), *Popular Politics, Riot and Labour: Essays in Liverpool History 1790–1940* (Liverpool: Liverpool University Press, 1992).

Belchem, John, 'Republican spirit and military science: the "Irish Brigade" and Irish-American nationalism in 1848', *IHS* 24, 113 (1994), pp. 44–64.

Belchem, John, '"Freedom and friendship to Ireland": Ribbonism in early-nineteenth century Liverpool', *International Review of Social History* 39 (1994), pp. 33–56.

Belchem, John, 'Nationalism, republicanism and exile: Irish emigrants and the revolution of 1848', *Past and Present* 146 (1995), pp. 103–35.

Belchem, John, 'The Irish in Britain, United States and Australia: some comparative reflections on labour history', in Buckland and Belchem (eds), *Irish in British Labour History*, pp. 19–28.

Belchem, John, 'The Liverpool-Irish enclave', in MacRaild (ed.), *The Great Famine and Beyond*, pp. 128–46.

Belchem, John, 'The immigrant alternative: ethnic and sectarian mutuality among the Liverpool Irish during the 19th century', in O. Ashton, R. Fyson, and S. Roberts (eds), *The Duty of Discontent: Essays for Dorothy Thompson* (London: Mansell, 1995), pp. 231–50.

Bell, Jonathan, 'Changing farming methods in Donegal', in Nolan, Ronayne and Dunlevy (eds), *Donegal: History and Society*, pp. 471–90.

Bernstein, Iver, *The New York City Draft Riots: Their Significance for American Society and Politics in the Age of the Civil War* (New York: Oxford University Press, 1990).

Bew, Paul, *C. S. Parnell* (Dublin: Gill & Macmillan, 1980).

Bew, Paul, *Conflict and Conciliation in Ireland 1890–1910: Parnellites and Radical Agrarians* (Oxford: Clarendon, 1987).

Bew, Paul, *John Redmond* (Dundalk: Historical Association and Dundalgan Press, 1996).

Bew, Paul, 'A vision to the dispossessed? Popular piety and revolutionary politics in the Irish Land War, 1879–82', in Devlin and Fanning (eds), *Religion and Rebellion*, pp. 137–51.

Bhreathnach-Lynch, Síghle, 'Framing the Irish: Victorian paintings of the Irish peasant', *Journal of Victorian Culture* 2, 2 (1997), pp. 245–63.

Bickford, Lawrence, 'Famine, emigration and Boston', in Crawford (ed.), *The Hungry Stream*, pp. 205–12.

Bielenberg, Andy (ed.), *The Irish Diaspora* (Harlow and New York: Longman, 2000).

Bielenberg, Andy, 'Irish emigration to the British Empire, 1700–1914', in Bielenberg (ed.), *The Irish Diaspora*, pp. 215–34.

Birdwell-Pheasant, Donna, 'The "home place": center and periphery in Irish house and family systems', in Donna Birdwell-Pheasant and Denise Lawrence-Zuniga (eds), *House Life: Space, Place and Family in Europe* (Oxford and New York: Berg, 1999), pp. 105–29.

Bishop, Erin (ed.), *'My Darling Danny': Letters from Mary O'Connell to her Son Daniel, 1830–1832* (Cork: Cork University Press, 1998).

Bishop, Erin, *The World of Mary O'Connell, 1778–1836* (Dublin: Lilliput, 1999).

Black, Eileen, 'Practical patriots and true Irishmen: the Royal Irish Art Union 1839–59', *Irish Arts Review Yearbook* 14 (1998), pp. 140–6.

Black, Ronald, 'Four O'Daly manuscripts', *Éigse* 26 (1992), pp. 43–7.

Blaney, Roger, *Presbyterians and the Irish Language* (Belfast: Institute of Irish Studies, QUB, 1996).

Blessing, Patrick J., *The Irish in America: A Guide to the Literature and the Manuscript Collections* (Washington, DC: Catholic University of America Press, 1992).

Boland, Eavan, *In a Time of Violence* (Manchester: Carcanet, 1994).

Bolster, Evelyn, *A History of the Diocese of Cork: The Episcopate of William Delany, 1847–1886* (Cork: Tower Books, 1993).

Bourke, Angela, *The Burning of Bridget Cleary: A True Story* (London: Pimlico, 1999).

Bourke, Angela, 'The baby and the bathwater: cultural loss in nineteenth-century Ireland', in Foley and Ryder (eds), *Ideology and Ireland in the Nineteenth Century*, pp. 79–92.

Bourke, Angela, Siobhán Kilfeather, Maria Luddy, Margaret MacCurtain, Gerardine Meaney, Máirín Ní Dhonnchadha, Mary O'Dowd and Clair Wills (eds), *Field Day*

*Anthology of Irish Women's Writing*: IV & V, *Irish Women's Writing and Traditions* (Cork: Cork University Press/New York: New York University Press, 2002).

Bourke, Joanna, *Husbandry to Housewifery: Women, Economic Change and Housewifery in Ireland 1890–1914* (Oxford: Clarendon, 1993).

Bowen, Desmond, *History and the Shaping of Irish Protestantism* (New York: Peter Lan, 1995).

Boyce, D. George, *Nineteenth-Century Ireland: The Search for Stability* (Dublin: Gill & Macmillan, 1990).

Boyce, D. George, Robert Eccleshall and Vincent Geoghagan (eds), *Political Thought in Ireland since the Seventeenth Century* (London: Routledge, 1993).

Boyce, D. George and Alan O'Day (eds), *Parnell in Perspective* (London: Routledge, 1991).

Boyce, D. George and Alan O'Day (eds), *The Making of Modern Irish History: Revisionism and the Revisionist Controversy* (London; Routledge, 1996).

Boyce, D. George and Roger Swift (eds), *Problems and Perspectives in Irish History Since 1800* (Dublin: Four Courts, 2004).

Boylan, Thomas and Timothy P. Foley, 'From hedge schools to hegemony: intellectuals, ideology and Ireland in the nineteenth century', in O'Dowd (ed.), *On Intellectuals*, pp. 98–115.

Boylan, Thomas and Tadhg Foley, *Political Economy and Colonial Ireland: The Propagation and Ideological Function of Economic Discourse in the Nineteenth Century* (London: Routledge, 1992).

Bradley, Anthony and Maryann G. Valiulis (eds), *Gender and Sexuality in Modern Ireland* (Amherst: University of Massachusetts Press, 1997).

Brady, Ciaran (ed.), *Ideology and the Historians* (Dublin: Lilliput, 1991).

Brady, Ciaran (ed.), *Interpreting Irish History* (Dublin: Irish Academic Press, 1994).

Breatnach, Pádraig A., 'Meascra ar an saol in Éirinn, 1841–44', *Éigse* 25 (1991), pp. 105–12.

Brewer, John D. and Gareth I. Higgins, *Anti-Catholicism in Northern Ireland, 1600–1998: The Mote and the Beam* (New York: St Martin's, 1998).

Briggs, Sarah, Paul Hyland and Neil Sammells (eds), *Reviewing Ireland: Essays and Interviews from Irish Studies Review* (Bath: Sulis, 1998).

Brihault, J. (ed.), *L'Irlande et Ses Langues* (Rennes: Presses Universitaires de Rennes n. d. [1992]).

Brockliss, Laurence and David Eastwood (eds), *A Union of Multiple Identities: The British Isles c.1750–c.1850* (Manchester: Manchester University Press, 1997).

Brown, Stewart J., and David W. Miller (eds), *Piety and Power in Ireland, 1760–1960: Essays in Honour of Emmet Larkin* (Belfast: Institute of Irish Studies, QUB, 2000).

Brown, Terence, *The Life of W. B. Yeats: A Critical Biography* (Dublin: Gill & Macmillan, 1999).

Brożyna, Andrea Ebel, *Labour, Love and Prayer: Female Piety in Ulster Religious Literature 1850–1914* (Belfast: Institute of Irish Studies/Montreal: McGill–Queen's University Press, 1999).

Buckland, Patrick and John Belchem (eds), *The Irish in British Labour History* (Liverpool: Institute of Irish Studies, University of Liverpool, 1992).

Buckley, Anthony D., 'The case of the Cushendall schoolmaster', *The Glynns* 20 (1992), pp. 30–5.

Buckley, David N., *James Fintan Lalor: Radical* (Cork: Cork University Press, 1990).

Bull, Philip, *Land, Politics and Nationalism: A Study of the Irish Land Question* (Dublin: Gill & Macmillan, 1996).

Bull, Philip, Frances Devlin-Glass and Helen Doyle (eds), *Ireland and Australia, 1798–1998. Studies in Culture, Identity and Migration* (Sydney: Crossing Press, 2000).

Bull, Philip, Chris McConville and Noel McLachlan (eds), *Irish-Australian Studies* (Melbourne: La Trobe University, 1991).

Burtchaell, Jack, 'A typology of settlement and society in County Waterford *c.*1850', in Nolan, Power and Cowman (eds), *Waterford: History and Society*, pp. 541–78.

Burtchaell, Jack, 'The demographic impact of the Famine', in Cowman (ed.), *The Famine in Waterford*, pp. 263–88.

Burtchaell, Jack, 'The South Kilkenny farm villages', in Smyth and Whelan (eds), *Common Ground*, pp. 110–23.

Busteed, Mervyn, 'The Irish in nineteenth-century Manchester', *Irish Studies Review* 18 (1997), pp. 8–13.

Busteed, Mervyn, '"I shall never return to Hibernia's bowers": Irish migrant identities in early Victorian Manchester', *The North West Geographer* 2 (2000), pp. 15–30.

Busteed, Mervyn, '"Persons who are in a species of exile": varieties of Irishness amongst Irish migrants in mid-Victorian Manchester', in Norquay and Smyth (eds), *Space and Place*, pp. 57–76.

Busteed, Mervyn, 'Little islands of Érin: Irish settlement and identity in mid-nineteenth-century Manchester', in MacRaild (ed.), *The Great Famine and Beyond*, pp. 94–127.

Busteed, Mervyn and R. I. Hodgson, 'Irish migrant responses to urban life in nineteenth-century Manchester', *Geographical Journal* 16, 2 (1996), pp. 139–53.

Busteed, Mervyn., R. I. Hodgson and P. F. Kennedy, 'The myth and reality of Irish migrants in mid-Victorian Manchester: a preliminary study', in O'Sullivan (ed.), *The Irish World Wide*, II, *The Irish in the New Communities*, pp. 26–51.

Buttimer, Neil, 'A Cork Gaelic text on a Napoleonic campaign', *Journal of the Cork Historical and Archaeological Society* 95 (1990), pp. 107–23.

Buttimer, Neil, 'A Gaelic reaction to Robert Emmet's rebellion', *Journal of the Cork Historical and Archaeological Society* 97 (1992), pp. 36–53.

Buttimer Neil, 'Pláig fhollasach, pláig choimhtheach: obvious plague, strange plague', *Journal of the Cork Historical and Archaeological Society* 102 (1997), pp. 41–68.

Buttimer, Neil, '"A stone on the cairn": the Great Famine in later Gaelic manuscripts', in Morash and Hayes (eds), *'Fearful Realities'*, pp. 93–109.

Buttimer, Neil, 'Gaelic literature and contemporary life in Cork, 1700–1840', in Buttimer and O'Flanagan (eds), *Cork: History and Society*, pp. 585–653.

Buttimer, Neil, 'Degré de perception de la France dans l'Irlande Gaélique de la pré-famine, 1700–1840', in *Irlande et Bretagne: Vingt siècles d'histoire* (Presses Universitaires de Rennes 1994), pp. 178–89.

Buttimer, Neil and P. O'Flanagan (eds), *Cork: History and Society* (Dublin: Geography Publications, 1993), pp. 585–653.

Byrne, Anne, Ricca Edmondson and Tony Varley, 'Arensberg and Kimball and Anthropological Research in Ireland', introduction to Conrad M. Arensberg and Solon T. Kimball, *Family and Community in Ireland*, 3rd edn ([1940]; Ennis: Clasp Press, 2001), pp. i–ci.

Byrne, Anne and Ronit Lentin (eds), *(Re)Searching Women: Feminist Research Methodologies in the Social Sciences in Ireland* (Dublin: IPA, 2000).

Callanan, Frank, *The Parnell Split 1890–91* (Cork: Cork University Press, 1992).

Callanan, Frank, *T. M. Healy* (Cork: Cork University Press, 1996).

Campbell, Julian, *The Irish Impressionists: Irish Artists in France and Belgium* (Dublin: NGI, 1984).

Campbell, Julian, *Nathaniel Hone* (Dublin: NGI, 1991).

Campbell, Malcolm, 'The other immigrants: comparing the Irish in Australia and the United States', *Journal of American Ethnic History* 14, 3 (1995), pp. 3–22.

Campbell, Malcolm, 'Exploring comparative history: the Irish in Australia and the United States', in Pelan (ed.), *Irish-Australian Studies*, pp. 342–54.

Campbell, Malcolm, 'Immigrants on the land: a comparative study of Irish rural settlement in nineteenth-century Minnesota and New South Wales', in Bielenberg (ed.), *The Irish Diaspora*, pp. 176–94.

Campbell, Matthew, 'Lyrical unions: Mangan, O'Hussey and Ferguson', *Irish Studies Review* 8, 3 (2000), pp. 325–38.

Campbell, Matthew, 'Thomas Moore's wild song: the 1821 Irish melodies', *Bullán* 4, 2 (2000), pp. 83–103.

Campbell, S. J., *The Great Irish Famine: Words and Images from the Famine Museum, Strokestown Park, County Roscommon* (Strokestown: Strokestown Famine Museum, 1994).

Canavan, B., 'Story-tellers and writers: Irish identity in emigrant labourers' autobiographies, 1870–1970', in O'Sullivan (ed.), *The Irish World Wide*, III, *The Creative Migrant*, pp. 154–69.

Canavan, Tony (ed.), *'Every Stoney Acre Has a Name': A Celebration of the Townland in Ulster* (Belfast: Federation for Ulster Local Studies, 1991).

Cannavan, Jan, 'Romantic revolutionary Irishwomen: women, Young Ireland and 1848', in Kelleher and Murphy (eds), *Gender Perspectives in Nineteenth-Century Ireland*, pp. 212–20.

Canny, Nicholas P., *Europeans on the Move: Studies on European Migration, 1500–1800* (Oxford: Clarendon, 1994).

Cardwell, Evelyn, 'Interpreting Famine emigration with children at Ulster-American Folk Park', in Crawford (ed.), *The Hungry Stream*, pp. 99–204.

Carroll, Denis, *Unusual Suspects: Twelve Radical Clergy* (Dublin: Columba, 1998).

Carroll, Michael P., *Irish Pilgrimage: Holy Wells and Popular Catholic Devotion* (Baltimore and London: Johns Hopkins University Press, 1999).

Casey, Marion R., 'The Irish', in Kenneth Jackson (ed.), *The Encyclopaedia of New York City* (New Haven, CT: Yale University Press, 1995), pp. 598–602.

Casey, Marion R., 'Friends in need: financing emigration from Ireland', *Seaport* (New York's History Magazine), May 1996, pp. 30–3.

Casey, Marion R., 'Refractive history: memory and the founders of the Emigrant Savings Bank', *Radharc* 3 (2002), pp. 74–107.

Cassell, Ronald D., *Medical Charities, Medical Politics: The Irish Dispensary System and the Poor Law, 1836–1872* (London: Royal Historical Society, 1997).

Cassidy, Tanya M., 'Alcoholism in Ireland', in Cleary and Treacy (eds), *Sociology of Health and Illness*, pp. 176–92.

Chandler, Edward, *Photography in Ireland: The Nineteenth Century* (Dublin: Edmund Burke, 2001).

Chinn, Carl, '"Sturdy Catholic emigrant": the Irish in early Victorian Birmingham', in Swift and Gilley (eds), *The Irish in Victorian Britain*, pp. 52–74.

Chuto, Jacques, *James Clarence Mangan: A Bibliography of his Works* (Dublin: Irish Academic Press, 1999).

Clark, Dennis, *Erin's Heirs: Irish Bonds of Community* (Lexington, Ky: University Press of Kentucky, 1991).

Clark, Samuel, *Social Origins of the Irish Land War* (Princeton NJ: Princeton University Press, 1989).

Clark, Samuel and James S. Donnelly, Jr (eds), *Irish Peasants: Violence and Political Unrest, 1780–1914* (Manchester: Manchester University Press, 1983).

Clarke, H. B. (ed.), *Irish Cities* (Cork: Mercier/Dublin: RTÉ, 1995).

Clarkson, L. A., E. M. Crawford and M. A. Litvack (eds), *The Occupations of Ireland, 1841*, 4 vols (Belfast: Department of Economic and Social History, QUB, 1995).

Clear, Caitriona, *Nuns in Nineteenth-Century Ireland* (Dublin: Gill & Macmillan, 1987).

Cleary, Anne and Margaret P. Treacy (eds), *The Sociology of Health and Illness in Ireland* (Dublin: UCD Press, 1997).

Clyde, Tom, *Irish Literary Magazines: An Outline History and Descriptive Bibliography* (Dublin: Irish Academic Press, 2002).

Cohen, Marilyn (ed.), *The Warp of Ulster's Past: Interdisciplinary Perspectives on the Irish Linen Industry, 1700–1920* (London: Macmillan/New York: St Martin's, 1997).

Cohen, Marilyn, *Linen, Family, and Community in Tullylish, County Down, 1690–1914* (Dublin: Four Courts, 1997).

Cohen, Marilyn and Nancy J. Curtin (eds), *Reclaiming Gender: Transgressive Identities in Modern Ireland* (New York: St Martin's, 1999).

Coleman, Anne, *Riotous Roscommon: Social Unrest in the 1840s* (Dublin, Irish Academic Press, 1999).

Colfer, Billy, *The Hook Peninsula* (Cork: Cork University Press, 2004).

Collins, B., 'The origins of Irish immigration to Scotland in the 19th and 20th centuries', in Devine (ed.), *Irish Immigration and Scottish Society*, pp. 1–18.

Collins, B., 'The Irish in Britain, 1780–1921', in Graham and Proudfoot (eds), *A Historical Geography of Ireland*, pp. 366–98.

Collins, B., 'The linen industry and emigration to Britain during the mid-nineteenth century', in Crawford, (ed.), *The Hungry Stream*, pp. 151–60.

Collins, Peter (ed.), *Nationalism and Unionism: Conflict in Ireland 1885–1921* (Belfast: Institute of Irish Studies, 1994).

Colman, Anne Ulry, *Dictionary of Nineteenth-Century Irish Women Poets* (Galway: Kenny's Bookshop, 1996).

Comerford, R. V., 'Comprehending the Fenians', *Saothar* 17 (1992), pp. 52–7.

Comerford, R. V., 'Fenianism revisited: past-time or revolutionary movement?', *Saothar* 17 (1992), pp. 46–52.

Comerford, R. V., Mary Cullen, Jacqueline R. Hill and Colm Lennon (eds), *Religion, Conflict and Coexistence in Ireland: Essays presented to Monsignor Patrick J. Corish* (Dublin: Gill & Macmillan, 1990).

Comerford, R. V. and Enda Delaney (eds), *National Questions: Reflections on Daniel O'Connell and Contemporary Ireland* (Dublin: Wolfhound, 2000).

Connell, Paul, *Parson, Priest and Master: National Education in Co. Meath, 1824–1841* (Dublin: Irish Academic Press, 1995).

Connolly, Claire and Stephen Copley (eds), Sydney Owenson (Lady Morgan), *The Wild Irish Girl* (1806; new edn, London: Pickering & Chatto, 2000).

Connolly, S. J. (ed.), *The Oxford Companion to Irish History* (Oxford: Clarendon, 1998; rev edn 2002).

Connolly, S. J. (ed.), *Kingdoms United? Integration and Diversity* (Dublin: Four Courts, 1999).

Connolly, S. J., 'Popular culture: patterns of change and adaptation', in Connolly et al., *Conflict, Identity and Economic Development*, pp. 103–13.

Connolly, S. J., R. A. Houston and R. J. Morris (eds), *Conflict, Identity and Economic Development: Ireland and Scotland 1600–1939* (Preston: Carnegie, 1995).

Cook, S. B. *Imperial Affinities: Nineteenth-Century Analogies and Exchanges Between India and Ireland* (New Delhi, Newbury Park and London: Sage, 1992).

Cooney, Dudley Livingstone, *The Methodists in Ireland: A Short History* (Blackrock: Columba, 2001).

Cooper, David (ed.), *The Petrie Collection of the Ancient Music of Ireland* (Cork: Cork University Press, 2002).

Corbett, Mary Jean, *Allegories of Union in Irish and English Writing, 1790–1870* (Cambridge: Cambridge University Press, 2000).

Corish, Patrick, *Maynooth College, 1795–1995* (Dublin: Gill & Macmillan, 1995).

Corkery, Daniel, *Synge and Anglo-Irish Literature* (1931; Cork: Mercier, 1966).

Corrigan, Karen P., '"For God's sake, teach the children English": emigration and the Irish language in the nineteenth century', in O'Sullivan (ed.), *The Irish World Wide*, II, *The Irish in the New Communities*, pp. 143–61.

Côté, Jane McL., *Fanny and Anna Parnell: Ireland's Patriot Sisters* (Dublin: Gill & Macmillan, 1991).

Cottrell, Michael, 'Green and Orange in mid-nineteenth century Toronto: the Guy Fawkes day episode of 1864', *Canadian Journal of Irish Studies* 28, 2 (July 1993), pp. 12–21.

Coulson, Anthony (ed.), *Exiles and Migrants: Crossing Thresholds in European Culture and Society* (Brighton: Sussex Academic Press, 1997).

Coulter, Carol, *The Hidden Tradition: Feminism, Women and Nationalism in Ireland* (Cork: Cork University Press, 1995).

Cowman, Des (ed.), *The Famine in Waterford 1845–1850: Teacht na bPrátaí Dubha* (Dublin: Geography Publications, 1995), pp. 263–88.

Cowman, Des, 'Trade and society in Waterford City 1800–1840', in Nolan and Power (eds), *Waterford: History and Society*, pp. 427–59.

Crawford, E. Margaret (ed.), *The Hungry Stream: Essays on Famine and Emigration* (Belfast: Institute of Irish Studies, 1997).

Crawford, E. Margaret, 'Migrant maladies: unseen lethal baggage', in Crawford (ed.), *The Hungry Stream*, pp. 137–50.

Crawford, John, *St Catherine's Parish, Dublin, 1840–1900: Portrait of a Church of Ireland Community* (Dublin: Irish Academic Press, 1996).

Crawford, W. H. and R. H. Foy (eds), *Townlands in Ulster: Local History Studies* (Belfast: Ulster Historical Foundation and Federation of Ulster Local Studies, 1998).

Cronin, Maura, *Country, Class or Craft? The Politicization of the Skilled Artisan in Nineteenth-Century Cork* (Cork: Cork University Press, 1994).

Crookshank, Anne and the Knight of Glin, *Irish Portraits 1660–1860* (London: Paul Mellon Foundation for British Art, 1969).

Crookshank, Anne and the Knight of Glin, *The Painters of Ireland c. 1660–1920* (London: Barrie & Jenkins, 1978).

Crookshank, Anne and the Knight of Glin, *The Watercolours of Ireland: Works on Paper, in Pencil, Pastel and Paint, c. 1660–1914* (London: Barrie & Jenkins, 1994).

Crookshank, Anne and the Knight of Glin, *Ireland's Painters 1600–1940* (New Haven and London: Yale University Press, 2002).

Crossman, Virginia, *Local Government in Nineteenth-Century Ireland* (Belfast: Institute of Irish Studies, QUB, 1994).

Crossman, Virginia, *Politics, Law and Order in Nineteenth-Century Ireland* (Dublin: Gill & Macmillan, 1996).

Crotty, R. D., *Irish Agricultural Production: Its Volume and Structure* (Cork: Cork University Press, 1966).

Crowley, Tony, 'Forging the nation: language and cultural nationalism in nineteenth-century Ireland', in Tony Crowley, *Language in History: Theories and Texts* (London: Routledge, 1996), pp. 99–148.

Crowley, Tony, *The Politics of Language in Ireland 1366–1922: A Sourcebook* (London: Routledge, 2000).

Cullen, Fintan, *The Drawings of John Butler Yeats, 1839–1922* (Albany NY: Albany Institute of History & Art, 1987).

Cullen, Fintan, 'Still a long way to go: recent Irish art history', *Art History* 15, 3 (1992), pp. 378–83.

Cullen, Fintan, 'Tackling the visual: recent studies in Irish art history', *Bullán* 2, 2 (1996), pp. 111–15.

Cullen, Fintan, *Visual Politics: The Representation of Ireland 1750–1930* (Cork: Cork University Press, 1997).

Cullen, Fintan, *Sources in Irish Art: A Reader* (Cork: Cork University Press, 2000).

Cullen, Fintan, *The Irish Face: Redefining the Irish Portrait* (London: National Portrait Gallery, 2004).

Cullen, L. M., 'Catholics under the penal laws', *Eighteenth-Century Ireland* 1 (1986), pp. 23–37.

Cullen, L. M., 'Poetry, culture and politics', *Studia Celtica Japonica* 8 (1996), pp. 1–26.

Cullen, L. M., 'Filíocht, cultúr agus polaitíocht', in Ní Dhonnchadha (ed.), *Nua-Léamha*, pp. 170–93.

Cullen, L. M., 'The growth of Dublin 1600–1900: character and heritage', in Aalen and Whelan (eds), *Dublin City and County*, pp. 251–78.

Cullen, L. M., 'Humphrey O'Sullivan's Callan: before and after', in McDonnell (ed.), *Callan Co-operative Agricultural and Dairy Society Ltd*, pp. 11–28.

Cullen, L. M. and F. Furet (eds), *Irlande et France XVII<sup>e</sup>–XX<sup>e</sup> Siècles, pour une Histoire Rurale Comparée* (Paris: Editions de l'école des hautes études en sciences sociales, 1980).

Cullen, Mary (ed.), *Girls Don't Do Honours: Irish Women in Education in the Nineteenth and Twentieth Centuries* (Dublin: Women's Education Bureau, 1987).

Cullen, Mary and Maria Luddy (eds), *Women, Power and Consciousness in Nineteenth-Century Ireland* (Dublin: Attic, 1995).

Cullinane, John P. 'Irish dance world-wide: Irish emigrants and the shaping of traditional Irish dance', in O'Sullivan (ed.), *The Irish World Wide*, III, *The Creative Migrant*, pp. 192–210.

Cunningham, John, *Labour in the West of Ireland* (Belfast: Athol, 1995).

Curtin, Chris, Donnan Hastings and Thomas M. Wilson (eds), *Irish Urban Cultures* (Belfast: Institute of Irish Studies, 1993).

Curtis, L. Perry Jr, *Anglo-Saxons and Celts: A Study of Anti-Irish Prejudice in Victorian England* (Bridgeport, CT: Conference on British Studies, 1968).

Curtis, L. Perry Jr, *Apes and Angels: The Irishman in Victorian Caricature* (Washington DC and London: Smithsonian Institution, 1997).

Curtis, L. Perry Jr, 'The four Erins: feminine images of Ireland, 1780–1900', *Éire-Ireland* 33, 3 & 4; 34, 1 (1998–9), pp. 70–102.

Curtis, L. Perry Jr, *Images of Erin in the Age of Parnell* (Dublin: NLI, 2000).

Dalsimer, Adele M. (ed.), *Visualizing Ireland: National Identity and the Pictorial Tradition* (Boston and London: Faber, 1993).

Dalsimer, Adele M. and Vera Kreilkamp (eds), *America's Eye: Irish Paintings from the Collection of Brian P. Burns* (Boston: Boston College Museum of Art, 1996).

D'Alton, Ian, 'A perspective upon historical process: the case of Southern Irish Protestantism', in Smith (ed.), *Ireland, England and Australia*, pp. 70–91.

Daly, Kieran Anthony, *Catholic Church Music in Ireland 1878–1903, the Cecilian Reform Movement* (Dublin: Four Courts, 1995).

Daly, Mary E., *Women and Work in Ireland* (Dundalk: Dundalgan Press, 1997).

Daly, Mary E. and David Dickson (eds), *The Origins of Popular Literacy in Ireland: Language Change and Educational Development 1700–1920* (Dublin: Trinity College and UCD History Depts, 1990).

D'Arcy, Fergus, 'The Irish trade union movement in the nineteenth century', in Nevin (ed.), *Trade Union Century*, pp. 9–18.

Davis, Graham, *The Irish in Britain, 1815–1914* (Dublin: Gill & Macmillan, 1991).

Davis, Graham, 'Models of migration: the historiography of the Irish pioneers in South Texas', *South Western Historical Quarterly* 99, 3(1996), pp. 327–48.

Davis, Graham, 'The Irish in Britain, 1815–1939', in Bielenberg (ed.), *The Irish Diaspora*, pp. 19–36.

Davis, Richard, *Revolutionary Imperialist: William Smith O'Brien 1803–1864* (Dublin: Lilliput, 1998).

Dawson, Ciarán, *Peadar Ó Gealacáin, Scríobhaí* (Dublin: An Clóchomhar, 1992).

De Brún, Pádraig, 'The Irish Society's Bible teachers, 1818–27', *Éigse* 24 (1990), pp. 71–120; *Éigse* 25 (1991), pp. 113–49; *Éigse* 26 (1992), pp. 131–72.

De Courcy, Catherine, *The Foundation of the National Gallery of Ireland* (Dublin: NGI, 1985).

De Fréine, Seán, 'An Gorta agus an Ghaeilge', in Póirtéir (ed.), *Gnéithe den Ghorta*, pp. 55–68.

De Paor, Liam, *Landscape with Figures* (Dublin: Four Courts, 1998).

Deane, Seamus (general ed.), *The Field Day Anthology of Irish Writing*, 3 vols (Derry: Field Day, 1991).

Deane, Seamus, *Strange Country: Modernity and Nationhood in Irish Writing since 1790* (Oxford: Clarendon, 1997).

Denman, Peter, *Samuel Ferguson: The Literary Achievement* (Gerrards Cross: Colin Smythe, 1990).

Denvir, Gearóid, 'Decolonising the mind: language and literature in Ireland', *New Hibernia Review* 1 (1997), pp. 44–68.

Denvir, Gearóid, 'Filíocht Antaine Raiftearaí', in Denvir, *Litríocht agus Pobal* (Indreabhán: Cló Iar-Chonnachta, 1997), pp. 295–307.

Department of the Environment and Local Government, *An Introduction to the Architectural Heritage of Fingal* (Dublin: Dúchas, The Heritage Service, 2002).

Devine, Ciaran, 'The Irish language in County Down', in Proudfoot (ed.), *Down: History and Society*, pp. 431–87.

Devine, Patrick F. and Harry White (eds), *The Maynooth International Musicological Conference 1995: Selected Proceedings, Part One*, Irish Musical Studies IV (Dublin: Four Courts, 1996).

Devine, Patrick F. and Harry White (eds), *The Maynooth International Musicological Conference 1995: Selected Proceedings, Part Two*, Irish Musical Studies V (Dublin: Four Courts, 1996).

Devine, T. M. (ed.), *Irish Immigrants and Scottish Society in the Nineteenth and Twentieth Centuries* (Edinburgh: John Donald, 1991).

Devlin, Judith and Ronan Fanning (eds), *Religion and Rebellion: Historical Studies* xx (Dublin: UCD Press, 1997).

Dillon, Charles and H. A. Jefferies (eds), *Tyrone: History and Society* (Dublin: Geography Publications, 2000).

Diner, Hasia, '"The most Irish city in the Union": the era of the Great Migration, 1844–1877', in Bayor and Meagher (eds), *The New York Irish*, pp. 87–106.

Doherty, Gillian, *The Irish Ordnance Survey: History, Culture and Memory* (Dublin: Four Courts, 2004).

Dolan, Jay, *The American Catholic Experience: A History from Colonial Times to the Present* (South Bend: University of Notre Dame Press, 1992).

Donnelly, James S. Jr, *The Land and the People of Nineteenth-Century Cork: The Rural Economy and the Land Question* (London: Routledge & Kegan Paul, 1975).

Donnelly, James S. Jr, 'The Marian shrine of Knock: the first decade', *Éire-Ireland* 28, 2 (1993), pp. 54–97.

Donnelly, James S. Jr, *The Great Irish Potato Famine* (Stroud, Glos.: Sutton, 2001).

Donnelly, James S. Jr, 'Mass eviction and the Great Famine', in Póirtéir (ed.), *The Great Irish Famine*, pp. 155–73.

Donnelly, James S. Jr, and Kerby A. Miller (eds), *Irish Popular Culture, 1650–1850* (Dublin: Irish Academic Press, 1998).

Dooley, Dolores, *Equality in Community: Sexual Equality in the Writings of William Thompson and Anna Doyle Wheeler* (Cork: Cork University Press, 1996).

Dooley, Terence A., 'Why Monaghan Protestants opposed Home Rule', *Clogher Record* 14, 3 (1993), pp. 42–6.

Dooley, Terence A., 'The organisation of unionist opposition to Home Rule in counties Monaghan, Cavan and Donegal, 1885–1914', *Clogher Record* 16, 1 (1997), pp. 46–70.

Dooley, Terence, *The Decline of the Big House in Ireland: A Study of Landed Families* (Dublin: Wolfhound, 2001).

Dorian, Hugh, *The Outer Edge of Ulster: A Memoir of Social Life in Nineteenth-Century Donegal*, eds Breandán Mac Suibhne and David Dickson (South Bend and Dublin: University of Notre Dame Press and Lilliput, 2001).

Doyle, David N., 'The Irish in Australia and the United States: some comparisons', *Irish Economic and Social History* 15 (1989).

Doyle, David N., 'The Irish as urban pioneers', *Journal of American Ethnic History* 10, 2 (1991).

Doyle, David N., 'Cohesion and diversity in the Irish diaspora', *IHS* 21, 123 (1999), pp. 411–34.

Doyle, David N., 'Irish elites in North America and liberal democracy 1820–1920', *Radharc* 3 (2002), pp. 51–73.

Doyle, David N., 'The Irish in North America, 1776–1845', in Vaughan (ed.), *A New History of Ireland*, v, 682–725.

Doyle, David N., 'The remaking of Irish-America 1845–80', in Vaughan (ed.), *A New History of Ireland*, vi, pp. 725–63.

Doyle, Eugene, *Justin McCarthy* (Dundalk: Historical Association and Dundalgan Press, 1996).

Duffy, P. J., *Landscapes of South Ulster: A Parish Atlas of the Diocese of Clogher* (Belfast: Institute of Irish Studies, QUB, 1993).

Duffy, P. J., 'Management problems on a large estate in mid-nineteenth-century Ireland: William Steuart Trench's report of the Shirley estate in 1843', *Clogher Record* 16 (1997), pp. 101–23.

Duffy, P. J., 'The nuts and bolts of making landscape in the mid-nineteenth century', *Group for the Study of Irish Historic Settlement Newsletter* 8 (1997), pp. 13–16.

Duffy, P. J., 'Locality and changing landscape: geography and local history', in Gillespie and Hill (eds), *Doing Irish Local History*, pp. 24–46.

Duffy, P. J., 'Trends in nineteenth- and twentieth-century settlement', in Barry (ed.), *A History of Settlement in Ireland*, pp. 206–27.

Duffy, Patrick J., 'Emigrants and the estate office in the mid-nineteenth century: a compassionate relationship?', in Crawford (ed.), *The Hungry Stream*, pp. 71–86.

Dunne, Tom, 'Subaltern voices? Poetry in Irish, popular insurgency and the 1798 Rebellion', *Eighteenth-Century Life* 22 (1998), pp. 31–44.

Dunne, Tom, '"Tá Gaedhil bhocht cráidhte": memory, tradition and the politics of the poor in Gaelic poetry and song', in Geary (ed.), *Rebellion and Remembrance in Modern Ireland*, pp. 93–111.

Eagleton, Terry, *Heathcliff and the Great Hunger: Studies in Irish Culture* (London: Verso, 1995).

Eagleton, Terry, *Crazy Jane and the Bishop, and Other Essays on Irish Culture* (Cork: Cork University Press, 1998).

Eagleton, Terry, *Scholars and Rebels in Nineteenth-Century Ireland* (Oxford: Blackwell, 1999).

Edwards, Owen Dudley, 'The Irish priests in North-America', in Shiels and Wood (eds), *Studies in Church History*, XXV, *The Churches, Ireland and the Irish*, pp. 311–52.

Edwards, Owen Dudley, 'The stage Irish', in O'Sullivan (ed.), *The Irish World Wide*, III, *The Creative Migrant*, pp. 83–114.

Edwards, Owen Dudley, 'Oscar Wilde: the soul of man under Hibernicism', in Briggs et al. *Reviewing Ireland*, pp. 105–14.

Edwards, Owen Dudley and Patricia J. Storey, 'The Irish press in Victorian Britain', in Swift and Gilley (eds), *The Irish in the Victorian City*, pp. 158–78.

Elliott, Marianne, *The Catholics of Ulster: A History* (London: Allen Lane, 2000).

Emmons, D. M., *The Butte Irish: Class and Ethnicity in an American Mining Town, 1875–1925* (Urbana: University of Illinois Press, 1989).

English, Richard and Graham Walker (eds), *Unionism in Modern Ireland* (Basingstoke: Palgrave Macmillan, 1996).

Evans, E. E., 'Some survivals of the Irish openfield system', *Geography* 24 (1939), pp. 24–36.

Evans, Richard J., *Rituals of Retribution: Capital Punishment in Germany, 1600–1987* (Oxford: Clarendon, 1996).

Fanning, Charles, *The Irish Voice in America: 250 Years of Irish-American Fiction*, 2nd edn (Lexington: University Press of Kentucky, 2000).

Fanning, Charles (ed.), *New Perspectives on the Irish Diaspora* (Carbondale: Southern Illinois University Press, 2000).

Feehan, John, *Farming in Ireland: History, Heritage and Environment* (Dublin: Faculty of Agriculture, UCD, 2003).

Fielding, Steven, *Class and Ethnicity: Irish Catholics in England, 1880–1939* (Buckingham: Open University Press, 1993).

Finnegan, Frances, *Do Penance or Perish: A Study of Magdalen Asylums in Ireland* (Piltown, Co. Kilkenny: Congrave Press, 2002).

Fitzpatrick, David, *Oceans of Consolation: Personal Accounts of Irish Migration to Australia* (Cork: Cork University Press, 1994).

Fitzpatrick, David, 'Emigration 1801–70', in Vaughan (ed.), *A New History of Ireland*, V, pp. 562–622.

Fitzpatrick, David, '"A peculiar tramping people": The Irish in Britain 1801–70', in Vaughan (ed.), *A New History of Ireland*, V, pp. 623–60.

Fitzpatrick, David, 'Emigration 1871–1921', in Vaughan (ed.), *A New History of Ireland*, VI, pp. 606–52.

Fitzpatrick David, 'The Irish in Britain, 1871–1921', in Vaughan (ed.), *A New History of Ireland*, VI, pp. 653–702.

Fitzpatrick, David, 'The Irish in Britain: settlers or transients?', in Buckland and Belchem (eds), *The Irish in British Labour History*, pp. 1–10.

Fitzpatrick, David, '"A curious middle place": the Irish in Britain, 1871–1921', in Swift and Gilley (eds), *The Irish in Britain*, pp. 10–59.

Fitzpatrick, David, 'The failure: representations of the Irish Famine in letters to Australia', in Crawford (ed.), *The Hungry Stream*, pp. 161–74.

Flannery, James W., *Dear Harp of My Country: The Irish Melodies of Thomas Moore* (Nashville: Sanders: 1997).

Fleischmann, Aloys (ed.), *Sources of Irish Traditional Music c.1600–1855*, 2 vols (London and New York: Garland, 1998).

Flot, Michel, 'Gerald Griffin et la conversion linguistique de l'Irlande', in Brihault (ed.), *L'Irlande et ses Langues*, pp. 147–56.

Fogarty, Anne (ed.), *Irish Women Novelists, 1800–1940, Colby Quarterly* 36, 2 (2000).

Foley, Marc. C and Timothy J. Guinnane, 'Did Irish marriage patterns survive the emigrant voyage? Irish-American nuptiality, 1880–1920', *Irish Economic and Social History* 26 (1999), pp. 15–34.

Foley, Tadhg and Sean Ryder (eds), *Ideology and Ireland in the Nineteenth Century* (Dublin: Four Courts, 1998).

Foley, T. P. et al. (eds), *Gender and Colonialism* (Galway: Galway University Press, 1995), pp. 210–24.

Ford, Alan, James McGuire and Kenneth Milne (eds), *As by Law Established: The Church of Ireland since the Reformation* (Dublin: Lilliput, 1995).

Foster, John, 'Completing the first task: Irish labour in the nineteenth century', *Saothar* 15 (1990), pp. 65–9.

Foster, John, Muir Houston and Chris Madigan, 'Distinguishing Catholics and Protestants among Irish immigrants to Clydeside: a new approach to immigration and ethnicity in Victorian Britain', *Irish Studies Review* 10, 2 (Aug. 2002), pp. 171–220.

Foster, R. F. (ed.), *The Oxford Illustrated History of Ireland* (Oxford: Clarendon, 1989).

Foster, R. F., *Paddy and Mr Punch* (Harmondsworth: Penguin, 1993).

Foster, R. F., *The Story of Ireland* (Inaugural lecture, University of Oxford) (Oxford: Clarendon, 1995).

Foster, R. F., *W. B. Yeats: A Life, Volume One* (Oxford and New York: Oxford University Press, 1997).

Foster, R. F., 'Parnell, Wicklow, nationalism', in McCartney (ed.), *Parnell*, pp. 19–35.

Fraser, Lyndon (ed.), *A Distant Shore: Irish Migration and New Zealand Settlement* (Dunedin: University of Otago Press, 2000).

Frazier, Adrian, *George Moore 1852–1933* (New Haven CT: Yale University Press, 2000).

Freeman, T. W., *Pre-Famine Ireland: A Study in Historical Geography* (Manchester: Manchester University Press, 1957).

Freeman, T. W., 'Land and people, c.1841', in Vaughan (ed.), *A New History of Ireland*, v, pp. 242–71.

Friel, Bernadette, 'Language change in Urris', *Donegal Annual* 50 (1998), pp. 66–75.

Friel, Brian, *Translations* (London: Faber, 1981).

Fulton, John, *The Tragedy of Belief: Division, Politics and Religion in Ireland* (Oxford: Clarendon, 1991).

Gallagher, T., 'The Catholic Irish in Scotland: in search of identity', in Devine (ed.), *Irish Immigration and Scottish Society*, pp. 19–43.

Gallman, J. Matthew, *Receiving Erin's Children: Philadelphia, Liverpool and the Irish Famine Migration, 1845–55* (Chapel Hill: University of North Carolina Press, 2000).

Gallogly, Daniel, *The Diocese of Kilmore, 1850–1950* (Monaghan: Cumann Seanchais Bhréifne, 1999).

Gatrell, V. A. C., *The Hanging Tree: Execution and the English People, 1770–1868* (Oxford: Clarendon, 1994).

Geary, Laurence M., 'A psychological and sociological analysis of the Great Famine in Ireland', in Robert Dare (ed.), *Food, Power and Community: Essays in the History of Food and Drink* (Kent Town, South Australia: Wakefield, 1999), pp. 181–92.

Geary, Laurence M. (ed.), *Rebellion and Remembrance in Modern Ireland* (Dublin: Four Courts, 2001).

Geary, Laurence M., *Medicine and Charity in Ireland, 1718–1851* (Dublin: UCD Press, 2004).

Geary, Laurence M., 'Australia *felix*: Irish doctors in nineteenth-century Victoria', in O'Sullivan (ed.), *The Irish World Wide*, II, *The Irish in the New Communities*, pp. 162–79.

Geary, Laurence M., 'Famine, fever and the bloody flux', in Póirtéir (ed.), *The Great Irish Famine*, pp. 74–85

Geary, Laurence M., '"The late disastrous epidemic": medical relief and the great famine', in Morash and Hayes (eds), *'Fearful Realities'*, pp. 49–59.

Geary, Laurence M., 'What people died of during the famine', in Ó Gráda (ed), *Famine 150*, pp. 95–111.

Geary, Laurence M. '"The living were out of their feeling": a socio-cultural analysis of the Great Irish Famine', in Ó Conaire (ed.), *The Famine Lectures*, pp. 308–28.

Geoghegan, Patrick M., *The Irish Act of Union: A Study in High Politics 1798–1801* (New York: St Martin's Press, 1999).

Gibbons, Luke, *Transformations in Irish Culture* (Cork: Cork University Press, 1996).

Gibbons, Luke, '"A shadowy narrator": history, art and romantic nationalism in Ireland 1750–1850', in Brady (ed.), *Ideology and the Historians*, pp. 91–127.

Gibbons, Luke, 'Between Captain Rock and a hard place: art and agrarian insurgency', in Foley and Ryder (eds), *Ideology and Ireland in the Nineteenth Century*, pp. 23–44.

Gibbons, Luke, 'Romanticism, realism and Irish cinema', in Rockett et al., *Cinema and Ireland*, pp. 194–257.

Gibbons, Stephen, *Captain Rock, Night Errant: The Threatening Letters of Pre-Famine Ireland* (Dublin: Four Courts, 2004).

Gillen, Gerard and Andrew Johnstone (eds), *A Historical Anthology of Irish Church Music*, Irish Musical Studies VI (Dublin: Four Courts, 2001).

Gillen, Gerard and Harry White (eds), *Musicology in Ireland*, Irish Musical Studies I (Dublin: Irish Academic Press, 1990).

Gillen, Gerard and Harry White (eds), *Music and the Church*, Irish Musical Studies II (Dublin: Irish Academic Press, 1993).

Gillen, Gerard and Harry White (eds), *Music and Irish Cultural History*, Irish Musical Studies III (Dublin: Irish Academic Press, 1995).

Gillespie, Raymond (ed.), *Cavan: Essays on the History of an Irish County* (Dublin: Irish Academic Press, 1999).

Gillespie, Raymond and Myrtle Hill (eds), *Doing Irish Local History: Pursuit and Practice* (Belfast: Institute of Irish Studies, 1998).

Gillespie, Raymond and Brian P. Kennedy (eds), *Ireland: Art into History* (Dublin: Town House, 1994).

Gillespie, Raymond and Gerard Moran (eds), *Longford: Essays in County History* (Dublin: Lilliput, 1991), pp. 63–91.

Gilley, Sheridan, 'Roman Catholicism and the Irish in England', in MacRaild (ed.), *The Great Famine and Beyond*, pp. 147–67.

Gilligan, Jim, *Graziers and Grasslands: Portrait of a Rural Meath Community 1854–1914* (Dublin: Irish Academic Press, 1999).

Giltrap, Risteárd, *An Ghaeilge in Eaglais na hÉireann* (Dublin: Cumann Gaelach na hEaglaise, 1990).

Glazier, Michael (ed.), *Encyclopedia of the Irish in America* (South Bend: Notre Dame University Press, 1999).

Gleason, Philip, 'Higher education', in Glazier (ed.), *Encyclopedia of the Irish in America*, pp. 243–5.

Gleeson, David T., *The Irish in the South, 1815–1877* (Chapel Hill: University of North Carolina Press, 2001).

Gordon, Michael, *The Orange Riots: Irish Political Violence in New York City in 1870–1871* (Ithaca, NY: Cornell University Press, 1993).

Gordon-Bowe, Nicola and Elizabeth Cumming, *The Arts and Crafts Movements in Dublin and Edinburgh* (Dublin: Irish Academic Press, 1998).

Grace, Robert J., *The Irish in Quebec: An Introduction to the Historiography* (Québec: New York Irish History Roundtable, 1995).

Graham, Brian and Catherine Nash, *Modern Historical Geographies* (Edinburgh: Pearson Education, 2000).

Graham, B. J. and Susan Hood, 'Town tenant protest in late nineteenth and early twentieth-century Ireland', *Irish Economic and Social History* 21 (1994), pp. 39–57.

Graham, B. J. and L. J. Proudfoot (eds), *An Historical Geography of Ireland* (London: Academic Press, 1993).

Graham, Colin, *Ideologies of Epic: Nation, Empire and Victorian Epic Poetry* (Manchester: Manchester University Press, 1998).

Granberg, Leo, Imre Kovach and Hilary Tovey (eds), *Europe's Green Ring* (Aldershot: Ashgate, 2001).

Grant, James, 'The Great Famine in County Tyrone', in Dillon and Jefferies (eds), *Tyrone: History and Society*, pp. 587–615.

Gray, Jane, 'Folk poetry and working-class identity in Ulster: an analysis of James Orr's "The Penitent"', *Journal of Historical Sociology* 6 (1993), pp. 249–75.

Gray, Jane, 'Rural industry and uneven development: the significance of gender in the Irish linen industry', *Journal of Peasant Studies* 20 (1993), pp. 590–611.

Gray, Peter, '"Potatoes and providence": British government responses to the Great Famine', *Bullán* 1 (1994), pp. 75–90.

Gray, Peter, *The Irish Famine* (London: Thames & Hudson, 1995).

Gray, Peter, *Famine, Land and Politics: British Government and Irish Society 1843–50* (Dublin: Irish Academic Press, 1999).

Gray, Peter (ed.), *Victoria's Ireland? Irishness and Britishness, 1837–1901* (Dublin: Four Courts, 2004).

Greeley, Andrew, 'Achievement of the Irish in America', in Glazier (ed.), *Encyclopedia of the Irish in America*, pp. 1–4.

Greenslade, Liam, 'White skin, white masks: psychological distress among the Irish in Britain, in O'Sullivan (ed.), *The Irish World Wide*, 11, *The Irish in the New Communities*, pp. 201–25.

Gribben, Arthur (ed.), *The Great Famine and the Irish Diaspora in America* (Amherst: University of Massachusetts Press, 1999).

Grindle, W. H., *Irish Cathedral Music* (Belfast: Institute of Irish Studies, 1989).

Grogan, Geraldine, *The Noblest Agitator: Daniel O'Connell and the German Catholic Movement 1830–1950* (Dublin: Veritas, 1991).

Guinnane, Timothy, *The Vanishing Irish: Households, Migration, and the Rural Economy in Ireland, 1850–1914* (Princeton NJ: Princeton University Press, 1997).

Guy, J. R. and W. S. Neely (eds), *Contrasts and Comparisons: Studies in Irish and Welsh Church History* (Llandysul and Keady: Welsh Religious History Society and Church of Ireland Historical Society, 1999).

Haines, Robin, *Charles Trevelyan and the Great Irish Famine* (Dublin: Four Courts, 2004).

Hall, Wayne E., *Dialogues in the Margin: A Study of the Dublin University Magazine* (Washington: Catholic University Press of America, 2000).

Harris, Mary, *The Catholic Church and the Foundation of the Northern Irish State* (Cork: Cork University Press, 1993).

Harris, Ruth-Ann M., *The Nearest Place That Wasn't Ireland: Early Nineteenth Century Labour Migration* (Ames: University of Iowa Press, 1994).

Harris, Ruth-Ann M., *The Search for Missing Friends: Immigrant Advertisements Placed in the Boston Pilot* (Boston: New England Historical Genealogical Society, I–IV, 1989, 1991, 1993, 1995).

Harris, Ruth-Ann M., 'Come all you courageously: Irish women in America write home', *Éire-Ireland* 36, 1 & 2 (2001), pp. 166–84.

Harris, Ruth-Ann M., 'Searching for missing friends in the *Boston Pilot* newspaper, 1831–1863', in Bielenberg (ed.), *The Irish Diaspora*, pp. 158–75.

Hatton, Helen, *The Largest Amount of Good: Quaker Relief in Ireland 1654–1921* (London & Toronto: McGill-Queens University Press, 1993).

Hatton, Timothy J. and Jeffrey G. Williamson (eds), *Migration and the International Labour Market, 1850–1939* (London: Routledge, 1994).

Hearn, Mona, *Below Stairs: Domestic Service Remembered in Dublin and Beyond, 1880–1922* (Dublin: Lilliput, 1993).

Hempton, David, *Religion and Political Culture in Britain and Ireland from the Glorious Revolution to the Decline of the Empire* (Cambridge: Cambridge University Press, 1996).

Hempton, David and Myrtle Hill, *Evangelical Protestantism in Ulster Society, 1740–1890* (London: Routledge, 1992).

Hickman, Mary J., *Religion, Class and Identity: The State, the Catholic Church and the Education of the Irish in Britain* (Aldershot: Ashgate, 1995).

Hickman, Mary J., '"Locating" the Irish diaspora', *Irish Journal of Sociology* 11, 2 (2002), pp. 8–26.

Hickman, Mary J., 'Alternative historiographies of the Irish in Britain; a critique of the segregation/assimilation model', in Swift and Gilley (eds), *The Irish in Victorian Britain*, pp. 236–53.

Hickman, Mary J., 'Incorporating and denationalizing the Irish in England; the role of the Catholic Church', in O'Sullivan (ed.), *The Irish World Wide*, V, *Religion and Identity*, pp. 196–216.

Hill, Jacqueline, *From Patriots to Unionists: Dublin Civic Politics and Irish Protestant Patriotism, 1660–1840* (Oxford: Clarendon, 1997).

Hill, Jacqueline and Colm Lennon (eds), *Luxury and Austerity: Historical Studies* XXI (Dublin: UCD Press, 1999).

Hill, Judith, *Irish Public Sculpture: A History* (Dublin: Four Courts, 1998).

Hindley, Reg, *The Death of the Irish Language: A Qualified Obituary* (London: Routledge, 1990).

Hogan, Edmund F., *The Irish Missionary Movement: A Historical Survey, 1830–1980* (Dublin: Gill & Macmillan, 1990).

Holmes, Finlay, *Irish Presbyterianism 1642–1992* (Belfast: Presbyterian Historical Society of Ireland, 1992).

Holmes, Finlay, *The Presbyterian Church in Ireland: A Popular History* (Blackrock: Columba, 2000).

Holmes, Janice, *Religious Revivals in Britain and Ireland, 1859–1905* (Dublin: Irish Academic Press, 2000).

Holmes, Janice and Diane Urquhart (eds), *Coming into the Light: The Work, Politics and Religion of Women in Ulster, 1840–1940* (Belfast: Institute of Irish Studies, 1994).

Holmes, Michael and Denis Holmes (eds), *Ireland and India: Connections, Comparisons, Contrasts* (Dublin: Blackwater, 1997).

Hooper, Glenn and Leon Litvack (eds), *Ireland in the Nineteenth Century: Regional Identity* (Dublin: Four Courts, 2000).

Hoppen, K. T., 'Grammars of electoral violence in nineteenth-century England and Ireland', *English Historical Review* 59 (1994), pp. 579–620.

Hoppen, K. T., 'Roads to democracy: electioneering and corruption in nineteenth-century England and Ireland', *History* 81 (1996), pp. 553–71.

Hoppen, K. T., *Ireland Since 1800: Stability and Change* (London: Longman, 1990; rev edn, 1999).

Hoppen, K. T., 'Nationalist mobilization and governmental attitudes: geography, politics and nineteenth-century Ireland', in Brockliss and Eastwood (eds), *A Union of Multiple Identities*, pp. 162–78.

Houlbrooke, Ralph, (ed.) *Death, Ritual, and Bereavement* (London: Routledge, 1989).

Houston, C. J. and W. J. Smyth, *Irish Emigration and Canadian Settlement: Patterns, Links and Settlers* (Toronto: Toronto University Press, 1990).

Hout, Michael and Joshua R. Goldstein, 'How 4.5 million Irish immigrants became 40 million Irish Americans: demographic and subjective aspects of the ethnic composition of white Americans', *American Sociological Review* 59 (1995), pp. 64–82.

Howe, Stephen, *Ireland and Empire* (Oxford: Oxford University Press, 2000).

Hoy, Suellen, 'The journey out: the recruitment and emigration of Irish religious women to the United States, 1812–1914', *Journal of Women's History* 6 & 7 (1995), pp. 64–98.

Hoy, Suellen and Margaret MacCurtain, *From Dublin to New Orleans* (Dublin: Attic Press, 1994).

Hunt, Lynn (ed.), *The New Cultural History* (Berkeley: University of California Press, 1989).

Hutchinson, John, *James Arthur O'Connor* (Dublin: NGI, 1985).

Hutton, Sean and Paul Stewart (eds), *Ireland's Histories: Aspects of State, Society and Ideology* (London: Routledge, 1991).

Hynes, Eugene, 'Nineteenth-century Irish Catholicism, farmers' ideology, and national religion: explorations in cultural explanation', in Roger O'Toole (ed.) *Sociological Studies of Roman Catholicism: Historical and Contemporary Perspectives*, Studies in Religion and Societies XXIV (Lewiston: E. Mellen, 1989), pp. 45–69.

Ihde, T. W. (ed.), *The Irish Language in the United States* (Westport, CT: Bergin & Garvey, 1994).

Innes, C. L., *Woman and Nation in Irish Society, 1880–1935* (New York and London: Harvester, 1993).

*Irish Arts Review Yearbook* 15 (Dublin, 1999), cumulative Index to vols. 1–15, 1984–99, pp. 229–44.

Izarra, Laura, 'The Irish diaspora in Argentina', *British Association of Irish Studies News Letter* 32 (Oct. 2002), pp. 5–9.

Jackson, Alvin, *Colonel Edward Saunderson: Land and Loyalty in Victorian Ireland* (Oxford: Clarendon, 1995).

Jackson, Alvin, *Ireland 1798–1998: Politics and War* (Oxford: Blackwell, 1999).

Jacobson, Matthew F., *Whiteness of a Different Color: European Immigrants and the Alchemy of Race* (Cambridge MA: Harvard University Press, 1998).

Jacobson, Matthew F., *Special Sorrows: The Diasporic Imagination of Irish, Polish, and Jewish Immigrants in the United States*, rev. edn (Berkeley: University of California Press, 2002).

Jalland, Pat, *Death in the Victorian Family* (Oxford: Clarendon, 1996).

James, Dermot and Séamas Ó Maitiú (eds), *The Wicklow World of Elizabeth Smith, 1840–1850* (Dublin: Woodfield Press, 1996).

Jefferies, Henry A., and Ciarán Devlin (eds), *History of the Diocese of Derry from Earliest Times* (Dublin: Four Courts, 2000).

Jeffery, Keith (ed.), *'An Irish Empire'? Aspects of Ireland and the British Empire* (Manchester: Manchester University Press, 1996).

Jenkins, William, 'Patrolmen and peelers: immigration, urban cultures and "the Irish police"', in Canada and the United States', *Canadian Journal of Irish Studies* 28, 2 (2002), pp. 10–29.

Johnston, Jack, 'Society in the Clogher Valley, c.1750–1900', in Dillon and Jefferies (eds), *Tyrone: History and Society*, pp. 543–65.

Jones, Greta, 'Catholicism, nationalism and science', *Irish Review* 20 (1997), pp. 47–61.

Jones, Greta, 'Contested territories: Alfred Cort Haddon, progressive evolutionism, and Ireland', *History of European Ideas* 24, 3 (1998), pp. 195–211.

Jones, Greta and Elizabeth Malcolm (eds), *Medicine, Disease and the State in Ireland, 1650–1940* (Cork: Cork University Press, 1999).

Jordan, Alison, *Margaret Byers, Pioneer of Women's Education and Founder of Victoria College, Belfast* (Belfast: Institute of Irish Studies, 1991).

Jordan, Alison, *Who Cared? Charity in Victorian and Edwardian Belfast* (Belfast: Institute of Irish Studies, QUB, 1992).

Jordan, Donald E., Jr, *Land and Popular Politics in Ireland: County Mayo from the Plantation to the Land War* (Cambridge: Cambridge University Press, 1994).

Jordan, Donald E., Jr, 'The Famine and its aftermath in County Mayo', in Morash and Hayes (eds), *'Fearful Realities'*, pp. 35–48.

Jupp, Peter and Stephen A. Royle, 'The social geography of Cork city elections, 1801–30', *IHS* (May, 1994), pp. 13–43.

Kanya-Forstner, Martha, 'Defining womanhood: Irish women and the Catholic Church in Victorian Liverpool', in MacRaild (ed.), *The Great Famine and Beyond*, pp. 168–88.

Keane, Maureen, *Mrs S. C. Hall: A Literary Biography* (Gerrards Cross: Colin Smythe, 1997).

Kelleher, Margaret, *The Feminization of Famine: Expressions of the Inexpressible?* (Cork: Cork University Press and Durham NC: Duke University Press, 1997).

Kelleher, Margaret, '*The Cabinet of Irish Literature*: a historical perspective on Irish anthologies', *Éire-Ireland* 38, 3 & 4 (2003), pp. 68–89.

Kelleher, Margaret, 'Irish Famine in literature', in Portéir (ed.), *The Great Irish Famine*, pp. 232–47.

Kelleher, Margaret, 'Women's fiction, 1845–1900', in Bourke et al. (eds), *Field Day Anthology of Irish Writing*, v, pp. 924–75.

Kelleher, Margaret and James H. Murphy (eds), *Gender Perspectives in Nineteenth-Century Ireland* (Dublin: Irish Academic Press, 1997).

Kelly, James and Dáire Keogh (eds), *History of the Catholic Diocese of Dublin* (Dublin: Four Courts, 2000).

Keneally, Thomas, *The Great Shame: A Story of the Irish in the Old World and the New* (London: Chatto & Windus, 1998).

Kennedy, K., T. Giblin and D. McHugh, *The Economic Development of Ireland in the Twentieth Century* (London: Routledge, 1998).

Kennedy, Líam, *Colonialism, Religion and Nationalism in Ireland* (Belfast: Institute of Irish Studies, QUB, 1996).

Kennedy, Líam, 'Out of history: Ireland, that "most distressful country"', in Kennedy, *Colonialism, Religion and Nationalism in Ireland*, pp. 182–223.

Kennedy, Líam, P. S. Ell, E. M. Crawford and L. A. Clarkson, *Mapping the Great Irish Famine: A Survey of the Famine Decades* (Dublin: Four Courts, 1999).

Kennedy, S. B., *Irish Art and Modernism 1880–1950* (Belfast: Institute of Irish Studies, QUB, 1991).

Kenny, Kevin, *Making Sense of the Molly Maguires* (Oxford and New York: Oxford University Press, 1998).

Kenny, Kevin, *The American Irish: A History* (Harlow: Longman, 2000).

Kenny, Kevin, 'Diaspora and comparison: the global Irish as a case study', *Journal of American History* 90 (2003), pp. 134–62.

Keogh, Dáire, *Edmund Rice, 1762–1844* (Dublin: Four Courts, 1996).

Keogh, Dáire and Kevin Whelan (eds), *Acts of Union: The Causes, Contexts and Consequences of the Act of Union* (Dublin: Four Courts, 2003).

Keogh, Dermot, 'Founding and early years of the Irish TUC 1894–1912', in Nevin (ed.), *Trade Union Century*, pp. 19–32.

Kerr, Donal A., '*A Nation of Beggars'? Priests, People and Politics in Famine Ireland, 1846–1852* (Oxford: Clarendon, 1994).

Kerr, Donal A., *The Catholic Church and the Famine* (Blackrock: Columba, 1998).

Kiberd, Declan, *Inventing Ireland: The Literature of the Modern Nation* (London: Cape, 1995).

Kiberd, Declan, *Irish Classics* (London: Granta, 2000).

Kiely, M. B. and William Nolan, 'Politics, land and rural conflict in County Waterford', in Nolan and Power (eds), *Waterford: History and Society*, pp. 459–94.

Kinealy, Christine, *This Great Calamity: The Irish Famine 1845–52* (Dublin: Gill & Macmillan, 1994).

Kinealy, Christine, *A Death-Dealing Famine: The Great Hunger in Ireland* (London: Pluto, 1997).

Kinealy, Christine, *The Great Irish Famine: Impact, Ideology and Rebellion* (Basingstoke and New York: Palgrave, 2002).

Kinealy, Christine, 'Potatoes, providence and philanthropy: the role of private charity during the Irish Famine', in O'Sullivan (ed.), *The Irish World Wide*, VI, *The Meaning of the Famine*, pp. 140–71.

Kinealy, Christine, 'The response of the poor law to the Great Famine in County Galway', in Moran and Gillespie (eds), *Galway: History and Society*, pp. 375–94.

Kinealy, Christine, 'The workhouse system in County Waterford, 1838–1923', in Nolan and Power (eds), *Waterford: History and Society*, pp. 479–596.

King, Carla (ed.), *Famine, Land and Culture in Ireland* (Dublin: UCD Press, 2000).

Knowlton, S. R., *Popular Politics and the Irish Catholic Church: The Rise and Fall of the Independent Irish Party, 1850–59* (New York and London: Garland, 1991).

Koseki, Takashi, *Dublin Confederate Clubs and the Repeal Movement* (Tokyo: Hosei University, 1992).

Kraut, Alan M. 'Illness and medical care among Irish immigrants in antebellum New York', in Bayor and Meagher (eds), *The New York Irish*, pp. 153–68.

Kreilkamp, Vera, *The Anglo-Irish Novel and the Big House* (Syracuse: Syracuse University Press, 1998).

Kselman, Thomas A. *Death and the Afterlife in Modern France* (Princeton NJ, Princeton University Press, 1993).

Laffan Kathleen, 'James Scurry (1790–1828): A South Kilkenny scholar', *Decies* 50 (1994), pp. 60–6.

Lagrée, Michel, 'Foi et langue en Bretagne et en Irlande au XIXᵉ siècle', in *Chrétientés de Basse-Bretagne et d'ailleurs: Les Archives au risque de l'histoire* (Quimper: Société Archéologique du Finistère, 1998), pp. 275–81.

Lalor, Brian (ed.), *Encyclopaedia of Ireland* (Dublin: Gill & Macmillan, 2003).

Lane, Fintan, *The Origins of Modern Irish Socialism, 1881–1896* (Cork: Cork University Press, 1997).

Lane, P. G., 'The Encumbered Estates Court and Galway land ownership, 1849–58', in Moran and Gillespie (eds), *Galway: History and Society*, pp. 395–417.

Larkin, Emmet, 'The devotional revolution in Ireland, 1850–75', *American Historical Review*, 77 (1972), pp. 625–52.

Larkin, Emmet, *The Roman Catholic Church and the Home Rule Movement in Ireland, 1870–1874* (Chapel Hill: University of North Carolina Press, 1990).

Larkin, Emmet, *The Roman Catholic Church and the Emergence of the Modern Irish Political System, 1874–78* (Dublin: Four Courts, 1996).

Larmour, Paul, *The Arts and Crafts Movement in Ireland* (Belfast: Friar's Bush, 1992).

Lee, J. J. (ed.), *Irish Historiography, 1970–9* (Cork: Cork University Press, 1981).

Lee, J. J., *Ireland 1912–85: Politics and Society* (Cambridge: Cambridge University Press, 1989).

Lee, J. J., 'Millennial reflections on Irish-American history', *Radharc* 1 (2000), pp. 1–76.

Leerssen, Joep, *Remembrance and Imagination: Patterns in the Historical and Literary Representation of Ireland in the Nineteenth Century* (Cork: Cork University Press and South Bend: University of Notre Dame Press, 1996).

Leerssen, Joep, 'Language revivalism before the twilight', in Leerssen (ed.), *Forging in the Smithy*, pp. 133–44.

Leerssen, Joep et al. (eds), *Forging in the Smithy: National Identity and Representation in Anglo-Irish Literary History* (Amsterdam: Rodopi, 1995).

Lees, Lynn Hollen, *Exiles of Erin: Irish Migrants in Victorian London* (Ithaca: Cornell University Press, 1979).

Legg, Marie-Louise, *Newspapers and Nationalism: The Irish Provincial Press, 1850–1892* (Dublin: Four Courts, 1999).

Leighton, C. D. A., *Catholicism in a Protestant Kingdom: A Study of the Irish Ancien Régime* (Dublin: Gill & Macmillan, 1994).

Leighton, C. D. A., 'Gallicanism and the veto controversy: church, state and the Catholic community in early nineteenth-century Ireland', in Comerford et al. (eds), *Religion, Conflict and Coexistence*, pp. 132–58.

Lenehan, Jim, *Politics and Society in Athlone, 1830–1885: A Rotten Borough* (Dublin: Irish Academic Press, 1999).

Letford, L. and C. G. Pooley, 'Geographics of migration and religion: Irish women in mid-19th century Liverpool', in O'Sullivan (ed.), *The Irish World Wide*, IV, *Irish Women and Migration*, pp. 89–112.

Litvack, Leon and Glenn Hooper (eds), *Ireland in the Nineteenth Century: Regional Identity* (Dublin: Four Courts, 2000).

Lloyd, David, *Nationalism and Minor Literature: James Clarence Mangan and the Emergence of Irish Cultural Nationalism* (Berkeley: University of California Press, 1987).

Lloyd, David, *Anomalous States: Irish Writing and the Post-colonial Moment* (Dublin: Lilliput, 1993).

Lloyd, David, *Ireland After History* (Cork: Cork University Press, 1999).

Loftus, Belinda, *Mirrors: William III and Mother Ireland* (Dundrum: Picture Press, 1990).

Loftus, Belinda, *Mirrors: Orange and Green* (Dundrum: Picture Press, 1994).

Long, Gerard (ed.), *Books Beyond the Pale: Aspects of the Provincial Book Trade in Ireland Before 1850* (Dublin: Rare Books Group of the Library Association of Ireland, 1996).

Loughlin, James, *Ulster Unionism and British National Identity Since 1885* ((London: Pinter: 1995).

Lowe, W. J., *The Irish in Mid-Victorian Lancashire: The Shaping of a Working Class Community* (New York: Lang 1989).

Luddy, Maria, 'An agenda for women's history in Ireland: Part II 1800–1900', *IHS* 28, 109 (1992), pp. 19–37.

Luddy, Maria, *Women and Philanthropy in Nineteenth-Century Ireland* (Cambridge: Cambridge University Press, 1995).

Luddy, Maria, *Women in Ireland, 1800–1918: A Documentary History* (Cork: Cork University Press, 1995; 2nd edn, 1999).

Luddy, M., C. Cox, L. Lane, D. Urquhart et al., *Sources for Women's History in Ireland* (Dublin: Women's History Project, 1999).

Luddy Maria and Cliona Murphy (eds), *Women Surviving: Studies in Irish Women's History in the Nineteenth and Twentieth Centuries* (Dublin: Poolbeg, 1990).

Lyons, Laura E., 'The state of gender in Irish studies', *Eire-Ireland* 32, 4; 33, 1 & 2 (1997/8), pp. 236–60.

Macaulay, Ambrose, *William Crolly: Archbishop of Armagh, 1835–1849* (Dublin: Four Courts, 1994).

Mac Cárthaigh, Críostóir and Kevin Whelan (eds), *New Survey of Clare Island*, 1, *History and Cultural Landscape* (Dublin: Royal Irish Academy, 1999).

MacDonagh, Oliver, *States of Mind: A Study of Anglo-Irish Conflict 1780–1980* (London: Allen & Unwin, 1983).

MacDonagh, Oliver and W. F. Mandle (eds), *Ireland and Irish-Australia: Studies in Cultural and Political History* (London; Croom Helm, 1986).

MacDonald, Brian, *'A Time of Desolation': Clones Poor Law Union 1845–50* (Enniskillen: Clogher Historical Society, 2001).

Mac Gabhann, Séamus, 'Salvaging cultural identity: Peter Gallegan, 1792–1860', *Ríocht na Midhe* 9, 1 (1995), pp. 70–86.

Mac Gabhann, Séamus, 'Forging identity: Michael Clarke and the hidden Ireland', *Ríocht na Midhe* 9, 2 (1996), pp. 73–96.

Mac Gabhann, Séamus, 'Father Paul O'Brien of Cormeen (1763–1820): folk-poet and Maynooth professor', *Ríocht na Midhe* 10 (1999), pp. 125–51.

Mac Lochlainn, Antain, 'The Famine in Gaelic tradition', *Irish Review* 17/18 (1995), pp. 90–108.

MacRaild, Donald M., 'Irish immigration and the "Condition of England" question: the roots of an historiographical tradition', *Immigrants and Minorities* 14, 1 (1995), pp. 67–85.

MacRaild, Donald M., *Culture, Conflict and Migration: The Irish in Victorian Cumbria* (Liverpool: Liverpool University Press, 1998).

MacRaild, Donald M., *Irish Migrants in Modern Britain, 1750–1922* (Houndmills: Macmillan, 1999).

MacRaild, Donald M. (ed.), *The Great Famine and Beyond: Irish Migrants in Britain in the Nineteenth and Twentieth Centuries* (Dublin: Irish Academic Press, 2000).

MacRaild, Donald M., 'Wherever Orange is worn: Orangeism and Irish migration in the nineteenth and early twentieth centuries', *Canadian Journal of Irish Studies* 28, 2 (2002), pp. 98–117.

MacRaild, Donald M., 'Crossing migrant frontiers: comparative reflections on Irish migrants in Britain and the United States during the nineteenth century', in MacRaild (ed.), *The Great Famine and Beyond*, pp. 40–70.

MacRaild, Donald M., 'Introduction: the Great Famine and beyond: Irish migrants in Britain in the nineteenth and twentieth centuries', in MacRaild (ed.), *The Great Famine and Beyond*, pp. 1–13.

MacWilliams, Patrick (ed.), *Ordnance Survey Memoirs of Ireland: Index of Peoples and Places* (Belfast: Institute of Irish Studies, QUB, 2003).

Mageean, Deirdre, 'From Irish countryside to American city: the settlement and mobility of Ulster migrants in Philadelphia', in C. G. Pooley and I. D. Whyte (eds), *Migrants, Emigrants and Immigrants* (London; Routledge, 1991), pp. 42–61.

Mageean, Deirdre, 'To be matched or to move: Irish women's prospects in Munster', in Christiane Harzig (ed.), *Peasant Maids – City Women: From the European Countryside to Urban America* (Ithaca: Cornell University Press, 1997), pp. 57–97.

Magray, Mary Peckham, *The Transforming Power of the Nuns: Women, Religion and Cultural Change in Ireland, 1750–1900* (New York: Oxford University Press, 1998).

Maguire, Martin, 'The organisation and activism of Dublin's Protestant working class 1883–1935'. *IHS* 29, 113 (1994), pp. 65–87.

Mahon, William (ed.), *Doctor Kirwan's Irish Catechism by Thomas Hughes* (Cambridge, Mass.: Pangur, 1991).

Mahon, William, 'Scríobhaithe lámhscríbhinní Gaeilge i nGaillimh 1700–1900', in Moran and Gillespie (eds), *Galway: History and Society*, pp. 623–50.

Malcolm, Elizabeth and Greta Jones (eds), *Medicine, Disease and the State in Ireland, 1650–1940* (Cork: Cork University Press, 1999).

Maloney, John N., *A Soul Came into Ireland: Thomas Davis 1814–1845: A Biography* (Dublin: Geography Publications, 1995).

Mannion, J. J., *Point Lance in Transition: The Transformation of a Newfoundland Outport* (Toronto: McClelland & Steward, 1976).

Martin, Augustine, et al. (eds), *The Collected Poems of James Clarence Mangan*, 4 vols (Dublin: Irish Academic Press, 1996–9).

Martin, J. H., 'Social geography of mid nineteenth-century Dublin City', in Smyth and Whelan (eds), *Common Ground*, pp. 173–88.

Mathews, P. J., *The Abbey Theatre, Sinn Féin, the Gaelic League and the Cooperative Movement* (Cork: Cork University Press, 2003).

Maume, Patrick, 'Parnell and the IRB oath', *IHS* 29, 115 (1995), pp. 363–70.

Maume, Patrick, *The Long Gestation: Irish Nationalist Life 1891–1918* (Dublin: Gill & Macmillan, 1999).

McBride, Ian (ed.), *History and Memory in Modern Ireland* (Cambridge: Cambridge University Press, 2001).

McBride, Lawrence W., *The Greening of Dublin Castle: The Transformation of Bureaucratic and Judicial Personnel in Ireland, 1892–1922* (Washington: CUA Press, 1991).

McBride, Lawrence W. (ed.), *Images, Icons and the Irish Nationalist Imagination* (Dublin: Four Courts, 1999).

McBride, Lawrence W. (ed.), *The Reynolds Letters: An Irish Emigrant Family in Late Victorian Manchester* (Cork: Cork University Press, 1999).

McBride, Lawrence W., 'The Reynolds letters: sources for understanding the Irish emigrant experience in America and England, 1865–1934', in Fanning (ed.), *New Perspectives on the Irish Diaspora*, pp. 131–51.

McCaffrey, Lawrence J., *The Irish-Catholic Diaspora in America* (Washington, DC: Catholic University of America Press, 1997).

McCaffrey, Lawrence J, *Textures of Irish-America* (Syracuse: Syracuse University Press, 1998).

McCaffrey, Lawrence J., 'Diaspora, comparisons and Irish-American uniqueness', in Fanning (ed.), *New Perspectives*, pp. 15–27.

McCarthy, Angela, '"In prospect of a happier future": private letters and Irish women's migration to New Zealand, 1840–1925', in Fraser (ed.), *A Distant Shore*, pp. 105–16.

McCarthy, Angela, 'The desired haven'? Impressions of New Zealand in letters to and from Ireland, 1840–1925, in Bielenberg (ed.), *The Irish Diaspora*, pp. 272–84.

McCarthy, Marie, *Passing it On: The Transmission of Music in Irish Culture* (Cork: Cork University Press, 1999).

McCartney, Donal (ed.), *Parnell: The Politics of Power* (Dublin: Wolfhound, 1991).

McCartney, Donal, *W. E. H. Lecky: Historian and Politician 1838–1903* (Dublin: Lilliput, 1994).

McCaughey, Davis, 'Patrick O'Farrell on the Irish in Australia', in Bull et. al., *Ireland and Australia*, pp. 267–70.

McCone, Kim et al. (eds), *Stair na Gaeilge* (Maynooth: Department of Old Irish, 1994).

McConville, Chris, 'Patrick O'Farrell on the Irish in Australia', in Bull et al., *Irish-Australian Studies*, pp. 258–63.

Mc Cormack, W. J., *From Burke to Beckett: Ascendancy, Tradition and Betrayal in Literary History* (Cork: Cork University Press, 1994).

McCracken, Dónal P., *Southern African-Irish Studies* (Durban; University of Durban, 1992).

McCracken, Dónal P., 'Odd man out: the South African experience', in Bielenberg (ed.), *The Irish Diaspora*, pp. 251–71.

McCready, Richard B., 'Revising the Irish in Scotland: the Irish in nineteenth-and early twentieth-century Scotland', in Bielenberg (ed.), *The Irish Diaspora*, pp. 37–50.

McDermot, Brian, *The Irish Catholic Petition of 1805: The Diary of Denys Scully* (Dublin: Irish Academic Press, 1992).

McDonnell, Noreen (ed.), *Callan Co-operative Agricultural and Dairy Society Ltd, 1899–1999* (Callan Co-operative, 1999).

McDowell, R. B. *Crisis and Decline: The Fate of Southern Unionism* (Dublin: Lilliput, 1997).

McFarland, Elaine, *Protestants First: Orangeism in Nineteenth Century Scotland* (Edinburgh: Edinburgh University Press, 1990).

McGowan, Mark. K., *The Waning of the Green: Catholics, the Irish and Identity in Toronto, 1887–1922* (Kingston: McGill-Queen's University Press, 1999).

McGrath, Thomas G., 'The Tridentine evolution of modern Irish Catholicism: a re-examination of the "devotional revolution" thesis', in Ó Muirí (ed.), *Irish Church History Today*, pp. 84–99.

McGrath, Thomas, *Politics, Interdenominational Relations and Education in the Public Ministry of Bishop James Doyle of Kildare and Leighlin, 1786–1834* (Dublin: Four Courts, 1998).

McGrath, Thomas, *Religious Renewal and Reform in the Pastoral Ministry of Bishop James Doyle of Kildare and Leighlin, 1786–1834* (Dublin: Four Courts, 1998).

McGuinne, D., *Irish Type Design: A History of Printing Types in the Irish Character* (Dublin: Irish Academic Press, 1992).

McKenna, Malachy. 'A textual history of *The Spiritual Rose*', *Clogher Record* 14 (1991), pp. 52–73.

McKenna, Patrick, 'Irish emigration to Argentina: a different model', in Bielenberg (ed.), *The Irish Diaspora*, pp. 195–212.

McKenna-Lawlor, Susan M. P., *Whatever Shines Should Be Observed* (Dublin: Samton, 1998).

McLeod, H., 'Popular Catholicism in New York', in Shiels and Wood (eds), *Studies in Church History*, XXV, *The Churches, Ireland and the Irish*, pp. 353–73.

McNally, Vincent J., *Reform, Revolution and Reaction: Archbishop John Thomas Troy and the Roman Catholic Church in Ireland, 1787–1817* (Lanham and London: University Press of America, 1995).

McParland, Edward, 'A bibliography of Irish architectural history', *IHS* 26, 102 (Nov. 1998), pp. 161–212.

Meagher, Timothy J., *Inventing Irish America* (South Bend: University of Notre Dame Press, 2001).

Melville, Joy, *Mother of Oscar: The Life of Jane Francesca Wilde* (London: John Murray, 1994).

Miller, D. W., 'Irish Catholicism and the Great Famine', *Journal of Social History* 9 (1975), pp. 81–98.

Miller, D. W., 'Mass attendance in Ireland in 1834', in Brown and Miller (eds), *Piety and Power in Ireland 1760–1960*, pp. 158–79.

Miller, David W., 'Irish Presbyterians and the Great Famine', in Hill and Lennon (eds), *Luxury and Austerity: Historical Studies* XXI, pp. 165–81.

Miller, Kerby A., 'Class, culture, and immigrant group identity in the United States: the case of Irish-American ethnicity', in Virginia Yann McLaughlin (ed.), *Immigration Reconsidered: History, Sociology and Politics* (New York: Oxford University Press, 1990), pp. 92–129.

Miller, Kerby A., '"Revenge for Skibbereen": Irish emigration and the meaning of the Great Famine', in Gribben (ed.), *The Great Famine and the Irish Diaspora*, pp. 180–95.

Miller, Kerby A., '"Scotch-Irish" myths and "Irish" identities in eighteenth- and nineteenth-century America', in Fanning (ed.), *New Perspectives on the Irish Diaspora*, pp. 75–92.

Miller, Kerby A. and Bruce D. Boling, 'Golden streets, bitter tears: the Irish image of America during the era of mass migration', *Journal of American Ethnic History* 10 (1991), pp. 16–35.

Miller, Kerby A. and Bruce D. Boling, with Liam Kennedy, 'The Famine's scars: William Murphy's Ulster and American Odyssey', *Éire-Ireland* 36 (2001), pp. 98–123.

Miller, Kerby A., David N. Doyle, Bruce Boling and Arnold Schrier, *Irish Immigrants in the Land of Canaan: Letters and Memoirs from Colonial and Revolutionary America, 1675–1815* (New York: Oxford University Press, 2003).

Miller, Kerby A., David N. Doyle and Patricia Kelleher, '"For love and liberty": Irish women, migration and domesticity in Ireland and America, 1815–1920', in O'Sullivan (ed.), *The Irish World Wide*, IV, *Irish Women and Irish Migration*, pp. 41–65.

Milne, Kenneth (ed.), *Christ Church Cathedral, Dublin: A History* (Dublin: Four Courts, 2000).

Mokyr, Joel, *Why Ireland Starved: A Quantitative and Analytical History of the Irish Economy 1800–1850* (London: Allen & Unwin, 1983).

Moloney, Colette, *The Irish Music Manuscripts of Edward Bunting (1773–1843): An Introduction* (Dublin: Irish Traditional Music Archive, 2000).

Moloney, Mick, *Far from the Shamrock Shore* (New York; Crown Books, 2002).

Moran, Gerard, *A Radical Priest in Mayo: Father Patrick Lavelle: The Rise and Fall of an Irish Nationalist, 1825–86* (Dublin: Irish Academic Press, 1994).

Moran, Gerard (ed.), *Radical Irish Priests, 1660–1970* (Dublin: Four Courts, 1998).

Moran, Gerard, *Assisted Emigration to North America from Nineteenth-Century Ireland* (Dublin: Four Courts, 2004).

Moran, Gerard and Raymond Gillespie (eds), *Galway: History and Society: Interdisciplinary Essays on the History of an Irish County* (Dublin: Geography Publications, 1996).

Morash, Christopher, *Writing the Irish Famine* (Oxford: Clarendon, 1995).

Morash, Christopher and Richard Hayes (eds), *'Fearful Realities': New Perspectives on the Famine* (Dublin: Irish Academic Press, 1996).

Moriarty, Theresa, *Work in Progress: Episodes from the History of Irish Women's Trade Unionism* (Brighton: Irish Labour History Society/Unison, *c.*1994).

Morrissey, Thomas, *William J. Walsh, Archbishop of Dublin, 1841–1921: No Uncertain Voice* (Dublin: Four Courts, 2000).

Muenger, Elizabeth A., *The British Military Dilemma in Ireland: Occupation Politics, 1870–1914* (Lawrence KA: University of Kansas Press, 1991).

Mulcrone, Mick, 'The Famine and collective memory: the role of the Irish American press in the early twentieth century', in Gribben (ed.), *The Great Famine*, pp. 219–38.

Murnane, Brian, 'The recreation of the urban historical landscape: Mountjoy Ward Dublin *circa* 1901', in Smyth and Whelan (eds), *Common Ground*, pp. 189–207.

Murphy, Ignatius, *The Diocese of Killaloe, 1800–1850* (Dublin: Four Courts, 1992).

Murphy, Ignatius, *The Diocese of Killaloe, 1850–1904* (Dublin: Four Courts, 1995).

Murphy, James H. *Catholic Fiction and Social Reality in Ireland, 1873–1922* (Westport, CT: Greenwood, 1997).

Murphy, James H., *Ireland: A Social, Cultural and Literary History, 1791–1891* (Dublin: Four Courts, 2003).

Murphy, Maureen (ed.), Asenath Nicholson, *Annals of the Famine in Ireland* (Dublin: Lilliput, 1998).

Murphy, Maureen (ed.), *The Great Irish Famine Curriculum* (New York: New York State Education Department, 2001).

Murphy, Paula, 'The O'Connell monument in Dublin: the political and artistic context of a public sculpture', *Apollo* (Mar. 1996), pp. 22–36.

Murphy, Paula, 'The politics of the street monument', *Irish Arts Review Yearbook* 10 (1994), pp. 202–8.

Murray, Damien, *Romanticism, Nationalism and Irish Antiquarian Societies 1840–80* (Maynooth: Department of Old and Middle Irish, NUI Maynooth, 2000).

Murray, Peter, *Illustrated Summary Catalogue of The Crawford Municipal Art Gallery* (City of Cork Vocational Education Committee, 1992).

Nash, Catherine and Brian Graham, 'The making of modern historical geographies', in Graham and Nash (eds), *Modern Historical Geographies*, pp. 1–9.

National Gallery of Ireland and Douglas Hyde Gallery, *Irish Women Artists: From the Eighteenth Century to the Present Day* (Dublin: NGI and Douglas Hyde Gallery, 1987).

Neal, Frank, 'A criminal profile of the Liverpool Irish', *Transactions of the Historic Society of Lancashire and Cheshire* 140 (1991), pp. 161–99.

Neal, Frank, 'English–Irish conflict in the north-west of England: economics, racialism, anti-Catholicism or simple xenophobia?', *Bulletin of the North-West Labour History Group* 16 (1991–2), pp. 14–25.

Neal, Frank, 'Lancashire, the Famine and the poor laws', *Irish Economic and Social History* 22 (1995), pp. 26–48.

Neal, Frank, *Black '47: Britain and the Famine Irish* (Houndmills: Macmillan, 1998).

Neal, Frank, 'The foundations of the Irish settlement in Newcastle-upon-Tyne: the evidence in the 1851 Census', in MacRaild (ed.), *The Great Famine and Beyond*, pp. 71–93.

Neal, Frank, 'Black '47: Liverpool and the Irish Famine', in Crawford (ed.), *The Hungry Stream*, pp. 123–36.

Neal, Frank, 'English–Irish conflict in the north-east of England', in Buckland and Belchem (eds), *The Irish in British Labour History*, pp. 59–85.

Neville, Grace, '"He spoke to me in English: I answered him in Irish": language shift in the folklore archives', in Brihault (ed.), *L'Irlande et Ses Langues*, pp. 19–32.

Neville, Grace, '"Land of the fair, land of the free": the myth of America in Irish folklore', in Coulson (ed.), *Exiles and Migrants*, pp. 57–71.

Neville, Grace, 'Rites de passage: rituals of separation in Irish oral tradition', in Fanning (ed.), *New Perspectives on the Irish Diaspora*, pp. 117–30.

Nevin, Donal (ed.), *Trade Union Century* (Cork and Dublin: Mercier, in association with ICTU and RTÉ, 1994).

Ní Bhroiméil, Una, *The Gaelic Revival and America, 1870–1915* (Dublin: Four Courts, 2003).

Ní Chonghaile, Áine, *F. H. O'Donnell 1846–1916: A Shaol agus a Shaothar* (BAC: Coiscéim, 1992).

Ní Dheá, Eilís, 'Mícheál Ó Raghallaigh – scríobhaí ó Inis Díomáin', *The Other Clare* (Apr. 1992), pp. 18–20.

Ní Dheá, Eilís, 'Mícheál Ó hAnnracháin agus a chomhscríobhaithe i gCill Ruis', *The Other Clare* (Apr. 1993), pp. 45–7.

Ní Dheá, Eilís, 'Ár n-oidhreacht lámhscríbhinní ó Dhún Átha Thiar agus ón gCeantar Máguaird', in Ó Fiannachta (ed.), *Ómós do Eoghan Ó Comhraí*, pp. 31–42.

Ní Dhonnchadha, Máirín, 'Neamhlitearthacht agus Gaeilge: eagna na staraithe?', *Comhar* 50 (1991), pp. 22–5.

Ní Dhonnchadha, Máirín (ed.), *Nua-Léamha: Gnéithe de Chultúr, Stair agus Polaitíocht na hÉireann c.1600–1900* (Dublin: An Clóchomhar, 1996), pp. 170–93.

Ní Liatháin, Íde, *The Life and Career of P. A. McHugh, a North Connacht Politician 1859–1909: A Footsoldier of the Party* (Dublin: Irish Academic Press, 1999).

Ní Mhóráin, Brighid, *Thiar sa Mhainistir atá an Ghaoluinn Bhreá: Meath na Gaeilge in Uíbh Ráthach* (Dingle: An Sagart, 1997).

Ní Mhurchú, Máire and Diarmuid Breathnach, *1782–1881: Beathaisnéis* (Dublin: An Clóchomhar, 1999).

Ní Shéaghdha, Nessa, 'Gairmeacha beatha roinnt scríobhaithe ón 18ú agus an 19ú céad', *Celtica* 21 (1990), pp. 567–75.

Ní Úrdail, Meidhbhín, *The Scribe in Eighteenth and Nineteenth-Century Ireland: Motivations and Milieu* (Münster: Nodus, 2000).

Nic Craith, Mairéad, *Malartú Teanga: An Ghaeilge i gCorcaigh sa Naoú hAois Déag* (Bremen: Verlag für E. S. I. S.-Publikationen, 1994).

Nic Eoin, Máirín, 'Irish language and literature in County Kilkenny in the nineteenth century', in Nolan and Whelan (eds), *Kilkenny: History and Society*, pp. 465–79.

Nic Pháidín, C., *Fáinne an Lae agus an Athbheochan, 1898–1900* (Dublin: Cois Life, 1998).

Nicholson, Asenath, *Annals of the Famine in Ireland*, ed. Maureen Murphy (Dublin: Lilliput, 1998).

Nilsen, K. E., 'The Irish language in nineteenth century New York City', in O. Garcia and J. A. Fishman (eds), *The Multilingual Apple: Languages in New York City* (New York: Mouton de Gruyter, 1997).

Nilsen, Kenneth, 'Mícheál Ó Broin agus Lámhscríbhinní Gaeilge Ollscoil Wisconsin', *Celtica* 22 (1991), pp. 112–18.

Nolan, Janet, *Ourselves Alone: Women's Emigration from Ireland 1885–1920* (Lexington: University Press of Kentucky, 1989).

Nolan, Janet, 'Education: Irish-American teachers in public schools: 1880–1920', in Glazier (ed), *Encyclopaedia of the Irish in America*, pp. 236–9.

Nolan, William, *Fassadinin: Land, Settlement and Society in South-East Ireland 1600–1850* (Dublin: Geography Publications, 1979).

Nolan, William, *Tracing the Past: Sources for Local Studies in the Republic of Ireland* (Dublin: Geography Publications, 1982).

Nolan, William (ed.), *Tipperary: History and Society* (Dublin: Geography Publications, 1985).

Nolan, William (ed.), *The Shaping of Ireland: The Geographical Perspective* (Cork and Dublin: Mercier and RTÉ, 1986).

Nolan, William, 'Society and settlement in the valley of Glenasmole *c*.1750–*c*.1900', in Aalen and Whelan (eds), *Dublin City and County*, pp. 181–228.

Nolan, William, 'New farms and fields: migration policies of state land agencies 1891–1980', in Smyth and Whelan (eds), *Common Ground*, pp. 296–319.

Nolan, William, T. P. Power and Des Cowman (eds), *Waterford: History and Society: Interdisciplinary Essays on the History of an Irish County* (Dublin: Geography Publications, 1992).

Nolan, William, Liam Ronayne and Mairead Dunlevy (eds), *Donegal: History and Society: Interdisciplinary Essays on the History of an Irish County* (Dublin: Geography Publications, 1995).

Nolan, William and Anngret Simms (eds), Ríonach Ní Néill and Yvonne Whelan (comp.), *Irish Towns: A Guide to Sources* (Dublin: Geography Publications, 1998).

Nolan, William and Kevin Whelan (eds), *Kilkenny: History and Society* (Dublin: Geography Publications, 1990).

Noone,Val, 'Commentary and analysis. Publications from the Irish-Australian Conferences', in Philip Bull et al. (eds), *Ireland and Australia*, pp. 349–66.

Norquay, G. and G. Smyth (eds), *Space and Place: The Geographies of Literature* (Liverpool: Liverpool University Press, 1998), pp. 57–76.

O'Brien, Gerard, 'Charles Gavan Duffy 1816–1903', in O'Brien and Roebuck (eds), *Nine Ulster Lives*, pp. 87–98.

O'Brien, Gerard and Peter Roebuck (eds), *Nine Ulster Lives* (Belfast: Irish Historical Foundation, 1992).

O'Brien, John and Pauric Travers (eds), *The Irish Emigrant Experience in Australia* (Swords: Poolbeg, 1991).

O'Callaghan, Margaret, *British High Politics and Nationalist Ireland: Criminality, Land and the Law under Foster and Balfour* (Cork: Cork University Press, 1994).

Ó Canainn, Aodh, 'An Cúlra', in Ó Canainn and Watson (eds), *Scian a Caitheadh le Toinn*, pp. 1–27.

Ó Canainn, Aodh and S. Watson (eds), *Scian a Caitheadh le Toinn: Scéalta agus Amhráin as Inis Eoghain agus Cuimhne ar Ghaeltacht Iorrais* (Dublin: Coiscéim, 1990).

Ó Cathaoir, Breandán, *John Blake Dillon: Young Irelander* (Dublin: Irish Academic Press, 1990).

Ó Cearúil, Mícheál (ed.), *Gníomhartha na mBráithre* (Dublin: Coiscéim, 1996).

Ó Ciosáin, Niall, 'Boccoughs and God's poor: deserving and undeserving poor in Irish popular culture', in Foley and Ryder (eds), *Ideology and Ireland*, pp. 93–9.

Ó Ciosáin, Niall, *Print and Popular Culture in Ireland, 1750–1850* (London: Macmillan, 1997).

Ó Ciosáin, Niall, 'Printing in Irish and O'Sullivan's *Miscellany*', in Long (ed.), *Books Beyond the Pale*, pp. 87–99.

Ó Conaire, Breandán (ed.), *The Famine Lectures: Comhdháil an Chraoibhín 1995–97* (Boyle: Roscommon County Council, 2001).

Ó Conchúir, Breandán, *Clár Lámhscríbhinní Gaeilge in Ollscoil Chorcaí: Cnuasach Uí Mhurchú* (Dublin: Institute for Advanced Studies, 1991).

Ó Conchúir, Breandán, 'Thomas Swanton, Réamhchonraitheoir in Iar Chairbre', *Journal of the Cork Historical and Archaeological Society* 98 (1993), pp. 50–60.

O'Connell, Anne, '"Take care of the immigrant girls": the migration process of late nineteenth-century Irish women', *Éire-Ireland* 35, 3 & 4 (2000–1), pp. 102–33.

O'Connell, Maurice R. (ed.), *Daniel O'Connell: Political Pioneer* (Dublin: IPA, 1991).

O'Connell, Maurice R. (ed.), *O'Connell, Education, Church and State* (Dublin: IPA, 1991).

O'Connell, Maurice (ed.), *People Power: Proceedings of the Third O'Connell Workshop* (Dublin: IPA, 1993).

O'Connor, Emmet, *A Labour History of Ireland 1824–1960* (Dublin: Gill & Macmillan, 1992).

O'Connor, Thomas (ed.), *The Irish in Europe, 1580–1815* (Dublin: Four Courts, 2001).

Ó Crualaoich, Gearóid, 'The "merry wake"', in Donnelly and Miller (eds), *Irish Popular Culture*, pp. 173–200.

Ó Cuív, Brian, 'Irish language and literature 1845–1921', in Vaughan (ed.), *A New History of Ireland*, VI, pp. 385–435.

O'Day, Alan (ed.), *'A Survey of the Irish in England' by Hugh Heinrich* (1872) (London: Hambledon, 1990).

O'Day, Alan, *Irish Home Rule 1867–1921* (Manchester: Manchester University Press, 1998).

O'Day, Alan, 'Revising the diaspora', in Boyce and O'Day (eds), *The Making of Modern Irish History*, pp. 188–215.

Ó Donnchadha, Rónán, *Micheál Óg Ó Longáin, File* (Dublin: Coiscéim, 1994).

O'Donnell, Edward T., '"The scattered debris of the Irish nation": the Famine Irish and New York City, 1845–55', in Crawford (ed.), *The Hungry Stream*, pp. 49–60.

O'Donnell, Sean, *Clonmel 1840–1900: Anatomy of an Irish Town* (Dublin: Geography Publications, 1999).

O'Dowd, Anne, *Spalpeens and Tattie Hokers: History and Folklore of Irish Migratory Agricultural Workers in Ireland and Britain* (Dublin: Irish Academic Press, 1991).

O'Dowd, Desmond, *Changing Times: Religion and Society in Nineteenth-Century Celbridge* (Dublin: Irish Academic Press, 1997).

O'Dowd, Liam (ed.), *On Intellectuals and Intellectual Life in Ireland* (Belfast: Institute of Irish Studies, 1996).

Ó Drisceoil, Proinsias, *Ar Scaradh Gabháil: an Fhéiniúlacht in 'Cín Lae Amhlaoibh Uí Shúilleabháin'* (Dublin: An Clóchomhar, 2000).

Ó Duígneáin, Proinnsíos, *The Priest and the Protestant Woman: The Trial of Rev Thomas Maguire, PP, December 1827* (Dublin: Irish Academic Press, 1997).

Ó Dúill, Gréagóir, *Samuel Ferguson: Beatha agus Saothar* (Dublin: An Clóchomhar, 1993).

Ó Dúshláine, Tadhg, 'Gealán Dúluachra: Seanmóireacht na Gaeilge c.1600–1850', in Ó hUiginn (ed.), *Léann na Gaeilge*, pp. 83–122.

O'Dwyer, Riana, 'Women's narratives, 1800–1840', in Bourke et al. (eds), *Field Day Anthology of Irish Writing*, V, pp. 833–94.

O'Farrell, Patrick, *Vanished Kingdoms: Irish in Australia and New Zealand: A Personal Excursion* (Kensington, NSW: New South Wales University Press, 1990).

O'Farrell, Patrick, *The Irish in Australia: 1788 to the Present* (Cork: Cork University Press, 2001).

O'Farrell, Patrick, 'Patrick O'Farrell on the Irish in Australia', in Bull et al. (eds), *Irish-Australian Studies*, pp. 271–4.

O'Farrell, Patrick, 'The Irish in Australia and New Zealand, 1791–1870', in Vaughan (ed.), *A New History of Ireland*, V, pp. 661–81.

O'Farrell, Patrick, 'The Irish in Australia and New Zealand, 1870–1990', in Vaughan (ed.), *A New History of Ireland*, VI, pp. 703–24.

O'Farrell, Patrick, 'Varieties of New Zealand Irishness', in Fraser (ed.), *A Distant Shore*, pp. 25–35.

O'Farrell, Patrick, 'Writing the history of Irish-Australia', in MacDonagh and Mandle (eds), *Ireland and Irish-Australia*, pp. 217–28.

Ó Fiannachta, Pádraig (ed.), *Maigh Nuad agus an Ghaeilge* (Maynoooth: An Sagart, 1993).

Ó Fiannachta, Pádraig (ed.), *Ómós do Eoghan Ó Comhraí* (Dingle: An Sagart, 1995).

O'Flanagan, Patrick and C. G. Buttimer (eds), *Cork: History and Society* (Dublin: Geography Publications, 1993).

Ó Glaisne, Risteárd, *Modhaigh: Scéal Pobail – Scéal Eaglaise* (Baile Átha Cliath: An Clóchomar, 1998).

Ó Gráda, Cormac, 'A note on nineteenth-century Irish emigration statistics', *Population Studies* 29 (1975), pp. 143–9.

Ó Gráda, Cormac, *The Great Irish Famine* (Dublin: Gill & Macmillan, 1989).

Ó Gráda, Cormac, *Ireland Before and After the Famine: Explorations in Economic History, 1800–1925* (Manchester: Manchester University Press, 1988).

Ó Gráda, Cormac, *Ireland: A New Economic History, 1780–1939* (Oxford: Clarendon, 1994).

Ó Gráda, Cormac (ed.), *Famine 150: Commemorative Lecture Series* (Dublin: Teagasc/UCD, 1997).

Ó Gráda, Cormac, *Immigrants, Savers and Runners: the Emigrant Industrial Savings Bank in the 1850s* (Dublin: Department of Economics, UCD, 1998).

Ó Gráda, Cormac, *Black '47 and Beyond: The Great Irish Famine in History, Economy, and Memory* (Princeton NJ: Princeton University Press, 1999).

Ó Gráda, Cormac and Tim Dyson (eds), *Famine Demography* (Oxford: Clarendon, 2002).

Ó hÁinle, Cathal, 'Ceo Meala: an Craoibhín agus na hAmhráin Ghrá', *Irish Review* 14 (1993), pp. 33–47.

Ó hÁinle, Cathal, 'Ó Chaint na nDaoine go dtí an Caighdeán Oifigiúil', in McCone et al. (eds), *Stair na Gaeilge*, pp. 745–93.

Ó hEarcáin, M., 'Meath na Gaeilge i gCluain Maine agus in Iorras', *Donegal Annual* 47 (1995), pp. 106–12.

O'Hearn, Denis, 'Innovation and the world-system hierarchy: British subjugation of the Irish cotton industry', *American Journal of Sociology* 100 (1994), pp. 587–621.

Ó hÓgáin, Éamon, 'Scríobhaithe lámhscríbhinní Gaeilge i gCill Chainnigh 1700–1870', in Nolan and Whelan (eds), *Kilkenny: History and Society*, pp. 405–36.

Ó hUiginn, Ruairí (ed.), *Léann na Gaeilge: Súil Siar, Súil chun Cinn* (Maynooth: An Sagart, 1996).

Ó hUigínn, Ruairí (ed.), *Scoláirí Gaeilge* (Maynooth: An Sagart, 1997).

O'Leary, Paul, *Immigration and Integration: The Irish in Wales 1798–1922* (Cardiff: University of Wales Press, 2000).

O'Leary, Paul, 'From the cradle to the grave; popular Catholicism among the Irish in Wales', in O'Sullivan (ed.), *The Irish World Wide*, V, *Religion and Identity*, pp. 183–75.

O'Leary, Paul, 'Religion, nationality and politics: disestablishment in Ireland and Wales, 1868–1914', in Guy and Neely (eds), *Contrast and Comparisons*, pp. 89–113.

Ó Macháin, Pádraig, *Catalogue of Irish Manuscripts in Mount Melleray Abbey, County Waterford* (Dublin: Institute for Advanced Studies, 1991).

Ó Macháin, Pádraig, 'Additions to the collection of Irish manuscripts at Mount Melleray Abbey', *Éigse* 30 (1997), pp. 92–108.

Ó Macháin, Pádraig, 'Patrick Carmody, Irish scholar', *Decies* 53 (1997), pp. 133–43.

Ó Muirí, Réamonn (ed.), *Irish Church History Today* (Armagh: Cumann Seanchais Ard Mhacha, 1991).

Ó Muirithe, Diarmaid, 'Prayers for O'Connell and emancipation', *Éigse* 25 (1991), pp. 102–4.

Ó Muirithe, Diarmuid, 'An t-Athair Pól Ó Briain', in Ó Fiannachta (ed.), *Maigh Nuad agus an Ghaeilge*, pp. 8–43.

Ó Muraíle, Nollaig, 'Seán Ó Donnabháin', in Ó hUigínn (ed.), *Scoláirí Gaeilge*, pp. 11–82.

Ó Murchú, Máirtín, 'Language and society in nineteenth-century Ireland', in Geraint Jenkins (ed.), *Language and Community in the Nineteenth Century* (Cardiff: University of Wales Press, 1998), pp. 341–68.

O'Neill, Marie, *From Parnell to de Valera: A Biography of Jennie Wyse Power 1858–1941* (Dublin: Blackwater, 1991).

O'Neill, Tim P., 'Famine evictions', in King (ed.), *Famine, Land and Culture in Ireland*, pp. 29–70.

O'Rourke, Kevin H. and Cormac Ó Gráda, *Migration as Disaster Relief: Lessons from the Irish Famine* (Dublin: UCD 1996).

O'Rourke, Kevin H. and Jeffrey G. Williamson, *Globalization and History: The Evolution of a Nineteenth-Century Atlantic Economy* (Cambridge, Mass: MIT Press, 1999).

O'Rourke, Kevin H., Jeffrey G. Williamson and Timothy J. Hatton, *Mass Migration, Commodity Market Integration, and Real Wage Convergence: The Late Nineteenth Century* (UCD, Centre for Economic Research, 1993).

Orser, Charles E. Jr, 'Archaeology and nineteenth-century rural life in County Roscommon', *Archaeology Ireland* 11 (1997), pp. 14–17.

Orser, Charles E. Jr, 'Of dishes and drains: an archaeological perspective on Irish life in the Famine era', *New Hibernia Review* 1 (1997), pp. 122–34.

Orser, Charles E. Jr, 'Can there be an archaeology of the Great Famine?', in Morash and Hayes (eds), *'Fearful Realities'*, pp. 77–89.

Orser, Charles E. Jr, 'Archaeology and modern Irish history', *Irish Studies Review* 18 (1997), pp. 2–7.

Ó Saothraí, Séamus, *An Ministir Gaelach: Uilliam Mac Néill 1774–1821* (Dublin: Coiscéim, 1992).

Ó Síocháin, Etáin (ed.), *Maigh Nuad: Saothrú na Gaeilge 1795–1995* (Maynooth: An Sagart, 1995).

Ó Súilleabheain, Eoghan, 'Scríobhaithe Phort Láirge 1700–1900', in Nolan et al. (eds), *Waterford: History and Society*, pp. 265–308.

O'Sullivan, Niamh, *Aloysius O'Kelly: Re-Orientations: Painting, Politics and Popular Culture* (Dublin, Hugh Lane Municipal Gallery of Modern Art, 1999).

O'Sullivan, Niamh, 'The iron cage of femininity: visual representation of women in the 1880s land agitation', in Foley and Ryder (eds), *Ideology and Ireland*, pp. 181–96.

O'Sullivan, Patrick (ed.), *The Irish World Wide*, 6 vols (London: Leicester University Press). I *Patterns of Migration* (1992); II *The Irish in the New Communities* (1992); III *The Creative Migrant* (1994); IV *Irish Women and Irish Migration* (1995); V *Religion and Identity* (1996); VI *The Meaning of the Famine* (1997).

O'Sullivan, Patrick, 'Developing Irish Diaspora studies: a personal view', *New Hibernia Review* 7, 1 (2003).

O'Sullivan, Patrick, 'The Irish joke', in O'Sullivan (ed.), *The Irish World Wide*, III *The Creative Migrant*, pp. 57–82.

O'Sullivan Patrick, 'London and the union: Ireland's capital, Ireland's colony', in Stewart (ed.), *Hearts and Minds*, pp. 291–308.

Ó Tuathaigh, Gearóid, 'Maigh Nuad agus Stair na Gaeilge', in Ó Síocháin (ed.), *Maigh Nuad: Saothrú na Gaeilge 1795–1995*, pp. 13–35.

Ó Tuathaigh, M. A. G., 'The Irish in nineteenth-century Britain: problems of integration' [orig. 1981] repr. Swift and Gilley (eds), *Irish in the Victorian City*, pp. 13–36.

Owens, Gary, 'Constructing the Repeal spectacle: monster meetings and people power in pre-Famine Ireland', in O'Connell (ed.), *People Power*, pp. 89–93.

Owens, Gary, 'Nationalism without words: symbolism and ritual behaviour in the Repeal "monster meetings" of 1843–5', in Donnelly and Miller (eds), *Irish Popular Culture 1650–1850*, pp. 242–69.

Owens, Gary, '"A moral insurrection": faction-fighters, public demonstrations and the O'Connellite campaign, 1828', *IHS* 30, 120 (1997), pp. 513–41.

Owens, Gary, 'Visualising the Liberator: self-fashioning dramaturgy and the construction of Daniel O'Connell', *Éire-Ireland* 33, 3 & 4; 34,1 (1998/9), pp. 103–30.

Owens, Gary, 'Constructing the image of Daniel O'Connell', *History Ireland* 7, 1 (1999), pp. 32–6.

Parkhill, Trevor, '"Permanent deadweight": emigration from Ulster workhouses during the Famine', in Crawford (ed.), *The Hungry Stream*, pp. 87–100.

Pašeta, Senia, *Before the Revolution: Nationalism, Social Change and Ireland's Catholic Elite, 1879–1922* (Cork: Cork University Press, 1999).

Peckham Magray, Mary, *The Transforming Power of the Nuns: Women, Religion, & Cultural Change in Ireland, 1750–1900* (New York: Oxford University Press, 1998).

Pelan, Rebecca (ed.), assisted by Noel Quirke and Mark Finnane, *Irish-Australian Studies: Papers Delivered at the Seventh Irish-Australian Conference July 1993* (Sydney: Crossing Press, 1994).

Pelly, Patricia and Andrew Tod (eds), *The Highland Lady in Ireland, Journals 1840–50 by Elizabeth Grant* (Edinburgh: Canongate, 1991).

Pine, Richard and Charles Acton (eds), *To Talent Alone: The Royal Irish Academy of Music 1848–1998* (Dublin: Gill & Macmillan, 1998).

Póirtéir, Cathal (ed.), *Gnéithe den Ghorta* (Dublin: Coiscéim, 1995).

Póirtéir, Cathal (ed.), *The Great Irish Famine* (Cork: Mercier, 1995).

Pooley, C. G., 'Irish settlement in north-west England in the mid-nineteenth century: a geographical critique', *North-West Labour History Journal* 16 (1991–2), pp. 26–35.

Pooley, C. G. 'Segregation or integration? The residential experience of the Irish in mid-Victorian Britain', in Swift and Gilley (eds), *The Irish in Britain*, pp. 60–83.

Proudfoot, Lindsay J. (ed.), *Down: History and Society: Interdisciplinary Essays on the History of an Irish County* (Dublin: Geography Publications, 1997).

Proudfoot, Lindsay J. 'Regionalism and localism: religious change and social protest, *c.*1700 to *c.*1900', in Graham and Proudfoot (eds), *An Historical Geography of Ireland*, pp. 185–218.

Proudfoot, Lindsay J., 'The Estate system in mid nineteenth-century County Waterford', in Nolan and Power (eds), *Waterford: History and Society*, pp. 519–40.

Prunty, Jacinta, *Dublin Slums, 1800–1925: A Study in Urban Geography* (Dublin: Irish Academic Press, 1998).

Prunty, Jacinta, *Margaret Aylward, 1810–1889: Lady of Charity, Sister of Faith* (Dublin: Four Courts, 1999).

Quigley, Michael, 'Grosse Île: The most important and evocative Great Famine site outside of Ireland', in Crawford (ed.), *The Hungry Stream*, pp. 25–40.

Quinlan, Carmel, *Genteel Revolutionaries: Anna and Thomas Haslam and the Irish Women's Movement* (Cork: Cork University Press, 2002).

Quinn, John F., 'The "vagabond friar": Father Mathew's difficulties with Irish bishops, 1840–56', *Catholic Historical Review* 78 (1992), pp. 542–56.

Quinn, Peter, *Banished Children of Eve* (New York: Penguin, 1994).

Rafferty, Oliver P., *Catholicism in Ulster, 1603–1983: An Interpretative History* (London: Hurst, 1994).

Rafferty, Oliver P., 'The Catholic Church and Fenianism, 1861–1870: some Irish and American perspectives', *Bullán* 3 (1997–8), pp. 47–69.

Rafferty, Oliver P., *The Church, the State and the Fenian Threat, 1861–75* (Houndmills: Macmillan, 1999).

Reece, Bob, 'Writing about the Irish in Australia', in O'Brien and Travers, *The Irish Emigrant Experience in Australia*, pp. 226–42.

Regan, Stephen, *Irish Writing: An Anthology of Irish Literature in English 1789–1939* (Oxford: Oxford University Press, 2004).

Richards, E., 'Voices of British and Irish migrants in nineteenth century Australia', in C. G. Pooley and I. D. Whyte (eds), *Migrants, Emigrants and Immigrants* (London: Routledge, 1991).

Riggs, Pádraigín, Breandán Ó Conchúir and Seán Ó Coileáin (eds), *Saoi na hÉigse: Aistí in Onóir do Sheán Ó Tuama* (Dublin: An Clóchomhar, 2000).

Robins, Joseph, *The Miasma: Epidemic and Panic in Nineteenth-Century Ireland* (Dublin: IPA, 1995)

Robinson, Tim, *Stones of Aran: Pilgrimage* (Mullingar and Dublin: Lilliput and Wolfhound, 1986).

Rockett, Kevin, Luke Gibbons and John Hill (eds), *Cinema and Ireland* (London: Routledge, 1987).

Roediger, David R., *The Wages of Whiteness: Race and the Making of the American Working Class* (London: Verso, 1991).

Rouse, Sarah, *Into the Light: An Illustrated Guide to the Photographic Collections in the National Library of Ireland* (Dublin: NLI, 1998).

Rowan, Alistair, 'Irish Victorian churches: denominational distinctions', in Gillespie and Kennedy (eds), *Ireland, Art into History*, pp. 207–30.

Royle, Stephen, *A Geography of Islands: Small Island Insularity* (London: Routledge, 2001).

Ryan, Joseph J., 'Nationalism and music in Ireland', PhD thesis, NUI, Maynooth, 1991.

Ryder, Sean, 'Male autobiography and Irish cultural nationalism: John Mitchel and James Clarence Mangan', *Irish Review* 13 (1992/3), pp. 70–7.

Ryder, Sean, *James Clarence Mangan: Selected Writings* (Dublin: UCD Press, 2004).

Ryder, Sean, 'Gender and the discourse of Young Ireland cultural nationalism', in Foley et al. (eds), *Gender and Colonialism*, pp. 210–24.

Sahlins, Peter, *Forest Rites: The War of the Demoiselles in Nineteenth-Century France* (Cambridge, Mass.: Harvard University Press, 1994).

Samuel, R., 'An Irish religion', in R. Samuel (ed.), *Patriotism: The Making and Unmaking of British National Identity*, 3 vols, II: *Minorities and Outsiders* (London: Routledge, 1989), pp. 94–120.

Sandford, Jeremy (ed.), *Mary Carbery's West Cork Journal, 1898–1901* (Dublin: Lilliput, 1998).

Saris, A. Jamie, 'Mad kings, proper houses, and an asylum in rural Ireland', *American Anthropologist* 98 (1996), pp. 539–54.

Saris, A. Jamie, 'Producing persons and developing institutions in rural Ireland', *American Ethnologist* 26 (1999), pp. 690–710.

Scally, Robert J., *The End of Hidden Ireland: Rebellion, Famine, and Emigration* (Oxford: Clarendon, 1995).

Scally, Robert J., 'External forces in the Famine emigration from Ireland', in Crawford (ed.), *The Hungry Stream*, pp. 17–24.

Scheper-Hughes, Nancy, *Saints, Scholars and Schizophrenics: Mental Illness in Rural Ireland* (Berkeley and London: California University Press 1979; expanded edn, 2001).

Seth-Jones, David, *Graziers, Land Reform and Political Conflict in Ireland* (Washington: CUA Press, 1995).

Shannon-Mangan, Ellen, *James Clarence Mangan: A Biography* (Dublin: Irish Academic Press, 1996).

Shaw Sailer, Susan (ed.), *Representing Ireland: Gender, Class, Nationality* (Gainesville: University Press of Florida, 1997).

Shea, Ann M. and Marion R. Casey, *The Irish Experience in New York City: A Select Bibliography* (New York: New York Irish History Roundtable, 1995).

Sheehy, David, 'Archbishop Murray of Dublin and the Great Famine in Mayo', *Cathair na Mart* 11 (1991), pp. 118–28.

Sheehy, Jeanne, *The Rediscovery of Ireland's Past: The Celtic Revival, 1830–1920* (London: Thames & Hudson, 1980).

Sheehy, Jeanne, *Walter Osborne* (Ballycotton, Co. Cork: Gifford & Craven, 1974).

Sheehy, Jeanne, *Walter Osborne* (Dublin: NGI, 1983).

Shields, Hugh, *Narrative Singing in Ireland: Lays, Ballads, Come-all-yes and Other Songs* (Dublin: Irish Academic Press, 1993).

Shiels, W. J. and D. Wood (ed.), *Studies in Church History*, xxv, *The Churches, Ireland and the Irish* (Oxford: Blackwell, 1989).

Silverman, Marilyn, *An Irish Working Class: Explorations in Political Economy and Hegemony, 1800–1950* (Toronto: University of Toronto Press, 2001).

Silverman, Marilyn and P. H. Gulliver (eds), *Approaching the Past: Historical Anthropology through Irish Case Studies* (New York: Columbia University Press, 1992).

Silverman, Marilyn and P. H. Gulliver, *Merchants and Shopkeepers: A Historical Anthropology of an Irish Market Town, 1200–1991* (Toronto: University of Toronto Press, 1995).

Simms, Anngret, 'Perspectives on Irish settlement studies', in Barry (ed.), *A History of Settlement in Ireland*, pp. 228–47.

Simms, Anngret and J. H. Andrews (eds), *Irish Country Towns* (Cork and Dublin: Mercier and RTÉ, 1994).

Simms, Anngret and J. H. Andrews (eds), *More Irish Country Towns* (Cork and Dublin: Mercier and RTÉ, 1995).

Simms, Anngret and Patricia Fagan, 'Villages in County Dublin: their origins and inheritance', in Aalen and Whelan (eds), *Dublin City and County*, pp. 79–120.

Skerrett, Ellen, 'New perspectives on Irish diasporic communities: the Irish of Chicago's Hull-House neighbourhood', in Fanning (ed.), *New Perspectives on the Irish Diaspora*, pp. 189–222.

Slater, Eamonn and Terrence McDonogh, 'Bulwark of landlordism and capitalism: the dynamics of feudalism in nineteenth century Ireland', *Research in Political Economy* 14 (1994), pp. 63–118.

Slotkin, Edgar, 'Two Irish literary manuscripts in the mid-west', *Éigse* 25 (1991), pp. 56–80.

Smith, F. B. (ed.), *Ireland, England and Australia* (Canberra and Cork: Australian National University and Cork University Press, 1990).

Smyth, Alfred P., *Faith, Famine and Fatherland in the Irish Midlands: Perceptions of a Priest and Historian: Anthony Cogan 1826–1872* (Dublin: Four Courts, 1992).

Smyth, Gerry, *Decolonisation and Criticism: The Construction of Irish Literature* (London: Pluto, 1998).

Smyth, W. J., 'Landholding changes, kinship networks and class transformation in rural Ireland: a case study from County Tipperary', *Irish Geography* 16 (1983), pp. 16–35.

Smyth, W. J., 'Land values, landownership and population patterns in Co. Tipperary for 1641–1660 and 1841–1850: some comparisons', in Cullen and Furet (eds), *Irlande et France*, pp. 59–84.

Smyth, W. J., 'Social, economic and landscape transformations in County Cork from the mid-eighteenth to the mid-nineteenth century', in O'Flanagan and Buttimer (eds), *Cork: History and Society*, pp. 655–98.

Smyth, W. J. and Kevin Whelan (eds), *Common Ground: Essays on the Historical Geography of Ireland* (Cork: Cork University Press, 1988).

Spence, Joseph, 'Isaac Butt, nationality and Irish Toryism, 1833–1852', *Bullán* 2, 1 (1995), pp. 45–60.

Stewart, Ann M., *Royal Hibernian Academy of Arts, Index of Exhibitors and Their Works, 1826–1979*, 3 vols (Dublin: Manton Publishing, 1985–87).

Stewart, Ann M., *Irish Loan Exhibitions 1765–1927*, I (Dublin: Manton Publishing, 1990).

Stewart, Ann M., *Irish Loan Exhibitions 1765–1927*, II–III (St Ouen, Jersey: John Appleby in association with Manton Publishing, 1995).

Stewart, Ann M., *Irish Art Societies and Sketching Clubs, Index of Exhibitors, 1870–1980*, 2 vols. (Dublin, Four Courts, 1997).

Stewart, Bruce (ed.), *Hearts and Minds: Irish Culture and Society under the Act of Union* (Gerrards Cross: Colin Smythe, 1999).

Stout, Geraldine, *Newgrange and the Bend of the Boyne* (Cork: Cork University Press, 2002).

Stout, Matthew, 'Emyr Estyn Evans and Northern Ireland: the archaeology and geography of a new state', in J. Atkinson, I. Banks, and J. O'Sullivan (eds), *Nationalism and Archaeology* (Glasgow: Cruithne, 1996), pp. 112–27.

Stout, Matthew, 'The geography and implications of post-famine population decline in Baltyboys, County Wicklow', in Morash and Hayes (eds), *'Fearful Realities'*, pp. 15–37.

Strickland, Walter, *A Dictionary of Irish Artists*, 2 vols. (Dublin and London: Maunsel, 1913) (facsimile edn, Shannon: Irish University Press, 1969).

Swift, Roger, *The Irish in Britain, 1815–1914: Perspectives and Sources* (Dublin: Gill & Macmillan, 1991).

Swift, Roger, 'Heroes or villains? The Irish, crime and disorder in Victorian England', *Albion* 29, 3 (1998), pp. 399–421.

Swift, Roger, *Irish Emigrants in Britain 1815–1914: A Documentary History* (Cork: Cork University Press, 2002).

Swift, Roger, 'The historiography of the Irish in nineteenth-century Britain', in O'Sullivan (ed.), *The Irish World Wide*, II, *The Irish in the New Communities*, pp. 52–81.

Swift, Roger, 'Historians and the Irish: recent writings on the Irish in nineteenth-century Britain', in MacRaild (ed.), *The Great Famine and Beyond*, pp. 14–39.

Swift, Roger and Sheridan Gilley (eds), *The Irish in the Victorian City* (London: Croom Helm, 1985).

Swift, Roger and Sheridan Gilley (eds), *The Irish in Britain, 1815–1939* (London: Pinter, Savage, MD: Barnes & Noble, 1989).

Swift, Roger and Sheridan Gilley (eds), *The Irish in Victorian Britain: The Local Dimension* (Dublin: Four Courts, 1999).

Taylor, Lawrence J., 'The language of belief: nineteenth-century religious discourse in South-west Donegal', in Silverman and Gulliver (eds), *Approaching the Past*, pp. 142–75.

Taylor, Lawrence J., '"Peter's pence": official Catholic discourse and Irish nationalism in the nineteenth century', *History of European Ideas* 16 (1993), pp. 103–7.

Taylor, Lawrence J., *Occasions of Faith: An Anthropology of Irish Catholics* (Dublin: Lilliput, 1995).

Thomas, Br. Conal, *The Land for the People: The United Irish League and Land Reform in North Galway 1898–1912* (Corruandulla, Co. Galway, Aannaghdown Heritage Society, 1999).

Taylor Fitzsimon, E. A. and James H. Murphy (eds), *The Irish Revival Reappraised* (Dublin: Fourt Courts, 2003).

Thomson, David and Moyra McGusty (eds), *The Irish Journals of Elizabeth Smith, 1840–1850: A Selection* (Oxford: Clarendon, 1980).

Thuente, Mary Helen, *The Harp Re-Strung: The United Irishmen and Rise of Irish Literary Nationalism* (Syracuse: Syracuse University Press, 1994).

Tilley, Elizabeth, 'Charting culture in the *Dublin University Magazine*', in Litvack and Hooper (eds), *Ireland in the Nineteenth Century: Regional Identity*, pp. 58–66.

Tóibín, Colm and Diarmaid Ferriter, *The Irish Famine: A Documentary* (London: Profile, 2001).

Tovey, Hilary, 'Creating and re-creating modernity: peasantisation and de-peasantisation in Ireland', in Granberg et al. (eds), *Europe's Green Ring*, , pp. 306–29.

Travers, Pauric, 'The financial relations question 1800–1914', in Smith (ed.), *Ireland, England and Australia*, pp. 41–69.

Turner, Michael, *After the Famine: Irish Agriculture, 1850–1914* (Cambridge: Cambridge University Press, 1996).

Turpin, John, *John Hogan: Irish Neo-Classical Sculptor in Rome 1800–1858* (Dublin: Irish Academic Press, 1982).

Turpin, John, *A School of Art in Dublin since the Eighteenth Century: A History of the National College of Art and Design* (Dublin: Gill & Macmillan, 1995).

Uí Fhlannagáin, F., *Mícheál Ó Lócháin agus An Gaodhal* (Dublin: An Clóchomhar, 1990).

Uí Ógáin, Ríonach, *Immortal Dan* (Dublin: Geography Publications, n. d. [1995]).

Urquhart, Diane, *Women in Ulster Politics, 1890–1940* (Dublin: Irish Academic Press, 2000).

Valiulis, Maryann G. and Mary O'Dowd (eds), *Women and Irish History: Essays in Honour of Margaret MacCurtain* (Dublin: Wolfhound, 1997).

Vallely, Fintan, (ed.), *Companion to Irish Traditional Music* (Cork: Cork University Press, 1999).

Vance, Norman, *Irish Literature: A Social History*, 2nd edn (Dublin: Four Courts, 1999).

Vance, Norman, *Irish Literature since 1800* (London: Longman, 2002).

Vaughan, W. E. (ed.), *A New History of Ireland*, v, *Ireland Under the Union, I: 1801–70* (Oxford: Clarendon, 1989).

Vaughan, W. E., *Landlords and Tenants in Mid-Victorian Ireland* (Oxford: Clarendon, 1994).

Vaughan, W. E. (ed.), *A New History of Ireland*, vi, *Ireland Under the Union, II: 1870–1921* (Oxford: Clarendon, 1996).

*Victorian Literature and Culture* 32, 1 (2004): Special issue on Victorian Ireland.

Vincent, Joan, 'Interpreting silences: an anthropological perspective on the Great Irish Famine', *Éire-Ireland* 32, 2 & 3 (1997), pp. 21–39.

Vincent, Joan, *The Anthropology of Politics: A Reader in Ethnography, Theory and Critique* (Oxford: Blackwell, 2002).

Vincent, Joan, *Seeds of Revolution: The Cultural Politics of the Great Irish Famine* (New York: Palgrave, 2004).

Vincent, Joan, 'A political orchestration of the Irish Famine', in Silverman and Gulliver (eds), *Approaching the Past*, pp. 75–98.

Walker, B. M., *Ulster Politics: The Formative Years 1868–86* (Belfast: Institute of Irish Studies, QUB, 1989).

Walker, Brian, *Dancing to History's Tune: History, Myth and Politics in Ireland* (Belfast: Institute of Irish Studies, QUB, 1996).

Walker, G., 'The Protestant Irish in Scotland', in Devine (ed.), *Irish Immigration and Scottish Society*, pp. 44–66.

Wallace, Valerie, *Mrs Alexander: A Life of the Hymn Writer: Cecil Frances Alexander, 1818–1895* (Dublin: Lilliput, 1995).

Walsh, James P., *The San Francisco Irish 1850–1976* (San Francisco: Irish Literary and Historical Society, 1979).

Walsh, Oonagh (ed.), *Ireland Abroad: Politics and Professions in the Nineteenth Century* (Dublin: Four Courts, 2003).

Walsh, Oonagh, '"A lightness of mood": gender and insanity in nineteenth-century Ireland', in Kelleher and Murphy (eds), *Gender Perspectives*, pp. 159–67.

Walsh, T. J., *Opera in Dublin 1798–1820* (Oxford: Clarendon, 1993).

Ward, Margaret, *The Missing Sex: Putting Women into Irish History* (Dublin: Attic, 1991).

Ward, Margaret, *Unmanageable Revolutionaries: Women and Nationalism in Ireland* (London: Pluto, 1983; rev. edn, 1995).

Warwick-Heller, Sally, *William O'Brien and the Irish Land War* (Dublin: Irish Academic Press, 1990).

Welch, Robert, *Changing States: Transformations in Modern Irish Writing* (London and NY: Routledge, 1993).

Weston, Nancy, *Daniel Maclise: An Irish Artist in Victorian London* (Dublin: Four Courts, 2000).

Whelan, Bernadette (ed.), *Women and Paid Work in Ireland, 1500–1930* (Dublin: Four Courts, 2002).

Whelan, Kevin, 'The Catholic parish, the Catholic chapel and village development in Ireland', *Irish Geography* 16 (1983), pp. 1–15.

Whelan, Kevin, 'The geography of hurling', *History Ireland* 1 (1993), pp. 27–31.

Whelan, Kevin, *The Tree of Liberty: Radicalism, Catholicism and the Construction of Irish Identity, 1760–1830* (Cork: Cork University Press and South Bend: University of Notre Dame Press, 1996).

Whelan, Kevin, 'The memories of "The Dead"', *Yale Journal of Criticism* 15 (2002), pp. 59–97.

Whelan, Kevin (ed.), *Daniel O'Connell* (Dublin: Keough Notre Dame Centre, 2002).

Whelan, Kevin, 'Daniel O'Connell: the Kerry proteus', in Whelan (ed.), *Daniel O'Connell*, pp. 22–9.

Whelan, Kevin, 'Beyond a paper landscape: John Andrews and Irish historical geography', in Aalen and Whelan (eds), *Dublin City and County*, pp. 379–424.

Whelan, Kevin, 'Landscape and society on Clare Island 1700–1900', in Mac Cárthaigh and Whelan (eds), *New Survey of Clare Island* I, pp. 73–98.

Whelan, Kevin, 'Pre and post-famine landscape change', in Póirtéir (ed.), *The Great Irish Famine*, pp. 19–33.

Whelan, Kevin, 'The Catholic Church in County Tipperary 1700–1900', in Nolan (ed.), *Tipperary: History and Society*, pp. 215–55.

Whelan, Kevin, 'The modern landscape: from plantation to present', in Aalen, Whelan and Stout (eds), *Atlas of the Irish Rural Landscape*, pp. 67–103.

Whelan, Kevin, 'The regional impact of Irish Catholicism 1700–1850', in Smyth and Whelan (eds), *Common Ground*, pp. 253–77.

Whelan, Kevin, 'Towns and villages', in Aalen, Whelan and Stout (eds), *Atlas of the Irish Rural Landscape*, pp. 180–96.

White, Harry, *The Keeper's Recital: Music and Cultural History in Ireland, 1770–1970*, Field Day Critical Conditions Series (Cork University Press and South Bend: University of Notre Dame Press, 1998).

White, Harry and Nicholas Carolan, 'Ireland', in Stanley Sadie (ed.), *The New Grove Dictionary of Music and Musicians*, 2nd edn (London: Macmillan, 2001), XII, pp. 556–68.

White, Harry and Michael Murphy (eds), *Musical Constructions of Nationalism: Essays on the History and Ideology of European Musical Culture 1800–1945* (Cork: Cork University Press, 2001).

Williams, Leslie, 'Irish identity and the *Illustrated London News*, 1846–1851', in Shaw Sailer (ed.), *Representing Ireland*, pp. 59–93.

Williams, W. H. A., *Twas Only an Irishman's Dream: The Image of Ireland and the Irish in American Popular Song Lyrics, 1800–1920* (Urbana: University of Illinois Press, 1996).

Wilson, Adrian (ed.), *Rethinking Social History* (Manchester: Manchester University Press, 1994).

Wilson, Thomas M. 'Themes in the anthropology of Ireland', in Susan Parman (ed.) *Europe in the Anthropological Imagination* (Upper Saddle River, NJ: Prentice Hall, 1997), pp. 107–17.

Witoszek, Nina and Pat Sheeran, *Talking to the Dead: A Study of Irish Funerary Traditions* (Amsterdam: Rodopi, 1998).

WITS, *Star, Shells and Bluebells: Women Scientists and Pioneers* (Dublin: Women in Technology & Science, 1997).

Wright, Frank, *Two Lands on One Soil: Ulster Politics before Home Rule* (Dublin: Gill & Macmillan, 1996).

Yager, Tom, 'What was rundale and where did it come from?', *Béaloideas* 70 (2002), pp. 153–86.

Zimmerman, Georges-Denis, *Songs of Irish Rebellion: Political Street Ballads and Rebel Songs 1780–1900* (Dublin: Allen Figgis, 1967).

# Index

❋

Crawford Gallery, 153
crime, 15
Crolly, Archbishop William, 64
Cronin, Maura, 22, 147
Crookshank, Anne, 154–5
Crossman, Virginia, 15, 55
Crowley, Tony, 140
Cullen, Louis M., 85, 94, 144–5
Cullen, Mary, 48
Cullen, Paul, 64
Culwick, James 174
Cumming, Willie, 97
Curtis, Lewis Perry, 161, 203

Dalsimer, Adele, 157, 159, 163
d'Alton, Ian, 74
Daly, Kieran, 176–7
Daly, Mary E., 29, 48, 55–6, 143
Dames, Michael, 68
Danby, Francis, 156
D'Arcy, Fergus A., 64
Darley, George, 120
Davis, Graham, 204, 221
Davis, Thomas, 12, 43, 120, 163
Dawson, Ciarán, 146, 150
Deane, Seamus, 5, 124, 127, 129, 132, 134,
    137–8, 139
death, culture of, 34–5
De Barra, Pádraig, 149
De Brún, Pádraig, 148
De Fréine, Seán, 136, 143
Delaney, Bishop William, 64
demographic trends, 31–2
Denman, Peter, 133
Denvir, Gearóid, 147
De Paor, Liam, 140
De Paor, Máire, 159
Derg, Lough, 70
De Veres, 120
Devine, Ciaran, 144
Devine, Patrick F., 170
Devine, Tom, 201
Devon Commission, 78
Devonshire, Dukes of, 91
diaspora, Irish, 90, 182–222
    concept of, 183–7
    *see also* emigrants, emigration

Dickens, Charles, 191
Dibble, Jeremy, 173–4
Dillon, John, 19
Dillon, John Blake, 12
Dillon, T., 196
Diner, Hasia, 52, 193
disease, 37, *see also* epidemics
disestablishment, 61
domestic service, 50
Donegal, County, 69, 143
Donnelly, James S., 29, 33–4, 38–40, 69, 84
Donnelly, Bishop Nicholas, 176
Down, County, 107–9, 115, 144
Doyle, David, 200
Doyle, Eugene, 19
Doyle, Bishop James, 64, 66, 158
Drennan, William, 130
Dublin City
    development of, 94–5
    slums, 35, 45, 72, 95–6
*Dublin Review*, 172
*Dublin University Magazine*, 12
Duffy, Francis, 65
Duffy, P. J., 90, 92, 97, 101
Dunne, Tom, 146
Dunsany family, 85
Durkacz, Victor, 147

Eagleton, Terry, 125–6, 127, 132–4
Easter Rising, 3
economic history, 79
economy, 5–6
Edgeworth, Maria, 118, 120, 124, 131, 132
Edmondson, Ricca, 116
education, 16, 144
    system, national, 65
    women's, 52–4
    *see also* music education
EIRdata project, 134
electoral system, 16
Elgee, Jane (Lady Wilde), 'Speranza', 131
Ell, Paul S., 30–1
Elliott, Marianne, 74
emigrants, 37
    British attitudes to, 221
    Catholic and Protestant, relations
        between, 201–4